"I had the opportunity to experience William Keck's passion for classic television when he produced a lovely *Waltons* cast reunion special for Hallmark Channel. But until I read *When You Step Upon A Star*, I had no idea the extraordinary lengths he employed to meet all of his favorite stars. I should consider myself lucky he didn't turn up uninvited to my wedding, as he did at Melissa Gilbert's and Meredith Baxter's."

—Michael Learned (*The Waltons*)

*   *   *

"Two days before the taping of a *Knots Landing* reunion show Will Keck produced for the Hallmark Channel, I tripped while out jogging and ended up with a sizable and quite noticeable black eye. A diva disaster! But 'chill Will' demonstrated his protection for his celebrity guests by convincing me I'd be well taken care of with camera angles and makeup (applied with a spatula!). And he was right! Thank you, Will, for making sure I didn't look like the Target dog … and for revealing in *When You Step Upon A Star* how you put your *Enquirer* 'bad boy' self in the past to become the classy, prolific writer/producer you are today!"

—Joan Van Ark (*Knots Landing*)

*   *   *

"I'm not sure if William Keck was one of the many sleuths on my trail back in the day. They were all pretty slippery and skilled at hiding their tracks. I came to know Will later in life—when he wrote a wonderful piece for *USA Today* on one of our *Knots Landing* reunion specials, before moving on to produce his own *Knots* reunion for the always-delightful *Home & Family*. The fact that he saw the error of his ways—and now has the guts to tell it like it was—shows me he is a really decent human being who is now bringing good into the world. And I applaud him. Thank you, Will, for giving us a book that offers a look behind the curtain … but also restores our faith in mankind."

—Donna Mills (*Knots Landing*)

*   *   *

"*When You Step Upon A Star* offers a rare look at my dear friend Adam West, and so many other beloved Hollywood legends, from the unique perspective of a celebrity reporter who was assigned to expose their secrets. The invaluable life lessons he learned during his outrageous encounters prove that any leopard can change its spots."

—Julie Newmar, *Batman*'s Catwoman

"All of us have done things in our lives we're not proud of. It takes guts to admit it. Especially publicly. That is what Will Keck does in his book, *When You Step Upon A Star*—cops to the lesser him from the more enlightened him he has matured into. He does it with brutal honesty and a lot of humor. Bravo!"

—Dee Wallace (*E.T.*)

* * *

"Years ago, young *National Enquirer* reporter William Keck turned up at our home right after Christmas wanting to write a story about our new baby girl. My husband Peter was very protective and wanted to send the kid away. But in the spirit of the holidays we gave him a chance and invited him in. He ended up writing a beautiful story. Now, he's written an unvarnished, gritty book confessing some of his other encounters that didn't go quite as well. His stories left me shocked, amused, touched … and grateful we got off so easy."

—Catherine Bach (*The Dukes of Hazzard*)

* * *

"Reading *When You Step Upon A Star* took me back to when I was a young inexperienced actress working on a hit network TV show and dreading Tuesdays— the day the new weekly tabloids were put out in stores. I realized early on that producers and others on our set would give 'stories' to the papers and that about 10% were sure to be true with a wide open field for the remaining 90%. While I'm grateful not to be one of the 'stars' Will stepped on, many of our *Love Boat* guest stars were not so fortunate. Will's stories reveal his evolution into the kind, generous man I've come to both know and trust. Enjoy the read!"

—Cynthia Lauren Tewes (*The Love Boat*)

* * *

"The confessions recounted in William Keck's *When You Step Upon A Star* tell the story of a former tabloid bad boy uncovering personal secrets of Hollywood's most notable and infamous figures. One of whom I personally worked with was Larry Hagman, who played Major Tony Nelson on *I Dream of Jeannie*. I have only fond memories of working with William, who initially wrote a story about me for *TV Guide* ahead of the release of my New York Times bestselling memoir, *Jeannie Out of the Bottle* in 2012. This just shows me that we all deserve the space and opportunity to evolve. I wish him all the best on his literary debut. Welcome to the club!"

—Barbara Eden (*I Dream of Jeannie*)

WHEN YOU
STEP
UPON A
STAR

WHEN YOU
STEP
UPON A
STAR

CRINGEWORTHY CONFESSIONS
OF A TABLOID BAD BOY

WILLIAM KECK

Jacobs/Brown Media Group

LIBRARY OF CONGRESS CATALOGING-IN-PUBLICATION DATA
Keck, William
When You Step Upon a Star
Edited by Mark Alfred
Editorial staff: Jack Bowers, Marc Cushman, Steven Kates
Publisher: Matthew Brown

Includes bibliographical reference

Hard cover ISBN 978-1-7355673-7-2
Paperback ISBN 978-1-7355673-8-9
Kindle ISBN 978-1-7355673-9-6

First edition hardcover and softcover 2024

Library of Congress Control Number: 2024932954

This book is a work of journalism, protected under the First Amendment, with information presented under "fair use" guidelines. It is not endorsed, sponsored, or affiliated with the *National Enquirer*, or other periodicals which the author had in the past associated with.

Up to 10% of each chapter may be reproduced as quotes, provided attribution to the author and publisher is made. Other use may be made only with prior permission in writing from the publisher.

Provenance has been given for archival information utilized in this book. Newspapers, magazines, websites, or writers wishing to request additional attribution or removal of material from future printings and e-books, please contact publisher.
Attributions for some of the photographs in this book were not possible due to the images spanning a time period of 65 years, with the many displayed on numerous websites across the internet without provenance. We have provided credit when possible, and given acknowledgment for websites on which many of the images have been found. To add provenance to any photo or to request its removal from future printings and e-books, please contact publisher.

Cover Design: Damonza
Back cover image (top), taken and used by permission of Vince Trupsin.

Hard cover edition manufactured in the United States of America

*Jacobs/Brown Press is an imprint of Jacobs/Brown Media Group, LLC
Los Angeles, California
www.JacobsBrownMediaGroup.com*

To my *National Enquirer* bureau chief and mentor, Jerry George, who sent me out on so many of these morally questionable, traumatizing, mafia-like assignments, but not without equipping me with invaluable life lessons.

"Choose your battles, Kecky." "Know when to get out." And most importantly, "Always be true to yourself."

CONTENTS

PART III: DANGEROUS DIVAS

PART IV: DOMESTIC DISTURBANCES

PREFACE

During my multi-decade career working in Hollywood as an entertainment reporter covering celebrities, I've written countless articles that I'm proud to claim as my own. Very personal profiles that received accolades not only from my editors, but also from the town's top publicists and the stars themselves. But you won't find any of those happily-ever-after stories in this book. Rather, within these pages are my missions that, for one reason or another, went horribly wrong. Typically to blame was the cavalier bravado I displayed while investigating morally questionable leads, pursuing controversial angles or asking probing questions that I thought might be of interest to my readers, but were regarded as overly invasive or unnecessarily rude by my subjects.

Take for instance Bruce Willis, who threatened to burn down my house, many years after little Drew Barrymore left the message "I'm going to fucking kill you" on my home answering machine.

Ellen DeGeneres told me, "I don't like you so much," while *The Nanny's* Fran Drescher gave me a rather aggressive verbal spanking.

Beloved *Mary Poppins* icon Dick Van Dyke prodded his TV star buddy Andy Griffith to give me a good smack in the face, while *Star Trek's* Leonard Nimoy took me to task over a casual question I posed about his Spock ears. Another of my sci-fi idols—*Bionic Woman* Lindsay Wagner—greeted me at her father's funeral with a soul-crushing "Fuck you," which was really nothing compared to being dragged away by security from John Candy's private entombment.

Desperate Housewives star Teri Hatcher put a period on our years-long friendship by telling me "you will (one day) look up at your reflection in your coffin and not like what you see."

I accidentally terrified a pair of child stars on Halloween and sent an actress from *Lost* fleeing our interview in tears.

Gorgeous *Dallas* star Victoria Principal—a longtime object of my near stalker-like obsession—threatened me with legal action, which was preferable to being roughed up by a three-time Emmy-winning '90s sitcom star outside his home.

Then there was the time I landed a spot on the Scientologists' "suppressives" list after an innocent misunderstanding with the late, great Kirstie Alley. And in his autobiography *So Far...*, Alley's *Cheers* co-star Kelsey Grammer called me out by name as "a despicable piece of flesh" whom he invited "to burn in Hell!!"

Oh man, I'm outta breath.

While the words and actions of those peeved celebrities may have been justified at the time, please believe me when I tell you I'm really not as bad as all that makes me out to be. It's true though. There's no denying that over the years I've done many things of which I'm *not* proud. For me, the process of accountability and redemption that inspired me to write this book has been slow and continuous. As you'll discover, my irreverent sense of humor and the questionable fact-finding tactics and sweet-talking skills I fostered at the *National Enquirer* followed me upon graduating to my role as a "legit" celebrity reporter for such respected publications as *USA Today*, the *Los Angeles Times*, *People*, *Entertainment Weekly* and *TV Guide*. Quitting tabloid journalism didn't necessarily mean its mindset and methodology had quit me. What it did offer was extraordinary access to A-list talent I never in a million years expected I'd have an opportunity to interview. The very same publicists who would hang up the phone or threaten my life when I called as a representative of the *Enquirer*, were now contacting me to offer up their talent for intimate 1:1 interviews to be conducted in private dressing rooms, on the closed sets of major film and TV projects, backstage at concerts or even in the celebrities' homes.

The pandemic provided me the time I needed to meticulously comb through the dusty reminders of my past, reflect on all I'd experienced, process what I'd learned and discover what I wanted to say about it all. Ultimately, I decided to confess everything—holding *nothing* back. I'm owning up to my most grievous lapses in judgment, confessing my most mortifying blunders, revealing the embarrassing sex stuff and also taking the opportunity to share a few valuable insights I gained along the way.

While everything is naturally told from my perspective, I fully understand there are always at least two sides to any story. In some instances, a few of those mentioned in the book have chosen to contribute their side, or speak on behalf of a former co-star. A couple others, such as Victoria Principal and *Batman* star Burt Ward, requested minor changes be made that had no significant impact on the stories being told. But I assure you, there's not a word in this book, to the best of my memory—well-supported by an extensive archive of article clippings, my original reporter notebooks, tape-recorded interviews and photographs—that isn't the God's honest truth. How I uncovered some of these tabloid truths, however, did at times require me to employ *imaginative* means, often by accessing my inner thespian or undercover spy.

This is the story of how I infiltrated the secret worlds of the rich and famous, while privately struggling to come to terms with secrets of my own.

Life, I've come to realize, is often like giving birth in the middle of a colonoscopy. Only through surviving extreme discomfort and unspeakable mess are we able to live life to the fullest and truly appreciate those duller, quiet moments when we don't have something invasive up our ass, or a young stranger retreating from between our legs.

So—if you think you can handle it—pick up your CSI blacklights and join me as I pull back the soiled sheets and expose the bizarre, sometimes ugly and always entertaining life of a reformed and deeply repentant tabloid bad boy.

INTRODUCTION

It was never my intention to become a predatory, car-chasing, garbage-stealing celebrity hunter who hid in trees and crashed weddings, private hospital rooms and funerals. Rather, when I came to Los Angeles in my early 20s, my intention was to polish the Hollywood stars I grew up adoring, not step on them and expose their cracks.

That's why, when I joined the *National Enquirer* (then the nation's #1-selling supermarket tabloid) in December 1993, it took me some time to learn the ropes. My bureau chief, Jerry George, would tell me that the editors in Lantana, FL, were so *un*impressed by my first few tryout weeks that they were about to sack me—when fate intervened. On January 17, 1994, at 4:31 in the morning, the 6.7 magnitude Northridge, CA, earthquake rendered my Sherman Oaks apartment complex uninhabitable. Though the building was constructed just three years prior, the windows shattered, doors came off their hinges and balconies detached. Inside my small studio unit, my fish tank cracked—spilling my finned pets onto the carpet and transforming them into sashimi. With my contact lenses lost in the rubble, I called out into the darkness for my newly rescued Lhasa Apso puppy, Austin. When I finally found the little guy, he was trembling behind my waterbed, a piece of glass having cut his eye. Then I started to hear the screams of neighbors both inside my complex and out in the streets. It was truly a nightmare. A nightmare that made Jerry take pity on me and campaign to his bosses to delay my dismissal. That added reprieve gave me just the time I needed to prove my abilities and worth.

The story I'm about to tell accomplished just that, but not without chipping away a bit at my heart and soul. I was reminded of this darkest of dark assignments when Kim Kardashian hosted *Saturday Night Live* in October 2021. The reality star's surprisingly edgy, take-no-prisoners monologue garnered praise from critics, impressed by her air of confidence as she brazenly mocked her entire family. Even her late father, attorney Robert Kardashian Sr., who had aided his longtime friend, O.J. Simpson, in his acquittal for the 1994 double murders of Simpson's ex-wife, Nicole Brown Simpson, and her friend Ron Goldman, was looped in for laughs.

Satirizing the barbaric slayings, Kim mentioned (without naming) the first black person she ever met, asking the audience, "Wanna take a stab in the dark who it was?" As the studio audience howled, Kim explained, "It's sort of weird to remember the first black person you met, but O.J. does leave a mark. Or several. Or none at all. I still don't know."

You may not know, Kim, but *I* certainly do. And so do the victims' families.

One person watching *SNL* that night in disbelief and horror was Nicole's sister, Tanya Brown, who called the jokes—made during Domestic Violence Awareness Month—"beyond inappropriate and insensitive." Brown went on to say, "If (Kim) and her family loved Nicole so much as they claimed … she easily could have said, 'This is inappropriate and disrespectful to everyone! Not only for Nicole and Ron, but for all the victims of domestic violence who were murdered by their significant others.' "

Nicole Brown and O.J. Simpson, circa 1984.

Perhaps Kim, only 13 at the time of the slayings, had been too focused on other things to remember the Brown and Goldman families sobbing heavily on TV, publicly grieving losses too brutal to comprehend. But I remember the time and events all too well. It had been five months since the Northridge earthquake when a call came into the *Enquirer's* L.A. bureau on the morning of June 13, 1994, alerting us to a gruesome crime scene discovered outside Nicole's Brentwood condo. Whatever celebrity stories we were investigating were instantly abandoned so our entire workforce could devote its collective energy into infiltrating every location remotely connected to this bloodbath. I was sent to Mezzaluna Trattoria, an Italian restaurant on San Vicente Boulevard in Brentwood, where Goldman had been working as a server when Nicole and her family came in for dinner the prior evening.

But I was hardly the first on the scene. The restaurant had been besieged by press, and the employees—in deep mourning for their butchered friend—were already fiercely on guard. So much so that I was turned away the second I arrived.

Four days later, Nicole was laid to rest. And then came the most macabre assignment of my career. One that still sends vibrations down my vertebrae. It all started with a dreaded call from the *Enquirer's* most fiercely-aggressive editor, Brian Williams—not the longtime NBC news anchor, but a former priest turned ghoulish editor in the Lantana, FL, home office who refused to ever take "no" for an answer. Receiving a call from Williams pretty much guaranteed your day was about to be ruined by some ghastly assignment. Basically, we were young gladiators being sent unarmed into lions' dens, while our editors in the Sunshine State called the shots from country clubs, golf courses and, occasionally, from behind their desks.

Williams' instructions this morning were clear, as if my job depended upon it. I was to put on some nice clothes, get in my car and immediately head south to Dana Point, the seaside town where Nicole's parents lived in a private, gated community called Monarch Beach. Once there, I was to employ any means necessary to gain entry into the community in order to secure an exclusive, on-the-record interview with the Brown family.

O.J., come kill me now!

Not surprisingly, the security guards were already on high alert for pesky journalists like me who were willing to make up any conceivable (or inconceivable) story necessary to get past their gates. So, when I tried to make a "grocery delivery," I was immediately turned away.

"Brian, it's not going to work," I called in to report.

"Will, you're a smart guy and you can do this," Brian encouraged me. "Find a way. Be creative."

I thought about just throwing in the towel and telling Brian to screw off, but this cunning fox had a way of getting inside your head—almost like an Italian

Godfather or cult leader, so that you wanted to make "daddy" proud. He'd pump up your ego to the point where there was no doubt you were capable of pulling off the most heinous acts.

(Above) The former *National Enquirer* Lantana, FL, home base (before its October 2001 anthrax-related closure), where our top-selling O.J. covers (like the one below) were conceived.

So I decided to drive just a little further down the coast to the beachfront Ritz-Carlton, Laguna Niguel luxury hotel. I valeted my car and marched through the lobby with my shoulders back, projecting my own fabricated Kardashian confidence so as not to arouse the suspicions of security. Once outside, I quickly descended the hotel's stone staircase leading down to Monarch Beach, which was shared by the hotel and the Browns' residential compound.

Now I'm the type of guy who can sweat like a pig in a snowstorm, so you can imagine how miserable it was traipsing through a sandy beach in the middle of a blistering June afternoon dressed in a suit and tie. But as I slipped off my dress shoes and rolled up my pants, my initial fears began to give way to a massive adrenaline rush. This insane plan might actually work! All of a sudden, I felt like Lucy Ricardo coming up with a screwball scheme to infiltrate the home of her favorite matinee idol Robert Wagner—just days after he'd buried Natalie Wood!

With little effort, I easily scaled the gate surrounding the Monarch Beach residences. Before I knew it, I was inside, rolling my socks back up my ankles and praying I wouldn't pass out before making my way up a steep hill to the address Brian had provided: 222 Monarch Bay Drive.

I hadn't even considered what I might do in the unlikely event that I actually made it to the Brown family home. So, when I found myself standing outside the luxurious house, all I could think to do was snap a photo. But I knew Williams would want more before allowing me to flee the scene. My anxiety was surging. Though O.J. had been arrested and charged with the double homicide the day after Nicole's burial (after hiding out in Robert Kardashian's home and leading police on his infamous Ford Bronco chase), what if he'd escaped and was on his way to visit his children at Grandma and Grandpa's?! The photo in my camera would at least exist as evidence of me having made it this far after police discovered my gutted and lifeless body in the bushes.

Brian was naturally elated when I called to tell him how far I'd come since our previous call. "I knew you could do it!" he said. "Now just go up and knock on the door."

"But what do I tell them?"

"Tell them the truth, Will. You're a journalist. You know what to do."

Sigh. He was right. I did know what to do, I just *really* didn't want to do it!

Outside the Browns' door, I took in one deep breath and just ... knocked. Moments later the door opened and I was greeted by a housekeeper. I smiled warmly, trying to control my quivering lip (and bladder) and cheerfully chirped, "Good morning. I'm here to pay my respects to Mrs. Brown." And just like that I was ushered inside the house and escorted to a small sitting room where Nicole's mother, Juditha, and her surviving daughters, Denise, Dominique and Tanya, were seated around a framed portrait of their slain Nicole with tears in their eyes.

Mrs. Brown immediately stood up and took my clammy hand in hers. My blood was racing. I'm lucky I didn't drop dead of a coronary right there on the spot. I suddenly had to pee really badly, but was pretty sure this wouldn't be the best time to ask to use the bathroom. Or maybe it would have, so I could have climbed out a window and escaped back down to the beach.

"Thank you for coming," said the surprisingly composed Brown matriarch. "How did you know my daughter?"

Gulp! I feared I was quite possibly about to be torn apart like a male warrior who dared infiltrate Wonder Woman's Amazonian birth island. But Juditha's eyes were kind and welcoming. I felt such a maternal warmth radiating from her little body that I somehow sensed I was safe. She had just lost a daughter to unspeakable violence and now yearned only for peace and justice. So I mustered up enough courage to tell the truth. The whole truth and nothing but.

"I am so very sorry for your family's loss," I started, with Mrs. Brown still holding my hand in hers. "And I'm so incredibly sorry for this intrusion. I'm with the *National Enquirer*."

I felt Mrs. Brown's hand clench mine just a bit tighter before letting go. The three sisters stood up in unison and led me out to the grand foyer toward the front door, with a clear insinuation that I was to go. Immediately. But despite my incredibly cold invasion of their privacy, the women remained remarkably calm and cordial. I was about to learn they were ripe to begin telling their side of the story.

Just as I neared the door, I heard Mrs. Brown softly ask in her German accent, "What do you want to know?"

Fuck if I knew! But I had to say *something*. I heard Brian coaxing me on. "Just start talking, Will. You know what to do."

"I guess I'd like to know how you told the children," I spoke softly.

It turned out to be just the right question. O.J. and Nicole's 8-year-old daughter, Sydney, and 5-year-old son, Justin, were the Brown family's only concerns. Keeping them safe from the man they believed murdered their mother was all that mattered.

Before she continued speaking, Mrs. Brown prefaced that under no circumstances would she discuss the children's father or even speak his name. I naturally understood.

And then, she told me.

"We sat the children on the sofa, held their hands and told them softly their mother was gone," said the proud matriarch with a steely strength that impresses me to this day, even after her own death. "We said 'Mommy's in heaven and she's not coming back. But she'll never stop loving you and you must never let her memory escape from your hearts.'"

I was told the confused children remained quiet and refrained from crying. Their grandmother told them they now had four mommies (herself and aunts Denise, Dominique and Tanya) who would be watching after them forever.

Then came the heartbreaking conversation about what a funeral was, and if the children wanted to attend. The choice was theirs.

"Sydney and Justin told us they didn't want to see their mommy in the coffin, but they did want to go to the funeral with their daddy," said Mrs. Brown, still careful not to speak of the man by name.

After all the attention her son-in-law had been getting, Mrs. Brown seemed almost grateful to have the opportunity to talk about the children whom she hoped would carry on their mother's legacy. She went on to recall how her grandchildren brought their mother a rose and held their father's hand throughout the service. "I know their mommy must have been so proud of them," she said, feigning a smile as best she could. "They were so brave and strong; just like Nicole always was."

Following the funeral, the children moved into the Browns' home. (Were they upstairs now? I wondered. Perhaps even crouched at the top of the stairs like curious Brady kids eavesdropping on mom and dad?)

A family priest, I was told, had been brought in to address questions the children's grandparents and aunts were not equipped to answer. The family's goal, Juditha explained, was to attempt to regain some sense of normalcy, meaning Sydney would resume ballet classes, Justin would return to karate and they would find other children in the neighborhood with whom they could play.

I found particularly touching one of the last things Mrs. Brown told me. "Every time I look into Sydney and Justin's eyes, I see their mother staring back," she said, almost as if she were reciting a prayer. "Nicole was the best mom, and these children are her greatest legacy. I promise to raise her children in a way she'd be proud of. They will never forget their sweet mother and always know how much she loved them."

Like my father's father (all three of us named William Keck), I've always been an emotional crier. The Irish in us. And as much as I wanted to maintain a professional demeanor, there was no way I could continue holding back my tears as Mrs. Brown and her daughters wept openly in front of me. Soon, Mrs. Brown was opening her heart without me having to ask questions.

"She was a perfect angel, and she was murdered. *Murdered!*" said Mrs. Brown, emphasizing that life-ending word with a rage she hadn't shown thus far. "That isn't right. It's not supposed to work that way. It's just not fair."

And finally, she did mention *his* name, telling me, "I don't know what her involvement with O.J. was. What I can tell you was she was the best mother to her kids. She loved them with all her heart, and someone robbed my grandchildren of their mother. They'll have to live with that for the rest of their lives." She also wanted to communicate—perhaps to O.J. himself via the *Enquirer*—which was about to become their mouthpiece, that she was not afraid of her former son-in-law.

I left with way more than I ever could have imagined I would ... or deserved. Rather than press my luck and ask for photos, I decided the best course of action would be to again express my sympathies and gratitude and hightail it the hell out of there before grandpa bear came home. Who knows if he would have shared his wife's genteel hospitality?

Though I'm sure they did not appreciate having their personal space invaded,

'**Mommy's in heaven and she's not coming back**'

Nicole Simpson's young children learned the tragic news of their mother's death from their heartbroken grandparents.

And in an exclusive ENQUIRER interview, Nicole's grieving mother reveals what she and her husband told the youngsters — Sydney, 8, and Justin, 5 — at their home in Dana Point, Calif., soon after Nicole's bloodied body was found.

HOW O.J.'S KIDS WERE TOLD OF THE TRAGEDY

"We sat the children on the sofa, held their hands and told them softly their mother was gone," said Judy Brown.

"We said, 'Mommy's in heaven and she's not coming back. But she'll never stop loving you and you must never let her memory escape from your hearts.'

"Sydney and Justin were very quiet. There were no tears.

"Nicole was a very strong woman — and she instilled that inner strength in her children.

"We told the children that they had four mommies now — me and Nicole's three sisters, Denise, Dominique and Tanya.

"We also explained to them what a funeral was and asked if they wanted to go.

"Sydney and Justin told us they didn't want to see their mommy in the coffin, but they did want to go to her funeral with their daddy.

"At the funeral, they brought Nicole a beautiful rose and held their daddy's hand. I know their mommy must have been so proud of them. They were so brave and strong — just like Nicole always was.

"Since then Sydney and Justin have been talking to a priest who is helping to answer their many questions.

"The children will be living here with us.

"We've filled our home with about 12 children for Sydney and Justin to play with — and soon we'll begin to establish some degree of normalcy.

"Sydney will continue her ballet lessons and Justin will pursue karate.

"We can never forget, but we must go on.

"Every time I look into Sydney and Justin's eyes I see their mother staring back.

"Nicole was the world's best mom and these children are her greatest legacy.

"I promise Nicole that I will raise her children in a way she'd be proud of. They will never forget their sweet mother. They will always know how much she loved them."

— WILLIAM KECK

"They brought Nicole a beautiful rose and held their daddy's hand" . . . The Simpson children with O.J. at their mother's funeral.

the Brown family ended up being so pleased with my respectful approach and accurate reporting that a relationship was formed between them and the *Enquirer* that continued for years. They had been well aware of the abuse their former son-in-law had inflicted upon their daughter and wanted to carry out Nicole's wishes that, should something happen to her, the world would know the identity of the culprit.

When I heard O.J. announce Juditha's passing in a November 2020 video posted on his Twitter account, I wasn't completely shocked to hear him say he'd maintained a close bond with his ex-mother-in-law all these decades later. Juditha had committed to doing *whatever* was necessary to maintain a close relationship with Sydney and Justin. And she'd clearly succeeded, with both visiting their dying grandmother just before she passed.

As it turned out, I would make one last visit to the Brown compound in the coming months. Back at the bureau, Jerry summoned me into his office and shut the door. I was certain I was about to be fired for something I'd done, or more likely, something I'd refused to do. Rather, Jerry got very serious and told me he had an important assignment for me. Like a scene straight out of a *Mission: Impossible* movie, he handed me a large manila envelope and told me I would be making a delivery.

When I asked what was inside, Jerry told me the contents were top secret.

Wait. *What*???!! I felt more than a little disrespected being asked to play delivery boy without being looped into his circle of trust. "Why all the secrecy?" I asked him.

"Look where you're going, Kecky."

I glanced down at the address written on the envelope: 222 Monarch Bay Drive. Why in the world was I being sent back *there*?! All became clear when I got down to the parking garage and, naturally, peeked inside the unsealed envelope. It was an artist's rendering of a badly bruised Nicole that was being sent to the Browns for their approval prior to its publication on the *Enquirer's* next cover. The accompanying story concerned Polaroid photographs Nicole had taken of herself and placed in her safety-deposit box as evidence of an alleged 1989 beating at the hands of O.J.

The savage beating had left Nicole bloodied and bruised and sent her to the hospital. O.J. had pleaded no contest to spousal abuse for the incident but served no jail time. Sealing away the photos, close friends and family believed, was Nicole's insurance policy. Should something tragic ever befall her, the deeply disturbing images should point directly to the man responsible. The artist's rendering was the *Enquirer's* shrewd way of revealing this shocking image to the world before the actual photos were officially released by the prosecution.

My initial uninvited intrusion into the Browns' sanctuary had established the beginnings of what would come to be a long-standing, mutually beneficial relationship between the Browns and the *Enquirer*. Despite our incredibly uncomfortable and awkward first encounter, Nicole's grief-stricken parents and sisters knew they now had a propagandist, enabling their slaughtered loved one to be heard from her grave. Though our shared goal of bringing Simpson to justice did not come to pass as we'd all expected, the Browns got to tell their side of the story, while the *Enquirer* earned newfound respectability as the most trusted source for O.J. exclusives. *The New York Times* cited us for "aggressiveness and accuracy," while the *Los Angeles Times* sent one of its reporters, Katy Butler, to spend a day in our bureau to get a behind-the-scenes look at our news-gathering operation. (To be sure, we were all on our very best behavior that day!)

But an investigative crime-scene journalist was the last thing I wanted to be. Just as being a snoopy tabloid reporter had never remotely been part of my plan. What had brought me to Hollywood was a burning desire to meet all the seemingly inaccessible movie and TV stars who had brought me such joy as an only child. My surrogate Hollywood families! Now, I'd somehow found myself working for an organization that could provide that access—by invading their private worlds and causing them undue distress.

How in God's name had I ended up in this position? And more importantly, how the hell was I going to find my way out?

PART I:
DISTURBING THE DEAD
(& NEAR DEAD)

> "AFRAID OF DEATH? NOT AT ALL. BE A GREAT RELIEF.
> THEN I WOULDN'T HAVE TO TALK TO YOU."
> — KATHARINE HEPBURN
> (TO AN ANNOYING INTERVIEWER, WHO
> REGRETTABLY, WAS NOT ME)

Chapter 1
THE GHOSTS OF BRADYS PASSED

(THE BRADY BUNCH CAST)

The Brady Bunch. Top row (l-r): Christopher Knight, Barry Williams, Ann B. Davis. Middle row (l-r): Eve Plumb, Florence Henderson, Robert Reed, Maureen McCormick. Bottom row (l-r): Susan Olsen and Mike Lookinland. (ABC Television)

WHO: Cast members of the 1969–1974 sitcom *The Brady Bunch.*

WHAT: On-the-record interviews for the *National Enquirer, USA Today* and *TV Guide*. Moderating a cast reunion panel.

WHERE: Various.

On April 10, 1974—just one month after *The Brady Bunch* aired its final episode—my father was sitting with my mother in front of their television set in Slingerlands, NY (a suburb of Albany). Playing that night was one of my dad's favorite films, *Tender Is the Night* (described in the film's trailer in a voiceover by star Jason Robards as "the story of the gayest, wildest era of our century"). According to my mom, little five-year-old Billy (that'd be me) had been put to bed early so as not to detract from the evening's entertainment. Well, as fate would have it, before the first commercial break aired, my father's 32-year-old

3

body went into violent spasms, and within about a minute went forever limp. He'd been diagnosed with a congenital heart condition with a long, very complicated name (idiopathic hypertrophic subaortic stenosis), and had been growing increasingly concerned that his days might be numbered after one of his most-liked crooners, Bobby Darin (of "Mack the Knife" and "Beyond the Sea" fame), succumbed to his own weakened heart just before Christmas '73. That night, William Aaron Keck took to the grave a closely guarded secret gay life that my mother's long been resistant to discuss. (As you can imagine, not her favorite subject. Though I'll share the little I know later on.)

This being the Wednesday night before a three-day Easter weekend, my mother Nancy elected to send me off to school the following morning to take part in a bunny-hop parade without revealing to me that my daddy was dead. One last day of childhood innocence before a five-year-old's entire world would be shattered.

It was also decided to keep me away from my father's wake and funeral so I'd be spared even a glimpse of the casket, much less his embalmed body.

Left: Me, shortly after my father's death, and (right) visiting his grave to honor the 50th anniversary of his 1974 passing.

That decision, while well-intended to protect innocent Billy's formative young mind, led to a haunting, sometimes overwhelming curiosity I secretly struggled with for years.

Was my daddy *really* dead? Or had he for some mysterious reason unknown to anyone faked his death just as some of the characters did on the soap operas our housekeeper Catherine would watch when she came to clean every other Wednesday? And if he really had been buried, what had his corpse looked like and how well was it holding up? What suit had he been buried in? Was he still wearing

4

his wedding ring, or his watch, which I had naturally liked to play with when I sat on his lap?

And why had my mother forbidden me from touching anything in his wardrobe? Did she want it left just as it was in case he might one day return?

These are the questions that swirl through a preschooler's naïve, hopeful and fantastical imagination. And while I never followed through on my ghoulish, *Addams Family*-like fantasies of sneaking into St. Agnes Cemetery late at night with a shovel to dig my father up and have a peek, I became forever obsessed with death and adopted surrogate TV Dads as my own. And #1 on that list was Robert Reed's Mike Brady.

This hunky *Brady Bunch* dad was IT for me—always loving, humorous and fair when doling out punishments to both his biological sons *and* adopted stepdaughters. Even Jan. And though I could never quite put my finger on what it was, there was something extra alluring about Reed. *Hmmm....*

Los Angeles Dodgers pitcher Don Drysdale's 1970 guest appearance provided a glimpse of what a gay version of *The Brady Bunch* might look like. (ABC Television)

Flash forward to May 1992, one week before I was to graduate from Hobart College in Geneva, NY. I was picking up some hair products at a CVS when I nearly fell to my knees. There on the cover of the new issue of *People* magazine were the faces of four *Brady Bunch* kids with an inset photo of their TV dad Reed, who'd apparently died. At the young age of 59. Of AIDS!!!

I finally knew what Mr. Brady's mysterious *something* was: he'd lived a secret gay life in the closet. Just as my own father had. And just as I feared I was doomed to repeat.

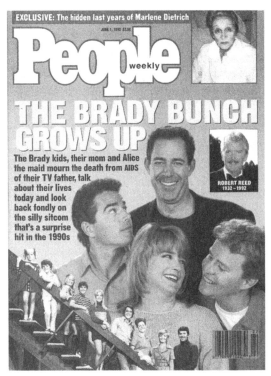

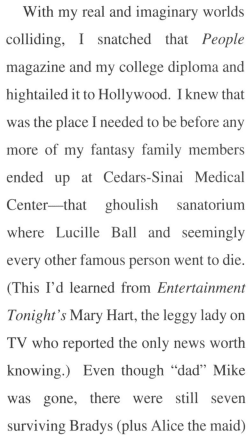

Above: The June 1, 1992, *People* cover that hurled me to Hollywood. Below: The iconic *Brady Bunch* house in Studio City, CA.

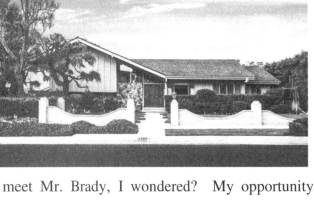

With my real and imaginary worlds colliding, I snatched that *People* magazine and my college diploma and hightailed it to Hollywood. I knew that was the place I needed to be before any more of my fantasy family members ended up at Cedars-Sinai Medical Center—that ghoulish sanatorium where Lucille Ball and seemingly every other famous person went to die. (This I'd learned from *Entertainment Tonight's* Mary Hart, the leggy lady on TV who reported the only news worth knowing.) Even though "dad" Mike was gone, there were still seven surviving Bradys (plus Alice the maid) waiting to welcome me into Robert Reed's vacated square in their Brady family three-by-three grid. If they so warmly welcomed annoying Cousin Oliver, then surely there could be a place for me.

But was it *really* too late to meet Mr. Brady, I wondered? My opportunity to explore that very unlikely paranormal scenario presented itself late the following year when I found myself standing on the doorstep to 11222 Dilling St. in Studio City, CA—also known as the famous *Brady Bunch* house (which HGTV sold in September 2023 for $3.2 million to a superfan who, sadly, was neither me or fellow *Brady*-phile Lance Bass). Perhaps it was some unconscious Freudian attempt to reconnect with my own dead father that inspired this fanciful search for a paternal poltergeist.

Here's the backstory on that. It was December 1993—my very first week at the *Enquirer*. And with zero sources to my name, I knew I needed to deliver something to keep me from getting the boot, which was looking like a real possibility.

Out of desperation, I ventured to the Beverly Hills offices of Aaron Spelling Productions, where I'd been employed as a production assistant on several series. There, I brazenly handed out business cards to underpaid guys I'd met in the mailroom who I knew could use a fast buck in exchange for celebrity scoop. One was this awkward, flushed-face chap named Beau. I should have known Beau wasn't equipped to handle such a nefarious invitation, he having once returned to our offices in a total tizzy after attempting a script delivery to the home of one of *Melrose Place's* hunky male leads. When there was no answer at the front door, sweet, simple Beau peeked over the backyard fence and discovered the boyish, wavy-haired actor sitting naked on the edge of his swimming pool—his lean, athletic body stretched back as he received a blowjob from another dude. *Shocking!!!*

I figure Beau had to have been the one who turned me in to my former boss, Sr. VP of Production Gail Patterson. That same day, Gail called to congratulate me on my new position with the *Enquirer*. "I really hope it works out," she said, "because you'll never work here again." After warning me to stay away from the building and her employees, she hung up the phone. It would be a few years until I was able to apologize to Gail when we found ourselves in the same elevator at the Beverly Hilton and enjoyed a brief, but friendly exchange.

Realizing it would be a no-go with Beau, I was excited to receive my first potential call-in source—an eccentric toupee stylist-to-the-stars claiming to have dirt on both William Shatner *and* parenticidal pretty boy Lyle Menendez. (My editors weren't impressed.)

So I continued taking calls from one nutjob "insider" after another, hoping one might prove legit. Excitedly, I'd type up random story submissions on the *Enquirer's* bright yellow lead sheets, praying one of my crazy suggestions would get approved for me to begin investigating.

I've saved a stack of these wild pitches, which reveal the true extent of my desperation at the time. Among the wackier ones:

- Shannen Doherty Shocker: Plotting Murder of *90210* Co-Star Tori Spelling!!
- Michael Jackson to Welcome a Baby Bear into His Family!!
- Imelda Marcos Practices Voodoo and Baby Sacrifices! (Which, I know, makes me sound like a real QAnoner.)

(Note: None of the above ever made it into print, but one was actually true! I'll leave you to guess which. Hint: a person named in the correct pitch may or may not have once flipped me off in a Hollywood nightclub after declining to take a photo with me.)

Allowing my imagination to run wild, I asked myself: What were the makings of a solid *Enquirer* story? I reasoned it should be centered around a celebrity who was familiar to most and, ideally, beloved. There should be an attention-grabbing, sensationalized headline. And, as I naïvely and incorrectly assumed at the time, it was always a plus if there was some tie-in to the supernatural. (An angry ghost, perhaps???)

Ah-ha; I had it!! What if the Shakespearean-trained Reed's disgruntled spirit was haunting the Brady house seeking revenge on the sitcom he'd long blamed for killing his career? To me, it sounded like just the kind of story the *Enquirer* would enthusiastically plaster on its front page: "BRADY HOUSE HAUNTED BY AIDS-RAVAGED TV GHOST!"

(Note to my fellow *Brady* fans: If any of you are thinking this ghost story shares a suspicious similarity to the Season One, Episode 23 "To Move or Not to Move" episode—the one where the kids pretend to be ghosts to sabotage the potential sale of the family home—I'm not denying I may have been *slightly* inspired. Regardless, in both instances the results proved disastrous.)

I took the elevator down to the parking garage of our Sunset Blvd. office building in West Hollywood, climbed into my red Firebird, and sped over Laurel Canyon to Studio City. Before I knew it, I was parked right in front of that sacred pop-culture mecca, trying to drum up enough courage to do my very first cold-door knock as a tabloid reporter.

I rang the doorbell, banking on my boyish enthusiasm to spare me a violent tirade from a frustrated homeowner who'd no doubt had it with fan intrusions. Might the door be slammed in my face, leaving me with a fat, swollen nose like the ugly one Marcia Brady received after getting hit in the face with a football?

As it turned out, my paranoia was unwarranted. To my great relief, Violet McCallister, the kindly woman who answered the door, was actually quite amused by my otherworldly suggestion that her house might be haunted.

"I'm sure you're aware that Mr. Reed hated doing the show," I told Violet, carefully studying her facial expression to see if my sales pitch was at all registering. "So, it wouldn't be at all surprising if he ... oh, I don't know, occasionally knocked over a vase, maybe...."

"Sorry, we haven't experienced anything out of the ordinary," she said. "I'd tell you if we did."

"You're absolutely certain you haven't heard anything strange at night? Rattling perhaps...?"

"Nope."

"Okay, just let me know if you hear anything…," I said, handing her one of my newly printed business cards. As I turned my back, I casually added, "There could be some good money in it for you."

"Well, hold on," said Violet, stopping me on her front yard walkway. "Now that you mention it...."

BINGO!!! I had persuaded my first source to come dance with the devil! I was now officially a tabloid reporter, and I couldn't wait to tell my editors the great news!

As soon as I got back to our bureau, I typed up my pitch with great enthusiasm and handed the lead sheet to my bureau chief, Jerry, to have him add his obligatory signature and then fax it to the home office in Lantana, FL. It was highly unusual for a tryout reporter such as myself to receive a direct phone call from our editor-in-chief—intimidating Harvard grad Steve Coz—so when the big boss called mere minutes later, I figured I must have really impressed the guy!

9

"How'd you hear the house was haunted, Keck?" Coz asked in his typical gruff, confrontational Massachusetts accent.

"Actually, I thought of it all myself," I said, proudly tooting my own horn. "But the homeowner's totally on board…."

It's not overexaggerating to say Coz became instantly enraged, cutting me off before I could finish my sentence. "That is NOT the way we do things around here, Keck!!" he screamed. "And if you think it is, you can pack up your desk today!!"

Aw shit.

I'd later learn that Coz and his team were already on high alert. Not long before I was brought on board there had been a promising new female hire who'd turned out to be a plant, secretly researching a terribly unflattering exposé on how the *Enquirer* fabricated certain stories. Now Coz worried I might be his next unwelcome mole.

Thanks to Jerry going to bat for me, I managed to keep my job. And within a short amount of time, I was assigned my first legit *Brady* story: an on-the-record interview with then 33-year-old Susan Olsen (Cindy Brady) about a pair of DUIs she'd received—one of which cost her two nights in the pokey. While the facts of the story were confirmed by Susan, who was delightfully forthright and self-mocking over the phone, my editors (as always) felt the story needed more "color" and encouraged me to sweeten the story with additional "she told a friend" quotes. The creation of these anonymous celebrity "friends" gave reporters free rein to fabricate outlandish and deeply personal quotes of questionable origin—magically reported from celebrities' private conversations, sometimes even from behind the closed doors of their bedrooms!

And it's not just tabloids like the *Enquirer* and *Star* that do this. A friend of mine who worked as an editor for *In Touch Weekly* and *Life & Style* confided to me how such celebrity rags fabricated years' worth of soap opera stories revolving around the Brad Pitt/Jennifer Aniston/Angelina Jolie love triangle, as if these real-life players were characters on *Days of Our Lives*. Publishers initially balked at the trio's obviously invented and increasingly outlandish reunions, break ups, pregnancies ("They're having TWINS!!"), engagements and secret weddings, all reported by "insiders" or "friends" … until they saw magazine sales go through the roof and looked the other way. And so long as there were never suggestions of mental illness, violence, terminal illness or addiction, the stars' publicists also agreed to give the rags a free pass, choosing to take the free publicity rather than engage in a series of endless lawsuits.

"Angelina *confided to a friend* that she'd finally laid down the law, telling Brad, 'I never want to hear the name *Jennifer* mentioned in our home again!!'"

"*According to a close pal*, Jada informed a disappointed Will, 'Separation or not, no more booty calls for you until you get your skinny ass back in the Academy!!'"

And in this case, Susan Olsen— forever tethered to her lisping childhood character—told a friend, "When I'm an old lady, they'll probably put my gray hair up in curls and charge admission to see 'Senior Citizen Cindy!'"

'Brady Bunch' sweetheart struggles to escape nightmare of booze

The show destroyed my life, she says

"Brady Bunch" kid Susan Olsen is battling to beat booze after she was arrested twice for drunk driving and landed in jail!

Susan — who captured America's heart as adorable pigtailed Cindy Brady — is undergoing counseling sessions at a court-ordered alcohol education program.

"Being jailed was the most horrifying experience of my life," Susan, 33, told a pal.

"It didn't matter that I was Susan Olsen or Cindy Brady. I was still treated like public enemy No. 1.

"I had to pay over $1,000 in fines and my driver's license was taken away for two years.

"I made a mistake — and I'm paying for it."

Sadly, Susan's troubles date back to the days when she played Cindy Brady on the show, which ran from 1969 to 1974.

"The kids at school teased me horribly.

"They called me 'stupid Cindy' and

'I was stereotyped as that sweet child from hell!'

made fun of my lisp," she told a close friend.

"Cindy was wholesome and everyone assumed I was just like her. But I wasn't! As soon as I turned 15, I rebelled. I began experimenting with drugs and alcohol.

"I did everything possible to escape that goody-two-shoes image. But I couldn't even land work on 'The Love Boat' because I was stereotyped as that sweet child came crashing down when she was ar-

NOW 33, Susan gets a hug from her TV mom Florence Henderson.

CHILD STAR Susan Olsen played goody-goody Cindy Brady — and hated it!

A funny quote, right? Too bad she never said it. Even so, Susan was fine with what ran.

But my interview with Cindy Brady had been a phoner. I desperately wanted to meet a real, live, in-the-flesh Brady. So with "Dad" gone, I decided to pursue my next Holy Grail: perpetually sunny Brady mom Florence Henderson.

Of course, this one went about as well as my Mr. Brady poltergeist debacle.

I'd discovered Florence and her licensed hypnotherapist husband, John Kappas, were scheduled to lead a lecture on hypnosis, which I thought might be of interest to *Enquirer* fans. And, fortunately, so did Florence, who immediately agreed to an interview with me at Kappas' Hypnosis Motivation Institute in Tarzana.

The interview could not have gone better. John, a kind, gentlemanly fellow reminded me of President Nixon's Secretary of State, Henry Kissinger (who passed away at the ripe old age of 100 in November 2023). Like Kissinger, John wasn't

Above left: Dr. John Kappas, me and Florence Henderson, circa 1995. Right: At ABC's 50th Anniversary party with (from left) Maureen McCormick, me, Ann B. Davis, Christopher Knight and Susan Olsen, 2003.

particularly known for his sense of humor, but Florence more than made up for that. She had fallen head over heels in love with the man who'd employed hypnosis to help her overcome deep depression and an intense fear of flying. The two married and, in short time, she too became a licensed hypnotherapist.

While it seems ridiculously amateurish now, I was so excited to meet Mrs. Brady that I brought her red roses. She appeared genuinely touched by my innocent gesture, and the day I spent with Florence and John turned out to be incredibly sweet—not to mention quite revealing.

Even though they were two very different peas in a pod, they'd found ways to make their marriage work by embracing their differences. For instance, Florence told me, "John loves yachting near our home in Marina del Rey, and I can't get enough sex. So, we love having sex down below deck."

"If Florence had her way," John piped in, "I'd never get out of bed."

As an added bonus, Florence contributed this bit of *buzzzzzworthy* advice to all of the *Enquirer's* lady readers: "Don't become over-dependent on vibrators. After a while, they can desensitize a woman to the point where no man will ever be able to please her again."

Naughty, naughty, Mrs. Brady.

Henderson had generously given me everything I needed and much more for a compelling, wildly entertaining tabloid story. In return, she made just one tiny request: that nowhere in the article would we reference her age. My editors agreed, and everyone seemed happy. Florence and John garnered some nice exposure for their growing hypnotherapy institute, while we got a fun, sexy interview with America's all-time favorite TV Mom.

I was thrilled to learn that my editors liked the story so much that they'd decided to promote it on the cover—with a photo inside of Florence holding the rose I'd given her. How cool!! And cover placement also meant there'd be a nice little bonus in my next paycheck.

In this age before digital photo transmissions were commonplace, the big reveal of the week's new issue came to us via a large cardboard box delivered to Jerry's attention. Jerry would have his mousy, Olive Oyl-like secretary, Jan, open the box and leave an issue on each reporter's desk. You can just imagine my reaction (sheer horror!!!) when I glanced at the cover and read: 'Brady Bunch' Mom, 61: "I Love to Make Love." Yup, they'd printed Florence's age on the damned cover, repeated again on the headline of the article inside: 'Brady Bunch' Mom, 61, Confesses: I'm Crazy About Sex.

What the fucking fuck??!!

I ran into Jerry's office, enraged by the betrayal. "How could this have happened, Jerry?" I about cried. "Not only is Florence's age in the article, it's also in the article headline—and on the cover of the whole damn issue!"

Jerry was surprised too, so we called up a senior editor in Florida who couldn't be bothered with our call. "What's she going to do, sue us?" he groaned. "Let her. She gave us an on-the-record interview and her age is public record."

I knew Florence would more than likely never work with the *Enquirer* again. Plus, she couldn't have been thrilled with how I'd been instructed to really play her up as a "sex-crazed" nympho with an "insatiable libido" which had led to the collapse of her first marriage.

I'd come to learn the *Enquirer* never placed value on the big picture or building relationships. "Who cares if Florence Henderson refuses to work with us ever again?" was the shared mentality among the editors. It was all about selling the most copies of that week's issue. But it was also, I felt, a not so subtle "F-you" to a celebrity who had the audacity to make even one "unreasonable" request to the nation's #1 tabloid.

That week, Florence became the first recipient of what would come to be many more apology bouquets of flowers I'd have messengered all over town. (To the *Enquirer's* credit, they did always allow me to include the receipts for these floral "Forgive Mes" in my expense reports.)

But then a few years later I hit pay dirt. In my new staff position with *USA Today*, I was able to interview not only Florence and Susan, but *all* the surviving Bradys (including Alice the maid!) in person to publicize their 35th-anniversary TV Land reunion show, *Still Brady After All These Years*. I'd say I'd died and gone to TV heaven, but alas, the specter of Robert Reed still failed to show.

When I arrived on set, I was pleasantly surprised to discover most of the cast—most especially Susan and Chris Knight (Peter)—were feeling overly chatty, revealing long-buried Brady secrets to me as if I were their clergyman, bartender or hypnotherapist from the John Kappas Hypnosis Motivation Institute. And I imagine because it was so soon after I'd "graduated" from the *Enquirer,* I totally exploited their complete transparency and neglected to employ any semblance of a filter to my all-access, behind-the-scenes observations.

When Barry Williams (Greg) welcomed me into his dressing room while he changed in front of me (a teenage dream come true!!), I described the gray hairs on his chest—noting they didn't match the dyed jet-black hair on his head. (By

September 2023, Williams was gracefully gray on top with a cleanshaven chest for his stint on *Dancing With the Stars*, while I was now dying my own gray hair.) I shared with my readers how an overly emotional Maureen McCormick (Marcia) broke down in tears, not because she was a diva, but because her mother had died just days earlier. I thought nothing of branding Eve Plumb (Jan) the "Black Sheep Brady" (only because she chose not to sit with her TV sibs at lunchtime), and revealed that Ann B. Davis (Alice) treated me like Sam the butcher's chopped liver.

Then, I exposed the *real* reason Olsen had not reprised her Cindy Brady character in the highly-rated 1988 TV reunion movie *A Very Brady Christmas*. Though it had been widely reported that Olsen was off on her honeymoon, she sat

Author (in *Brady* T-shirt) moderating a 45th-anniversary panel in 2014 with Brady boys (from left) Mike Lookinland, Christopher Knight and Barry Williams. And (below) with Eve Plumb in 2016 on the set of *Home & Family*.

out the special because (as Knight told me) she'd been offered so little cash after producers backed up the Brink's truck to meet McCormick's hefty quote. And that certainly tracks with what I was told by Jodi Lyn Ritzen, organizer of a 2014 *Brady Bunch* 45th anniversary fan convention, to which I'd been invited to moderate cast Q&A panels. To put in an appearance, McCormick had allegedly requested $75k (a total steal compared to Plumb's $90k quote) as well as a private room away from her co-stars, with whom she would not appear in photos.

But my major misstep in covering the cast's 35th

anniversary reunion was my undeniably cruel description of Olsen's appearance (*before* she'd had a chance to sit for hair and makeup). "Wearing super-short denims and throwing back a Diet Coke," I wrote, "Olsen, at 43, looks more like a mutated Britney Spears than the youngest Brady in pigtails."

A mutated Britney Spears?? Good God, what was I thinking??!! If I'd ever needed an editor to wield a red pen, it was then and there. Unfortunately, the line ran untouched, and I remain forever embarrassed and apologetic to Ms. Olsen.

Why I repeatedly chose to skewer my beloved Bradys after dreaming of meeting them since I was a boy, I honestly can't say. My only guess would be that, as my article revealed, they genuinely did not seem all that happy to be together on that particular occasion. And that deeply disappointing discovery—that the Bradys were just as dysfunctional as every other family—sent me over the edge and sparked some sort of subconscious fury that came out in my writing. (It probably all started after Mr. Brady's untimely death burst my bubble.)

When I later ran into Knight at a party, he commended my story for finally telling it like it was with no sugarcoating. But I'd also heard that it had brought Olsen to tears. I was no better than that despicable Buddy Hinton (the sitcom's cruel school bully who'd tormented Cindy over her lisp). And like Buddy, I

Return of the Bradys

Brady Bunch reunites after 35 years — and they're not a happy family

deserved a direct punch to the teeth. I reached out to Susan via email and was surprised to get back an almost immediate response. And much kinder than I expected or deserved:

"Will. There may be a bit of misunderstanding. Frankly, I rather liked the article. I loved that my twisted humor got in. I wasn't sure about the word 'mutated' (but) I asked a friend who said, 'Hey Susan, you're 43 and someone is making a comparison to Britney Spears—that's a good thing!' In general, it may have seemed that you were trying to make us out to be rather sour people and I know a few readers perceived it that way. It was really a very truthful article. I really didn't have a problem with it and sent a link to a friend because I was so happy that my

16

pigtail line made it in…. No problem. My friends ... are very protective of me. I was probably less disturbed than they were by the M word. Take Care, Susan Olsen."

Now, that's class. So, several years later, in the summer of 2021, I was more than happy to make it up to Susan by offering her a whopping $500 to appear in a Brady-themed skit I thought up for the Discovery Channel late-night talk show, *Josh Gates Tonight*. That figure was bargained down from the two grand her manager had originally requested. What can I say? I was working off a tight budget and needed a Brady on the cheap!

(Note: With his own healthy, irreverent sense of humor about his Brady heritage, Chris Knight would have been my other choice. But I opted for Susan because I knew his Christopher Knight Home online furniture sales were skyrocketing—even Prince Harry and Meghan Markle are customers! So my measly $500 offer probably wouldn't have been much of an incentive.)

The wacky comedy bit I pitched Susan found our host, Josh Gates, picking her up in his car for a routine interview, only to discover she had hatched a devilish prank to seek revenge on the '70s sitcom *Happy Days*. Susan had been harboring a (totally fabricated) grudge against Fonzie and Friends dating way back to 1974 when *Happy Days* became ABC's new darling, prompting the network to cancel *The Brady Bunch*. The two would head over to the old *Happy Days* house in Hancock Park—not far from the Paramount lot where both sitcoms had taped—and vandalize the shit out of it.

As far out as that all may seem, it went off without a hitch. Well, *nearly*. Susan and Josh totally trashed the "Cunningham home" with a dozen rolls of TP and several cartons of eggs. And then—just as Josh stepped onto the front step about to release his last egg—the front door opened and out popped *Happy Days* mom Mrs. C, played by beloved TV icon Marion Ross. At 92, Ross had agreed to come out of retirement to give the two vandals a proper tongue-lashing. And as a fan of vintage TV who worshipped *Happy Days* nearly as much as *The Brady Bunch*, my day couldn't have been happier.

But on the morning of the shoot everything nearly imploded. This was right when the COVID pandemic was raging and all TV shows were taking all necessary precautions to protect their staffs and talent. When Susan arrived at our production

17

office just before we were all about to head over to the *Happy Days* house, she told me I needn't bother wearing my face mask around her because she was an anti-vaxxer. *Aw shit!* How had I forgotten that Olsen had once worked as an outspoken, conservative Republican radio host??!! So now I was in a position of possibly killing both our host *and* America's most beloved, surviving TV mom (with Florence having passed in 2016).

I made the call to clue in Josh since he was my boss and the one who would be spending most of his day in a confined car next to Susan. Then at the location, I would keep Marion safely protected inside the *Happy Days* house with the homeowner and his family (all of whom had been vaccinated) and as far away from the troublemaking Trumper as possible.

My plan worked just fine—that is until right after we wrapped when I discovered Susan and Marion posing together side-by-side in a photo with Josh. *Crap!* Since there was no turning back time, I jumped into the shot as fast as I could and then immediately whisked Marion away from Susan and into her waiting limo to take her straight home.

To my great relief, Ross exhibited no flu-like symptoms in the happy days ahead and tuned in to watch her sketch with great delight. Had it gone the other way, I can only imagine what truly tasteless headline the *Enquirer* might have plastered on its cover to exploit my fatal faux pas:

From left: Discovery Channel host Josh Gates, *Happy Days* mom Marion Ross, Susan Olsen and me, 2021.

"HAPPY DAYS HOUSE HAUNTED BY VIRUS-RAVAGED TV GHOST!"

Lesson Learned: Perhaps I wasn't meant to be a Brady after all. Perhaps, rather than focusing on the loss of my dad, I should be more grateful for the blessing of the real life stepfather who came into my life—bringing with him three very lovely stepsiblings: Teresa, Tamara and Brad. Two even had hair of gold like their father. Close enough, right?

A WORD FROM THE BRADY BUNCH'S CHRISTOPHER KNIGHT

Walking down memory lane is something I'm asked to do often. People use Bradys like signposts or timepieces. In the same way a song instantly takes you back to a moment in time, "Brady" evokes fond memories. And from my experience, those memories are almost always from childhood—the strongest kind.

I met Will back in 2003 and over the years we've run into each other on several occasions. But the memories of our interviews had faded into the distance. Of course, after reading Will's Brady chapter, the memories flooded back. And like that scene in *The Wizard of Oz*, where the film goes from black & white to color, new details emerge.

Upon reading Will's passages about his childhood connection to the Bradys, it dawns on me how his connection is like the root of a tree put down long ago. I see it's fundamental to who Will is and what he's become.

So, why did Will ask for my thoughts in his book? Because to Will I've been a lifelong friend. I wasn't being asked to contribute because of the normal metrics of friendship, but because I'm his metaphysical brother. Peter is being asked to comment, through Chris. The Bradys have been like the dirt around his roots. They've been there, supporting him and nurturing him for a lifetime. If this sounds odd, it's not. It's no longer a unique experience for me to be treated as a lifelong friend or family member, even by someone I've only just met. To be an important part of someone's life is a privilege. (Even if it wasn't really me who was there being important.)

In hearing Will fantasize on being a Brady, wanting Mike Brady as his father and dreaming of being a substitute for Oliver, I hear again a common refrain: "I wished to have been in the Brady family." Though the family was created as television entertainment, it transcended its original purpose long ago. It's become a touchstone of sorts. A depiction of a functional family and an alternative family to many. What kid wouldn't want to grow up in a safe, nurturing environment; have helpful, encouraging brothers and sisters and an understanding mother and father who listen and dispense lessons with love, compassion and regularity? What's not to like about living in a home where trust is expected, individualism admired and togetherness cherished?

I get it, Will. I truly do! Mike and Carol were awesome. They'd be proud of you, and I'm sure happy to hear you're no longer a gossipist. They were patient with Peter when he abused the power of the press, helping to channel his creativity away from making stuff up. They were also there to pick up the pieces when Peter fantasized of being someone different. Peter and you do seem to share a lot in common. Now, if only Mike was here he could give you this lecture … I'll give it a shot:

All we can do is try our best, with honest intent, to work to understand each other. Respect comes to those who respect. The real and imagined are different. Make room for fantasy so it makes room for you, but bring a map so you know the way back. And finally, this … "Here's the story" … was a story! The Bradys were a Bunch, of actors playing roles. We weren't family. We *played* a family and all of us wished our own families were as wonderful as the Bradys.

If some of our past behavior disappointed you, I'm sorry. Shattering illusions can be upsetting. But those Bradys who you described as not being happy to be together, well they weren't Bradys. That house you went up to with ideas of Mike Brady hauntings, it wasn't the Brady house. (Okay, maybe it's recently become the Brady House, but technically, *not* the house.) And neither Bob Reed or Mike Brady even knew where that house was. His spirit would have gotten lost trying to find it. The Bradys are, and always have been, fiction. They can only be seen on TV and in your mind. Aspire to be like them, not us mortal humans who portrayed them.

Still stalking my Brady siblings at HGTV's *A Very Brady Renovation*
premiere party, 2019. Top (l-r): McCormick, Plumb and Olsen.
Bottom (l-r): Williams, Knight and Lookinland.

Chapter 2
BRAVE LAST DAYS

(DEAN MARTIN)

Dean Martin in the 1970s.

WHO: Dean Martin (1917–1995). Golden Globe-winning movie & TV actor/comedian. Las Vegas nightclub crooner. Member of the infamous Rat Pack. Honored posthumously by the Grammys with their 1999 Hall of Fame Award (for his rendition of "Everybody Loves Somebody") and their 2009 Lifetime Achievement Award.

WHAT: Documenting his declining health and crashing his 1995 funeral for the *National Enquirer*.

WHERE: La Famiglia restaurant, Beverly Hills, CA. Pierce Brothers Westwood Village Memorial Park and Mortuary, Westwood, CA.

When I was a kid growing up in Slingerlands, NY, after school let out, I'd enjoy riding my bike to a convenience store to buy packs of baseball cards. And by "baseball cards," I of course mean *Three's Company* and *Charlie's Angels* trading cards—the ones that always included a rock-hard rectangular shard of unchewable gum dusted with sugar to make it appear somewhat edible. This is where I'd also spend as much time as possible flipping through the latest adventures of *Green Lantern* or *The Flash* before I'd catch the stern eye of the cashier, letting me know it was time to either buy something or bolt. I don't remember ever paying much attention to the tabloids in the magazine racks until one unforgettable afternoon in 1979.

At 10 years old, I was jolted by a photo on the *National Enquirer*'s front page. It was of Ethel Mertz—Lucille Ball's treasured sidekick from *I Love Lucy*—accompanied by three chilling words I'll never forget: Brave. Last. Days. The full headline, as I recall, was "Vivian Vance, Beloved *I Love Lucy* Star. Her Brave Last Days."

I was instantly struck by the stinging realization that the immortal sitcom characters I so loved watching on TV were in fact played by real people who got sick and died.

Vivian, who I'd watch on afterschool reruns of *The Lucy Show*, reminded me so much of my Nana— my mom's mom, Ruth. They shared not only a similar body type and always perfectly coiffed hairdos, but also razor-sharp

Vivian Vance (left, circa 1975, CBS Television) and my Nana, Ruth (right).

comedic timing. And the thought that wacky Ethel Mertz was dying, or perhaps by now already dead, brought my psychological candy-conveyer belt to a grinding halt.

Who could have possibly guessed that some 15 years later I'd be reporting my own "Brave Last Days" stories as a tabloid reporter?

Because my *Enquirer* editors were well aware of my obsession with Hollywood's last remaining Golden Age stars, I was assigned an inordinate amount of these "Brave Last Days" or "BLD" stories. And truth be told, I was beyond grateful to be given the chance to slip inside these dying legends' private domains—

and perhaps even breathe their same air—before they were gone from this planet forever … like Lucy and Viv.

But as I'd come to learn, some things are best left unseen.

Very few know this better than my extremely private and professionally discreet next-door neighbor Tyler. As owner of the celeb-filled Hollywood Forever Cemetery, Tyler either inherited or acquired the remains of such legends as Rudolph Valentino, Mickey Rooney (whom you'll read about later), *Golden Girls'* Estelle Getty, Burt Reynolds and Anton Yelchin (*Star Trek*'s Chekov 2.0). Whenever another big star dies, I'll casually ask Tyler, "Did ya get him?"

"Trying," he'd occasionally shrug before disappearing into his house.

Back in January 2017, Tyler got to meet Judy Garland—not in the flesh, but in the bone—nearly 50 years after her fatal drug overdose. Per the wishes of her daughters, Liza Minnelli and Lorna Luft, mama Judy's remains were to be interred in Hollywood Forever's newly-christened Judy Garland Pavilion. But first, her body had to be exhumed from New York's Ferncliff Cemetery. For security reasons, Tyler was required to eyeball the Oscar winner in her coffin—both before her flight west, and then again once the two landed in L.A. As much as I've pried, I've been unsuccessful in getting tight-lipped Tyler to spill any details of what he saw inside her casket. He's eternally loyal to his clients, long after the earth settles. "Was Judy's skeleton decked out in Dorothy's iconic blue and white gingham dress and ruby slippers?" I so wanted to ask. "Was whatever was left of her hair done up in pigtails?" "Was there a little mummified gray Cairn Terrier placed beside her?" (The answer to that last one is "no." However, you can find an honorary memorial monument featuring a bronze sculpture of Dorothy's dog Toto on the Hollywood Forever grounds.)

But Tyler wouldn't even tell me which celebrity he was flying east to collect until after he'd completed his top-secret mission and news of Garland's relocation had become public.

Since Mary Tyler Moore had just died on the East Coast prior to his departure, I double downed on her. Though MTM turned out *not* to be his secret celebrity acquisition, Tyler did tell me he'd spoken with a colleague during his trip to New York City who had personally glimpsed Moore's naked corpse laid out on a cold slab for embalming. (But probably better to remember her tossing that crocheted tam o'shanter up in the air, right?)

So, here's my question for you. And try to answer truthfully. Would you have snuck a peek at Judy or Mary if you'd been given the chance? I honestly don't know how I'd answer. It's not like I haven't seen dead bodies before. There was that one motorcyclist on the side of the freeway. My grandparents at their funerals. And in Egypt I got to spy King Tut.

Speaking of Tut, after what duration of time does a once-sacred burial place become an archeological "find" acceptable for unearthing to have a look-see?

In November 2007, Egypt's most famous pharaoh was removed from his sarcophagus in his Valley of the Kings tomb and placed in a climate-controlled acrylic glass box to give visiting tourists an up-close glimpse of Tutankhamun's blackened and cracked-skin corpse. Since that provoked no great outcry from the public, perhaps it's time to send Marilyn Monroe and James Dean out on glitzy international tours for the ticket-buying public.

As macabre and unbelievable as that may sound, I was recently told by a close publicist friend that he was trying to block the son of one of his former clients (a true Broadway legend) from putting his mother's ashes up for auction as a piece of Hollywood memorabilia.

There's no denying that a major star's death can translate into big bucks for any vulture willing to capitalize on such tragedies. One of the best examples of this occurred back in August 1977, when Elvis Presley dropped dead of a heart attack. Though the Presley family had issued a strict edict that no cameras were to be allowed during public viewings of the body, the *Enquirer* paid Elvis' cousin $18,000 to snap a photo of what became known as "The King in the Casket." The infamous black-and-white image ended up on the tabloid's cover, selling a record-breaking 6.5 million copies and skyrocketing circulation. People just couldn't resist having one last look at their beloved King, just as they wouldn't be able to turn away from published post-mortem photographs of John Lennon, Michael Jackson, River Phoenix and Whitney Houston. So given the chance, I'd bet a good majority of you would have elected to have a look at Judy on the Jet or Mary in the Morgue. And yeah, I suppose I would have too.

I did get a chance to snap my own photo of a corpse-like star back in 1994 as part of my ongoing investigation into the "Brave Last Days" of Dean Martin. This much-adored Vegas crooner/comedic film star made headlines as recently as 2021—more than 25 years after his death—when photos taken in 1952 resurfaced of him showering naked at the Palm Springs El Mirador Hotel with his comedy partner Jerry Lewis. The scandalous image, which proved just how "big" a star Martin actually was, fetched a cool $4,500 on eBay.

Photo of Dean Martin in Beverly Hills, taken by the author shortly before the singer's death at age 78.

Sometimes known as "Dino" or "The King of Cool," Martin was a member of the infamous Rat Pack (also comprising Frank Sinatra, Sammy Davis Jr., Joey Bishop and Peter Lawford). He'd also starred in the original 1960 version of *Ocean's 11*, which was remade in 2001 with Clooney, Pitt and Damon.

Every few months (often when it was a slow news week), the *Enquirer* would have me report another ghoulish "Dean Martin: Brave Last Days" story whenever some paparazzo would submit the latest photograph of the frail alcoholic. The ravages of endless martinis, smokes and rich Italian food had rendered Dino barely recognizable from his suaver years when he presented as the epitome of style.

It wasn't hard to find Dino, whose broken heart never healed following the tragic death of his beloved son Dean Paul in a 1987 military jet crash at the young age of 35. Every night the perpetually mourning father would haunt the same Italian restaurant in Beverly Hills—a routine that went on for years. And should one of his favorite eateries close, he'd just move on to a similar Italian restaurant for his nightly dinners and cocktails. The problem with these photographs was that despite being taken months or even years apart, the photos always looked as though they could have been snapped on the same evening. That's because in place of his signature tuxedo, Martin now wore the exact same outfit night after night: ill-fitting gray trousers, a baby-blue collared shirt and a navy racing jacket.

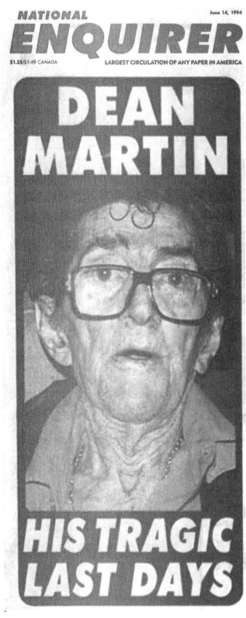

The *Enquirer* copy editors would sometimes switch to "Tragic Last Days" to accompany a particularly unflattering photo.

Always seated at the same table twirling his spaghetti, Mr. Martin would welcome me with a warm smile, while dribbling white clam sauce down his shirt. "One day you'll see me back up on the stage," he'd promise. It was positively heartbreaking. The only silver lining: I'd always dine at an adjoining table and order a hearty chicken parmigiana dinner that I'd include in my monthly expense report.

My first "Dino: BLD" story ran in March 1994. I reported that Dean had wasted away to a skeletal 120 pounds and could be spotted arriving to Beverly Hills' La Famiglia restaurant nearly every evening between 7:30–8:30 "with a Scotch in one hand, and a cigarette in the other." Curiously, Martin's ex-wife Jeanne would sometimes accompany him, but—like me—sit at an adjoining table. I'd jot down in my notepad how his loud, phlegmish coughing fits would startle the other patrons.

He also had no objection to me taking my own photos. Had I asked him to drop his trousers and show me his impressive manhood rather than his manicotti, perhaps I could have sold my own photo on eBay for $4,500.

After my visits with Dean, the next step in writing my distasteful pre-obits involved breaking the news that the star was again facing his "brave last days" to Martin's celebrity friends, hoping they'd provide comment. And I had three regulars I could always count on to pick up the phone and give me on-the-record quotes.

First, there was comedy great Morey Amsterdam, a mensch of a guy best known for playing sidekick Buddy Sorrell on *The Dick Van Dyke Show*. I'll never forget the time I paid one of my surprise visits to Morey when he was recovering in a hospital room, and he told me, "The *Enquirer* sends over a 'Get Well' bouquet of flowers even before I know I'm sick!" (Now *that's* how you deal with the tabs!)

Author with *Dick Van Dyke Show* co-stars Rose Marie and Morey Amsterdam in the mid-'90s.

Then there was crotchety comedy legend Milton Berle, beloved to TV audiences as Uncle Milty or Mr. Television, who was known to whip out his enormous cock at the drop of a hat. (I would have asked for a showing, but my conversations with Milty were mostly over the phone, which would have made that request even extra weird.)

And finally, there was Red Buttons, a sweet ginger-haired comic I knew best from the original versions of *Pete's Dragon* and *The Poseidon Adventure*. Red would always end our phone chats by saying, "Bless your heart for remembering Dean, William. Hey, if I give you my address, would you send me a copy when your article comes out?" I'm embarrassed to say I always told Red I would, but never did. Not because I was lazy or inconsiderate, but because I had a gut feeling that these would in fact turn out *not* to be Dean's brave last days, and I didn't want to send this dependable source a physical reminder of our latest flub.

While Red could not have been more cordial, Uncle Milty was just plain mean. And I mean *mean!!* And he'd always get my name wrong.

27

"Listen, *Peck*," he'd scream into the phone.

"Actually, it's Keck," I'd correct.

"I'll call you Peck if I wanna call you Peck, PECK!!" he'd holler back in my ear before calming down and giving me the quotes I needed.

In June 1995, we were so sure Dino's time had finally come that the overconfident editors went so far as to craft his "final" words.

"I'm not sorry about leaving this world," the editors claimed Dean had told loved ones. "There's nothing left in it for me." (How lovely.) This time we were just half a year early. Ironically, when Dean finally did take his last breath on Christmas Day 1995, our staff was off celebrating the holidays with our families. We were completely blindsided. Perhaps it was Dean's revenge.

Missing his exit, I sure as hell wasn't about to miss his funeral, which was to be held just three days later. Next to perhaps to absconding Kelsey Grammer's garbage (that story's coming up), this was the most stereotypical tabloid stunt I ever pulled off.

Dean was to be interred at the star-studded Pierce Brothers Westwood Village Memorial Park and Mortuary—one of the stops where I always take out-of-town guests hoping to spot a big Hollywood star. They're also guaranteed an "autograph" by way of a headstone etching, and these stars never balk at selfies.

Among Westwood Village Memorial's most famous residents are, curiously enough, an inordinate amount of former on-screen co-stars who seemingly wanted to spend eternity together. These include: Jack Lemmon & Walter Matthau; *Green Acres* spouses Eddie Albert & Eva Gabor (later joined by a handful of her older sister Zsa Zsa's ashes); *Hogan's Heroes* stars Bob Crane & Richard Dawson; *Family Affair* co-stars Brian Keith & Sebastian Cabot; and *Poltergeist* sisters Dominique Dunne & Heather O'Rourke. (And here's a little exclusive scoop I've never shared: *Poltergeist* mom JoBeth Williams told me she's instructed her sons, Will and Nick, to scatter some of her own ashes near Dominique and Heather when her time comes. A bit macabre, but also quite sweet, eh?)

Also crammed into this tiny plot of land hidden behind a Wilshire Blvd. cineplex: Natalie Wood, Donna Reed, Farrah Fawcett, Hugh Hefner, Jim Backus, Don Knotts, Rodney Dangerfield, Merv Griffin, Kirk Douglas, Florence

Henderson, Carroll O'Connor, **Doris Roberts**, novelist Truman Capote and their *cremè de la creme* guest of honor, **Marilyn Monroe**. (With so little real estate left, I'm guessing they must be plotting to evict nobodies like you and me to make space for future A-listers.)

As you can probably guess, with a rich treasure trove the likes of this, Westwood Village Memorial's security detail is equivalent to Fort Knox's. When I arrived there early in the day before Dean's evening memorial service, guards were already posted at the gates. My game plan was simple—come pay my respects to some random dead person, and then just wait it out a few hours on the lawn to casually enter the chapel with the invited guests. But I was sent scrambling in the mid-afternoon when the guards began clearing the grounds for a "special private event." Only in L.A. do cemeteries have VIP lists!

Suddenly I was shit out of luck. What to do? What to do...?

Well, as it turned out, there was a neighborhood of private homes just on the other side of the tall cinder-block wall surrounding the cemetery. As I walked the perimeter, I discovered the sturdy branch of a large tree in one homeowner's backyard extended over the cemetery wall—directly above the entrance to the small chapel where Dean's mourners would soon be entering! Five hundred bucks was all it took for the homeowner to agree to rent me his tree for the night. And in no time, my photographer and I scurried up that tree like hungry monkeys trying to reach a bunch-a-bananas.

Directly below our perch, a lectern had been placed where guests would sign their names in a registry book. Bingo! Through my binoculars, I'd have a bird's-eye view of every Oscar, Emmy and Grammy winner who'd be entering that chapel!

All we had to do was wait it out. And wait. And wait.... I was up in that doggone tree for nearly four hours, and it was now starting to get chilly. And very dark. By the time the service finally began a little after 7pm, it was too dark for my photographer to get any decent shots. Using a blinding flash could have given Don Rickles a coronary and necessitated a second, impromptu funeral. So my disappointed photographer had no choice but to climb down our tree, leaving me all by myself.

Fortunately, there was just enough moonlight for me to make out the faces of such famous mourners as Bob Newhart, Angie Dickinson, Jerry Lewis, Shirley MacLaine and Tony Danza. Having more than enough color for my story, I too could have left my perch when the chapel doors closed and the service began. But since I had the tree for a few more hours, I decided to stick it out. And thank goodness I did! About an hour in, up there under the stars, I was treated to a private concert by the great Rosemary Clooney (George's aunt)—her unmistakable deep, warm voice emanating from inside the chapel and crooning the Dino standard, "Everybody Loves Somebody (Sometime)."

Ah, now that's amore! I'm just grateful my tree branch didn't give out, sending me crashing down on Danza.

Lesson Learned: Even in the most awkward and uncomfortable situations, you can always find something (like Dino's spaghetti and martinis) to make you smile.

A Q&A WITH COMEDIAN RICH LITTLE
ON THE REAL BRAVE LAST DAYS OF DEAN MARTIN

(Courtesy of Rich Little)

KECK: Rich, tell us who the real Dean Martin was in his later years.

LITTLE: A loner. A very private person who didn't socialize much at all. I compare him to Johnny Carson. They both were very similar in that they kept to themselves and were a little hard to get to know. When we did *The Dean Martin Celebrity Roasts* at the MGM Grand in Las Vegas, Dean didn't even know who we were going to roast until about ten minutes before. I remember we were walking right up to the dais, and Dean turned to me and said, "Rich, who are we honoring tonight?" I said, "*What???* You don't know? Oh my God—it's Michael Landon." And Dean said, "Oh, that's a good choice; I like him." He just sailed through life doing what he wanted—playing golf and watching old Westerns on TV.

KECK: He ended up drinking himself to death in the end, but back in his glory years, was he really bombed when we saw him on stage swirling his scotch?

LITTLE: One time after one of the roasts, I remember going over to where Dean was sitting and picked up his glass to sniff it. And I didn't detect booze, which surprised me. The only time I ever saw Dean smashed was at the Ronald Reagan *All-Star Inaugural Gala* (1981 TV Special) when I was standing between Dean and Frank Sinatra. Dean was about to go on in five minutes and he was loaded. Frank told him, "You're not going on." And Dean said, "Fuck you, I'm going on!" And Frank told him, "You're not fit to go on; you're going to make an ass of yourself. I'm doing you a favor. Go back to the hotel right now and sleep this off!" Dean said, "You can't tell me what to do," and Frank said, "Yes I can," and got two guys to drag him away. Frank saved him from saying something terrible.

KECK: How much did Dean's essence change following the 1987 death of his son, Dean Paul?

LITTLE: It was pretty well over for him after his son died. He never recovered from that and became secluded. It was kind of sad at the end to see this decayed Dean Martin, as he was.

KECK: Did you ever make an attempt to visit him during those final years when he was at his worst?

LITTLE: No. One time a driver picked me up who said he also drove Dean. Dean had apparently told him, "Nobody comes to my house and I never see anybody."

KECK: How did you react when you'd see those *Enquirer* paparazzi photos of Dean looking so frail and forlorn?

LITTLE: We didn't want to look at those pictures. We wanted to remember him as he was.

KECK: You were invited to Dean's memorial service at the Westwood Chapel, but were out of town performing. Knowing Dean as you did, how do you believe he would have felt knowing I was perched up in that tree spying on all the goings-on?

LITTLE: (laughs) Oh, he would have gotten a kick out of it. He probably would have guessed you were Death coming to take him off to heaven.

KECK: I can't imagine Mr. Sinatra would have appreciated me crashing his friend's service?

LITTLE: No, no. Frank would have probably chopped the tree down.

KECK: How do you believe Dean should be remembered?

LITTLE: As a fun guy who did what he wanted. He didn't care about coming off polished, and everyone loved him for that.

L-R: Dean Martin, Frank Sinatra, Milton Berle and Rich Little.
(Courtesy of Rich Little)

Chapter 3
ASHES, ASHES

(DINAH SHORE)

Dinah Shore in the 1970s.

WHO: Dinah Shore (1916–1994). Multiple Emmy-winning singer, actress and host of the 1974–1980 daytime talk show *Dinah!* Highly publicized romance with actor Burt Reynolds.

WHAT: Crashing her 1994 funeral for the *National Enquirer.*

WHERE: Hillside Memorial Park, Culver City, CA.

When I was a teenager, I used to babysit this precocious kid in the neighborhood named Joshua. After I'd put little Josh to sleep, I'd sneak into his parents' bedroom to sample his father's massive collection of *Penthouse* magazines and the grainy Polaroids he'd snapped of his topless wife. I much preferred the magazines—a far more alluring incentive than the $5/hour I earned to give up my Saturday nights.

But then one Saturday—to my sheer horror—I discovered that all of the magazines had been dumped in the trash! Vowing to rescue this spank mag treasure trove before garbage collection day, I conspired with my best friend Tom to sneak away from our homes in the middle of the night and, as quietly as possible, roll my stepdad's wheelbarrow a quarter of a mile down the winding road to Joshua's house. The covert mission was well worth our efforts, as we ended up absconding with a 39-gallon lawn-and-leaf bag filled with more than enough porn to get us through the long, sweaty summer months ahead. But where do two horned-up teens stash such a valuable windfall? Tom and I decided to bury the bulging Glad bag in a giant gaping hole we dug in the woods across from his parents' house. Our very own secret XXX library where we could freely check out "inspirational" reading material as needed … which, for a couple 15-year-olds, was nightly.

But tragically—within mere days—the owner of that land, Larry Bjurstrom, unearthed our buried booty, and back in the trash all that fabulous flesh went. This time lost forever. It was nothing short of devastating. And to further rub salt in our wounds, we knew he'd share this humiliating story with our parents and other neighborhood adults over one of the fireside chats he hosted around the campfire he'd built within yards of our exposed hole. And to be sure, no one would question the identities of the neighborhood porn pirates.

One weekend night when I was back babysitting Josh after the great *Penthouse* tragedy, I somehow got to chatting with the kid about an afternoon talk show I'd watched when I was his age. The show, *Dinah!* (yep, the exclamation point was actually in the show's title!) was a breezy afterschool precursor to *Ellen* and *The Kelly Clarkson Show,* hosted by a lovely singer from the south named Dinah Shore. When I mentioned her name to Josh, he burst out laughing, convinced I'd made it up.

"What's so funny?" I asked the kid.

"Dino-*saur*?" Joshua repeated back to me, with a quizzical expression. "The show was hosted by a dinosaur??"

In all the years I'd watched her welcome stars like Lucille Ball, Florence Henderson and Betty White onto her sofa, it had never once occurred to me just how close Dinah's name was to a Jurassic reptile. Nor could it have occurred to me at the time that just 10 years later I would be in attendance at Dinah's funeral ... with my parents and grandmother as my guests!

Here's how that all went down. And it actually begins with the story of how I ended up working for the *Enquirer* in the first place.

After I relocated to L.A., my mom Nancy, stepdad Jim and nana Ruth would fly out west to visit me once a year, usually in February to escape their chilly upstate New York winters. And during these visits, I'd always get them into tapings of one

34

of their favorite TV sitcoms, like *Cheers*, *Coach* or *The Golden Girls*. But what impressed them most was when I scored them seats to the February 21, 1992, taping of *The Tonight Show Starring Johnny Carson*. This was arguably one of the most A-list *Tonight Show* tapings of all time, with special guests Michael Douglas—coming on to promote his thriller, *Basic Instinct*—and, in her only appearance with Johnny EVER, the legendary Dame Elizabeth Taylor. Six days shy of 60, Taylor had slimmed down, gotten off the tranquilizers and was looking hipper than ever with a full head of sultry, sable hair and a studded black leather motorcycle jacket that exposed ample cleavage. (It was a far different Liz from the one I'd be chasing down the winding roads of Bel Air just a few years later, as you'll read all about in my upcoming Dangerous Divas section.)

Dame Elizabeth making her one and only *Tonight Show* appearance in 1992.

I'd been able to secure my family these incredible tickets because I'd landed myself a coveted position as an NBC page during the final months of Carson's epic 30-year run as America's #1 late night talk show host. Leading up to his retirement, all the town's biggest stars were jockeying to drop in and bid their last goodbyes before Johnny forever disappeared behind his rainbow-striped curtains.

And as you might imagine, demand for audience tickets to one of these star-studded tapings was at an all-time high. Excited ticket holders who had flown in from all over the world were lining up outside our studio doors for several hours—or, as we crept ever closer to Johnny's May 1992 send-off—*days* before show tapings. And naturally, those who'd waited it out at the very front of the line (sometimes overnight, shivering in the pouring rain) expected they would be rewarded with the best seats in the house, which wasn't necessarily the case.

Per the edict of Mr. Carson and his longtime executive producer Freddie de Cordova—neither a spring chicken at the time—only young (under age 25), good-looking men and women were to be seated in the front rows to give the impression that Johnny was still relevant to younger generations. (These genetically privileged peeps were known to us as DFs, as in Down Fronts.) Jay Leno had already been lined up as Johnny's successor, and Johnny was determined to not exit looking like some Dinah Shore. Err, dinosaur.

It put all of us NBC pages in an incredibly awkward position, having to canvas the crowd and pull camera-friendly candidates. Since we naturally couldn't tell our gray-haired grannies that they were being hidden in the dark "because you're an old fart," we had to come up with creative (read: lame) excuses like, "Oh, those seats up front are reserved for Mr. Carson's VIPs." Or, "Actually where we're seating you offers the best vantage point so the cameras won't block your view."

Though this unspoken and ageist seating arrangement is the general standard for all TV shows that turn their cameras on their audiences (just check out *American Idol* or *America's Got Talent*), it understandably provoked a serious stink from some of the more vocal seniors who questioned why they were being seated so far from Johnny's desk. One particularly peeved gentleman ripped up his ticket and threw the torn pieces in my face!

With this crummy policy increasingly gnawing at me, I vented my frustrations to a fellow page, who clued me in to a way I could expose Johnny's dirty little secret and at the same time earn some extra rent money.

"Why not sell the story to the *National Enquirer*?" he suggested.

Though I'd flipped through the *Enquirer* for years in supermarket checkout lines to read *Dallas* and *Dynasty* storyline spoilers, the thought of actually being one of their secret paid sources had never so much as crossed my mind. And under

Above: *The National Enquirer*'s L.A. Bureau in the mid-'90s. Among the notables: (from left) senior reporter Mike Glynn (who recruited me), me, my regular partner in crime Suzanne Ely, the late great Neal Hitchens (in the ball cap) and (far right with the champagne) our Bureau Chief Jerry George, my mentor, to whom this book is dedicated. Below: My 1996 *Enquirer* press pass.

normal circumstances, I would never have even considered ratting out my own employer, but these were not normal circumstances. What we were being asked to do was pretty shady, so I went ahead and had my friend introduce me to *Enquirer*

senior reporter Michael Glynn, who ended up paying me a couple grand for my ageism tip.

At the time, $2,000 was like winning the Mega Millions lottery. Only later would I learn the real reason the *Enquirer* shelled out that much dough for a story that ended up being buried as a small item in the gossip pages. The editors were being overly generous because they knew having a snitch inside *The Tonight Show,* with its never-ending carousel of stars, could prove invaluable.

While I never again sold another story about Mr. Carson (or any other employer, for that matter), the *Enquirer* succeeded in seducing me into their mafia-like family with an offer I couldn't refuse. An actual job that would all but guarantee my immediate access to those Hollywood legends I'd come west to meet. And that, kids, is how William Keck first ended up becoming a tryout tabloid reporter, paid to extract Hollywood secrets and exclusive news-making quotes.

Though I'd arrived a little too late to the game to meet Lucy or Mr. Brady, I'd finally found my "in" and could now commence madly checking names off my "Must Meet Before They Kick the Bucket" bucket list. And I actually was fortunate enough to meet Dinah Shore in the flesh before her February 1994 death, which turned out to be the very same week my parents and grandmother arrived in town for their annual family visit!

Rather than just leave them alone in their hotel while I crashed Dinah's funeral, I thought, "Why not bring them along?" Not only could they get a glimpse into the insane world in which their "little Billy" had found himself, but my attending the service with more mature adults would actually help me blend in with the other mourners.

Our car was the very first to arrive at Hillside Memorial Park, a Jewish cemetery in Culver City, CA. (And I should note that this may have been the only time that my notoriously late mom and I *ever* arrived anywhere early.) Though we had no invitation, we had something better—a shiny white Cadillac, which helped us steer right past the unsuspecting security guard.

Even though she had the best sense of humor of possibly anyone I've ever known, and oftentimes a wicked one at that, Nana was also a Catholic who had buried her Jewish husband just four years earlier, and deemed my assignment to be a bit distasteful. So, while she elected to stay in the Caddy with the air conditioner on full blast, I led my mom and Jim right up to the funeral register book.

Due to a rather remarkable coincidence, my straightlaced Southern church-going stepfather had no problem signing our names as the first entries. That's because wayyy back in the 1930s, Jim's considerably older sister, Liz, had actually attended Hume-Fogg High School in Nashville, TN, with the deceased, who back

38

then was a popular cheerleader known to her schoolmates as Fannye Rose. *How about that?!* Talk about serendipity!! We were practically Fannye's kin!

Judging by the 50 or so folding chairs set up on the lawn facing the mausoleum where Dinah would be interred, this was to be a small service of only family and close friends, meaning keeping a low profile would prove extra challenging. We chose to sit in the second-to-last row to be as unobtrusive as possible as the other guests began to arrive.

And what an esteemed guest list it was!

My mom had really been hoping she'd see movie star Burt Reynolds—Dinah's boy toy from decades earlier—but he was a no-show. The *Enquirer* reported it had been a stressful week for Burt on the set of his sitcom *Evening Shade*, where he'd apparently gotten into a rather heated altercation with that week's guest director, *Cheers* star John Ratzenberger. According to an eyewitness, Burt slapped John so hard that his glasses flew off his face, as Marilu Henner and guest star Kathie Lee Gifford looked on in horror.

But even without Burt, my mom was far from disappointed. First to arrive and taking a seat in the row in front of us was comedian Dick Martin—host of the 1968–1973 variety show *Rowan & Martin's Laugh-In*—who had also briefly dated Dinah back in the '50s. (That girl "shore" got around!)

Next to Dick sat (the always reliable funeral attendee) Angie Dickinson, with the two sharing a laugh over just how much the crypt wall reminded them of post office boxes. The laughter ceased with the arrival of former President of the United States Gerald Ford and his wife Betty Ford. Because Betty took the seat one down from Jim, my frustrated mom had to strain her neck to unobtrusively eyeball what jewelry our former First Lady was wearing.

Other mourners trickling in included *M*A*S*H* star Wayne Rogers and longtime Motion Picture Association president Jack Valenti.

Since I obviously couldn't whip out my notebook and expose my true identity, I was furiously making mental notes of every detail that *Enquirer* subscribers would be able to read in next week's issue. (Yes, this was the era when "news" could still hold as news for minutes, hours or even a week after an event occurred.) I would have the exclusive scoop. Or so I thought until *he* arrived.

Securing an invitation to just about every damn happening in town—funerals, weddings, brises or his traditional first position on the Academy Awards red carpet (while I always had to sneak in through back doors)—was Army Archerd. *Variety's* trusted and well-respected veteran Hollywood newsman was always dressed in suits that fit him far better than his oversized toupee—a silvery slice of Hollywood memorabilia that should really be on permanent display at the Academy Museum of Motion Pictures under a dome of protective glass. So, when I saw Army arrive with his wife Selma, I knew I could kiss my *Enquirer* exclusive bye-bye, as Army's coverage would appear in the pages of next morning's *Variety*.

But I was equally aware that with Army's good taste and limited column space, we'd very likely be reporting different details. My rival's reporting was always predictably harmless. He'd list off who was there, mention a couple of nice quotes said over Dinah's urn and end with a respectful sign-off that would ensure he'd be invited to every future funeral up to and including his own.

That meant I had to keep my eyes peeled, and my ears open, for tidbits Army would never dream of reporting. For instance, the last big name to arrive was comedy legend Bob Hope, who was escorted by his valet to a seat directly behind ours. Poor Bob—90 at the time—started complaining loudly the minute he arrived. And JUST. WOULDN'T. STOP.

"I'm too warm," Bob grumbled to his patient valet, who then moved Bob to a folding chair under the shade of a nearby tree. Then moments later, it was, "I'm freezing." So back Bob went to his place in the sun. My mom actually suggested going back to our Cadillac to fetch Bob a sweater. My alternative suggestion: Why not just invite Bob to join Nana in our temperature-controlled Caddy? *"Look what I brought you, Nana: BOB HOPE!!"*

More than any of the kind tributes expressed during the quick memorial, what my parents and I remember most—and still laugh about to this day—was Dinah's unforgettable entry: in a simple urn, carried out on a sterling silver serving tray right alongside a large aluminum coffee urn and Styrofoam cups! I can only assume the frenzied cemetery worker was trying to save herself a trip. But the bizarre grouping very easily could have lent itself to a terribly distasteful faux pas.

"Coffee, tea … or Dinah?" my **naughty mom** whispered in my ear, suggesting one of the VIPs might accidentally **stir up a cup** of instant ashes. It took everything we had to maintain our respectful **demeanors** so as not to get tossed out on our Fannyes by President Ford's Secret Service detail.

With so much colorful **material to work with,** I couldn't wait to write it all up. And I thought I did a commendable **job balancing** the humor with the proper reverence due America's **Sweet'N Low Sweetheart** who had raised millions for charities via her **Club Skirts Dinah Shore Weekend** women's golf tournament. Held annually in Palm Springs, CA, **the fundraiser has** strangely morphed—to Dinah's dismay—into what has become the largest lesbian dance party in the world. Go figure??!)

I was excited to hand the article to my grandmother as proof that not everything in the *Enquirer* was made up. So you can imagine my incredible disappointment when I discovered that not a single word of my thorough, accurate, first-hand, on-the-scene reporting made it into the rag's two-page tribute. Rather, the editors in **Lantana,** FL, decided, as always, to take the tried-and-true "Brave Last Days" angle (with reporting from unnamed "insiders"), claiming that Dinah had commissioned a $3,000 wig after losing all her hair to chemo. They also heavily played **up** some fabricated nonsense claiming "Burt broke down" when he heard of his former lover's death.

Incredibly, the Hope-less story made no mention of the funeral or any of its famous attendees—including a former

President and First Lady! I could have just spent the day with my family at the San Diego Zoo watching gorillas sniff their fingers.

It's terribly discouraging when you go that extra mile to offer your readers the very best exclusive scoop, only to realize the "devastated Burt Reynolds" angle had been the plan all along.

I'd experience that same disappointment years later when I covered the SAG (Screen Actors Guild) Awards for *Entertainment Weekly*, managing to gather buzz-worthy red carpet quotes from all the A-list nominees and presenters. But in place of my reporting, *EW* opted to run a shockingly sexist photo grid displaying closeups of several actresses' allegedly saggy breasts with a caption along the lines of "Sag Awards Proves to be a Real Bust." Readers were invited to try to identify whom each set of tits belonged to. I'm sure the Guild (not to mention Meryl Streep and Dame Helen Mirren) appreciated that booby prize as much as I did. Can you even imagine *EW* printing such trash today (that is if it hadn't ceased publication in 2022)?

I felt like I was right back at the *Enquirer*, coming to realize that the lines separating supermarket tabloids from so-called "legitimate" entertainment news outlets were fading fast.

Lesson Learned: Before you stack too much on one tray just to save time, consider making two trips to save face. And find a more secure foxhole to stash your porn.

Chapter 4
CANDY CRASH

(JOHN CANDY)

John Candy as Johnny LaRue on *SCTV*, 1981.

WHO: John Candy (1950–1994). *SCTV* alum and comedic star of numerous big-screen comedies of the '80s & '90s, including *National Lampoon's Vacation, Splash, Spaceballs, Uncle Buck* and *Planes, Trains & Automobiles*.

WHAT: Attempting to crash his 1994 funeral and interment for the *National Enquirer*.

WHERE: St. Martin of Tours Catholic Church, Brentwood, CA. Holy Cross Cemetery and Mortuary, Culver City, CA.

When I was 16, my high school French class took a trip to Paris. While I was of course excited to ascend the 674 steps to reach the second floor viewing platform of the Eiffel Tower, it was another of the City of Light's landmarks that truly left me spellbound: The Tomb of Napoleon Bonaparte in the grand rotunda of Les Invalides. It is here that the diminutive Emperor's 5'6" body is entombed in a series of coffins made of tin, mahogany, lead and ebony—all set inside a gargantuan (16.4' tall, 13' long, 6.5' wide) sarcophagus constructed from a rare reddish-purple quartzite mined from Russia.

The epic proportion of "Le Petit Corporal's" funerary box was intended, of course, as a deferential tribute to man of short stature, but larger-than-life grandeur.

A real king-size king: The massive Tomb of Napoleon Bonaparte. Taken by the author in 1985 during his high school French class' trip to Paris, France.

It was *not* a design of necessity, as was the oversized casket created to house the substantial body of late comedic genius John Candy.

When Candy died in 1994, my *Enquirer* editors desperately wanted an exclusive photo of that super-sized "Candy wrapper," knowing all too well it would draw curious eyes—akin to a carnival barker inviting patrons inside a freak-show tent to marvel at the fat lady. Lucky me—assigned this morbid mission of fat-shaming a dead man I'd idolized ever since discovering him impersonating celebrities like Orson Welles and Julia Child on the '70s Canadian sketch comedy show *SCTV*.

I think one of the reasons I've long had an affinity for heavier comics the likes of Candy, Oliver Hardy, Dom DeLuise and *Modern Family's* Eric Stonestreet is because, in my early teens, I saw myself as an awkward fat kid who tried to get by with humor. I was never FAT fat; more like … oh, pudgy Jerry O'Connell in *Stand By Me* or a doughy pre-*Guardians of the Galaxy* Chris Pratt.

Shockingly, my extra prepubescent pounds were the result of a combination of factors, including a diet consisting primarily of mozzarella sticks and Fritos dipped in peanut butter, zero exercise (apart from once trying to break the pogo stick jumping world record) and (surprise, surprise!!!) watching an ungodly amount of television. The pudge really only became a problem one summer in the early '80s when I discovered I'd developed boy boobs and was suddenly shy about taking off my T-shirt at the town pool.

As I matured, the problem improved considerably, with the boobs shrinking in size to something more akin to nipple cups. But they still weren't working for me, ya know? So as soon as a surgeon diagnosed my tiny tits as "gynecomastia," I scheduled a procedure to correct the problem. A radical mini-mastectomy if you

44

will. And viola—I woke from the anesthesia with a chest that at long last looked more Tarzan than Jane.

While I still occasionally develop chipmunk cheeks, typically after wine-tasting weekends, I haven't considered myself "fat" since high school. It's true what they say, though: That fat kid always lurks somewhere inside. Not that you'd ever be able to find any photographic evidence of him. Oh no, I took care of that!

The photographer in our family was my perpetually jovial Uncle Tom. Not an Easter, wedding or First Communion went by without Tom snapping away to fill his many albums … whether we liked it or not. (And oftentimes I did not.) To that end, whenever I'd visit him, my Aunt Karen and my cousins Patrick, Timothy, Katy and Andrew in Syracuse, I'd sneak downstairs after everyone fell asleep to pull out every last fat photo I could find and flush 'em all down the toilet.

How horrible, then, that some ten years later I'd be scheming to photograph evidence of a man's excessive weight *after* he was dead.

Then just 43, Candy had been down in Durango City, Mexico, shooting the film *Wagons East* when he suffered a fatal heart attack in the middle of the night. While news of his sudden passing was tragic, it wasn't terribly shocking considering he'd been a chain-smoker who had weighed north of 300 pounds for most of his life and was rumored to have had a weakness for cocaine. On top of all that, it had been reported that he'd died after consuming a hearty lasagna dinner the night before.

So off I scampered to another funeral—hopeful that I'd return with a photo of Candy's XXL coffin to make my editors so happy that they'd welcome me back to the office with a giant slab of piping hot lasagna lightly sprinkled with cocaine in honor of the deceased.

But this proved no easy task, and one I ultimately failed miserably due to overconfidence and insufficient planning. When I arrived at Brentwood's St. Martin of Tours Catholic Church, there was no overhanging tree for me to rent or family Cadillac to hide inside; only a burly bouncer checking names on his clipboard as if he were posted outside Studio 54. The frenzied scenario I'd found myself in wasn't all that far off from a late- '70s NYC club scene, as I tried to blend into a crowd that included Tom Hanks, fellow *SCTV* alum Rick Moranis and

Saturday Night Live vets Chevy Chase, Bill Murray, Jim Belushi and Dan Aykroyd (who was to deliver Candy's eulogy).

With panic setting in as I neared the clipboard Nazi, I thought good fortune may have afforded me an unanticipated "in" when I spotted yet another of Candy's *SCTV* co-stars among the mourners—actress/comedienne Catherine O'Hara. While the world knows O'Hara as the mom from *Schitt's Creek* and the *Home Alone* movies, I'd come to know her personally. Well, *barely*. We shared a hairdresser at the since-shuttered Elle Salon in Beverly Hills and occasionally our appointment times would overlap, allowing me a few moments to chat Catherine up as Patty gave her a blowout.

(Incidentally, Elle was also the all-star salon Nancy Reagan visited every Wednesday without fail, always accompanied by her tall, handsome Secret Service bodyguard. After a few months, I noted the former First Lady's routine and booked my perm [*yes, perm*] appointments concurrent with hers. That's how I got Mrs. Reagan to personally autograph a copy of her autobiography, *My Turn*, as a special gift for my Nana Ruth, who shared the same February 6 birthday as Nancy's husband Ronnie.)

Granted, it was pretty tacky of me to approach O'Hara in the first place to ask if she could sneak me into her pal's funeral as if this were the movie premiere for *Best in Show*. And it was perfectly understandable when she politely declined. Now coming face to face with the keeper of the clipboard, the only story I could come up with on the fly was that my name was William Keck (true!), part of the philanthropic W.M. Keck Foundation family (crushingly not true) which funded *Sesame Street* (true) and our family friend (not true) John Candy had co-starred with Big Bird in the *Sesame Street* spin-off movie *Follow That Bird* (true).

No surprise that I was politely asked to immediately leave the grounds. As I walked back to my car in shame, Candy's hearse drove right past me, disappearing behind a plastic tarp that had been carefully positioned to block the view of that plus-size casket from intrusive paparazzi and reporters like me. But I refused to admit defeat! As they say, it ain't over 'til the fat … er, scratch that. I knew I'd have one last shot at the Culver City cemetery where Candy's casket was to be interred.

So after the service ended, I steered my car south on to the 405 Freeway to merge with the legit mourners in the long funeral procession. Noticing all the other drivers had been handed bright orange "Funeral" placards upon their exit from the church to display on their dashboards, I knew I had to break from the pack and beat Candy and Co. to the Holy Cross Cemetery as fast as I could. *Vrooommmm vrooommm*!!

Fortunately, this time luck was on my side! The clueless security guard posted at the cemetery gates kindly directed me up the hill to a mausoleum where a short ceremony was to be held. I was in!

As soon as I entered the imposing, dimly lit, all-marble mausoleum, I continued walking with feigned confidence straight ahead toward a small chapel where another service—delivered all in Spanish—was concluding for a hairdresser named Gilda Gutierrez. Out of the corner of my eye, I took note of stanchions and a red velvet rope that had presumably been erected to keep the Gutierrez *familia* (and me!) out. Knowing full well that I'd stand out like a Kardashian at Kmart if I dared step anywhere near this VIP area, I decided instead to slide into one of the chapel pews and drop to my knees for Gilda. As the sole Caucasian in the congregation, I stood out here too, but none of the Gutierrezes seemed to give a shit.

I remained there on my knees with my eyes closed in silent prayer long after every member of the Gutierrez family had exited the chapel. (Her passing had no doubt impacted me the hardest.) When a member of Candy's security detail gently touched my shoulder and explained the chapel had to be cleared for the next service, my Hail Marys for Gilda turned into desperate prayers for my own ass.

"I'm still praying," I told the man, with my eyes firmly shut.

"You have two minutes," he answered coldly, clearly on to my game.

At that point I casually glanced back over my shoulder and spotted a small gathering of people outside the mausoleum waiting for me to vacate the premises. The first two faces I spotted: Danny DeVito and his wife Rhea Perlman. Though diminutive in size, this Hollywood power couple was hard to miss. And they looked even tinier standing beside their late friend's gargantuan coffin. Yes, the rumors were 100% true. That thing was HUGE! But with all eyes on me, there was just no way I could get away with taking a photo with the small camera I'd concealed in my jacket.

I knew what I was doing was seriously reprehensible, and I'm not sure I've ever felt like more of an outsider. I was now actually holding up John Candy's service from starting, and the guard had understandably run out of patience.

"Okay, sir, you're going to have to come with me ... NOW," he said firmly, grabbing my arm and pulling me to my feet.

As I got up, I quickly made the sign of the cross I'd learned in Catholic Mass (modified in my frenzied brain to "Father, Son and Holy *crap*!"), and tried my best to avoid making eye contact with the DeVitos as I was carted off to a small, dark holding office.

"We know you're the same guy who was trying to get into the church," said a second taller guard. "Who are you?!"

I foolishly kept with my lame story that I was a friend of the family desperate to pay my respects. But it was pointless, and by this point, pathetic. I was busted and ended up being held in that cemetery prison for the duration of Candy's service until all the famous mourners had cleared out and Candy's coffin had been forever sealed away from view behind a marble slab. There'd be no photo, and most assuredly no celebratory lasagna dinner. By the time security finally told me I was free to leave, I felt like crawling inside the nearest crypt and praying the Lord my soul to take.

While I'd failed in the eyes of my editors, I'm grateful that casket photo doesn't exist. Because unlike all my fat photos swiped overnight from my Uncle Tom's albums, there'd be no going back and erasing that exploitative image from the eyes of Uncle Buck's legions of fervent fans.

Lesson Learned: If you're going to crash a funeral, don't ya dare get caught with your hand in the Candy jar.

Chapter 5
BIONIC BOY TOY

(LINDSAY WAGNER)

WHO: Lindsay Wagner (b. June 22, 1949). Winner of the 1977 Outstanding Lead Actress Primetime Emmy for her role as crime-solving cyborg Jaime Sommers on *The Bionic Woman* (1976–1978).

WHAT: Crashing her father's funeral for a *National Enquirer* investigation into her new romance with a younger man.

WHERE: Panorama Presbyterian Church, Panorama City, CA.

Lindsay Wagner as the *Bionic Woman* (ABC).

I only recently discovered a fascinating study conducted in the mid-1970s that blamed a new genre of television shows featuring independent, "aggressive" heroines such as *Wonder Woman*, *The Bionic Woman* and *Charlie's Angels* for inciting young girls to grow into violent women who were more likely to engage in chokings and knife fights. *Yikes!!* What this terribly troubling report neglected to address: how those very same pop culture programs inspired girls (and their gay brothers) to turn jump ropes into golden lassos to seize Nazis, to mimic the bionic *"whooooop"* sound effect as they feigned leaping in slow motion over walls in pursuit of sinister Russian spies and to chase abusive pimps into alleyways while

49

balancing themselves on roller skates. In other words: demonstrating how anyone, regardless of sex, can become a hero.

Over the years, I've been incredibly blessed to interview all of these inspiring female role models, including the wonderful Lynda Carter and the eternally angelic Jaclyn Smith, Kate Jackson and Cheryl Ladd. (Farrah Fawcett, I spied only once—eating a plate of waffles all by herself at a coffee shop across the street from the Chateau Marmont.) But more than any other ass-kicking action hero, it was bionic beauty Lindsay Wagner

Author with Wonder Woman Lynda Carter at her 2019 cabaret show (above) and (below) *Charlie's Angels* co-stars Jaclyn Smith and Cheryl Ladd at the 2010 *TV Land Awards*.

whom I was most anxious to meet when I came west searching for my favorite stars.

That's because, as a kid, I never missed an episode of this *Six Million Dollar Man* spin-off centered around Jaime Sommers, a top-ranking tennis pro who is critically injured in a tragic skydiving accident—necessitating life-saving, state-of-the-art upgrades to her legs, an arm and an ear. In return for her extravagant upgrade, she's recruited by the United States government to engage in dangerous top secret missions that constantly put her life in jeopardy. In my eyes, Jaime was the most incredible woman in the world, and the license plate on my car—BIONIC—is a testament to my enduring adoration.

Not long after I started at the *Enquirer*, I let my editors know that if a Lindsay Wagner story ever arose, I'd jump at the chance to work it. Well, be careful what you wish for. When that golden opportunity did present itself, it grabbed me by the nuts and squeezed them harder than Jaime compressing fuzzy tennis balls in her bionic fist.

Here's what happened. After receiving a tip from a caller offering up personal info on Ms. Wagner, our bureau chief Jerry excitedly waved me into his office.

"Okay Kecky," he announced. "Here's the story you've been waiting for!"

But the elation I initially felt upon learning I'd potentially be interviewing my childhood idol ended abruptly when I was told the nature of the assignment. Lindsay's father, Bill Wagner, had died and I was to "cover" his funeral. Under normal circumstances, the *Enquirer* wouldn't have cared less about the passing of a '70s TV star's cremated relative, but this time there was another angle. Lindsay, then 45, was dating a 28-year-old buck who was closer in age to her two sons. The *Enquirer* wanted me to crash the funeral and get photos and info on Lindsay's bionic boy toy.

I know ... just HORRIBLE!!! Even so, I was in no position to turn down an assignment I'd basically begged for, so off I traipsed to the Panorama Presbyterian Church, not having a clue what I'd say if I were to come face-to-face with the grieving daughter.

Accompanying me on my covert operation was our very heavyset, bearded English paparazzo, Vincent Eckersley. Eckersley was a tabloid legend—never above attempting any means necessary to get his shot. Before Elvis Presley's cousin successfully snapped that previously referenced 1977 "King in the Casket" *Enquirer* cover photo, Vincent had shamelessly disguised himself as a Catholic priest in his own failed attempt to capture that very same taboo image with a camera he'd concealed within a hollowed-out Bible. Compared to that outlandish stunt, this assignment would be a piece of Victoria Sponge Cake!

Vincent did his best to hide his 300 pounds behind a bush with his camera lens aimed across the street at the chapel courtyard. Meanwhile, I was in the packed parking lot searching for a spot as far away as possible from the church so as not to draw attention to my car's BIONIC license plates that had recently arrived from the DMV.

Stepping into the courtyard, I saw no sign of Lindsay. But there was no missing her tall, olive-skinned beau—standing by himself and appearing almost as uncomfortable and out of place as I was feeling. When I introduced myself (leaving out my professional affiliation), he told me his name was "Tony" and that he was dating the deceased's daughter.

"And here she comes now …," said Tony, welcoming my childhood crush into his arms with a warm, comforting embrace.

Gulp! There she was. After all these years. Just a couple feet away and even more beautiful in person. Offering me a kind smile I didn't deserve, the actress greeted me with a friendly "Hello, I'm Lindsay."

"Oh, I know," I answered nervously.

"You knew my dad?" she asked, leaving me to scramble for a response.

While a well-formulated lie may have served other *Enquirer* reporters at this oh-so-awkward moment, there was no way I could ever deceive the Bionic Woman, even though she herself had assumed countless secret identities. (To pull off her top secret missions to save the world from mad scientists, killer robots and an alien Sasquatch, Jaime had gone undercover as a pro wrestler, a stewardess, a beauty pageant contestant and even a nun.)

"I'm so sorry for the intrusion," I prefaced sheepishly, followed by sycophantic babbling to stall for time. "I want you to know I'm a huge fan. Seriously—huge. I have a framed photo on my apartment wall of you lifting a car over your head with one hand. And my car, parked right outside behind the church, has the license plate BIONIC."

Rather than call for security to escort this obsessive stalker off the premises, Lindsay once again smiled, seemingly amused that one of her fans had brazenly infiltrated her dad's funeral. But I wasn't *just* a fan, I admitted.

"I'm with the *National Enquirer*," I blurted out, "and they want to do a story about you and Tony. We actually have a photographer over there across the street who managed to get some shots of you both."

When I pointed to the bush where Vincent was hiding, Lindsay and Tony looked across the street, prompting Vincent to reveal himself (and his wide lens) with a cordial wave.

With my identity now exposed, I prepared for Lindsay to pick me up with her bionic arm and toss me through one of the church's stained glass windows. But instead, she ... smirked, appearing calm and completely void of rage.

"So, if you already got photos, what do you need?" she asked.

Not wanting to blow this unanticipated opportunity with an unreasonable request for a full interview, I whispered, "Maybe just ... a caption for the photos ...."

"You want a caption?" she answered. "Okay, I'll give you a caption: *'FUCK YOU.'*"

And there it was. Exactly what I prayed *wouldn't* happen. But I could hardly blame her. And that's just what I told her: I had it coming. I apologized for the gross intrusion and turned my back in shame. But as I started back toward the parking lot, Ms. Wagner must have sensed my deep humiliation and broken heart.

"Hold on," she said, summoning me back.

Lindsay Wagner, 45, in hot romance with 28-year-old toy boy

"Bionic Woman" Lindsay Wagner has fallen hard for a handsome hunk who's 17 years her junior!

The 45-year-old actress has put four failed marriages behind her and is having the time of her life with artist Tony Proctor, 28.

She's starry-eyed again after 4 failed marriages

"BIONIC WOMAN" Lindsay Wagner found happiness on a mountaintop with young artist and auto detailer Tony Proctor.

"Tony has shown me what it's like to really feel loved. He is a true southern gentleman. I haven't touched a doorknob since I met him," Lindsay told The ENQUIRER in an exclusive interview.

"If I forget and open a car door myself, he makes me get back into the car."

Lindsay — who will star with "Six Million Dollar Man" Lee Majors in the upcoming TV movie "Bionic Everafter?" — added: "Tony and I had our first date last January — and it was perfect!

"He took me hiking in the mountains. Believe it or not, when we got to the top, we saw a double rainbow! We connected on that mountain and we've been close ever since.

Really??!! I was elated!!!

Lindsay properly introduced me to her boyfriend, Tony Proctor (*Score! I now had his full name!!),* who said I could print that he was in love with her, adding "there's nothing I wouldn't do to make her happy."

I thanked them both for their generosity and said I would now leave to allow them time to spend with family and friends. Lindsay asked for my business card, assuring me she'd follow up with a call (I feared from her attorney). But as it turned out, Lindsay—like many of us—hadn't always had the closest relationship with her dad. And in a stroke of unexpected serendipity, she and Tony were just about to launch their own Native American-inspired jewelry line. So when Lindsay reached out just as she said she would, we were able to collaborate on an on-the-record story that acknowledged the couple's romance, and at the same time brought publicity to their colorful baubles. They even submitted a lovely photo of themselves—each sporting earrings from their line. One bionic hand washing the other.

Years later when I was producing the celebrity segments for Hallmark Channel's morning lifestyle show *Home & Family*, I twice welcomed Lindsay onto our show. And on one of those visits, I asked her to join me for a photo op on the bumper of my Jeep—with that very same BIONIC license plate that had been carefully concealed in the parking lot outside her dad's service. Afterwards, she invited me up near her mountain home to attend one of her delightful "An Evening With Lindsay Wagner" events, where she screened clips from her various projects, shared wildly entertaining behind-the-scene memories and took questions from the audience.

Admittedly, I never had the guts to remind her of our very first meeting, because even in her mid-60s, Lindsay still looked fit enough to rip off my face and expose me as some devious Fembot.

Author posing on his Jeep's Bionic bumper with on the set of *Home & Family*, 2017.

Lesson Learned: Sometimes our stalkers can become our friends. But then other times … well, just wait until you get to my Victoria Principal chapter.

Chapter 6
WHO FORGOT YA, BABY?

(TELLY SAVALAS)

Telly Savalas as Kojak, with his trademark sucker.

WHO: Telly Savalas (1922–1994). Winner of the 1974 Best Lead Actor Primetime Emmy for his role as lollipop-sucking police detective Theo Kojak on the 1973–1978 police drama *Kojak*. 1963 Oscar nominee for *Birdman of Alcatraz*. Played the villainous 007 villain Stavro Blofeld in 1969's *On Her Majesty's Secret Service*, the inspiration for Mike Myers' Dr. Evil character. Jennifer Aniston's godfather and Nicollette Sheridan's former stepfather.

WHAT: Investigation into his burial for the *National Enquirer.*

WHERE: Forest Lawn Cemetery, Hollywood Hills, CA.

In 2021, my mom and I paid a visit to her parents' mausoleum at the Beth Emeth Cemetery in Glenmont, NY, to unlock the heavy metal gates and take care of some long-overdue spring cleaning. As we swept away cobwebs and removed dead flowers, we never stopped to think just how difficult it might have been to locate the crypt in its overpopulated necropolis had her family's name (Sporborg)

Cleaning out the family mausoleum, 2021.
(I took some flak on social media for wearing shorts and flip flops.)

not been etched in the stone. For not every grave is so carefully marked, as I discovered back in 1994.

More than his roles as '70s TV detective Kojak or James Bond villain Ernst Stavro Blofeld (in 1969's *On Her Majesty's Secret Service*), Telly Savalas is perhaps most noteworthy today for being the Greek actor selected by Jennifer Aniston's late father (*Days of Our Lives*' John Aniston) to be her godfather. However, it was I—*not* a Savalas or Aniston—who intervened to get a grave marker installed above Telly's unmarked plot at Forest Lawn Cemetery in the Hollywood Hills.

If you've never heard of Telly and have yet to see his take on Blofeld, I'll tell ya all you need to know. Savalas was known for his shiny bald head, gold chains and deep raspy voice. His *Kojak* character was always sucking on a lollipop while investigating the murder of the week. And his trademark line: "Who Loves Ya, Baby?" became a pop-culture catchphrase.

The one-time de facto stepfather of *Desperate Housewives* vixen Nicollette Sheridan (whom you can read all about later in the book), Savalas enjoyed a colorful lifestyle—romancing three wives and doting over his six biological children. For the last 20 years of his life, he'd resided at the Sheraton Universal Hotel, which was typically filled with Universal Studios theme park tourists who could oftentimes find Telly at the bar (which for a period of time, was named "Telly's"). And near the end of the actor's life, he popped up on late-night TV ads endorsing the Players Club, a service offering members exclusive savings and gambling privileges in Las Vegas and Atlantic City. These ads were so overplayed that comedian Phil Hartman portrayed Savalas in *Saturday Night Live* spoofs that promoted the "Player *with Yourselves* Club," whose members received exclusive masturbation privileges in hotel rooms all over the world ... for just 15 minutes with unlimited amounts of Kleenex.

Savalas was undoubtedly a TV icon, so it was surprising when the *Enquirer* received an anonymous tip four months after his 1994 death that no identifying stone had been placed at his gravesite. And guess who was assigned to get to the bottom of this travesty.

With its shooting fountains, impeccably landscaped hedging and impressive marble statues, Forest Lawn is the place for those seeking VIP access to heaven. With a little help from a groundskeeper, I was able to locate a beautiful grassy alcove where Telly had supposedly been laid to rest. And sure enough: no marker to speak of! One of our photographers snapped a shot of me—notepad in hand—pointing down to the barren plot of grass, a photo that actually made it onto page 20 of the *Enquirer's* May 31, 1994, issue. What a proud moment for the Keck family that was!

And this certainly wasn't the first time such an unfortunate oversight involving a beloved celeb had occurred. In his own 2004 memoir, titled *The Untold Story*, my former *Enquirer* boss Iain Calder recalled pointing his own finger at an unstable "hole in the wall" crypt where the body of Judy Garland had been temporarily stored for more than a year while her family debated a suitable final resting place.)

Besides the grave being unmarked, a little investigating uncovered that Savalas' burial fees had mysteriously gone unpaid, with none of the actor's heirs forking over the modest $196 annual fee for weekly placements of fresh flowers on his grave.

Here's a sampling of my shocking world-exclusive exposé that somehow failed to earn me a place on *60 Minutes'* crack investigative team:

"When the *Enquirer* visited Telly's burial site four times during an 11-day period in May, we found just a pathetic plot of unmarked land. The only sign of devotion was dying flowers floating in a cheap vase of moldy water."

Contacted for comment, Telly's widow, third wife Julie, told us through her attorney that she was having an artist friend design a special $10,000 marble grave marker that would be ready for installation in a month's time. There was just one problem with that: Forest Lawn allows only bronze grave markers. Oopsy-daisy!

A cemetery spokesperson told me he couldn't go on record about what was causing the holdup, but he insinuated that there'd been a lack of communication between Julie and Telly's children. "It's a private family matter and they do not wish for us to comment on it at all," is all I was told.

So back over the hill to Forest Lawn I'd schlep week after week only to discover nothing but grass and more grass. A

Me pointing to Telly's unmarked grave in the *National Enquirer*.

follow-up story let *Enquirer* readers know that another month had gone by with still no stone. Truth be told, it was now summertime, and I was tiring of making these repetitive treks in the L.A. heat. So, anxious to bring some resolution to this matter and spare the Savalas family any further embarrassment, I hatched a plan …

On behalf of the family, I placed a call to the cemetery to find out what the hell was going on.

"The *National Enquirer* is raking (the family) over the coals that (Telly's) grave still doesn't have a marker," I told a Forest Lawn rep who'd been dealing with the Savalas family. "What's the hold-up? I'd like to just get this taken care of as quickly as possible."

The man on the other end of the line who was assigned to the Savalas account didn't question a thing, informing me, "We've had his plaque here for some time. As we've been told, there are issues within (the family), and we've just been waiting to hear from someone about getting this in the ground."

"Well, that's true," I answered with unwavering confidence. "Sadly, certain family members aren't speaking to one another at the moment. Maybe you can do everyone a big favor. Would you place some calls and let them know the stone will be installed next week?"

"I'd be happy to," said the rep. "Just let me know what day."

"How about Thursday," I suggested. "Around 4?"

"That should work just fine."

And it was as easy as that! On Thursday, July 28, 1994, our national nightmare ended when Kojak at long last got his grave marker. I was fairly confident that my photographer and I would be the only Savalas "loved ones" in attendance. So you can imagine my surprise (*dread!*) when the cemetery rep approached from behind and gently placed his hand on my arm. "Oh look," he said. "Uncle Gus (Telly's brother) made it!"

That was our cue to exit.

Uncle Gus, it turned out, was the one who ultimately paid for his brother's gravestone out of his own pocket. And when he discovered the *Enquirer's* involvement, he was rightly outraged.

The way I see it, even if I was out of line, at least I had the decency to show up to pay my respects. And with the stone finally set in place, I was finally able to rest in peace.

Telly, now you know who loved ya, baby!

Telly Aristotle Savalas

January 21, 1922 – January 22, 1994

"The hour of departure has arrived,

and we go our ways —

I to die and you to live.

Which is better God only knows." — Aristotle

Lovely quote, right? Too bad Aristotle never said it. The credited speaker was, in fact, Aristotle's philosophical predecessor, Socrates. Oops!

Note to Savalas Family: when you call in your order for a replacement, make sure the engravers understand the corrected marker should *not* read Telly Socrates Savalas.

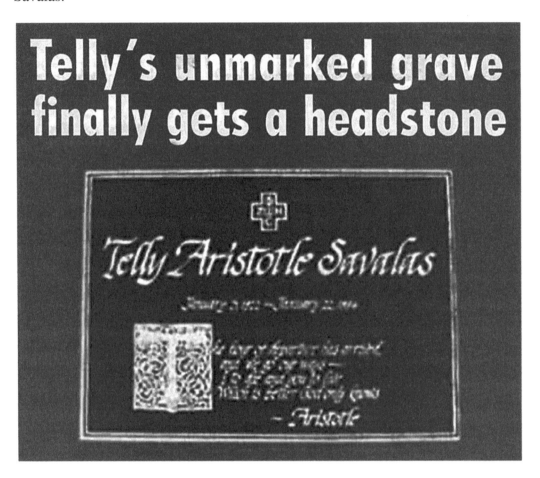

Lesson Learned: Before taking your last breath, make sure you've assigned someone trustworthy to carry out your final wishes. If not, your legacy may be left in the hands of a total stranger.

Chapter 7
A-TEAM STAR/F-MINUS ETHICS

(GEORGE PEPPARD)

George Peppard in his starring role in NBC's *Banacek*. (1973, Wikimedia Commons)

WHO: George Peppard (1928–1994). Handsome film and television star best known for his roles as Hannibal Smith on the 1983–1987 action series *The A-Team*, and Audrey Hepburn's love interest in the 1961 big-screen classic *Breakfast at Tiffany's*.

WHAT: Investigating his 1994 death for the *National Enquirer.*

WHERE: UCLA Medical Center, Westwood, CA.

As I began writing this entry, I was hunkered down in a hospital room in Fairbanks, Alaska. A critical case of pneumonia had cut short my mom's dream cruise, and she was now on a ventilator fighting for life. After a few truly agonizing days, by the grace of God (and a top-notch team of young docs straight out of *Grey's Anatomy*), she recovered. But for a while it was a terrifying ordeal, and it could have gone either way. Never in my wildest dreams could I have imagined that less than two years later a global pandemic would leave *millions* fighting for their own lives on respirators, with their loved ones barred from even holding their hands. It's a nightmare scenario beyond my comprehension.

With that pandemic perspective, I now see how lucky I was to have been able to keep vigil at my mom's bedside, protectively watching the door and making sure no one entered her room with anything less than one hundred percent compassion and respect. Heaven help that one student nurse who kept disturbing my mom's sleep by constantly checking on one vital after another. I may have gone just slightly Shirley MacLaine on her.

In times of a health crisis, there is nothing more sacred than a family's steadfast protectiveness of their loved one. However, back in the mid-'90s, the *Enquirer* routinely called upon me to invade hospitals and defy that sacred right to privacy. This was one of the very worst parts of my job. And in the case of the assignment I'm about to share, the famous patient had already taken his last breath, which somehow made it extra insidious. The deceased was handsome actor George Peppard, who fought alongside Mr. T on NBC's *The A-Team* and wooed Audrey Hepburn in the film classic *Breakfast at Tiffany's*.

Incidentally, *Breakfast at Tiffany's* was the movie playing in the background when I lost what I refer to as "my straight virginity" to my singer friend, Lauren, who always reminded me of *Beverly Hills, 90210's* Jennie Garth. It happened in her small Hollywood apartment, with the film's haunting theme song, *Moon River*, serenading us at my moment of climax. For many closeted gay guys like I was at the time, you get to lose your virginity twice—typically, the first time to a girl as part of a last-ditch effort to make Mom (and Jesus) happy, and then ultimately to the guy you pictured in your mind during that earlier encounter. My second cherry-popping at age 23 was with Scott, a gorgeous, blond, cowboy type who'd played a lifeguard on the NBC soap opera *Santa Barbara* and sent me home with a lovely parting gift of freshly-picked avocados from his backyard that I turned into the best guacamole I've ever had.

But back to Peppard.

My marching orders came from our most feared editor, Brian Williams. I was to immediately head over to UCLA Medical Center, where the other half of Hollywood goes to die when they can't get a reservation at Cedars. My mission: gather up whatever details I could about Mr. Peppard, who—according to the hospital employee who'd stuffed him in a body bag—had just passed on in his private room surrounded by family.

There are times in this book when I point blame towards others for the distasteful actions I was called to carry out during my formative tabloid years, but this one was all on me. Sure, Williams wouldn't let me leave the hospital until I unearthed some dirt. "C'mon, Keck," he'd push. "You're part of a team and you've got to be a team player." Still, I was ultimately the one who picked up the shovel.

Going through the nurse who had been treating Peppard, I was granted an interview with his doctor in the very room where he'd just died.

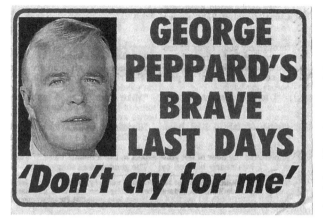

The Peppard family had released a statement about their patriarch's cause of death (cancer), but there were many details left out that the family felt didn't need to be shared publicly. These (of course) were the details Williams wanted most. I was informed by the doctor that George had actually been battling leukemia and had bravely refused stronger painkillers so as to remain as alert as possible in his final hours. Joined by a clergyman, and surrounded by fifth wife Laura and his children from previous marriages, George passed peacefully with the family having formed a circle around him.

But the quote from the doctor I remember most was, "It takes an extraordinarily brave man to sit in the center of this room talking to his family while seated on a bedside commode."

After learning more details than could ever fit into one story, I bolted out of the hospital and informed Williams that I had everything he wanted and much more. "That's my boy," he said. I was made to feel the hero. If the *Enquirer* gave out medals for bravery on the battlefield, he surely would have awarded me one that day. That was the sick, mafia-like way of the tabloid world: Praise for reprehensible behavior, while any expressions of moral reservations were met with accusations of weakness and insubordination. Just as on the battlefield, or working for Tony Soprano, the only way you can get the job done is by repressing personal ethics and going in for the kill!

63

Not surprisingly, I felt little pride when my story came out in the new issue, which on the front page teased "George Peppard's Brave Last Days."

As if I didn't feel slimy enough, after the article came out bearing my byline (which the *Enquirer* now wisely omits to protect their reporters' covers), I received a phone call that reduced me to the size of a hospital bed bug. I'd given my phone number to Peppard's nurse, should she think of any additional details she'd like to share. After reading my article, she in fact did have something to add: "I hope you're proud of yourself; you tricked us all," the nurse scolded. "Just know wherever Mr. Peppard is now, is a place you'll never see."

I assume she meant I'd be burning in Hell, which I can only imagine is a better fate than returning to a hospital in Fairbanks, Alaska.

Lesson Learned: "First, do no harm" needn't only be a pledge for physicians or Hippocrates. Hospitals are for the sick, not the sick and twisted. Get out of the way and let medical professionals do their damn jobs.

Chapter 8
DOWN IN THE MEADOWS
(AUDREY & JAYNE MEADOWS)

WHO: Audrey Meadows (1922–1996), winner of the 1955 Primetime Emmy for her 1952–1957 role as *The Honeymooners*' Alice Kramden. Audrey's older sister, Jayne Meadows (1919–2015), known for various co-starring roles including Billy Crystal's mother in *City Slickers* and several appearances on *The Love Boat* and *Fantasy Island.*

(Left) Audrey Meadows with her *Honeymooners* co-stars Jackie Gleason and Art
Carney, circa 1955. (Wikimedia Commons)
(Right) Audrey's sister Jayne Meadows with husband Steve Allen at the 1987
Emmy Awards. (Alan Light/Wikimedia Commons)

WHAT: Investigation into Audrey's health (and subsequent death) for the *National Enquirer.*

WHERE: Cedars-Sinai Medical Center, L.A.; The Friars Club, Beverly Hills.

As sleazy as my previous chapter's George Peppard hospital caper had been, I at least got my facts right: George was unquestionably dead. But what happens when you incorrectly report that a dead celebrity is alive? *Ugh.* I found out the hard way in 1996.

You don't often hear the word "ghoul" thrown around these days. It's one of those words like "pansy" that, thankfully, has been all but retired. Around Halloween time you'll hear it every so often, much like "poltergeist," as an alternative to the over-used "ghost." But it's hardly ever used in everyday language. Still, I was once called a "ghoul" by Jayne Meadows, a red-haired actress best known not for her body of work, but for being the wife of legendary comic and pre-Johnny Carson *Tonight Show* host Steve Allen—a characterization she deeply resented as slighting the rest of her wide-ranging life. Jayne also had to contend with a far more famous sister: actress Audrey Meadows, who played Alice Kramden—the long-suffering wife of New York City bus driver Ralph Kramden on the 1950s sitcom *The Honeymooners.* Too young to remember that very non-PC show? Suffice it to say the studio audience would howl whenever Ralph (as portrayed by comedic giant Jackie Gleason) would bunch up his fist in Alice's face and physically threaten her with his LOL catchphrase, "One of these days, Alice, POW, right in the kisser!"

Can't quite imagine Jay saying that to Gloria on *Modern Family*, can you?

So, here's what went down that labeled me a "ghoul." My *Enquirer* bureau chief Jerry had received a tip from his secret source at Cedars-Sinai Medical Center that poor Audrey had been admitted for an unknown diagnosis. So lucky me—I had to do what I hated most—a hospital room "eyeball," which basically meant I had to sneak a quick look at Audrey to see how bad, or hopefully good, she appeared.

I can't begin to tell you how many bogus bouquets of flowers I delivered to hospital rooms during my *Enquirer* years. They helped me look the part whenever I had to hurry through hospital lobbies and past security guards under the pretense of visiting sick relatives. Fortunately, this particular mission didn't take much snooping, as Jerry's source had given us Audrey's exact floor and room number. So up I went, stepping off the elevator, walking swiftly down the hall past the nurses' station, always appearing confident that I knew exactly where I was headed so as not to draw suspicion.

When I found Audrey's room, her door was open. There was Alice Kramden lying in bed, now looking more as she did in her later years as Ted Knight's nagging mother-in-law, Iris, on the ABC sitcom *Too Close for Comfort*. She was sitting up having a conversation with a well-dressed gentleman when I walked in with my colorful bouquet.

I was hoping our hospital-room interaction might be similar to one I'd had earlier that year with comedian Morey Amsterdam of *The Dick Van Dyke Show* (my go-to whenever I needed a quote for those Dean Martin deathwatch stories). For that particularly memorable "eyeballing" assignment, I'd located diminutive Morey in Cedars room #5008, propped up in bed, chatting with his lovely wife, Kay. When I told Morey I was a reporter with the *National Enquirer*, he smiled graciously and invited me to pull up a chair. He assured me he wasn't in danger of dying just yet. He'd only been experiencing a little shortness of breath, but would be sure to let me know when he *was* dying. Before I knew it, Morey was trying out some of his "new" jokes on me, poking fun at such current newsmakers as George Washington, Christopher Columbus and Joan of Arc.

It was a pleasant, laugh-filled experience for us both, and—as a result—only positive reporting ended up in the paper. While I'd certainly never be so forward as to suggest celebrities need show similar graciousness to the press in such a private, vulnerable setting, it's definitely a way to avoid an ugly confrontation and take control of a potentially negative story.

Audrey Meadows chose not to take that approach. Initially, she lit up when she saw the bountiful bouquet that I'd had my regular West Hollywood florist arrange.

"How lovely," said Audrey, reaching for her flowers.

Since I'd identified myself as an *Enquirer* reporter in the card she was opening, I had no choice but to clue her in right away. Her extreme displeasure was instantaneous. "Oh no. No, no, no."

Audrey held onto the flowers as her companion swiftly ushered me to the door. This was the moment that, from my experience, could go several ways. I could be arrested for trespassing, which wasn't my first choice. I could make a clean getaway, having sufficiently "eyeballed" my subject. Or—as happened on the rarest of occasions—I might actually be granted a reprieve. A rare invitation back inside the room for an exclusive sit-down interview that would make me the hero of the day back at the office. I decided to gamble.

"If you'll just read the card," I begged the gentleman, as the door shut in my face.

And then I heard Audrey's strong, rasping voice shout out, "Hold on."

Yes, I thought! She'd read my kind card and was going to invite me back. She realized I was different from the typical *Enquirer* scumballs who had no doubt terrorized her friends for years.

And sure enough, the door opened, the gentleman poked out his head and said, "Thank you for the flowers." My spirits briefly soared, until a half-second later, when he continued, "You can go now."

Crap.

'HONEYMOONERS' STAR BATTLES BACK FROM BRINK OF DEATH

TV legend Audrey Meadows — who played Jackie Gleason's wife on the classic sitcom "The Honeymooners" — was prepared to die when she was recently rushed to a hospital with severe pneumonia.

The 69-year-old actress ordered her doctors not to resuscitate her if she could no longer breathe on her own after her lungs filled with fluid due to a respiratory infection.

"As far as being kept alive on a respirator, I've always felt that there comes a time when you have to know when enough is enough," Audrey told a pal after her touch-and-go battle for life.

TV's beloved Alice Kramden was burning with fever and gasping for breath when she was admitted to Cedars-Sinai Medical Center in Los Angeles on January 24, under the name "Audrey Six."

"The poor soul was white as a ghost and moaning in pain," said a source close to the star. "Her lungs were filled with fluid from an acute bronchial infection that turned into pneumonia.

"It quickly became a life-and-death fight because Audrey had told her doctors she wanted no means of artificial respiration used on her if she could no longer breathe on her own.

"Plain and simple, if her lungs ceased to work Audrey would have been a goner. It was her choice and she's obviously one very brave lady.

"Everyone thanked God that she quickly responded to the massive antibiotic therapy the doctors gave her intravenously.

"The staff was able to keep her lungs clear of fluid and within 24 hours she turned the corner and was soon out of the woods.

"Audrey was transferred out of Intensive Care on January 26 and admitted to a VIP room. She was kept on oxygen and antibiotics and will have to take it easy for a while.

"This condition has left her weak as a kitten. But one thing for sure, she's a fighter. She wouldn't still be here if she wasn't."

— ALAN BUTTERFIELD
and WILLIAM KECK

AUDREY MEADOWS told doctors not to resuscitate her if she became unable to breathe on her own.

By the time I returned to the bureau, Jerry had talked to his source, who assured him that Ms. Meadows was merely battling pneumonia and was on her way to a complete recovery. And that's the story Jerry needed me to write ASAP, even though my visit had confirmed nothing of the sort. This isn't normally how things worked at the *Enquirer*, and I wasn't at all comfortable with what I was being asked to do. Audrey hadn't granted me an interview and I didn't get a look at her medical chart. But Jerry was on deadline to close the issue and was desperate for this story to fill a hole. "Kecky," he pleaded. "I need you to do this. *Please*. Just do it for me."

Jerry had been a staunch supporter of mine, both professionally and personally. He'd bailed me out of trouble on more than one occasion and had even fought for my job when the executive editors wanted me sacked before I'd had a chance to impress them.

So, I did it. I gave Jerry the quotes he coerced me to attribute to his "secret source": that Audrey had been hospitalized for "an acute bronchial infection that turned into pneumonia," but was now "out of the woods" and would soon be released.

Well, I got part of the story right. Just a few days later, Audrey would be released—to a funeral home! *Ugh.* How awful. One of my actual worst fuck-ups of all time.

Realizing after my unwanted intrusion that the *Enquirer* was most likely on to her fatal diagnosis (giving us more credit than we deserved), Audrey had elected to beat us to the punch by issuing a press release that she was sadly fighting a losing battle to terminal lung cancer. Unfortunately, our new issue had already gone to press, with my byline on an article assuring *Enquirer* readers that America's beloved Alice Kramden was joyously on the mend. By the time the new issue hit the stands, Audrey Meadows was dead.

(As a side note, no story in the *Enquirer* is ever "inaccurate." We just "explained" that after we'd gone to press, Audrey's health had taken a tragic and unexpected turn. *Very* unexpected.)

I was MORTIFIED. I wanted to strangle Jerry, but with him being my boss, all I could do was mope around a bit to communicate I'd been done dirty and would never again submit unsubstantiated quotes. And I'm proud to say I never did.

If only it had ended there.

During those horribly uncomfortable few days between Audrey's tragic announcement and the release of our new issue which would celebrate her recovery, the *Enquirer's* new publisher dropped into our L.A. bureau to meet the staff. When I introduced myself, his first words were, "William Keck … you wrote the Audrey Meadows piece. *Nice work.*"

I was hardly in a position to defend my tarnished reputation by explaining what had really happened, thereby throwing Jerry under the bus. So, I just grumbled, "Yes, that was unfortunate. We'll be much more careful going forward."

To his credit, Jerry did feel horrible. So, what did he do to make it up to me, you might ask? Immediately after Audrey released her statement—*before* she was even dead—he assigned me to write her obituary for the follow-up issue!!

What I didn't know at the time was that, prior to her public announcement spurred by my intrusion, Audrey had kept her true diagnosis a secret—even from her beloved sister Jayne, who had been falsely led to believe Audrey was merely being treated for a blood clot and phlebitis. Now reeling from the shocking true nature of her sister's grave condition, Jayne was preparing for the worst—which didn't stop Jerry from instructing me to call her at home to get quotes for Audrey's (pre)obituary which would soon be going to press. (Another big gamble: this time that unpredictable Audrey would in fact be dead by the time the new issue hit stands.)

To make matters even worse, Jayne had been left alone at home to process this news, while her husband Steve was out of town performing dinner theater in Florida with wild-haired comedienne Phyllis Diller. When Jayne answered the phone in tears, I introduced myself as respectfully as possible, asking if she might perhaps like to supply the *Enquirer* with some personal family photos for our tribute to Audrey—who, I can't stress enough, *was still alive!*

Jayne could have chosen many words to describe my extreme gall, but what I very clearly heard her say over the phone was, "You ghoul!" And with the dictionary definition of "ghoul" being "an evil spirit, especially one that robs graves and feeds on dead bodies," I think she nailed me: A big ole *Walking Dead* ghoul!!

One might assume (i.e., hope) that would be the final time I'd speak with Jayne, but our paths were destined to cross one more time.

Phyllis Diller somehow ended up becoming a friend. I liked to tell people at the time that we were "casually dating"—me in my twenties and she approaching 80. (You can read more about our sordid *Harold & Maude*-like affair in Phyllis' upcoming chapter.) Not long after Audrey's funeral, Phyllis invited me to be her escort (i.e., sober driver) to some special event being held at the Friars Club in Beverly Hills—a bawdy show business club founded by Milton Berle that had

70

hosted countless roasts and only admitted women as members in 1987 after being ordered to do so by the courts. Following a legal battle with the New York Friars Club and the deaths of most of its members, the building on South Santa Monica Boulevard closed its doors and was demolished in 2011.

When I arrived to pick up Phyllis at her Brentwood mansion, I had no clue that the event I'd been invited to was a banquet honoring Jayne Meadows and Steve Allen! And guess what? We were sitting at their table!! *Aw, Hell!* Phyllis must have seen the blood rush out of my face when I heard the news, because she didn't waste any time telling me, "I know; don't worry."

"I don't think you *do* know, Phyllis," I tried explaining, all befuddled. "You see, I...."

"I know all about it, and it's been settled," said Phyllis, calmly explaining that she and Jayne had spoken on the phone earlier in the day. Upon learning the name of Phyllis' "plus one," Jayne swirled my name around in her head.

"William Keckkk...," she repeated to Phyllis a couple times. "That name sounds *familiar....*" As soon as Phyllis told her I worked at the *National Enquirer*, Jayne put the pieces together, yet miraculously didn't nix my attendance.

"Are you absolutely sure?" I asked Phyllis. "Jayne did call me a *ghoul.*"

While I hate speaking ill of the dead (I much prefer robbing their graves and feasting on their rotting flesh), Phyllis told me that Mrs. Steve Allen had made her own share of enemies over the years and then went on to call Jayne the "c" word ... and I *don't* mean comedienne! As Phyllis explained, all the famous attendees that evening would be coming only in support of Steve, who (according to Phyllis) had apparently fallen out of love with Jayne many, many years earlier.

"It's a loveless marriage," Phyllis claimed. "Steve had fallen in love with actress Jennifer Jones, but when he admitted his affair to Jayne, she'd threatened him that if he ever left her, she would destroy his reputation." And from that point on, they allegedly put on a front all the way up until his death in 2000.

When we arrived at the Friars Club, the first thing I noticed was Jayne scurrying from table to table, madly rearranging the place cards. And shocker— Phyllis and I were no longer seated at the table of honor.

The evening quickly nosedived from somewhat uncomfortable to dismally unbearable as the hours dragged on and on and on. I've been to a few stinker events over the years, but this one easily took the cake. (In fact, the *only* good thing about the night was the cake: lemon buttercream with raspberry filling.) Having spent decades in Steve's shadow, Jayne had made sure this one night would be all about HER. She'd painstakingly supervised the editing of the couple's tribute video, including just ONE grainy 90-second black-and-white clip of Steve, followed by an excruciatingly long compilation reel showcasing clips of every walk-on bit part Jayne had been able to salvage from her dusty vault dating all the way back to the 1940s. Have you seen Jayne as Mildred Havelend in 1946's *Lady in the Lake*? Well, I have!

I will say this. Jayne and Steve were at least fortunate that so many of their surviving friends showed up in their very best wigs and toupees to celebrate them. By the time Phyllis turned 80 in 1997, the only person her birthday-gala organizers were able to scrounge up to play MC was *Diff'rent Strokes* child star Gary Coleman. "I don't even know that twerp," poor Phyllis cried on my shoulder, giving serious consideration to canceling her event altogether. "That just shows you how many of my friends are DEAD." Most notably Audrey Meadows. Last I checked.

Lesson Learned: Before you send "Get Well" flowers, make sure the card shouldn't instead read "My Sympathies."

Chapter 9
NO FUN WITH DICK & ANDY

(DICK VAN DYKE & ANDY GRIFFITH)

WHO: Dick Van Dyke (b. Dec. 13, 1925) and Andy Griffith (1926–2012). A pair of television legends recognized through many awards and distinctions for their classic eponymous sitcoms, *The Dick Van Dyke Show* (1961–1966) and *The Andy Griffith Show* (1960–1968). In the '90s, both gentlemen made TV comebacks as stars of their own hit mystery series: Van Dyke in *Diagnosis Murder* (1993–2001) and Griffith in *Matlock* (1986–1995).

Andy Griffith welcomed pal Dick Van Dyke on to a 1986 episode of *Matlock.* (NBC)

WHAT: On-the-record interviews for the *Los Angeles Times* and *USA Today*.

WHERE: Dick and Arlene Van Dyke's Malibu home. Set of the CBS legal drama *Family Law*.

We all dread receiving that phone call that someone we love has passed. I've mentioned my sweet Nana Ruth a few times already. In 2002, she was 90 and had been in and out of the hospital suffering from congestive heart failure, but she'd rebounded enough for me, my boyfriend Jim and my parents to plan a getaway to Spain. When Jim and I were at the airport just about to board our return flight to Los Angeles, my name was called over the public-address system to please pick up

Easter 1972 with my Nana
(and her wig).

the nearest white courtesy phone. When I did, I no longer had a Nana. Just like that. I'm grateful I was at least fortunate enough to have had the news broken to me gently by the calming Southern drawl of my stepdad (also named Jim).

We aren't always that lucky.

On January 17, 1996, I had the horrible misfortune of being asked by one of my *Enquirer* editors to phone Andy Griffith at his home to inform the TV legend that his 38-year-old adopted son, Andy Griffith Jr. (who went by the name "Sam"), had overdosed that morning in his North Hollywood home after a heavy night of partying.

Andy Griffith with TV son **Ron Howard**, circa 1961. (CBS)

For those too young to remember, Griffith Sr.'s most famous role was Andy Taylor in the 1960–68 situation comedy, *The Andy Griffith Show*, which cast the beloved actor as the right honorable sheriff of Mayberry, NC. Taylor was also the widowed father of a young boy named Opie, played by child actor Ron Howard many years before he grew up to star in *Happy Days* and become an Oscar-winning director of several Hollywood blockbusters. This macabre phone call made me feel as if I were calling Sheriff Andy Taylor to inform him that Opie had OD'd.

Sam was Andy's only son. The troubled youth had been found slumped over his desk by his roommate, who attempted to administer CPR. But it was too late. To add an extra layer of unbearable heartache to the tragedy, after years of animosity between Sam and Andy, an unfinished letter of apology addressed to his father had been found at Sam's feet.

I can still remember my editor, Larry Haley, providing me Andy's home phone number in North Carolina where the TV legend had relocated when he was shooting *Matlock*, a 1986–95 detective series later rebooted with Kathy Bates.

"What do I do if Andy picks up?" I asked Haley.

"You tell him and get his reaction," I was instructed emphatically, without a drop of empathy or compassion.

Phoning the long-since disconnected 910-473-6274 (don't bother dialing; Andy won't pick up!) was without a doubt the worst call I ever had to make in my life. As I pressed the final number, I prayed to the Gods of Mayberry that he wouldn't answer. Please, please, PLEASE don't pick up.

But he did. The sad "Hello" on the other end of the line was unmistakable. He sounded tired and pained and I wondered if he'd already heard the news.

"Mr. Griffith," I prefaced softly. "This is William Keck with the *National Enquirer* in Los Angeles."

"Oh God, no," he said. "Is it true?"

"Then you've heard?" I asked.

"I received a call earlier, but I was praying it wasn't true."

"I'm afraid it is, sir," I said.

Without a bit of anger, Mr. Griffith thanked me for calling, but said he had to hang up. I reiterated my sympathy and let him go without trying to "work" him for heartbreaking quotes to fill the story I'd be tasked with writing.

After taking a moment to decompress, questioning if that had actually just happened, I phoned Haley back to let him know I'd broken the news to Mr. Griffith. Haley was very excited and wanted to know everything the father in mourning had told me.

"He was too devastated and in shock to speak," I reported back. Haley was not pleased. "Give him a while and call him back," he ordered. It was one of the few times I flatly refused an editor's request.

A short time later, another editor, Charlie Montgomery, phoned with instructions to call *The Andy Griffith Show* co-stars Don Knotts and Jim Nabors to get their reactions to Sam's death. I didn't do that either.

Perhaps another reporter phoned Andy back to get all the "exclusive" quotes that surprisingly ended up in the story—quotes about Andy being "hammered with pain" and "ravaged with guilt." But more likely than not they were all made up, as so often happened.

The 1996 "Andy Griffith Heartache" *Enquirer* article (left), and (right) me with Andy's longtime friend and co-star Don Knotts, whom I flatly refused to phone.

There was also a discussion among the editors about having me refer in my story to Sam—who had struggled with drugs for many years—as "Dopie," under the attention-grabbing headline, "Andy Griffith Heartache: 'I Tried My Best, But My Boy is Going Straight to Hell.'" But I successfully fought that as well.

It was becoming clear in the *Enquirer* home offices that this Keck fella in the L.A. Bureau was reaching his limit and potentially going soft. I began sensing a definitive shift in the way I was treated. No longer was I brought into some of the more "sensitive" discussions. Doors were closed in my face, while eager new hires were invited in to receive their marching orders.

The unsavory source who called in the scoop about Sam's death also offered us a copy of a detailed book proposal for Sam's in-the-works, tell-all memoir, *I'm No Opie*, which somehow ended up in my possession. (I rediscovered this forgotten manuscript in my *Enquirer* files while researching this book.) Some of the titles of the never-to-be-published chapters were "Wreaking Havoc on the Mayberry Set," "The Day My Father Took Ronnie Howard Instead of Me For a Ride in the Car," "Mom—the Better Actor," "The *Real* Don Knotts," "Dad's All-Night Parties on Deserted Islands," and, my personal favorite, "Dad Marries My Sister's Best Friend."

Hoping to further cash in on the tragedy, the source told me that Sam had been having a difficult time selling the book because, remarkably, he didn't have any photos of himself with his father, and Andy wouldn't provide him any. From that point on, knowing one day I'd write this book, I never missed an opportunity to grab a photo with a TV legend, something I should have requested from Mr. Griffith the one time I met him in person.

That was in 2001 when I was on assignment for the *Los Angeles Times*. I'd been invited to the set of a new CBS TV legal drama called *Family Law* to interview one of its stars, the late great Dixie Carter of *Designing Women* fame. I consider that highly emotional interview to be among my all-time best. I remember Dixie tearing up as she recalled how her daddy back on their Tennessee plantation had to lower their long-waving Confederate flag after its symbolism changed from a sign of Southern pride to a racist and hurtful reminder of slavery. This established a trust with Dixie that enabled me to easily get her on the phone shortly thereafter for a profile I was writing for the *Times* on her former best friend, Delta Burke. Having not spoken for years after a very public falling out over issues that lead to Burke's sudden exit from *Designing Women*, Delta and Dixie were so touched by the kind quotes each offered the other in my article that I ended up getting the two to meet for lunch. That was the beginning of their reestablishing a bond that continued until Dixie's passing in 2010. So even though it's not the focus of this book, my reporting has accomplished *some* good over the years.

But no good came from unexpectedly meeting Griffith on the *Family Law* set, where he was shooting a special guest appearance. My sensitivity filter was apparently malfunctioning when I included in my article a reference to the then-75-year-old's "little spotted hand," which I'd noticed when he'd extended it toward me for a cordial handshake. I should have known that *Times* readers—many seniors themselves around Andy's age—wouldn't appreciate that unnecessary descriptive. And as it turned out, one of those readers was Griffith's close pal and fellow TV comedy legend Dick Van Dyke, whom I'd worshipped all my life. But, honestly, who hasn't?

In his letter to the editor that addressed me personally, Dick schooled me good. "Mr. Keck," he wrote. "Andy Griffith lives in South Carolina, so it's unlikely he read your column. However, if he did, I'm sure he'd be anxious to put his 'little spotted hand' right in your face."

JUST FOR VARIETY

ARMY ARCHERD

GOOD MORNING: The L.A. Times is learning it cannot write off Dick Van Dyke. The actor's show, "Diagnosis Murder," according to the paper's William Keck, "is considered by most critics to be the sexless, prune juiced-down sibling of 'ER' or 'NYPD Blue.'" Van Dyke quickly e-mailed the paper, "I don't need prune juice myself but I'm sure those who do would find good use for the paper containing your article."

Above: Variety columnist Army Archerd's column. Below: The star of The Dick Van Dyke Show with co-stars Mary Tyler Moore and Larry Mathews, circa 1963. (CBS)

Ouch!! But Dick was right (except for the South Carolina reference, as Griffith's home was in *North* Carolina). I give him huge props for taking the time to defend his friend and all seniors, who obviously deserve our utmost respect. As a hot-shot punk in my 30s, I was naïve and couldn't yet see the full picture. But I sure as heck do now ... along with more than a few sunspots on my own hands.

I'd already been on the *Mary Poppins* star's shit list after an article I'd written earlier that year for the *Times*, which stated that many TV critics viewed his mystery series, *Diagnosis Murder*, as "the sexless, prune juiced-down sibling of *ER* or *NYPD Blue*." Though I'd attributed that harsh critique to various reviewers who'd routinely taken potshots not only at Van Dyke's show, but also Angela Lansbury's *Murder, She Wrote*, Dick took *me* to task by rather brilliantly taking my own words and using them as ammunition. "I don't need prune juice myself," he wrote my *Times* editor. "But I'm sure those who do would find good use for the paper containing your article."

Van Dyke's clever quotes were then picked up by my nemesis, Army Archerd, who ran them in his *Variety* column.

Yes, Dick was saying that my articles were wipe-worthy. And, in hindsight, showing anything other than great deference for two men who had provided such joy to fans all over the world was indeed a dirty-ass move on my part.

At home with Dick Van Dyke in 2013.

But as my career advanced, I was fortunate enough to have had opportunities to make things up to both men. In 2013, Mr. Van Dyke invited me into his Malibu home for an interview timed to his Screen Actors Guild Life Achievement Award. Personally greeting me at the door, the then-87-year-old could not have been more hospitable as he showed me his treasured collection of Laurel & Hardy memorabilia. And waiting for me in the kitchen with a pitcher of freshly-squeezed lemonade was his lovely new 42-year-old bride, Arlene.

I was relieved to discover Dick wasn't at all the grumpy curmudgeon that my earlier reporting had provoked him to be. And with a conscientious commitment to clean up my spotty record, my tribute article wisely made no references to anyone's hands, proving a leopard can, in fact, change his spots!

And a year earlier, when Griffith passed, I had the great honor of getting to round up his last surviving *Andy Griffith Show* co-stars—including

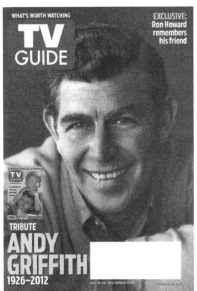

Ron Howard (Opie), Jim Nabors (Gomer) and Betty Lynn (Thelma Lou)—for a cover-story tribute I wrote for *TV Guide*.

Howard generously took time to pen a heartfelt, more than half-page tribute to his former TV dad. In particular, Howard praised Griffith's pledge to use his family-friendly television programs to show people how they can live with integrity and make huge differences in the lives of others. These were words I very much needed to hear at that time.

What was *my* work contributing to the world? And what did I want my own legacy to be…?

Lesson Learned: While racism, sexism, sizeism and all isms are abhorrent, ageism comes with an added layer of stupidity in that every one of us who is fortunate enough to achieve longevity will, as a result, suffer some form of persecution. It was a sobering truth I learned while still in my twenties when the Enquirer *employed a team of Hollywood special effects makeup wizards to transform me into what we called a "Golden Oldie"—from my Dick Van Dyke chimneysweep cap all the way down to my little spotted Andy Griffith hands!*

Chapter 10
LIVER WITH SOME BEANS AND A NICE CHAMPAGNE

(LARRY HAGMAN)

WHO: Larry Hagman (1931–2012). Two-time Emmy nominee and four-time Golden Globe nominee for his iconic role as the villainous oilman J.R. Ewing on the 1978–1991 primetime soap *Dallas*. Astronaut Maj. Anthony Nelson on the 1965–1970 sitcom classic *I Dream of Jeannie*.

Larry Hagman as J.R. Ewing on *Dallas*, 1980s. (CBS)

WHAT: Investigation into his 1995 liver transplant for the *National Enquirer*. Various on-the-record interviews for *USA Today* and *TV Guide*.

WHERE: Northern California low-income apartment complex. Southfork Ranch, Parker, TX.

In my upcoming Victoria Principal chapter, you'll learn the full extent of my (at times unhealthy) obsession over the CBS primetime soap opera, *Dallas*. Suffice to say for now that back during my years attending Bethlehem Central High School in Delmar, NY, while the other kids were out on Friday nights getting drunk, stoned and laid, I was perfectly content staying in to watch the show's filthy-rich Ewing clan get drunk (Sue Ellen), stoned (Lucy) and laid (J.R.). And I wasn't alone. A whopping 83 million Americans and 350 million international viewers tuned in for *Dallas*'s November 1980 resolution of its "Who Shot J.R.?" cliffhanger. This was a phenomenon unlike any other, making Larry Hagman—the man who played ruthless, womanizing, double-crossing Texas oil man J.R. Ewing—the most famous celebrity in the world.

And Hagman would have been the first to tell you that. And also that he shared much more in common with his misbehaving *Dallas* character than the gentlemanly NASA astronaut he'd played years earlier on the '60s sitcom *I Dream of Jeannie.*

I learned much about Hagman's darker side from his *I Dream of Jeannie* co-star Barbara Eden at her home in 2011.

I was once invited into the home of Jeannie herself, actress Barbara Eden, who clued me in to some of Hagman's sophomoric, unprofessional on-set antics, including wild temper tantrums, vomiting and urinating all over the set to express his dissatisfaction with scripts, humiliating guest star Sammy Davis Jr. and terrorizing a group of elderly nuns.

I got my own taste of Larry's devilish nature when I visited the Southfork Ranch in Parker, TX, (where the series shot its exterior scenes) to cover the filming of a 2004 *Dallas* reunion special.

Out by the corrals, I'd struck up a conversation with the male hairstylist of Linda Gray (my actress friend who played the role of J.R.'s boozy wife, Sue Ellen), when Hagman casually walked by, lowered his hat politely and said, "Evenin', boys."

"Mr. Hagman," I called out to the Fort Worth native. "You know Texas about as well as anyone. It's my first time visiting your state. Anything you'd recommend?"

"Two things," Hagman said. "First, get yourself a fuzzbuster. These Texas cops can be real assholes. They'll getcha if you don't stop for school buses. Second thing you want to make sure you get: PUSSY! Texas has the best pussy of any state in the country."

With that, Larry chuckled just like J.R. and waltzed off, leaving my mouth agape.

Had I really heard him right? Considering he'd been married to his wife Maj going on 50 years, was the then-73-year-old still a connoisseur of that particular Texan delicacy? Besides that, he surely knew Linda's hairstylist, a man he was traveling with, was as queer as I was.

"That's Larry for ya," the unfazed hairstylist shrugged.

Another time, I asked Larry if he could recall J.R.'s "Three B's"—the bribes his character would routinely throw around Texas to land shady business deals. "Booze!" Hagman shouted out immediately, followed seconds later by "Broads and Booty."

Hagman got his good share of all three, but it was the booze that proved to be his undoing. While Larry always managed to handle his liquor, his soaked liver could hold out for only so long.

"The booze started around seven in the morning," I was told of Hagman's drinking habits by his best friend, actor Patrick Duffy, who played J.R.'s little brother, Bobby Ewing. "Larry would pop a bottle of champagne and … would just keep it going all day long. We figure he must have spent about $80,000 a year on booze, and Larry once told me, 'I wasted (the equivalent of) a Mercedes a year for like 40 years.'"

By my calculations, that meant Hagman would have spent over a million dollars on liquor during the original *Dallas*' 13-season run. I don't know about you, but that figure alone leaves me with one helluva hangover!! Advil, anyone?

"By the end of the day, a half a dozen bottles of champagne would have been consumed, and only by him," continued Duffy. "It was constant. And that kind of drinking affects the liver."

Uh, ya think?

Though it was only ever reported that Hagman received one liver transplant, he was actually the recipient of two, his co-stars confirmed to me. The first was in 1995. While on a waiting list for a new liver, Hagman ventured out with Duffy on their yearly fishing trip to Vancouver. "He was within weeks, a couple of months at most, of just not being able to keep going," Duffy recalled. "I knew if he didn't get a liver soon, I'd be saying goodbye to my friend. And when they opened him up, his liver just dissolved as they were taking it out. It was that close."

What neither Duffy nor Hagman knew was the secret role I'd played in this transplant saga. One morning in September 1995, I was awakened by what I'd by now come to accept as my lot in life: *another* of those wake-up calls from my *Enquirer* pimp Brian Williams. I would be taking on a major top-secret assignment that involved travel. These last-minute trips meant having to scramble to pack an overnight bag and find someone to look after Austin, my epileptic Lhasa Apso (who coincidentally had been named after his rescuer, Teri *Austin,* an actress from the *Dallas* spinoff *Knots Landing*). But Williams would hear no excuses. In just a couple of hours—doggy sitter or not—I'd be flying to Northern California to break the news to a grieving woman that her dead partner's liver had been transplanted into the body of a TV superstar.

As Williams explained to me, a hospital insider had tipped us off that Larry's new liver had been harvested from the body of a Puerto Rican gentleman named William Ruben Gonzalez III, who'd left behind a girlfriend and infant daughter after his truck rolled three times. Besides a massive cerebral hemorrhage that left him in a coma, his body was relatively unscathed, making him the perfect organ donor upon his body's arrival at the San Bernadino County Medical Center.

(Many years later, Cynthia Cidre, the Latina executive producer of TNT's *Dallas* reboot, told me Hagman used to joke with her that receiving Gonzalez's liver had made him "part Mexican.")

Once again, I'd be paired with our photographer Vincent, the same obese English bloke who'd been hiding in the bushes outside Lindsay Wagner's father's funeral. Once our plane landed, we would head directly to the dusty, run-down apartment complex in Citrus Heights where Gonzalez's fiancée Jeanette Goins was still trying to process how dramatically her life had changed since her Bill's fatal August 21st accident.

Aw shit. This assignment was a really slimy one.

Vincent and I had little trouble locating the dreary Sunrise Center apartment complex, which consisted of several small cement bungalows surrounding a dusty playground with rusty slides and broken swing sets. Surveying the depressing complex, I saw through my tabloid glasses the sleazy direction this story would no doubt take. Tragic Goins was struggling in squalor with her now-fatherless baby Monique, while daddy's liver was living the good life in a multi-million-dollar Malibu beach house. The perfect recipe for a tabloid exposé!!

I would paint Goins as the sad victim to whom Hagman would most certainly have to reach out for fear of being branded (by the *Enquirer*) a cold, heartless bastard. And that's pretty much how this sleazefest played out.

Vincent and I decided that the most important component to this story was the photo of the lonely mother and child. Without that heartbreaking image, there was no story. But what if this woman refused to pose? Or even worse, called the police on us? Assuming she was even home. And what if she had a gun? While I am a registered organ donor, I wasn't looking to donate any of mine that day. Although, how poetically karmic would it have been had the day ended with a "Who Shot Will Keck?" murder mystery?

We decided that Vincent would snap an unsolicited shot of Goins just as soon as she opened her apartment door. I was to play the good guy—apologizing for the intrusion, but quickly explaining that I'd come bearing BIG news. News that could potentially prove tremendously beneficial and change her life! It was a warped version of those old Publishers Clearing House Prize Patrol doorstep ambush TV commercials from the '80s, where shocked housewives with their hair up in curlers would open their doors and be handed large cardboard checks.

After Goins recovered her vision from Vincent's camera flash going off in her face, she consented to pose for a few shots holding baby Monique. (Phew! Part one of our mission accomplished!!) Then when Vincent felt he had gotten all the shots he needed, he took off with the film, leaving me to drop the bomb.

I sat Goins down at a rotted picnic table stained with dried ketchup and bird crap and told her why I'd come. It did indeed involve Bill, I confirmed.

"Bill was an organ donor, wasn't he?" I asked gently.

"Yes," she sheepishly nodded.

"Well, it turns out a very famous person received Bill's liver."

Tears started flowing down Goins' face. "Who?" she asked softly.

"Well ... have you ever seen *Dallas*?"

And that's all I needed to say.

"I knew it!" she said. "I just had a feeling as soon as I heard that man playing J.R. had received a transplant. I knew in my heart it was Bill's liver."

Defending her man, Goins went on to tell me, "Bill wouldn't have cared if the person who got his liver was a big star or a truck driver like himself. The way he saw it, a human life is a human life. And Mr. Hagman should be happy to know that Bill never touched alcohol."

(Regrettably, Bill's virgin liver would soon get its first taste of booze thanks to its new host's old habits.)

One of the last things she told me was, "When our little Monique is old enough, I'll show her Mr. Hagman's TV show—so she can see the man her daddy saved." (I suggested she perhaps start Monique off with *I Dream of Jeannie* before introducing the impressionable tot to a philandering cowboy who called his alcoholic wife a "slut" and pounded away on one secretary after another.)

But then came an unforeseen twist that turned what I'd intended to be a heartwarming hero story into a tasteless exposé. Unbeknownst to me, my "classy" editors had pulled Gonzalez's arrest records, which revealed that Bill had another side. A dark side. He had been convicted of assault with a deadly weapon, traffic convictions, burglary, check forging and, curiously, *stealing water*??? Suddenly, the victim was to be depicted as a real lowlife: "a tough ex-convict who abused drugs, belonged to a gang, and brutally beat his common-law wife," is how it read in print.

Sigh. Talk about kicking a guy when he's down (like six feet under) and can no longer defend himself. At least his widow, Jeanette, got a thousand dollars from us, with smaller amounts paid out to other Citrus Heights sources who agreed to keep the story quiet until our story hit the stands.

After the story ran, I was instructed to write a follow-up piece. Regardless of Hagman's reaction to the initial story, we were going to claim that he now felt beholden to this poor fatherless family. In other words, we were going to publicly guilt ole J.R. into writing a check to the Goins clan. One of the more creative *Enquirer* writers in Florida used my legit reporting to invent bullshit "dialogue" for Hagman, claiming he'd "told a friend" that his "eyes fill with tears of gratitude" that "somebody had to die so I could live. I want to repay him for giving me a second chance at life."

The cheese level intensified at the very end of the article, with this bogus quote attributed to Hagman: "Every day I'll toast the memory of Bill Gonzalez, but the glass I lift will be filled with orange juice, because I have to look after Bill's liver." *Barf!*

As I mentioned, Larry wouldn't be able to stay away from the liquor for long, necessitating a transplant redux. So, in essence, Bill's donated organ sadly was little more than a placeholder until the arrival of liver #3—a fact that thoroughly disgusts my friend Jack Bowers, who struggled to stay alive for 14 years on a liver transplant list, coming *this close* to death's door before receiving his one and only replacement.

Now, I'm not saying that Hagman didn't feel authentic appreciation toward Gonzalez (I'm sure he did!), but anyone who actually knew this colorful showman would tell you he never spoke like that. Not by a long shot. He would have said something more along the lines of, "Poor Mexican bastard. Just hope his south-of-the-border liver doesn't give me the *turistas*!"

For a brief period, Goins and I remained in touch, with my editors occasionally asking me to secure quotes from her for follow-up articles. The quotes they wanted were always very specific, designed to set up the next "story" in our ongoing Rich Man/Poor Man transplant saga.

Among the "quotes" Goins allowed us to attribute to her: "Bill was a charitable man who wouldn't have expected any show of gratitude from Mr. Hagman … If Mr. Hagman wishes to contact me when he's feeling stronger, I would be happy to speak with him. After all, through these tragic circumstances we will be forever connected."

When Goins suddenly stopped returning my calls, I knew Hagman had finally paid for her silence. This was all but confirmed in Hagman's 2001 autobiography, *Hello Darlin'*: *Tall (and Absolutely True) Tales About My Life,* in which the actor wrote that each morning, "I brush my teeth while looking at a framed photo of my liver donor, which I have courtesy of the *National Enquirer.*"

Ironically, on a bookshelf outside my own bathroom is an autographed copy of Hagman's memoir, which makes me think of him—every time I flush.

Back at Southfork Ranch in 2012 for TNT's *Dallas* reboot with (from left) Jesse Metcalfe, Brenda Strong, Patrick Duffy, Linda Gray, Larry Hagman, me, Charlene Tilton, Steve Kanaly, Marlene Forte, Josh Henderson and Jordana Brewster.

When cancer finally did take Larry down in November 2012, it also necessitated the death of J.R. Ewing, who'd been back causing trouble on TNT's *Dallas* reboot. I booked a flight to Texas to cover the character's funeral for *TV*

Guide, and decided to dress in black just in case the on-set producers needed an extra mourner in the scenes shooting that day.

But at the Burbank airport, I went into sheer panic when I missed my flight by mere seconds. The evil flight attendant who was closing the door to the jet bridge as I came running towards her screaming "I have to get to a funeral" remained smug as she locked the door and blocked me from boarding. I ran back to security to see if I could reclaim the bottles of unopened hair products I'd had to surrender thanks to that fucker Osama bin Laden (no dice!), and then drove like a madman down to LAX. Miraculously—without getting into an accident—I managed to catch the next available flight and made it to the "Dallas Petroleum Club" before J.R.'s casket closed. And if you ever catch that standout season two episode, titled "J.R.'s Masterpiece," you'll see me paying my respects right alongside Bobby, Gary, Sue Ellen, Lucy, Ray, Cliff, Mandy and Cally.

J.R. Ewing's 2013 memorial service with (from left): Ken Kercheval, Steve Kanaly, Deborah Shelton, Linda Gray, Patrick Duffy, Cathy Podewell, me, Charlene Tilton and Ted Shackelford.

Lesson Learned: Whether you live in a beachfront Malibu mansion or the Sunrise Center apartment complex, there's no escaping death. But you sure as hell have a better shot at getting an organ transplant (or two) if your address is in Malibu.

A WORD FROM HAGMAN'S *DALLAS* TV WIFE LINDA GRAY

When I first met Will we were at Southfork Ranch. He obviously loved our cast and told us stories of growing up with us as his family. Our biggest fan.

He has such a boyish excited quality about him that it's infectious. Loved by the entire cast, we loved it when we knew he was coming to interview us. Will was always fun, ready with interesting questions and soon became a friend. He never missed a trick, noticing everyone and everything around him. The interviews were well-researched, thought out and always interspersed with humor.

With lovely Linda Gray on the set of *Home & Family*, 2014.

I remember one interview in particular. I'd arrived at an appointment early so that I could park my car and sit in it without any outside interference while I spoke to Will about a very sensitive subject: Larry Hagman's passing. I told Will about the day that Patrick Duffy and I went to Larry's hospital room. It was two days before he passed. We walked into the room where Larry, propped up in his bed, sat wearing a Southfork Ranch baseball hat. He said that he had two weeks to live and that he was not afraid of dying. I reminded him that we had a J.R./Sue Ellen scene together on Monday and he had promised me a ride in the new Tesla car that he had bought. He smiled and said, "Oh, that's right, darlin'; I forgot all about that!"

When we walked out of the hospital, we were thrilled that he looked so good and seemed in great spirits. I was looking forward to that Monday.

The good news is that Will had known Larry and me for years and knew of our deep friendship. The questions about Larry—personal and necessary for the article he was to write for *TV Guide*—were asked with such love and respect that it made it a bit easier to speak of his passing. Will was so sensitive to my feelings as well as to the delicate subject.

The world loved Larry and Will was the one responsible for making sure that all the details were correct so that the fans could say goodbye to Larry and J.R. Ewing at the same time. Not an easy task!

Knowing that Will grew up watching *Dallas* in his home always brought a smile to my face. I could see him feeling like we were his family ... *but who in their right mind would want to be a part of the Ewing Family?*

Chapter 11
DISHONORING DACK

(DACK RAMBO)

How appropriate that this confession should turn out to be Chapter 11—as this was the one time in my life and career when I felt 100% morally bankrupt. This is the story I have *never ever* dared tell anyone for fear of being branded, as Kelsey Grammer so eloquently put it, a despicable piece of flesh damned to burn in Hell.

This chapter nearly didn't make it into the book at all, with a few concerned parties advising that I'd be wise to keep this particular admission to myself. Let this skeleton stay buried! But I ultimately made the decision that disclosing this dishonorable act was the honorable thing to do. Not for myself so much, but for the gentleman who was so grievously wronged by what I watched happen (even if he's sadly no longer alive to see the truth come out).

Dack Rambo, circa 1974.
(Wikimedia Commons)

This is the story that, regrettably, earned me my very first *National Enquirer* byline. But instead of instilling in me any sense of pride, seeing my name in print attached to this journalistic disgrace made me feel only deep shame.

My involvement in this mess began by accident in January 1994, just a few weeks after I'd been brought in to the *Enquirer* as one of their tryout reporters to prove my worth. I was assigned a desk at the Los Angeles bureau on the Sunset Strip and tutored on how to answer the phone.

There was the "safe" phone line that could be answered *"National Enquirer,"* and then a generic "Hello" line that had been set up to receive calls from unsuspecting innocents who weren't to know the origin of the callback number they'd been given by undercover reporters looking to land new sources.

One afternoon when I answered a call on the "safe" line, an anonymous voice told me she had a juicy story to sell and wanted to know, as they all did, what it might be worth. She purported to work at Kern Medical Center in Bakersfield, CA, and claimed to have access to patient records. There was a TV star from a long-running, successful primetime soap opera who was in the final stages of AIDS. It had been more than eight years since movie idol Rock Hudson's death from that dreaded disease following a short stint on *Dynasty*, and I recalled all too well how the tabloids had exploited that tragedy to the hilt with a wave of sensationalized cover stories. With that in mind, I knew this could potentially be another big tabloid story. And I was also fairly certain I knew the secret identity of the dying actor.

In 1991, *Dallas* soap stud Dack Rambo had bravely come out publicly as bisexual and HIV-positive, which was deeply impactful for me to hear as a young, closeted gay man who had secretly lusted after the hunky star during his three-year stint as J.R. Ewing's Speedo-bulging cousin, Jack Ewing. It just had to be him, I guessed, which turned out to be spot-on.

I took down the source's contact info and shared the tip with my bureau chief Jerry, who instructed me to type up the potential story on one of our lead sheets. But I was never ever to put in writing that any information had originated from confidential hospital records, as that would have been in violation of privacy laws. After the lead sheet was faxed to the *Enquirer's* home office in Lantana, FL, for editorial approval, it didn't take long for "my" story to be greenlit.

Since I had no clue how this whole reporting thing actually worked, as I'd never even taken a single journalism course in college, Jerry paired me with a newly-hired, heavyset, hotshot named Brad Weissberg. Instantly rubbing me the wrong way, Brad was the tabloid's gay shining star who somehow managed to hit a home run with every story he was assigned. If I wanted to make it as an *Enquirer* reporter and excel in the cutthroat tabloid world, this was the guy I was told I'd be wise to emulate. So, off Brad and I drove to Bakersfield in search of an ailing *Dallas* star.

As we made the two-hour drive north, I remember feeling both intrigued and terrified, wondering what exactly we'd discover upon our arrival. Specifically, I was curious what Dack might look like in this early era of the plague before life-saving medication was introduced to combat the disease's devastating side effects.

According to my source (whose mother, it turned out, was the one who actually worked at the hospital as a nurse), Rambo had been checked in by a male friend the night before. Because of his weakened condition, he could only scratch an X on the forms in place of his signature. He'd tried to shield his carcinoma-covered face behind a sheet, and though alert, appeared confused. For the initial tip, the caller was to receive a guaranteed payment of $860, with a $400 bonus should the story appear on our cover, which was pretty much a guarantee if we succeeded in our nefarious mission: to land Dack Rambo's exclusive deathbed interview!

Talk about trial by fire! This assignment was about as horrible as they came, made all the worse because it was centered around a man I greatly admired. And not only that, the subject matter was treading dangerously close to my own secret life that I'd been desperately trying to shield from my mother, friends, co-workers and the rest of the world. Rubbing even more salt in the wound was my being trapped in a car with Brad, who—in my then-homophobic mind—presented himself as a bitchy, gruff, egotistical, raspy-voiced "fag." The very antithesis of the man I wanted to be, but also, per my new bosses, *exactly* who I should aspire to be.

Sigh. What in God's name had I gotten myself into?

When we arrived at Kern Medical Center, Brad could sense my quivering nerves and hesitation to even get out of his car. He told me, as if I were a virgin, to just relax and let him guide me through it. And just like a virgin, I ended up getting screwed without knowing what had just happened to me.

My source had supplied me with Rambo's room number (346), which, upon our arrival, I discovered was located directly across from the nurses' station. Taking Brad's lead, we walked casually past the room's open door, noting that the bed was empty.

This didn't seem real. On TV shows, the discovery of an empty hospital bed with freshly pressed linens was always an indicator that a patient had recently died.

How many times on *ER* or *Grey's Anatomy* have we seen a loved one enter an empty hospital room before making a frenzied rush to the nurses' station and asking hysterically, *"What happened to my husband in room 408?!!!"*

"Are you a relative of the patient, ma'am?" the compassionate TV nurse would whisper before delivering the blow. "I'm so sorry to inform you that your husband passed away just a short time ago. Can I get you something … a pudding, perhaps?"

Well, I really, *really* needed a pudding … spiked with whatever spare Oxycontin, Vicodin, Xanax and Percocet Nurse Jackie might have stashed away in the hospital pharmacy.

Despite my virginal status, I suspected that the discovery of an empty bed didn't mean we were quite off the hook just yet. And sure enough, Brad said we would head back down to the lobby for a brief respite before making another attempt. When that too revealed only an unoccupied room, I worried where our snooping might take us next. Please, *please* not the morgue!! To my relief, Brad surprised me by announcing, "Okay, we can go now. We got everything we need."

"Everything we need to do *what*?" I asked.

"Write the story. You don't want to spend the whole day here, do you?"

So just like that, Brad drove us to a nearby greasy-spoon diner, where my new mentor announced it was time to write the interview.

"What interview??!" I questioned, completely dumbfounded. "We got no interview."

"No one has to know that," Brad informed me. Then swearing me to secrecy like some sadistic fraternity brother, he whipped out his notebook and began writing Dack Rambo's deathbed interview—including the actor's "final words"—over a drippy Reuben sandwich.

I was aghast. Were all the *Enquirer* stories I'd read over the years fabricated? Was this what it meant to be a tabloid "reporter"—someone who replaced actual reporting with creative writing?

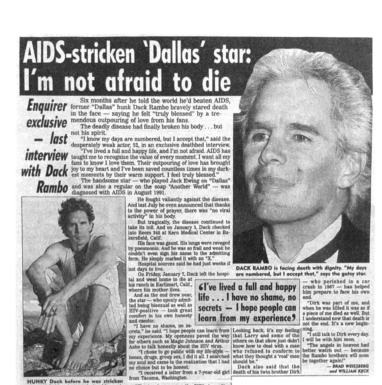

**AIDS-stricken 'Dallas' star:
I'm not afraid to die**

Enquirer exclusive — last interview with Dack Rambo

Six months after he told the world he'd beaten AIDS, former "Dallas" hunk Dack Rambo bravely stared death in the face — saying he felt "truly blessed" by a tremendous outpouring of love from his fans.

The deadly disease had finally broken his body... but not his spirit.

"I know my days are numbered, but I accept that," said the desperately weak actor, 52, in an exclusive deathbed interview. "I've lived a full and happy life, and I'm not afraid. AIDS has taught me to recognize the value of every moment. I want all my fans to know I love them. Their outpouring of love has brought joy to my heart and I've been saved countless times in my darkest moments by their warm support. I feel truly blessed."

The handsome star — who played Jack Ewing on "Dallas" and was also a regular on the soap "Another World" — was diagnosed with AIDS in August 1991.

He fought valiantly against the disease. And last July he even announced that thanks to the power of prayer, there was "no viral activity" in his body.

But tragically, the disease continued to take its toll. And on January 3, Dack checked into Room 346 at Kern Medical Center in Bakersfield, Calif.

His face was gaunt. His lungs were ravaged by pneumonia. And he was so frail and weak he couldn't even sign his name to the admitting form. He simply marked it with an "X."

Hospital sources said he had just weeks if not days to live.

On Friday, January 7, Dack left the hospital and went home to die at his ranch in Earlimart, Calif., where his mother lives.

And as the end drew near, the star — who openly admitted being bisexual as well as HIV-positive — took great comfort in his own honesty and candor.

"I have no shame, no secrets," he said. "I hope people can learn from my experience. My openness paved the way for others such as Magic Johnson and Arthur Ashe to talk honestly about the HIV virus.

"I chose to go public with my life-style — booze, drugs, group sex, I did it all. I searched my soul and came to the realization that I had no choice but to be honest.

"I received a letter from a 7-year-old girl from Tacoma, Washington.

"She too is carrying the HIV virus. She said I was her hero — not because I was some Hollywood star, but because I was not afraid to tell people the truth.

"I spoke out, and she is proud that someone was listening!"

The actor once revealed that Larry Hagman made his life hell on "Dallas" because Dack was gay. But he now says he has only forgiveness in his heart for Larry and his costars.

"I've done a lot of thinking about the treatment I received in Hollywood and the problems I experienced on the set.

"At the time it hurt horribly.

DACK RAMBO is facing death with dignity. "My days are numbered, but I accept that," says the gutsy star.

HUNKY Dack before he was stricken with AIDS. He admits to being bisexual.

TWINS Dirk and Dack Rambo before Dirk (left) was killed in a 1967 car crash. "I will be with him soon," says Dack.

"I've lived a full and happy life... I have no shame, no secrets — I hope people can learn from my experience"

— who perished in a car crash in 1967 — has helped him prepare to face his own end.

"Dirk was part of me, and when he was killed it was as if a piece of me died as well. But I understand now that death is not the end. It's a new beginning.

"I still talk to Dirk every day. I will be with him soon.

"The angels in heaven had better watch out — because the Rambo brothers will soon be together again!"

Looking back, it's my feeling that Larry and some of the others on that show just didn't know how to deal with a man who refused to conform to what they thought a 'real' man should be."

Dack also said that the death of his twin brother Dirk

— BRAD WEISSBERG and WILLIAM KECK

The article came out a few weeks before Dack's valiant battle ended in March 1994 at age 52 in his hometown of Delano, CA. Whatever last words, if any, were actually spoken by the once gorgeous silver fox with a perfectly-placed mole on his left cheek, we'll never know. In the years since, the actor's mother, Bea (who'd already buried Dack's twin brother, Dirk, following a tragic 1967 auto accident) and his siblings, Bill and Beatrice, all passed.

In my vast archive of article clippings exists this poorly-written, completely fabricated *National Enquirer* "final interview" that reads like bad soap opera writing. Dack's "exclusive quotes" absolved Hagman for reported on-set homophobia and acknowledged a letter Dack had supposedly received from a 7-year-old girl in Tacoma, WA, who was also battling HIV. Even though the article painted Rambo as a proud, brave, grateful and benevolent soul who died with dignity, they weren't his words and never should have appeared in print. It's shameful. Even though I didn't write a single word of the story, it was attributed to me for everyone to see. Yep, here was my name in print—William Keck—right beneath the name Brad Weissberg.

While I am guilty in having known about this abomination, I did try to intervene somewhat before the story went to press. When my source clued me in that Dack had checked out of the hospital to return to his then 84-year-old mother's home to die, I sent a memo off to our editor-in-chief Steve Coz, suggesting that the words "deathbed interview" be struck from the story. I also requested that my name not appear in the byline. Both requests were denied. But knowing Coz as I do, I can tell you this. If he'd gotten wind of Weissberg's extreme creative writing tactics, his ass would have been out the door faster than a bullet aimed at ole J.R.'s heart.

Though I elected to continue my *Enquirer* apprenticeship—which led rather quickly to a multi-year staff position—I did so vowing that no matter how other reporters may have culled their interviews, I'd always do my damnedest (aside from the occasional "told a friend" quotes we were required to include) to ensure my reporting was rooted in legitimate investigations. When I made that one regrettable exception to my steadfast rule never to fabricate entire interviews—as I revealed in Chapter 8 about the Meadows sisters—the results proved disastrous, only further solidifying my oath to stick to the truth, the whole truth and nothing but.

And for the most part, my colleagues at the *Enquirer* also worked their asses off to get to the truth. Brad Weissberg was ultimately exposed as an unfortunate anomaly and didn't stick around long after I arrived. In 2020, Brad himself succumbed to a fast-growing cancer at age 56. (I haven't a clue what his final words might have been.)

I'm well aware that confessing the role I played in this unforgiveable transgression will win me no fans, and perhaps even understandably lead some to question the authenticity of the other stories in this book. That's your choice. I've already told you everything within these pages is true.

But keeping what I've now told you in mind, I invite you all to always consider the source of the "news" you allow to seep into your brains. Never shy away from questioning its authenticity. Though I'm hardly a fan of the individual who popularized the term "fake news," in this AI-generated world in which we've suddenly all found ourselves living, there's more of it going around than at any other time in history.

Lesson Learned: Take responsibility for the sins of your past without expecting forgiveness.

A WORD FROM DACK'S *DALLAS* CO-STAR SHEREE J. WILSON

Author with *Dallas* and *Walker, Texas Ranger* actress Sheree J. Wilson in 2018.

I was so pleased when Will invited me to help set the record straight by sharing with you who the *real* Dack Rambo was. The lovely man I got to know in 1986 when I joined *Dallas* as Dack's character's ex-wife, April Stevens.

Dack was so charming and had this smile that was infectious. Just as sweet as the day is long. My very first scene was with Dack, and—as you can imagine—I was terribly nervous about joining this long-running show I'd watched since high school. Even though we were playing adversaries, he couldn't have made me feel more comfortable. He told me, "Just relax. We're all friends here and you'll find that to be true."

Gay, bi, whatever ... I remember that cute little twinkle in his eye. He was definitely checking me out, and I was just so flattered. Everyone liked him on the set, but being as spiritual and humble as he was, Dack was never one of Larry (Hagman's) good 'ole, belly-up-to-the-bar boys drinking Bourbon & Branch. That wasn't him. And he sure had some big boots to fill after Patrick (Duffy) left the show.

After Patrick came back (from the dead) in the shower in such a big way, my conniving character was part of the reason Dack's character, Jack, was written out. The town wasn't big enough for both April *and* Jack, which left me feeling saddened with a twinge of guilt.

Then years later when I heard the news that he'd passed, I was like, "*What*; that can't be." Dack was so fit, good-looking and seemed the epitome of health. It was way too soon and just heartbreaking. But for Dack to make the brave choice to be among the first to use his celebrity to educate people and to bring awareness to AIDS—so that there wasn't as much stigma and fear and judgment—took tremendous courage. Especially in the darkest days when it was happening to him. That is his legacy.

PART II:
DOWN & DIRTY

XXX WARNING: THIS SECTION'S CHAPTERS DISCUSS
SALACIOUS SUBJECT MATTER
(MORE *BREAKING BAD* THAN *BRADY BUNCH*)

Chapter 12
MAGGOTS & HOOKERS

(KELSEY GRAMMER)

Kelsey Grammer, 2010.
(Wikimedia Commons)

WHO: Kelsey Grammer (b. February 21, 1955). Multiple Emmy and Golden Globe winner for his role as Dr. Frasier Crane on *Cheers* and its *Frasier* spinoffs.

WHAT: Numerous investigations into his personal life for the *National Enquirer*.

WHERE: Grammer's former Agoura Hills, CA, residence. Cow's End, Venice Beach, CA. The Mirage Hotel and Casino; various strip clubs, Las Vegas, NV.

Blood-splattered crime scenes and hospital rooms aren't the only locations where fluid-detecting CSI blacklights come in handy. During my celebrity-snooping years, there was no shortage of *other* Hollywood DNA waiting to be discovered as I infiltrated the forbidden worlds of adult-film stars, Sin City strip clubs, a suspicious "health" club and a Palm Springs nudist resort. And I have *Frasier* star Kelsey Grammer to personally thank for allowing me to drop some DNA of my own.

Before I get into that sordid tale, it's worth mentioning that Mr. Grammer also gave me a shout-out in *So Far...*, his own 1995 autobiography. It is available as an audiobook if you would like to hear Kelsey personally read the following passage from page 230—*his* version of a conversation I had with his then-fiancée, Tammi Jo Baliszewski, at a Venice Beach, CA, coffee house:

Kelsey Grammer So Far...

...On the day before our engagement party, for instance, a despicable piece of flesh approached her at her favorite coffee bar in Venice. Obviously, he'd been following her, and when he spoke to her, he introduced himself as William Keck, a reporter – and I use the term loosely – from the *National Enquirer*. "Tammi," he said, "we're going to run a story that Kelsey is HIV-positive, and we have proof."

Tammi asked, "What kind of proof? Do you have a blood test?"

"Oh, well, we've followed him and he lives a really wild life," said Keck. "Look, we don't care if you help us or not – we're going to run this story anyway. But if you do, we'll pay you up to $50,000 and we won't use your name so Kelsey will never know of your cooperation."

They never did run the story for obvious reasons, but these are the kind of tactics the "rags" employ – regrettably, they work more often than not.

It terrorized Tammi, and I invite this young man to fry in hell. But that's probably a done deal already. William – I'm speaking to you directly now – your mother must be very, very proud.

Well, now. That doesn't paint a very pretty picture of your kindly author, now does it? While I chose not to scream "slander" at the time (reasoning I wasn't exactly a saint in all of this, and *might* even had some bad karma coming), I am relieved that after all these years—conveniently following Paramount+'s *Frasier* reboot—I'm finally getting the chance to share *my* account of that meeting.

Understandably, Kelsey was hearing his fiancée's version of the events— sanitized *significantly* to protect her role in this ugliness. The truth is, during their unhealthy three years together, Tammi routinely spilled her guts to me about what she experienced. And the majority of what we discussed—including the most shocking reveals—remained between us and never saw the light of day. Nor will they be revealed in this chapter.

So, when Kelsey writes that I "approached" Tammi at her favorite coffee house, presuming I'd followed her, what he didn't know was that I'd phoned Tammi and *she'd* chosen the Cow's End coffee house in Venice as our secret meeting spot. There'd been no following Tammi or Kelsey or faking blood tests. Rather, we had close insiders feeding us intel—namely, Grammer's own half-brother, John—a longtime source who "belonged" to my fellow *Enquirer* reporter Marc Cetner, and who ultimately revealed his identity publicly in exchange for compensation. It certainly was never my style to falsely claim (i.e., threaten) that a story was all set to run before it was properly investigated. As was the case more often than not, the HIV tip we'd received turned out to be nothing more than a bogus rumor that would have been forever buried, had Grammer himself not elected to bring it up in his memoir.

When I first heard the Julliard School-trained thespian (in that wonderfully theatrical, polished voice of his) tell this tale on tape, I opted to find humor in the absurdity of it all. And as it turned out, while perhaps not "proud," my mother *and* grandmother also got a real kick out of it. For a while, I even played a portion of Kelsey's book narration on the outgoing message of my answering machine.

This was all back in the mid-'90s when *Frasier* was one of TV's top shows and Kelsey's off-screen antics were reported routinely on various tabloid covers. The demand for dirt on Kelsey was so high that on one unforgettable evening I was sent to do what is called a "garbage run" outside the actor's former Agoura Hills estate. That entailed finding out what day of the week he put out his garbage (Tuesdays), and then literally stealing his trash from the containers left on the side of the road for the following morning's pickup. After tossing the stinky, overstuffed bags into the trunk of my Toyota Celica, I headed back to the *Enquirer* bureau to examine the contents of my treasure hunt.

It was fast approaching midnight when I arrived with Kelsey's trash at our office atop a Sunset Strip high-rise. I really should have thought all this out more carefully, but this was my virgin garbage run. And like a virgin, I was anxious to get this whole thing over and done with so I could take a shower, wash off the filth and get some sleep. Although there was no shortage of newsprint that I could have laid out on our bureau's floor, I wasn't thinking clearly and just emptied all the trash directly onto the carpeting—completely oblivious to what might fall (*or squirm*) out.

I could only imagine what shocking items I might uncover. Nude photos? VD medication? The top-secret pages of an upcoming *Frasier* script or Grammer's Paramount contract with unreasonable salary demands? As I weeded through food cartons and toiletries, I failed to notice the white creepy crawlies that were inching their way toward every corner of the room. Yep—maggots! *Loads* of 'em that had been pleasantly feasting on Kelsey's gnawed sirloin bones before I disrupted whatever it is maggots do at the midnight hour.

By the time I spotted them, they were already under my co-workers' desks and making their way toward our archives. *Aw, hell!!* Trying my best to keep a straight head during yet another of my twisted *I Love Lucy* moments, I hurried out to the hallway and caught an elevator down to the lobby to ask the late-night guard if I could borrow the cleaning crew's vacuum for an "emergency situation." The guard had already spotted me carrying the trash bags in from the parking garage, so perhaps assumed I'd been upstairs dismembering a corpse. (Those crazy *Enquirer* kids!)

When I got back up to the office with the vacuum, the maggots were, well ... well-settled into their new home, and I couldn't help but think how appropriate it was that the offices of America's #1-selling supermarket tabloid had literally been infested with maggots. Clooney surely would have had a field day.

But then I started to panic. I could be jeopardizing my job! I imagined Jerry, along with my other colleagues, returning to work the following morning only to discover the hideous maggots had matured overnight into swarms of vengeful Hitchcockian flies—each bearing Kelsey's maniacal, laughing face.

But nothing exciting like that happened. I managed to vacuum up every last squirmer, and aside from a few straight porn (yawn) VHS video boxes and discarded prescription meds, I'd struck out big-time. Even the salvaged skin flicks could theoretically have belonged to Grammer's gardener or neighbor. The whole evening had been a colossal waste of time, succeeding only in reminding me that this was absolutely *not* my life's calling. I was better than this. Or at least I hoped to be.

Though I never dug through Grammer's rubbish again, loads of the sitcom star's "trash" would be delivered to me. Because shaming and disparaging is not the mission of this book, we'll just leave all of that in the junkyard where it belongs.

As for Kelsey's fiancée, Tammi, I always liked the kid. Like me, this Kansas-bred strawberry-blonde was in over her head and never cut out for the flashy Hollywood lifestyle. While Tammi and I have remained friendly all these decades later, that was not in the cards for her and Kelsey. Before any "I do's" were exchanged, she claims she was driven to the breaking point by three (unsubstantiated) surprise bedroom discoveries involving one of her friends, a dress and her caged pet cockatiel.

After landing a tasteful spread in *Playboy*, as well as bit parts (under the name Tammi Alexander) in an episode of *Baywatch* and a Tom Green comedy called *Bob the Butler*, she turned toward a career in holistic medicine and found work assisting a New Age doctor. I tried supporting Tammi's new venture by submitting some of my blood to the quack, who claimed he could determine what foods were toxic to the body and should be avoided. The results proved fascinating. Apparently, I was highly allergic to strawberries—my favorite fruit to which I most definitely was *not* allergic. And even more curious, shellfish—a food I was diagnosed as being deathly allergic to starting at age 12 when I'd turned a crab claw into a finger puppet at my stepdad's office clambake, was now suddenly perfectly safe to consume.

Not surprisingly, I kept popping strawberries to my heart's content and continued avoiding crabs.

Avoiding crabs was also on my mind when I was sent to Las Vegas to poke my nose into Tammi's pre-Kelsey past. With deepest apologies to my mother, here's what happened.

One afternoon I was called into Jerry's office and handed a torn page from one of those tawdry free papers they distribute on the Vegas strip. You know, the ones promoting "gentlemen's clubs" and in-room "dancers." This particular ad, which I still have, featured a naked woman who looked just like Tammi. With her back arched seductively, only a pink satin sheet shielded her breasts. There was a 24-hour number to call if you wanted to order a "Licensed Female Entertainer" (which in Vegas-speak, of course, meant a hooker), who'd perform a lot more than a foxtrot if the

price was right. If you needed further evidence that this was not an advertisement for the Arthur Murray Dance Studio, there were three red "Xs" positioned near the blond woman's exposed thigh, along with a guarantee in writing that "You'd be *hard pressed* not to love us."

So, my assignment was basically to fly to Vegas and find out whether or not Kelsey was engaged to a prostitute.

To make the most of my trip, I brought along my two best friends, Tim and Brad, who went off drinking and gambling while I tried tracking down the photographer who'd taken the photos of Tammi. From a lead we'd been provided, it didn't take long to find John, the man who had held on to the negatives and confirmed the obvious—Tammi was indeed the girl in his photos. But the guy claimed to have no idea whether or not she herself turned tricks. He'd merely snapped the images and sold them to the operation. This should be a cautionary tale to all unsuspecting models posing for photos: You could unwittingly end up becoming a spokesperson for herpes, erectile dysfunction or hookin'! Read your contracts, boys and girls!

So, next on my checklist was determining if Tammi was in any way connected to the service. Since the business of course wouldn't confirm anything over the phone when I tried calling the number in the ad, I had no choice but to dial back in a different voice and order a "dancer" to my room at the Mirage.

While I admit I found this all rather titillating, as I was desperately trying to squeeze out any last ounce of remaining straight-boy testosterone, I was not happy to be missing what at the time was Vegas' hottest ticket in town: Siegfried and Roy—just about six years before poor Roy Horn got mauled and permanently disfigured by a tiger. With Tim and Brad already in the theater saving my empty seat, my intention was to wrap up business as quickly as possible and catch the second half of the show. Well, you know what they say about best "laid" plans....

After waiting in my room for what seemed like an eternity, the phone finally rang in my hotel room. A security guard, standing watch by the elevators, was on the other end of the line, informing me that a young woman had arrived, but I'd have to come down to personally escort her up to my room. Oh Lord; how embarrassing!

When I got down to the lobby, it was as if I'd come face to face with a Sasquatch. My "dancer" turned out to be an Amazonian woman (easily over 6 feet in heels), with short, spiky, bleached-blond hair, chomping away on a wad of gum. She was dressed just as you'd picture a prostitute in an episode of *Three's Company* after an innocent misunderstanding landed Janet and Mrs. Roper in a jail cell with a motley crew of good-time gals. Noticing the knowing smirks I was attracting from the security guard and a Midwest dad who'd just checked in with his family, I hurried Bigfoot up to my room as fast as I could.

With the door closed, I didn't waste any time pulling it out ... "it" being Tammi's magazine ad. I forget the girl's name, but based on her exaggerated Bronx accent, let's just call her "Roxie."

"I swea-uh," said Roxie. "I've nevuh seen that gurl before in my life." (The only word missing from that sentence: "Offusuh.")

Now, if I'm going to be honest, here's where the story gets a little sketch. (Yeah, right here, as if it hadn't gone there already). I'd basically fulfilled the requirements of my assignment by getting one of the dancers to deny having any connection to Tammi. But the taboo allure of ordering a prostitute to my room on the *Enquirer's* dime now had me a little worked up, so to speak. Let me just say it: I was horny as all hell. But Roxie just wasn't doing it for me. Since Roxie had told me she was relatively new in town and hadn't had much contact with any of the agency's other "dancers," I justified that it was perfectly within reason to solicit a second opinion.

Not wishing to hurt Roxie's feelings, I told her that she reminded me of my sister, and that I'd be more comfortable with a different girl. Roxie crossed her legs on one of my room's two queen-sized beds and took a moment to stare me down before dialing up her agency and relaying my disappointment. "He wants another gurl," said Roxie. "He says I look like his sistah."

She handed me the phone and I made a fast arrangement with her employer (read: pimp) to pay Roxie 50 bucks for her trouble. Then, as soon as she was out the door, I described the kind of dance partner I'd prefer. Still way too closeted to request a Derek Hough, the order I placed was more akin to Derek's kid sister and fellow *Dancing With the Stars* personality Julianne Hough. Blonde was fine, but her hair should be longer than Roxie's (ideally, longer than mine). Preferably under 5'10" (my height), and it would be nice if she came dressed a little more ... demurely.

Well, kudos to this agency for besting Domino's at getting my order right. In 30 minutes or less, I was called back down by the elevator guard to meet what appeared to be an even cuter version of Reese Witherspoon, dressed all in white lace. Sure, I got that same raised eyebrow from the elevator guard who by now must have thought I was a real sex fiend, but this time I proudly escorted my lady friend right past him with my head held high.

I don't have to invent a name for this young lady because I'll never ever forget it. Her name was Shawna Sorrenson. And while it was in all likelihood her "stage" name, I was inclined to believe every word that came out of her mouth. She told me she was a single mom with a young daughter, who was working her way through law school. Funny, I'd made that Reese Witherspoon comparison, as this turned out to be a real-life Elle Woods! Rather than working as a cocktail waitress down in the casinos, she figured she could earn her law degree a lot faster by sucking cock. And I wouldn't be at all surprised to discover that Shawna was now one of our country's most successful District Attorneys. Perhaps even headed for the Supreme Court! I tried tracking her down on Facebook, and quite a few Shawna Sorrensons came up. I thought one or two possibly could have been her, but what kind of message would I send? "Sorry to bother you, Judge Sorrenson. Your husband and children are very attractive, and I happen to be a Dachshund lover too! By any chance did you give me a BJ back in the mid-'90s...?"

I didn't think it likely I'd get a response.

That night in my hotel room, Shawna basically told me what I suspected all along. There was no way of knowing for certain that Tammi hadn't worked for the agency, but more likely than not they'd just purchased a photo of an attractive woman they knew would drive horny out-of-town businessmen (like me!!) to call the number for a little in-room Electric Slide.

I still had $450 left in my pocket after the $50 I'd handed Roxie to go away, so I decided to just donate it all to Shawna's law-school fund. Shawna was extremely appreciative and asked me what I wanted in return.

Whaaa-huh????

"Well, I hadn't really thought about it," I told her innocently. "What can I get?"

"For $450, pretty much whatever you want."

While my closeted life hadn't afforded me all that much action with either guys or girls at this point, I wasn't exactly desperate and had zero interest in having full-on intercourse with a Vegas prostitute. Plus, I know it sounds ridiculous, but I'd gotten to know Shawna a little by then and didn't want to totally take advantage of her.

"I guess a blow job would be nice," I told her, probably sounding like Ron Howard's wholesome *Happy Days* character, Richie Cunningham.

(Mom, if you haven't already, it would be a good idea to stop reading now.)

I sat back on the queen-size bed closest to the window that afforded the best view of the strip, unbuckled my trousers and closed my eyes. The sensation I felt next was not what I'd been expecting.

"Is that really necessary?" I asked Shawna, as she rolled down a condom.

"I'm sorry," she explained. "It's the only way I do it."

To this day, it goes down in the books (now literally) as the worst blow job I've ever received. (The latex's fault, Shawna; not yours.) I figured Shawna was looking toward her future in the courtroom where she'd have a much better chance swaying the jury without a mouth riddled with active sores. So, I made the most of it and caught the last 20 minutes of the tiger act.

But my assignment wasn't quite done yet. The *Enquirer* editors desperately wanted Tammi to be a hooker.

So, the next evening, my investigation took me to the since-shuttered Olympic Garden and Crazy Horse Too strip clubs. I was able to make contact with a stripper named "Platinum Peaks," who helped me get in touch with a woman named Cecilia Crippen. Then known as "the Heidi Fleiss of Vegas," Crippen was in charge of booking the town's main female models. But Cecilia informed me that Tammi, while quite "popular at parties," was, alas, not a hooker. She posed for the photos hoping to become either a *Playboy* centerfold or *Baywatch* lifeguard—two

goals she came close to achieving.

Upon filing my story, my disappointed *Enquirer* editors back in Lantana, FL, took all my reporting and painted Tammi as "a nude model for sleazy escort services that were actually fronts for prostitution rings."

The resulting article went on to expose Kelsey's church-going lady love as "a two-fisted drinker who had no qualms about shedding her top and dropping her pants for the camera." Per Tammi, the article led Kelsey to interrogate her, with the two committing to try healing their fractured relationship by working with their pastor at St. Monica Catholic Church in Santa Monica. (The very same church, I should note, that my bureau chief attended regularly with his family.)

I would come to cross paths with Mr. Grammer yet again in the summer of 2021 when I was producing the celebrity segments for the late night talk show, *Josh Gates Tonight*. Besides being the popular TV personality whom I sent out to vandalize the *Happy Days* house with Cindy Brady, Gates is basically Discovery Channel's very own khaki-wearing Indiana Jones who spends most of the year scouting lost cities, buried treasure ... and sharks. One unforgettable afternoon, Gates came storming toward my office, announcing to the entire staff, "Keck—this has got to be the biggest fuck-up of your career!" While admittedly alarmed, I could tell he was amused by whatever he was about to reveal.

Gates had just wrapped a Zoom interview segment I'd produced with Grammer, who'd been booked at the last minute to fill a hole during Discovery's highly-hyped Shark Week programming block, when every guest is required to share some story related to sharks. While the other celeb guests we'd secured for that week (Tiffany Haddish, William Shatner, Brad Paisley, Super Bowl champ Rob Gronkowski) had all gone shark diving in Discovery specials and thus had no shortage of shark tales to share, Grammer had absolutely no shark tie-ins whatsoever. Or so we thought.

As it turns out, Kelsey has a rather morbid connection to the sharp-toothed predators, a discovery I would have made had I been granted a pre-interview, an essential practice for most all daytime and late-night TV talk shows. Putting celebrity guests on the phone with a producer before their actual on-air interview ensures the celebrities will have entertaining stories to share with the host, and— perhaps even more importantly—prevents uncomfortable questions from being asked.

But in this particular instance, because of my previous clashes with Kelsey, I was relieved when his rep told me he would be too busy for a pre-interview. Would he have even recognized my name when I introduced myself all those years later?

Probably not. But I certainly didn't want to risk him putting two and two together and pulling out of the show. So, I just asked Grammer's publicist if her client had any memorable dorsal-finned encounters he might be able to share with our host.

"I don't know," she said casually. "Josh can just ask him during their interview."

As I prepared a rather extensive list of interview questions for Gates to ask Grammer, my deep dive reminded me of how the actor's early life had been marred by one unimaginable tragedy after another. That Kelsey was able to not only survive each of these heartaches, but thrive as he has, is a truly remarkable achievement (to say the least) that gives me enormous respect for this man.

When Kelsey was 12, the grandfather who raised him dropped dead of a heart attack.

The following year, his father, Frank, was shot to death outside his home.

When Grammer turned 20, his beloved kid sister, Karen, was kidnapped outside a Red Lobster where she'd been waiting tables and raped for several hours before being viciously stabbed to death.

Five years later, Grammer's two half-brothers, Stephen and Billy, drowned in a freak scuba-diving accident.

And then in 2008, Kelsey himself suffered a heart attack while out paddle-boarding in Hawaii.

"So when you bring up sharks," I cautioned Gates, "probably best to avoid any specific references to ocean sports."

Gates agreed. So when it finally came time for the big interview, the host simply asked, "Got any fun shark stories, Kelsey?"

At that point, as Gates recounted to me and all within earshot, Grammer turned suddenly stoic before answering, "I wouldn't say I have any *fun* stories about sharks, but I had a brother *eaten* by one."

Oh SHIT! How could I have missed THAT?

To my great misfortune, the web stories I pulled up relating to Stephen and Billy's scuba accidents had left out one major detail: Billy's body was never recovered and had, yes, presumably been consumed by a shark.

Thank GOD the interview did not air live, allowing us the opportunity to edit out the cringeworthy moment and, with his irate publicist's eventual blessing, respectfully move Grammer's entire segment into a different episode airing post-Shark Week. It was indeed a fuck-up on my part, but hardly the "biggest fuck-up of your career," as Gates will discover if he reads this book.

There are a couple final Kelsey footnotes to share. My Nana Ruth absolutely adored *Frasier*. So, when she and my parents flew west for their annual visit, I was determined to get them seats to a show taping on the Paramount lot. I called in some favors and, remarkably, was able to secure Kelsey's own personal house seats. Thankfully, Kelsey never came over to greet his mystery VIP guests. We did, however, get to meet Moose—the late Jack Russell Terrier who portrayed Frasier's foil Eddie—and he couldn't have been lovelier.

Cut to several years later when I was positioned outside the Shrine Auditorium covering the Emmy Awards red carpet for *Entertainment Weekly*. As I was wrapping up an interview, I discovered Kelsey's revered publicist, Stan Rosenfield, walking the actor straight towards me. Before I could duck for cover, Kelsey flashed a big smile and offered me his hand.

"Hello there," he said warmly. "Have we met before?"

Gulp!

Without blinking an eye, I swallowed up all my courage and unapologetically introduced myself as ... William *Peck*. As much as I wanted to, I just couldn't get out that K.

It's important for me to take this opportunity to apologize to both Kelsey and Tammi for that unfortunate day at the Cow's End coffee house that no doubt legitimately did terrorize her, as Kelsey described in his book. And hitting her up the day before the couple's engagement party—a fact I hadn't known—made it even more reprehensible. At that time in the mid-'90s, AIDS was a raging epidemic. For me to have posed even the unverified *suggestion* that Kelsey may have tested positive for HIV was epically irresponsible.

I can remember all too well the great anxiety I'd experienced having to wait days for the results of my own various HIV tests over the years. To instill that terror in Tammi, and—I can only imagine—possibly force Kelsey to show her the results of a negative test to appease her fears, is something I will always deeply regret.

And we at the *Enquirer* should have known better, having had the privilege of working alongside our colleague, Neal Hitchens, a remarkable man who so valiantly raised AIDS awareness as an award-winning author and activist.

Personally, I most remember Neal's spot-on impression of *Bewitched*'s befuddled Aunt Clara (as played by actress Marion Lorne) that had me in stitches no matter how many times I heard it. Neal was also my first gay role model, demonstrating that one could be out, proud and happy.

Whenever I think of Neal—only 43 when he died in 2000—I am reminded of the previously referenced Robert Reed, Dack Rambo and the 40-some million others this merciless disease has taken from the planet. Just about that same number are living with HIV today, and thankfully living longer, healthier lives with medications that sadly hadn't been available to Neal. Had I not remained in the closet for as long as I had, I very possibly would not be alive today to tell these stories.

It's traumatizing enough to receive confidential results from an accredited doctor in a medical clinic. But to be on the receiving end of such gossip from a punk tabloid reporter in a coffee house, knowing there's a possibility that this private information may be blasted on the cover of the *National Enquirer*, well ...

I can only hope, as I imagine Kelsey does, that we are not defined and forever damned by choices made during our reckless youth. Satan, spare me your flames.

Lesson Learned: If you dig through someone else's garbage, not even the most durable latex gloves can protect your hands from getting soiled. Scrub away as you may, that antiseptic-resistant stench has a way of lingering years after the trash has been hauled off to the city dump.

A HAPPILY-EVER-AFTER UPDATE FROM TAMMI BALISZEWSKI

What can I say about William Keck? He's a very likable, intelligent and charming guy, and seemed so trustworthy, even though I knew he worked for a tabloid. This worked to his advantage during conversations; he just listened so well! (Something I was not accustomed to.) Also to my detriment (not just with Will but life in general), I was a people pleaser with very little self-worth and no concept of boundaries or discernment.

Will was right; I was in over my head in Los Angeles and with Kelsey. Though Kelsey and I had the best of intentions, the relationship was doomed from the start. I was attracted to him because he was wounded and he was attracted to me because I was sad. Not a rock-solid foundation.

When the inevitable demise of our relationship occurred, I was devastated. He met another woman and our therapist broke up with me on his behalf. We never spoke again. I felt I had made such a mess of my life that suicide was the only option; the only way to stop the pain. And though I considered myself spiritual, it was not until this event occurred that I started praying and meditating in earnest. During a meditation I "heard" the message that if I had the courage to keep breathing and look for signs, I would be guided, and life would eventually be wonderful. I was skeptical but agreed to keep breathing ... for a while.

I was indeed guided, and found myself in school. I became a hypnotherapist and then completed two master's programs in Spiritual Psychology, which supported me in my personal healing and prepared me to be a counselor. I went on to receive two PhDs and wrote two spiritually based self-help books.

These days I am so grateful for my peaceful life with my beautiful horses and my incredible husband of 20 years. I am also grateful for the painful life lessons, challenges, heartache and hardships. They were all vital for my "soul level learning." I am a living example that our past, and even our present, does not have to dictate our future. My message to anyone who is struggling is: no matter where you have been, or where you are, take responsibility for yourself, forgive everyone everything, and align with your soul and Spirit. If you are willing to do this, happily ever after is not only possible, but promised.

Chapter 13
TOYS FOR TOTS

(MICKEY ROONEY)

Mickey Rooney, circa 1979. (Bernard Gotfryd/Wikimedia Commons)

WHO: Mickey Rooney (1920–2014). Diminutive former child actor turned top box-office superstar who was awarded two honorary Oscars. Co-starred with Judy Garland in many musicals, including *Babes in Arms*.

WHAT: *National Enquirer* investigation into a rape allegation.

WHERE: The West Hollywood, CA, apartment of power publicist Ruth Webb.

Part of our job as *National Enquirer* reporters was to field the occasional calls from certified nut jobs. You'd try to be as polite as possible when breaking the news to the faceless tipster on the other end of the line: "No, I'm sorry; I don't think we'd be interested in a story about Pamela Anderson's hair extensions being harvested from concentration camps."

But every so often on a slow afternoon you'd get a tip so over-the-top that it'd be worth looking into … maybe even to file away in case one were ever to, oh say … write a book. In this particular instance, it was the irresistible combination of "Mickey Rooney" + "sex toys" that had me hooked!

Personally, I've never been much into sex toys. I think they're funny to look at, and for a few months my friend Tim and I enjoyed a back-and-forth swap of a leather fisting glove he'd picked up at a white-elephant holiday gift exchange. But

I can assure you, it never left the box! As for getting that same assurance from Tim: *"Raise a hand, buddy—that is, if you have one free."*

The most used sex toys I ever saw piled in one place had allegedly belonged to actor Mickey Rooney. Once the biggest box-office star in the world between the late 1930s and early '40s, Rooney had, by this time, long faded from notoriety.

MGM publicity still of Rooney, Judy Garland (in her Dorothy dress) and studio head Louis B. Mayer. (Wikimedia Commons)

At a height of just 5'2", Rooney had held his own opposite such glamorous leading ladies as Elizabeth Taylor and Judy Garland. He sired nine children and assembled a total of eight wives—including a one-year marriage to gorgeous screen star Ava Gardner, who would go on to marry Frank Sinatra.

The tipster alleging to have inherited Mickey's collection of kink was legendary talent agent Ruth Webb—who'd once repped Mickey! (Another reason I couldn't say no to this one.) In her initial call, Webb had promised me an "explosive" story if I'd come over, right away, to her Hollywood apartment where she insisted the interview take place. Besides Rooney, Webb had also represented several other since-deceased stars whose stories appear in this book, including Phyllis Diller and Tammy Faye Bakker. But her glory years representing such Tinseltown legends as Gloria Swanson and Dorothy Lamour had long passed. Approaching 80, she was now taking on non-actors who'd landed at the center of some sordid scandal or another. Among her roster: O.J. Simpson sidekick Kato Kaelin, vixen-on-skates Tonya Harding, Divine Brown (the prostitute who gave Hugh Grant his infamous BJ) and John Wayne Bobbitt, a former bar bouncer who was dabbling in porn after his wife Lorena chopped his dick off with her kitchen knife. But now Ruth was turning the tables on one of her own—one whose career she claimed to have resurrected more than once.

Never your run-of-the-mill agent, Webb famously worked out of her bedroom dressed in her nightgown, which is exactly how she greeted me at her apartment door. She wasted no time ushering me into her boudoir and pointing to the waterbed.

"Mickey Rooney raped me!" she charged. "And it had happened right here!!"

Despite the dramatic reveal, it in fact did not happen right there. Webb went on to describe the exact course of events. "I had been in bed with the flu," Ruth told me. "He chased me out of bed and into the bathroom. I can usually outrun him, but not this time. He backed me up against the toilet

Publicist Ruth Webb in her 70s, around the time she hosted the author in her boudoir.

seat. I said 'No,' but he started to masturbate and stuck it into me. I protested, screaming, 'No, Mickey, no... (You're *not* so fine; you're *not* so fine; you *don't* blow my mind; NO MICKEY!).' But he finished himself off and ejaculated inside of me." She referred to him as her "fast draw rapist," and claimed he had attempted this crime on many previous occasions. "He was always in too much of a hurry to ever satisfy a woman."

This was quite an accusation. And I couldn't do a story without proof, I told her.

"Oh, I have proof!" she insisted, clearly out for blood.

And with that, Webb opened her closet door and pulled out a large plastic bag. "Here's all the proof you need." My jaw dropped as I watched this eccentric woman in her mid-70s empty the bag's contents onto her pink satin bedspread. Out fell every size, texture, shape and color of sex toy you could imagine. And probably more than a few you couldn't.

She explained that Mickey had spent hundreds on "masturbation devices," but that Mickey's favorite toy was a sex doll he'd picked up in New York City that had inspired him to develop a movie titled *Introducing Susie*, in which he would have played a lonely bank clerk who falls in love with a blow-up doll. All is good until one day she explodes. (Pretty sure I saw Ryan Gosling in that.)

"These are all Mickey's!" she said. "He kept them here because he couldn't have them at home."

What I remember most about the toys, and I'm sorry to gross you out, was the repellent stench. They obviously hadn't been cleaned properly, and still smelled of Mickey or whomever had last "played" with them. When I suggested that there was no way of proving that the toys were Mickey's, Ruth grew agitated. DNA testing was a hot topic at the time because of the O.J. trial, so Ruth suggested I

Photo taken by author of Mickey Rooney (waving a free hand) with wife Jan at the 2009 Academy Awards.

have the toys tested for any remaining Rooney residue. The *Enquirer*, of course, would never invest in such an expense. Even if the toys were Mickey's, that in no way could corroborate Ruth's rape claim that he'd slipped her his mickey. And I knew it was way too late to DNA-test Ruth.

So, to Ruth's great dismay, Mickey got off, as she'd claimed he had so many times before in a synthetic pocket pussy she shoved in my face. Mickey finally passed away in 2014 at age 93, taking all his sex toy secrets to the grave.

Lesson Learned: This one's easy. After playtime, clean your toys, boys and girls. Preferably with Clorox!

Chapter 14
THE HILLS ARE ALIVE

(MAX BAER JR.)

WHO: Max Baer Jr., 6'4'' (b. December 4, 1937). Best known for playing dimwit Jethro Bodine on the 1962–1971 sitcom *The Beverly Hillbillies.*

WHAT: *National Enquirer* investigation into a rape allegation. On-the-record interview for *TV Guide.*

WHERE: Home of porn star Gayle "Beverlee Hills" Sutro, Poway, CA. Westin Los Angeles Airport Hotel.

Max Baer Jr. in a 1962 promotional photo for *The Beverly Hillbillies.* (CBS)

Before we delve into all the sordid details involving my backwoods/backdoor investigation into the world of porn stars and hillbillies, let's jump back in time to one of the get-rich-quick schemes I tried launching in the mid-'90s with my best buddy, Tim. Our venture was to be called "The Celebrity Strip"—basically celebrity look-alike strippers we would send to perform at bachelorette and stag parties. Working in the Warner Bros. casting department (on such series as *Knots Landing* and *Lois & Clark*), Tim knew the basics of how to go about recruiting "talent." First order of business: taking an ad out in *Drama-Logue* magazine. After that, we printed up business cards and rented a legit Studio City audition space on Ventura Blvd. for our first round of castings. And to protect ourselves from being perceived as junior Harvey Weinsteins-in-training, we wisely invited Tim's casting associate, Debbie, to join us for the Saturday-afternoon auditions where we'd be asking aspiring actors to strip down to their skivvies.

We set up a sign-in table outside the audition room, hoping the 50 job applications we'd printed would be sufficient for the onslaught of hopefuls we were certain had seen our ad. As it turned out, we slightly overestimated the response, as only four performers showed.

They included:

A leggy, female Cher impersonator who came decked out in the legend's iconic "If I Could Turn Back Time" fishnet body stocking. (The only performer we could have actually sent out on auditions!)

A diminutive male comedian who performed two characters: a spastic Pee-wee Herman and an elderly George Burns—the latter of whom pulled a cigar out of his tighty-whities and smoked it.

A not-so-attractive Latin man trying to pass himself off as a dead ringer for Jean-Claude Van Damme, the big-screen action star/martial artist (who Tim was convinced he'd recently seen at a Hollywood orgy). But when the fella took off his clothes, all he revealed was an acne-covered back and a bulge-less teal-colored Speedo—a look that could have inspired Matt Damon's less-than-flattering chartreuse swimsuit reveal in *The Talented Mr. Ripley*.

And then finally there was Niecy, a bone-thin, strung-out, obvious prostitute, who was accompanied by her burly bodyguard/pimp. Since Niecy had not identified on the sign-in sheet which celebrity she'd be impersonating, our obvious first question was, "And who are you supposed to be?"

"I dunno," she mumbled, glancing over at her friend.

Tim and I looked at each other, neither sure how to proceed.

"Well, we have to mark you down as some celebrity," I explained.

"Okay," Niecy sighed. "How about one of them Cosby kids?"

"Which one?" Tim asked, trying to stifle a laugh.

"The middle one," Niecy said.

Hmmm. Now that still left some doubt. Assuming she wasn't referencing the early '70s "Hey, Hey, Hey" *Fat Albert and the Cosby Kids* animated series, we could immediately rule out Dumb Donald and Mushmouth. But that still left six

Many years after auditioning the stripping "Vanessa Huxtable," I interviewed the real Vanessa, actress Tempestt Bledsoe (right) with (left) her *Cosby Show* kid sis, Keshia Knight Pulliam (Rudy).

sitcom options: Sondra, Denise, Vanessa, Rudy, Olivia and Theo. After a quick once-over (presumably) eliminated Theo, we instructed Debbie to mark the candidate down as "Vanessa." As soon as Tim gave Niecy a thumbs up to start her audition, the pimp hit "play" on the boombox he'd brought and the Huxtable hopeful started her dance, which was actually more like a slow sway. Without even an attempt to strip.

"She's not stripping," Tim whispered to me.

"I know," I answered.

"Well, tell her to start taking off her clothes."

"Oh my God," I winced. "You tell her."

We both turned to Debbie, who kindly informed Niecy, "Just a friendly reminder, this is a *stripping* audition…"

Niecy rolled her eyes and glanced over at her expressionless friend, who nodded his approval. And with that, Niecy stopped dancing altogether, sat her ass on the floor and started prying off her knee-high vinyl boots. And yes, it was just as mortifying as one might imagine.

We thanked Niecy for her time and told her we'd seen enough. *More* than enough. And right then and there, Tim and I knew we weren't cut out for the adult-entertainment business.

A few months later I was reminded of that smart decision when I was sent out on one of my seediest assignments. One that, unfortunately, involved another of my TV idols: Max Baer Jr.

I grew up loving (and kind of crushing on) Baer, the 6'4" ox of a man who played dimwit cousin Jethro Bodine on *The Beverly Hillbillies,* one of my all-time favorite 1960s sitcoms. (Yeah, I know—I have *lots* of "all-time favorites.") In the many years since his sitcom had gone off the air, Baer—son of 1930s World

Heavyweight Boxing champ Max Baer Sr.—had become a fixture on the Nevada scene with a long unrealized dream of building a *Hillbillies*-themed hotel/casino. I'd been shown concept drawings for the elaborate resort planned for somewhere in Nevada—first Reno, and later Carson City, before Baer finally settled on Douglas County. The main casino would have been modeled after the Clampett mansion with a flame-spewing oil tower out front. Inside, patrons would have had their choice to dine at either Granny's Vittles and Hog Tales Restaurant or the more upscale Drysdale's Fancy Eating. (Incidentally, I would have been in hog heaven at this place and am so disappointed that Baer's dream never came to fruition.)

But in 2013, I did get my chance to spend a day with the very salty star and his last surviving *Hillbillies* co-star: the Christian, ultra-proper actress Donna Douglas, who'd played Jethro's cousin, Elly May Clampett, and was now sharing inspiring words from the gospel at churches near her home just outside Baton Rouge, LA. This would be their first reunion since they'd come together in 2003 to bury Buddy Ebsen (who'd played her hillbilly pa, Jed), and it would sadly prove to be their last before Douglas' own death in 2015.

Before the interview began, I'd been forewarned by Douglas' rep that under no circumstances was I to bring up her long-ago affair with Elvis Presley. As I was told, Elvis had been the great love of Donna's life and had broken her heart. And although it had been nearly 50 years, the pain was still too great to revisit. If I even dared bring up The King, she would get up immediately and walk out!

(Not wanting to be a hound dog, I dutifully obeyed and earned my bone.)

And then came a second warning—from Baer himself. "I have known Donna 50 years and I have never heard her say anything bad about anybody; I have never even heard her curse," said the 75-year-old, who'd come dressed in a black tank top which showed off his still impressive musculature. "But she is the most bizarre girl I have ever met. I'm nuts—but I know I'm nuts. And I think she thinks she's sane, but she's not."

He was right! At 80, Douglas wore frilly white and pink lace with her blond hair (presumably a wig) done up in curls—the very same look she'd sported every day of her life since being cast as Elly May way back in 1962, as if she were forever auditioning for a remake of *Whatever Happened to Baby Jane?* I had to wonder:

Author with *Beverly Hillbillies* cousins Max Baer Jr. (Jethro) and Donna Douglas (Elly May) at their final reunion before her 2015 death.

Had the two never received notice from CBS that their show had been cancelled in 1971 and they were free to stop playing hillbillies? I found their interaction disturbingly similar to how Jethro and Elly May had sparred back in the day.

At one point, without any prompting from me, Donna wrestled Max down to the floor and got him in a headlock just as her tomboy character had been known to do. It was one of those jaw-dropping "Is this actually happening?" moments.

Bickering constantly as real kinfolk do, these two had weathered a lot together over the years. As difficult as it may be to believe with the insane salaries paid to today's top TV stars ($1 million+ per episode for the *Friends* cast), each had earned a paltry $500 an episode during *Hillbillies'* first season. That meant most weekends and over their summer hiatus, Douglas, Baer and Irene Ryan (who played their Granny) had to hit the road and make personal appearances at malls, car shows and rodeos to earn enough dough to pay the bills. (Just imagine David Schwimmer and Lisa Kudrow turning up to sign autographs and rope cattle at the National Little Britches Rodeo.)

In fact earlier that very day, Baer and Douglas had spent hours signing autographs and posing for photos with paying fans in a hotel near the Los Angeles Airport.

What I didn't tell Baer that day was that our paths had crossed many years earlier during my *Enquirer* years when I received a tip about his connection to infamous porn actress Gayle Sutro.

I'd heard for years that Max had developed an interest in the adult-film industry—as both a silent producer and fan of the genre's big-bosomed stars. "I like girls that are built like Dolly Parton," is how Baer had once described his personal preferences to me. "It's just a fact of life." And in the porn biz, there were no bigger boobs than Sutro's.

Above: Promotional photo from *The Beverly Hillbillies* featuring (l-r) Irene Ryan (Granny), Baer Jr. and Douglas. (Filmways Television/CBS Television Network)
Below: Author's photo of Baer and Douglas recreating that moment in 2013.

With a 55-inch bust (triple F cup), Sutro had starred in some 30 adult films under the stage names Gina Gianetti and (no kidding) Beverlee Hills. If you're lucky, you may have caught her in such classics as *Million Dollar Mellons* (yes, strangely spelled with two Ls) or *Between My Breasts #15* (you don't need to have seen the previous 14 to follow the storyline). But tragically, Sutro's inflating career suddenly collapsed when her breasts became infected with gangrene, resulting in an emergency operation to remove her diseased implants.

Sutro told me she had first become involved romantically with Baer after he'd seen her in *Penthouse* magazine and asked her out on a date. But she was now accusing her former lover of having driven from his Las Vegas home to her house in Poway, CA, to rape her!! To prove her allegations, she claimed to possess videos of the two having sex (joined by other men!!) and his dried semen on her bedsheets!

She also claimed that she'd been driven by a detective to Pomerado Hospital where she'd had her vagina scraped for semen and hair samples taken.

As the lucky reporter assigned to this potential Pulitzer, I really hoped it was all some horrible misunderstanding. Sure, Jethro was dumb as a rock, but a rapist??!! I couldn't "Baer" the thought. It made me question how fair a jury trial for an accused celebrity could possibly be with those in the jury box having to determine the guilt or innocence of a celebrity they'd known for years only as a benevolent character in a sitcom.

I began my investigation by placing repeated calls to the accused. But each time I dialed Baer's home number in Vegas, the voice on the other end of the line—*unmistakably* Jethro's—claimed to be merely a "business associate" taking calls

for Baer who was supposedly out of town (and unreachable) on a long fishing trip.

Max's side of the story, through his attorney, was that he and Sutro had indeed been romantically involved in the past, but—with her drinking having spiraled dangerously out of control—he had now selflessly taken on the role of caregiver. Baer claimed that one night Sutro had begged him for sex, and—feeling sorry for her—had climbed into her bed for some platonic cuddling. But there had been no sex. And certainly no rape.

When I finally got my chance to interview Baer (after he'd returned from that "fishing trip"), he told me Sutro "was crawling all over me, telling me, 'If you don't make love to me, you don't love me.'" He claimed he'd found her on the floor in a floral dress covered in vomit. He then cleaned her up, put her in fresh clothes and fed her Rally's hamburgers. (A crime if I've ever heard one.)

It was a case of hillbilly said, porn star said. About the only fact I was able to 100% confirm during my research was that Sutro regularly placed orders for bottles of Scotch from—I kid you not—the nearby Twin Peaks Liquor store.

According to Boobpedia (yes, it exists; just try Googling it), Gayle (or as she was also known, Gail, Cassie, Beverly and Beverlee) went on to become publisher of *Juggs* magazine before  succumbing to cancer in 2003 at the relatively young age of 51. She took to her grave further unsubstantiated sexual accusations against Jethro that, if true, would make it impossible for me to ever again watch *The Beverly Hillbillies* without getting totally wasted on Granny's moonshine.

Had angelic Donna heard any of this salacious gossip, I can only imagine her entire head would have developed gangrene!!

And oh—one last footnote about that failed Celebrity Strip business. A few weeks after our disastrous auditions, I managed to land one of the four hopefuls an actual paying gig! And believe it or not, the lucky lookalike was Niecy! As a 25th-birthday surprise for Tim, I hired "Vanessa Huxtable" to bring him up on stage at Dimples Karaoke bar in Burbank and perform (to his sheer horror) a sexy striptease as all his friends hooted and hollered like hillbillies. No one louder than yours truly.

Y'all come back now, ya hear?

Lesson Learned: "No" means "no," which is what I should have said to this backwards backwoods assignment!

Chapter 15
THE PRINCESS & THE PEE-PEE

(ZSA ZSA GABOR)

Zsa Zsa Gabor and Frédéric Prinz von Anhalt photographed in Switzerland, mid-1990s. (Wikimedia Commons)

WHO: Zsa Zsa Gabor (1917–2016). Hungarian-born Beverly Hills socialite who was the Paris Hilton of the '50s–'80s. Famous for infamously slapping a Beverly Hills cop and her *nine* marriages, the last (from 1986 until her 2016 death) to the eccentric Frédéric Prinz von Anhalt, who had adopted the title of Prince.

WHAT: Investigations for the *National Enquirer* into Prince Frédéric's injury by a hit-and-run driver and his expulsion from a health club for alleged indecent exposure.

WHERE: Zsa Zsa's Bel Air, CA, home. The Beverly Hilton, Beverly Hills, CA. Bally Total Fitness health club, Hollywood, CA. UCLA Medical Center, LA, CA.

Of all the many birthday parties I've attended, none could hold a candle (or 95) to the 95th birthday celebration held for scandalous socialite Zsa Zsa Gabor in her hilltop Bel Air mansion. But before we get to that surreal circus, I should probably explain who this glamorous "princess" was, for those too young to remember.

Zsa Zsa Gabor, left, circa 1959. (Wikimedia Commons) And (right) her younger sister Eva Gabor (with *Green Acres* co-star Eddie Albert) in 1965. (CBS Television)

Zsa Zsa and Eva Gabor were wealthy, beautiful and terribly glamorous Hungarian sisters famous (for the most part) for being famous, paving the way for future "It Sisters" like the Hiltons and Kardashians. Eva was most known for her starring role in the 1965–71 sitcom *Green Acres*, playing a glitzy society woman trying her best to live without luxury on her new husband's farm in a community

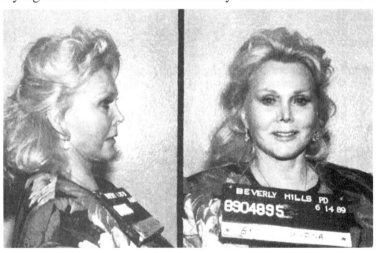

Zsa Zsa Gabor's 1989 mug shot taken after slapping a Beverly Hills cop.

filled with eccentric oddballs. It was no doubt an inspiration for Paris Hilton's reality series *The Simple Life* (see sidebar) and the Eugene Levy/Catherine O'Hara comedy *Schitt's Creek*.

Zsa Zsa, meanwhile, was most renowned for collecting husbands and for her outlandish headline-making behavior—like slapping a Beverly Hills cop across the face. Were she not bedridden in her final years, I have no doubt this lover of publicity would have taken part in that disturbing early 2010s trend (made popular by Paris, Lindsay Lohan and Britney Spears) of stepping out of limos while "accidentally" offering panty-free pussy peeks to the paparazzi. (That image reminds me of *Everybody Loves Raymond* grandma Doris Roberts, who once described her vagina to me—at an opening night performance of *The Vagina Monologues*—as a "cute little gray bunny rabbit.")

Eva's Fourth of July 1995 sudden death after slipping in a bathtub while vacationing in Mexico kicked off a series of back-to-back tragedies that rocked what had been a life of great privilege. Two years later, Zsa Zsa's 100-year-old mother, Jolie, died on April Fool's Day; no joke. And then just two months later her older sister Magda bid the world adieu on June 6—D Day! (Oh, those Gabors sure knew how to celebrate the holidays!)

Despite her many marriages, Zsa Zsa birthed but one child, a stout comedienne named Francesca Hilton, who struggled financially throughout her life while waiting for her mother's inheritance and, as a result, was one of my regular well-paid *Enquirer* sources.

Zsa Zsa had long claimed Francesca to be the child of a 1946 rape committed by her then-husband Conrad Hilton (Paris' great-grandpappy). She would go on to get revenge on Conrad by revealing an affair she claimed to have had during their marriage with his own teenaged son, Conrad Jr., who would then go on to marry Elizabeth Taylor. (Even the Kardashians would have one helluva time keeping up with Zsa Zsa's theatrics!)

Reaching her 90s, Zsa Zsa's tragic losses escalated at an alarming rate. She reportedly lost millions in the Bernie Madoff scheme. Then, in 2011, she had her right leg amputated (but reportedly didn't discover it was gone until *three years later* during a fleeting respite from her dementia). And in 2015, Francesca suffered a fatal stroke, dying at age 67 on January 5 (which turns out to be National Whipped Cream Day) at Norms coffee shop on La Cienega.

Now let's jump back a few years and amputations to 2012, when I received an emailed invitation from Zsa Zsa's ninth and final husband, Prince Frédéric von Anhalt, to attend his wife's 95th-birthday celebration at their Bel Air home.

Born Hans Georg Robert Lichtenberg in Germany in 1943, Freddie became a prince through unconventional means: adoption in his 30s by an 80-something financially strapped former German royal. From that he took the name "Prinz," which makes him about as much of a prince as Freddie Prinze Jr. Apparently, he was one of some 35 other "adopted" princes. And then Frédéric continued paying it forward (and getting paid to pay it forward) by allegedly collecting sums (rumored to be up to 50 grand apiece) from other handsome young men wanting to be knighted, while others were rumored to pay upwards of two million to be adopted as princes themselves. Just how much of a hands-on daddy he continued to be to his posse of puppy princes is known only to him.

Still, the ploy convinced Zsa Zsa—26 years his senior—to marry him in 1986, thus making herself a princess. In a brilliant case of rebranding, I remember seeing her as one of the celebrity panelists on *Hollywood Squares* going by the name "Princess Zsa Zsa"—completely decked out in royal regalia—crown and all.

Posing in front of a portrait of the Gabor women at Zsa Zsa's creepy 95th-birthday party.

On the evening of her macabre 95th-birthday party, caterers out in the driveway cooked up Zsa Zsa's favorite goulash and Hungarian sausage, while inside a few famous faces like Larry King and Connie Stevens milled about the musty mansion that looked (and smelled) more like a neglected museum. Many of the star's closest friends opted to skip the party—as well as her well-publicized funeral four years later—believing the events to be nothing more than exploitative press opportunities orchestrated by her carnival-barker husband. Also strangely absent from the birthday celebration: the guest of honor—who'd rarely been seen in public since her amputation. Rumors were circulating of a possible appearance later in the evening, but ultimately, when the cake was wheeled out, I along with roughly

130 other partygoers found ourselves singing "Happy Birthday" to a large framed oil painting of Zsa Zsa hung on a wall. With no one to blow out the candles, they all just sort of slowly flickered out and melted down into the frosting.

I felt sorry for Rex, the "plus one" I'd brought as my date, who'd really hoped to get a ZZ sighting before the night was done. But Freddie had turned Zsa Zsa's bedroom into a makeshift VIP lounge, and was only lifting the curtain to select celebrities and one photographer who'd been granted the exclusive for a brief viewing of the sleeping birthday beauty.

"Step right up, ladies and gentlemen, and marvel at a nearly bald, one-legged, 95-year-old authentic royal princess!"

After we left the party, as Rex and I were making our way down the driveway, I yanked him into the bushes outside Zsa Zsa's bedroom—enabling us a fleeting glimpse through sheer curtains of a nearly bald Ms. Gabor being spoon fed birthday cake by a nurse. I'd never seen Rex so happy.

As bizarre and unbelievable as all this may sound, Freddie's over-the-top antics had become routine amusement for me. Like Francesca, he too had been one of my longtime paid sources. And boy did that prince deliver the goods!

Marrying a Hollywood legend was not enough for this publicity-loving prince, who delighted at seeing his name in the *Enquirer* every week. To accomplish that, he'd dream up creative stunts—many that left his princess feeling publicly humiliated. But I couldn't get enough of the guy. He had a marvelous sense of humor, could charm the pants off practically anyone (and often did!) and was up for practically anything.

When he called in February 1996 to tell me he'd had his membership revoked from Bally's Total Fitness health club in Hollywood—a gym then composed primarily of elderly Russian immigrants, gay men and porn stars—he was threatening to file a multi-million-dollar lawsuit. As he explained it, he'd been given the boot because some of the old Russian ladies were "complaining they could see my manhood through my white Speedos."

(And yes, Freddie actually used the word "manhood," which I thought was only ever used in cheesy romance novels or "Dear Penthouse Forum" letters when the words "penis," "dick" and "cock" were overused.)

133

He'd been pulled out of the 40-person jacuzzi by the club's manager, accompanied by a beefy security guard and escorted to the locker room while they watched him change. "The other people in the jacuzzi were laughing at me," he said. "I felt like a prisoner in Alcatraz getting a strip search. I am no common criminal—I am Prince Frédéric von Anhalt!"

He went on to argue that his VPL or visible penis line (a term popularized when paparazzi photos of freeballing *Mad Men* big boy Jon Hamm began circulating) was barely noticeable and much ado was being made about nothing. "I'll have you know these trunks are from a stylish collection in Paris," he went on. "It's impossible to see through them because they're double-lined in the front. I paid a fortune for this swimsuit—nearly $48!" (Keep in mind this was the '90s. But even so, it was only $48.)

The Prince told me one of the most humiliating things he'd ever had to do was break the news to Zsa Zsa when she returned home after an exhausting day out on location filming her cameo for *The Brady Bunch Movie*. So furious was the princess that she commanded her husband to slip on the suit so she could have a look for herself. "Have these women nothing better to do than look between your legs?" she told von Anhalt. "Maybe some of those women don't have a good-looking husband like you and are jealous!"

Freddie even managed to get Zsa Zsa on the phone to comment for my *Enquirer* story, calling the allegations "horribly absurd … Frédéric is far too shy to go showing off his stuff. I've seen him in the bathing suit and I can't see a thing."

With vengeance on his mind, Freddie began hurling scathing accusations against Bally's members, who he claimed "are there not to exercise, but to cruise for sex partners" and "have sick feet with diseases that can easily be transmitted to others … many strange things that go on at the club that I can't speak of … far too much time spent looking between people's legs … someone has to be punished for the things that go on there!"

To unsheathe the truth, I came up with a wild idea to meet Freddie at the Beverly Hills Hotel pool with my trusted photographer Vincent to photograph the Prince in his tight, white Speedo before taking a dip. We would then get a dampened "after" photo to see what all the fuss was about. Crouching down in front of a prince to

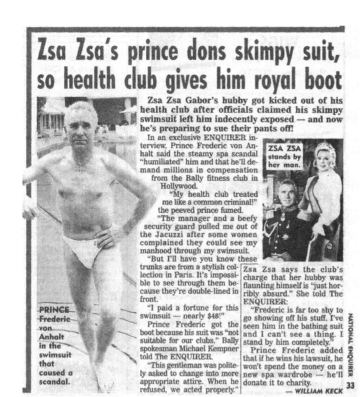

Zsa Zsa's prince dons skimpy suit, so health club gives him royal boot

Zsa Zsa Gabor's hubby got kicked out of his health club after officials claimed his skimpy swimsuit left him indecently exposed — and now he's preparing to sue their pants off!

In an exclusive ENQUIRER interview, Prince Frederic von Anhalt said the steamy spa scandal "humiliated" him and that he'll demand millions in compensation from the Bally fitness club in Hollywood.

"My health club treated me like a common criminal!" the peeved prince fumed.

"The manager and a beefy security guard pulled me out of the Jacuzzi after some women complained they could see my manhood through my swimsuit.

"But I'll have you know these trunks are from a stylish collection in Paris. It's impossible to see through them because they're double-lined in front.

"I paid a fortune for this swimsuit — nearly $48!"

Prince Frederic got the boot because his suit was "not suitable for our clubs," Bally spokesman Michael Kempner told The ENQUIRER.

"This gentleman was politely asked to change into more appropriate attire. When he refused, we acted properly."

ZSA ZSA stands by her man.

Zsa Zsa says the club's charge that her hubby was flaunting himself is "just horribly absurd." She told The ENQUIRER:

"Frederic is far too shy to go showing off his stuff. I've seen him in the bathing suit and I can't see a thing. I stand by him completely."

Prince Frederic added that if he wins his lawsuit, he won't spend the money on a new spa wardrobe — he'll donate it to charity.

— WILLIAM KECK

PRINCE Frederic von Anhalt in the swimsuit that caused a scandal.

NATIONAL ENQUIRER 33

see if I could make out his crown jewels had to have been one of my crowning achievements. And in the end, it was a tough call. So we published them to allow *Enquirer* readers to judge for themselves.

Overjoyed with his coverage (or lack thereof), Freddie claimed my article helped secure him a lucrative $1.5 million deal from Hom, the manufacturer of his skimpy swimsuit, to be their spokesperson for a year. "I'll be flying to Paris to pose in sexy new swim fashions," he told me. "I can't thank the *Enquirer* enough for this rather peculiar exposure. Who could have guessed I could make so much money simply by dropping my pants?"

For her part, Zsa Zsa forbade her overexposed husband from joining any more "health" clubs, advising he stay home and enjoy the pool and jacuzzi in their own backyard. Frédéric's need for so much jacuzzi soaking, he claimed, was related to a "hit and run" incident he'd been involved in a year earlier. And I just so happened to have had a front seat to that one too!

His Royal Highness had personally phoned me from the emergency room of UCLA Medical Center claiming to be in critical condition after being struck by a car while jogging through Bel Air. I had to question just how "critical" he was, considering he was on the other end of the line. But regardless, he insisted that Zsa Zsa was rushing to his bedside and if I hurried, I'd most likely be able to get some quotes and photos of her. "But hurry!" he urged.

I hurried as fast as I could, but by the time I arrived at the ER, Freddie was sitting up on a gurney and his princess had come and gone.

"You missed her," he sighed, clearly disappointed with me. "I told you to hurry."

"I hurried as fast as I could," I explained. "Where'd she go?"

"She had to go home to do an interview with *Entertainment Tonight* about my accident."

"So, she just left you here?"

"Yes, yes," he said, seemingly unfazed by his abandonment. "I told her to go. The hospital wouldn't allow cameras in here, so she had to rush home to meet them in time to get the story on tonight's show."

"But I thought you'd promised *me* the exclusive."

"You *are* getting the exclusive," he insisted. "The *hospital* exclusive. *ET's* getting the at-home exclusive."

The author visits Zsa Zsa Gabor at home with husband Prince Frédéric, after he was struck by a car.

Uh-huh. This guy.

Even though they'd put a neck brace on him, Frédéric's injuries appeared to be restricted to some wear and tear on his tracksuit. But after a thorough dry cleaning, he was expected to make a full recovery.

"So, when are they discharging you?" I asked.

"We can go anytime." That's when I realized I was Frédéric's ride home. So, I got the Prince into my Toyota Celica and made the short trip to Bel Air. Along the way, he filled me in on his brush with death.

He said, "I'll show you where it happened when we pull through the gates."

When we arrived at the scene of the crime, I asked Freddie to get out of my car and point to the place of impact, which he was more than happy to do. Getting all the photos I needed for my story, I drove him back to Castle Gabor, where Zsa Zsa was all made up for the *ET* cameras.

Zsa Zsa didn't seem particularly pleased to learn I'd had her husband recreate his near-fatal accident. But she did appreciate that I'd brought his ass safely home. If only they'd had a spare Speedo, I would have joined them in the jacuzzi.

The princess ended up hanging on until December 18, 2016, when she passed at age 99. A newsmaker 'til the very end, she made her final public appearance at Beverly Hills' Church of the Good Shepherd on December 30. In front of a less than star-studded congregation that included soap opera actress Kate Linder (a.k.a. Esther the maid on *The Young and the Restless*) and reality TV star Bobby Trendy, her grieving widower pulled her boxed ashes out of a Louis Vuitton dog carrier that she'd used to tote around her beloved shih tzu, Macho Man. Von Anhalt then continued toting his late wife's remains around the globe in that same designer bag all the way through 2021, when ¾ of her was finally buried in Budapest, with the remaining ¼ landing in her little sister Eva's plot at Westwood Memorial Park.

Lesson Learned: Some charming princes may be more trouble than they're worth. Or merely frogs in disguise, who just got damn lucky.

PARIS & NICOLE ... DOGGY STYLE

Since we're talking Gabors, Hiltons and purse puppies, I thought here would be a good place to fess up to the time I took things too far with Paris Hilton back in 2004. The pink princess, along with her one-time BFF Nicole Richie, were promoting the second season of their FOX reality show, *The Simple Life*, and I was assigned to write a feature on the pair for *USA Today*. There had been a lot of talk that the two were on the outs—a rumor I chose to play up in my cheeky introduction, which read:

Lounging at home with Paris and her litter.

"The thin, spoiled one in the wild pink fashions is the aggressor, while the fuller-bodied crazy girl is the more passive." I went on to cite a source who'd seen the two "going to the bathroom outdoors in public places," followed up by a quote from the show's producer, Jonathan Murray, who confided, "One was a little more potty-trained than the other," while her friend had left "a little present on the rug" of her host family.

Having grabbed the attention of my readers with these sensational quotes, only then did I reveal that the renegade defecators turned out *not* to be Paris and Nicole, but rather the female pocket pups they toted around in their designer purses. *Oops!*

138

Chapter 16
PEEKABOO PENIS

(TAMMY FAYE BAKKER)

Tammy Faye Bakker, circa 2004.
(Wikimedia Commons)

WHO: Tammy Faye Bakker Messner (1942–2007). Former televangelist and Heritage USA Christian theme-park founder who faced disgrace in the '80s when she stood by her pastor husband, Jim Bakker. Bakker had allocated their church's funds to silence his rape accuser while he and Tammy Faye lived a life of extreme luxury.

WHAT: A *People* magazine feature chronicling Tammy Faye's surprise visit to a nudist resort.

WHERE: *The Surreal Life* house, Hollywood Hills, CA. The Desert Shadows Inn, Palm Springs, CA.

In March 2022, actress Jessica Chastain collected the Best Lead Actress Oscar for her spot-on portrayal of disgraced televangelist Tammy Faye Bakker in the biographical drama *The Eyes of Tammy Faye*. Chastain had told the *Los Angeles Times* that the prosthetics and layers upon layers of heavy makeup required for her transformation had left her with "permanent damage" to her skin.

But there was just no other way to portray Tammy Faye.

So known was the real Tammy Faye for her clown-like makeup and river of tears, that I used her as the inspiration for the lead character of a comic strip I created for my college newspaper. *The Squeelers* was a send-up of pop culture and politics with a cast of colorful characters based upon real-life newsmakers whom I transformed into pigs. And "Spammy Faye Bacon" was my star: a pudgy, heavily-made-up porker prone to hysterics and sobbing fits.

Spammy Faye Bacon

I can actually credit these silly swines for helping me land my college internship with the ABC daytime soap opera *All My Children*. Not long after my arrival on the Hobart College campus, I learned there was a tenured English professor among the faculty named Grant Holly, whose daughter, Lauren Holly, was an actress on *AMC*. So in an effort to foster a relationship with Grant and Lauren, I incorporated them both into my comic as Grunt and Lauren Hoggy, she being an actress on the soap opera *All My Piglets* that took place in the fictional town of Swine Valley (a spin on *AMC*'s Pine Valley). While that all may sound ridiculous, my plan paid off bigtime—with Lauren helping set up the interview for my *AMC* internship. And by spring 1989, I was handing scripts to the soap's star, Susan Lucci!

Those few months I spent with the *AMC* actors was a dream come true! And in 2017—six years after the soap ended its 41-year run on ABC—I was delighted to repay the kindness they'd shown me by inviting many of them to participate in a two-hour cast reunion I put together for Hallmark Channel's *Home & Family*.

Back in the '80s, while Lucci's iconic Erica Kane was stirring up trouble on daytime TV, Tammy Faye Bakker's real life was playing out like a soap opera with one scandalous twist after another covered on all the nightly news programs. But by the time I met her in 2003, she'd successfully turned her life around. Having divorced Rev. Jim Bakker while he was serving out a prison sentence for fraud, Tammy Faye had published two autobiographies (*Tammy: Telling It My Way* and *I Will Survive ... and You Will, Too!*), co-hosted a daytime talk show (*The Jim J. and Tammy Faye Show*), found lasting love in a second marriage to her ex's former business partner, Roe Messner, and won my heart (as well as the hearts of others in the LGBTQ community) for her outspoken support of gay rights and compassion for those battling HIV/AIDS. So what a rare treat it was when *People* magazine invited me to spend a day with her and a motley crew of other "celebrities" (Vanilla Ice, *CHiPs* actor Erik Estrada, porn legend Ron Jeremy)— all looking to enjoy a 16th minute of fame—sequestered together in a run-down Hollywood Hills home for the MTV reality series, *The Surreal Life*.

Out of everyone in the cast, Tammy Faye was the one with whom I instantly bonded. Having battled cancer on and off since 1996, she'd received a devastating call just the day before from her doctor informing her that her lung cancer, which had been in remission, had returned with a vengeance. While Tammy told me she was relying on faith and the power of prayer to get her through this latest ordeal, I could tell the prognosis was grim. And she knew it too.

But this day was to be a welcome distraction—with the cast getting to leave the house for a mystery road trip to a surprise location. Unfortunately, the trip would end with Tammy, as always, in tears.

The Surreal Life producers had clued me in to our secret destination where the cast would be spending the night: the Desert Shadows Inn—a Palm Springs nudist resort!! While the initial thought of spending a day in the sun surrounded by a bunch of swinging schlongs and bouncing boobs was quite titillating, my fantasy image looked nothing like the reality we encountered. How shall I describe Desert Shadows? Hmmm... well, let's just say it looked less like a college Spring Break party in Fort Lauderdale and more like the San Diego Zoo's gorilla enclosure, if all the primates were in the pool swatting volleyballs over nets and lounging spread-eagle on inflatable pool floats. The bouncing boobs, I should mention, belonged to the mostly older men with hair in all the wrong places, while the pale, bare-naked ladies were jiggling from their necks all the way down to their thighs. And all the patrons at the come-as-you-are café got up from their vinyl chairs with waffle-shaped impressions left on their ass cheeks.

Those sneaky producers had plotted this risqué display specifically with Tammy Faye in mind. How would a devout Christian, who had once overseen the development of the ill-fated Heritage USA family vacation resort, react to a bacchanal of exposed flesh and out-of-control pubes? The answer ... not well! Not

141

well at all. And even though I'd bonded with Tammy Faye in the luxury party van on our nearly two-hour drive to the desert, I didn't dare spoil the producers' plans by giving her a heads-up.

By the time we arrived, the camera crew was already in place—ready to capture Tammy's anticipated theatrics as the cast filtered into the Desert Shadows lobby. Once Messner, Estrada, Jeremy and all the others were assembled in front of the check-in desk, the resort manager popped out from behind a door wearing nothing beneath his t-shirt. When Tammy got one look at his low-hanging danglers, she shook her head, burst into tears and ran straight out to the parking lot. Living up to the title of the show, the whole thing was truly surreal.

But the producers got *exactly* what they wanted: vintage Tammy Faye reduced to the same emotional wreck that had made her a famous circus clown some 16 years earlier.

Not thinking of the cameras, I ran right up to comfort her.

"Are you okay?" I asked.

"No, I'm *not* okay!" Tammy told me with the tears flowing hard. "It's just not right."

"What's not right?"

"I'm a married woman. The only man I should see naked is my husband."

And that's when I noticed it—her heavy mascara dripping down her face, identical to the pastel streaks I'd seen on *Nightline* when she and Jim had been grilled by newsman Ted Koppel about their ministry's misappropriated funds, their lavish lifestyle and sex scandal hush money. It was as if my little college comic strip had evolved Disney-style into a full-fledged theme park with a living, breathing Spammy Faye Bacon character sobbing uncontrollably right before my eyes.

The Surreal Life producers were understandably none too pleased that I'd stepped into their money shot, and I was immediately (and aggressively) yanked away by the show's angry executive producer who tried to coax Tammy back into the resort. But girl wasn't having it.

"Forget it!" she told the man emphatically. "I'm not setting one foot back in that horrible place. You're going to have to find me another place to stay the night or I'm outta here. It's just not right!"

After the fallout, Tammy Faye was put up in a nearby, clothing-*required* hotel, while I got to rejoin the skin safari to see which celebs might drop trou. Not surprisingly, Ron Jeremy was the first to volunteer.

A director friend of mine, who'd worked closely with Ron Jeremy in the adult film industry, told me that following their season of *The Surreal Life*, the porn star and Tammy had gone on to develop an unlikely kinship. While she was undergoing her cancer treatments, she would often reach out to Ron for support and he was always happy to give Tammy all the time she needed to work through her fears.

Now let's take just a moment to ponder that, shall we? If a devout Christian and a porn star known as "The Hedgehog" can look beyond their differences to bond as compassionate human beings, might it not be worth us at least attempting to do the same with folks who don't share our own beliefs?

About a year after our trip to Desert Shadows, a much frailer-appearing Tammy Faye invited me to her house for a very personal at-home interview with her and Roe. Both having weathered serious health challenges, Tammy Faye wanted it known that she was planning to leave this Earth with deep gratitude in her heart. By the time she passed on July 20, 2007, she had atoned for what she considered to be her sins, made peace with her scandalous past, given thanks for her many blessings, offered kindness and compassion to others and was ready to take her place in heaven. And isn't that how we'd all hope to take our final bow?

But for sweet Tammy Faye's sake, I only hope everyone in the Garden of Eden has their fig leaves properly placed.

Lesson Learned: My own personal checklist before heading out to the nudist resort:

    1) Hit up the gym.

    2) Take care of all essential manscaping.

    3) Light spray tan.

    4) Don't overdo it on the mascara.

Chapter 17
DICK FOR DILLER

(PHYLLIS DILLER)

WHO: Phyllis Diller (1917–2012). Wild-haired, eccentric comedienne known for mocking her age, appearance and husband, Fang.

WHAT: Social visits and on-the-record interviews for the *National Enquirer*.

WHERE: Diller's home, Brentwood, CA. Jimmy's restaurant, Beverly Hills, CA.

I was thrilled to learn from reading my literary idol David Sedaris' 2021 book, *A*

Phyllis Diller in the 1970s.
(Allan Warren/Wikimedia Commons)

Carnival of Snackery, that the two of us share something rather unusual in common. We'd both developed friendships with self-deprecating, wild-haired comedienne Phyllis Diller. I don't think it would even be too much of an exaggeration to say Ms. Diller and I casually dated back in the late '90s—when I was in my twenties and the comedy legend was in her eighties. And by "dated," I mean I squired her to a few industry events and served as her designated driver when she was craving guacamole and margaritas from her favorite Mexican restaurant. That's where I discovered my wacky gal became a nasty drunk after the third cocktail sunk in. Although there were a couple of nights when Phyllis ended up nearly passed out in the passenger seat of my Toyota Celica, I promise you I never took advantage of her. Well, at least not sexually.

In case you weren't lucky enough to grow up seeing Phyllis make the rounds telling her cheesy jokes on various TV specials and game shows, I'll "Phyl" you in. *Ba-dum BUM!* Besides that wonderful untamed hair, she was also known for her Technicolor muumuus and an exaggerated, unmistakable cackle that made her a dependably entertaining talk and game show guest. She was never averse to laughing at her own jokes, as I would come to learn the first time she invited me into her Brentwood mansion. Meticulously catalogued in a mammoth filing cabinet under such subject headers as "Husbands," "Old Age" and—the fattest file by far—"Ugly," were thousands of old jokes, each typed on 3-x-5 index cards. When she read me a few of her favorites, she'd guffaw hard as if she'd just thought 'em up.

"On my honeymoon, I put on a peekaboo blouse. My husband peeked and booed." *Ahhh-hahahaa.*

"I went to a beauty parlor in France. They applied for foreign aid." *Ahhhh-hahahahaaa.*

"My mother entered my picture in a beauty pageant. They sent it back with a note, 'Sorry, no pets allowed.'" *Ha-ha-ha-HA!*

"I have so many liver spots I should come with a side of onions." *Bahhahahhahaaa.*

Either you love this kind of humor or you don't. I couldn't get enough, making me the perfect audience for Phyllis to test Prehistoric jokes that she was considering reviving. It is said that at the time of her 2012 death, Diller had amassed some 53,000 jokes. They're now in the possession of Washington, D.C.'s Smithsonian Institution.

While she may have started out "beauty challenged" like her pal Joan Rivers, by the time I met Phyllis, nearly 20 procedures had transformed her into a halfway-decent-looking old broad. I remember one time helping her look through stacks of photos when I came across a series of images that made me gasp out loud. They were before-and-after photos taken of Phyllis in the process of undergoing a chemical peel that left her face looking like raw hamburger meat.

"Wow, these are great!" I told her. "Can we print them?"

PHYLLIS DILLER: MY PLASTIC SURGERY NIGHTMARE

NATIONAL
ENQUIRER
LARGEST CIRCULATION OF ANY PAPER IN AMERICA
$1.39/$1.69 CANADA
December 31, 1996

"I don't see why not," she said with a grin. (They ran in the *Enquirer* the following week, along with a new one-liner from Phyllis: "The sight of my face was uglier than a shot of Dennis Franz' behind on *NYPD Blue*." (Yeah, that one's majorly dated. Even so, I appreciate an era when there were classy comedians who still called a badonkadonk a behind.)

Another of Diller's decades-long running gags involved a never-seen fictitious husband she'd invented for her act named "Fang," whose laziness was matched only by his extreme thriftiness. In reality, there never was a "Fang," just a pair of ex-husbands named Sherwood and Warde, who I'm sure were grateful to have never made it into the act. Instead, it was always "Fang." But with Phyllis now in her senior years, Fang wasn't mentioned so much anymore. He'd been replaced chiefly by jabs at her own advancing years: "The best contraceptive for old people is nudity!" *Bahahahaha!!*

Over the years, the filing cabinet's "Fang" section had grown yellow and dusty—much like Phyllis herself. (Trust me, she would have applauded that zinger.) So, I got into my head an idea that it might be a good time to find the then-79-year-old a new Fang. She positively lit up when I suggested we launch a national contest in the pages of the *Enquirer*, which was hands-down her favorite newspaper. We would invite eligible bachelors (well-groomed and physically fit, upon her insistence) to submit one current photo, along with their age (between 50–80), marital history and a brief essay (50 words or less) stating why they thought they'd be her perfect "Fang." It was *The Golden Bachelor*—27 years before the world was introduced to Gerry Turner. Our winner, to be personally chosen by Ms. Diller herself, would be treated to a romantic night out on the town with the woman of his dreams—or nightmares, as the case may be.

"Frankly, I'm sick of dating my mortician," Phyllis told our readers in a solicitation I helped her write. "He says he's already spent so much money on me that when I croak, he won't earn a cent." And no "freeloaders, married men or toyboys need apply," she cautioned. "I'm making 80 my cutoff because if the guy turns out to be hot stuff,

The *National Enquirer* contest to find Phyllis Diller her next husband.

I'd like to have him around for a while to enjoy him." A doctor, she said, would be ideal, "in case I collapse during the night." And he should share her love for theater, art exhibits, jazz and her favorite TV show *Frasier*—starring the *Enquirer's* favorite cover boy.

The response was tremendous. Letter upon letter arrived from all over the country from men of all ages, races and—no surprise—sexual orientations. (The queens loved their Phyllis!) I could tell Phyllis was really hoping to actually get laid by the end of this. While she adored her gay following, she didn't want any following her into her bedroom to try on her wigs. So, any guy with too many highlights in his hair, or wearing more makeup than Phyllis, was the first to have his photo tossed in the reject pile.

When it was time to make the final selection, Phyllis was drawn to an attractive retired financier from Palm Desert who shared her love of golf. Once he was selected as a finalist, a phone interview was arranged to see if there was any chemistry—and there was! Phyllis was excited, thinking that what started out as a silly contest might actually go somewhere. But I felt there was something about the guy that seemed too ... I don't know, safe. Too conservative. I worried he'd bore Phyllis, who had spent decades mingling with Hollywood glitterati. I mean, her best friend was Bob Hope, whom she had on permanent display as a ginormous painted portrait under a spotlight in the middle of her dusty ballroom. (Yes, she had a ballroom.)

No, Phyllis needed someone matching her larger-than-life caliber. And I believed I was holding that photo in my hand!!

It was a black-and-white headshot of a gorgeous man who looked like Sir Laurence Olivier in his prime. Dr. Emile Franchel, a widower from Littlerock, CA. He sent a heartfelt letter and a handsome photo that he admitted was taken "a few years ago," but asserted that he'd maintained his active lifestyle and good looks. And best of all—he was a doctor—which had been tops on Phyllis' wish list. Yes, Dr. Emile Franchel was the man I wanted for Phyllis, and I finally managed to convince Phyllis to let boring Mr. Palm Desert go and instead take a chance on the silver fox, who had his very own limousine and valet.

The date was set. They were to meet in Beverly Hills at Jimmy's, Phyllis' favorite old-time restaurant, for the early-bird special. I remember Phyllis acting like an excited schoolgirl going to prom, and I felt like her dad ... equally excited, but also feeling protective and hopeful that the man I'd chosen would live up to his glowing pitch.

Finally, the moment arrived. The maître d' hurried into the dining room to announce that Emile's limousine had just pulled up. I gave Phyllis a gentle hand-squeeze to wish her good luck, and told Vincent, my photographer, to make sure he was ready to capture the moment when the two lovebirds first set eyes on each other.

But as soon as I ran out to greet the gentleman caller and got one look at his hideous, purplish, 1970s-era, hearse-like limousine, I knew we were in serious trouble. As for the valet, he was actually Dr. Franchel's nurse, as I discovered just as soon as a frail, elderly, bespectacled man with but a wisp of remaining white hair atop his freckled head, struggled to get out of his car. His physical limp, he explained, was the result of dropping a large rock on his foot and breaking a toe just the day before.

That stunning photo he'd submitted turned out to be 40 years old!! And when I saw what he was wearing—a patterned blazer straight out of a 1970s Sears catalog, I considered pushing him right back into his funerary coach and jumping right in there with him to make a clean getaway. Beneath his untucked shirt, I could see trousers stained with what appeared to be dried, yellowish residue. Perhaps from a previous meal. Mustard? Phlegm?

And while it was true he was a doctor, it turned out he was in actuality a retired hypnotherapist, which was dangerously close to a no-no on her wish list. "No psychiatrists," she'd stipulated. "They're all nuts!" But Emile wasn't any ordinary hypnotist. Back in 1955 he hypnotized people on live TV in his very own series: *Adventures in Hypnotism*. I was hoping he might put Phyllis under his spell, but there was no having it.

I felt terrible for Phyllis. But, then again, we'd billed the contest as a search for the next Fang, and this guy certainly had all the makings of the skinflint she referenced in her act. Maybe she'd see the humor in it and make the most of the evening. Alas, that turned out not to be the case. One look at Emile, and Phyllis looked as though she was going to murder me. I was worried she was going to call the whole thing off and make me drive her home before any photos were taken. But despite her fury, Phyllis was a pro. She grinned through her disdain and posed

for the obligatory champagne toast and first dance.

She explained to her readers that she forgave Emile for submitting the ancient photo because the photo the *Enquirer* had run of her to announce the contest was itself 30 years old. "Even though he's no John

Me with good-sport comedienne Phyllis Diller and the disappointing suitor I found for her.

Travolta on the dance floor," she said, "I give him credit for even attempting to dance with a broken toe."

But I knew Phyllis' hopes of getting laid had been dashed, and my heart genuinely ached for her. While we never saw Dr. Emile again after his valet took him back to his crypt, I did learn that Phyllis—all on her own—reached out to the runner-up in Palm Desert, and that the two had made plans to meet for a golf date. Whether or not Phyllis scored a hole in one, I can only hope.

Lesson Learned: Sometimes even the greatest comedians can't see the punchline coming.

Chapter 18
MY #METOO MOMENT

(RICHARD MULLIGAN)

WHO: Richard Mulligan (1932-2000). Two-time Emmy winner for his roles on the sitcoms *Soap* and *Empty Nest*.

WHAT: My #MeToo encounter. Crashing a celebrity fundraiser.

WHERE: The Pasadena Civic Auditorium, Pasadena, CA. The Beverly Hilton Hotel, Beverly Hills, CA.

Richard Mulligan as Dr. Harry Weston in *Empty Nest*. (NBC)

The week before actress Alyssa Milano coined the phrase "Me Too" in her groundbreaking October 2017 Tweet that prompted such other brave celebrities as Gwyneth Paltrow, Ashley Judd and Jennifer Lawrence to come forward with sexual harassment and assault stories of their own, I got an advance peek at the crusade to come.

It was October 10th on the set of Hallmark Channel's *Home & Family*. Oscar-winning actress Mira Sorvino had been booked as that day's guest and I had been assigned to produce her segment. As I was going over her interview's talking points with our hosts, we got word that *The New Yorker* magazine had prematurely published an online version of Ronan Farrow's explosive exposé on film producer Harvey Weinstein—which for the first time revealed Sorvino's blistering sexual-harassment accusations. Her protective PR team wasted no time canceling all of Mira's planned television appearances for the day. All except ours. Though she was still in a state of shock, and physically shaking when she arrived to our set, I gave Mira all the time she needed to collect herself, assuring both Mira and her team that her interview would be solely focused on her new film *6 Below: Miracle on the Mountain*. And it was.

Mira was so appreciative of how gently and respectfully she'd been handled that she offered me a warm hug as I walked her out to her car.

I was on the receiving end of a much different kind of touch in August 1991 when I was #MeToo'd by one of my favorite sitcom stars. It was the day before a Primetime Emmy Awards telecast and all the presenters swung by the Pasadena Civic Auditorium to rehearse. As a way to break into "show business" before joining the *Enquirer,* I got myself hired as a Pinkerton security guard and expressed to my new bosses a desire to work high-profile celebrity events. You can imagine my delight when one of my first assignments found me guarding the actual Emmy statuettes that would be handed out the next day on live TV.

From where I was positioned on this rehearsal afternoon, I had a primo view of the stage where one celebrity after another, dressed in casual weekend attire, walked out to read their dialogue on a teleprompter, just as they would the next day dressed in their tuxedos and glamorous gowns. Every once in a while, one of the actors would grumble, "I'm not going to say that," and their line would be rewritten on the spot. It was thrilling!

Though there were much bigger stars coming and going throughout the afternoon, one I was particularly excited to see was 58-year-old sitcom star Richard Mulligan. Mulligan had starred as wacky Burt Campbell on the 1977–1981 ABC sitcom *Soap* (yet another of my all-time faves) and was now up for Outstanding Lead Actor in a Comedy Series for his role as Dr. Harry Weston—the harried, widowed father of two daughters—on *The Golden Girls* spin-off *Empty Nest*.

When Mulligan left the stage, he came walking right toward me. Although new to the job, I was well aware that autograph and photo requests were strictly forbidden. (It would be a few years before I'd adopt my "fuck it" attitude and turn every legendary celebrity encounter into a Kodak moment.) But I couldn't resist introducing myself and attempting to mimic the finger-snap/hand-wave ritual his delusional *Soap* character would execute to turn himself invisible. Seeming amused by this fanboy, Mulligan smiled and casually chatted me up—inquiring

154

where I was from and what had brought me out to L.A. Then, before politely excusing himself, he very casually reached down between the legs of my cheap Pinkerton polyester pants and gave my "pinkerton" a gentle squeeze. With that, he pulled back his hand, slyly offered me one of those cool "point and wink" gestures and exited the auditorium.

Richard Mulligan (top right) with the cast of *Soap*, 1977. (ABC)

Oh. My. God. I'd had my very first sexual encounter since arriving in Los Angeles, and it was with Burt from *Soap*??!! Had I been forewarned that I was going to be fondled by a "Burt" at the Emmys, I would have made a beeline for Burt Reynolds. Even Bert from *Sesame Street* probably would have been preferable. To be sure, Richard Mulligan would not have been among my top 500 molestation picks.

To be honest, at the time I wasn't so offended as much as completely dumbstruck, as in "What the hell just happened??!!" I got the impression Mulligan thought he was giving me some sort of parting gift in lieu of an autograph. An auto-*grab*.

Anyway, because of that uninvited grope, a few years later I felt completely justified in taking Mulligan's seat at the *Empty Nest* cast table when I snuck into *That Girl* star Marlo Thomas' annual St. Jude charity gala in The Beverly Hilton hotel. I wasn't alone this time. My accomplice was fellow *Enquirer* reporter, Suzanne Ely, who shared my absurd sense of humor and love of classic TV sitcoms.

Upon entering the ballroom, the *Empty Nest* table was the first we could find with two empty seats (which had been reserved for no-shows Mulligan and Kristy McNichol, the actress who played his daughter Barbara). The only two cast

155

members who were actually seated at the table were Park Overall (the show's sarcastic nurse Laverne) and David Leisure (annoying neighbor Charley).

Almost immediately after taking our seats, Overall asked us in her strong Southern drawl, "How y'all looped in with St. Jude?"

Ummm ... Suzanne and I looked at each other, waiting for the other to answer. Since I remembered Marlo's father, sitcom legend Danny Thomas (whose son, Tony Thomas, produced *Empty Nest*), appearing in TV spots talking about the charity he founded that had some connection to hospitals, I just spat out, "We're volunteers."

Well, Park could not have been more overjoyed to share this news with the entire table. "Did ya hear that, y'all? These two are St. Jude volunteers."

And then came applause from everyone seated at the table, expressing their gratitude for all the good we did. All Suzanne and I could do was smile back politely and ask if they wouldn't mind passing the dinner rolls—always the best part of those Beverly Hilton rubber-chicken dinners. It could have just ended there and we all would have had a fine evening, but Park just had to come back with a follow-up question. "So ... how'd y'all end up volunteering for St. Jude?" she asked.

Again, I looked over at Suzanne, hoping she'd take this one, but instead she just sipped her wine, waiting to hear how in fact we did end up volunteering our services for this mystery charity.

After a long uncomfortable pause with the whole table staring at us as I chewed my roll to stall for time, I finally broke the deafening silence. "My grandfather," I offered. "St. Jude helped him out when he was sick. He wouldn't have made it without St. Jude."

I thought I'd sold my story pretty well, but all I got back were blank stares, except for Overall who was nodding quizzically trying to make sense of what I'd said. Then suddenly, as if on cue, the lights went down, and Marlo took the stage. After saying a few kind words about her late father, Marlo threw to a video package that began playing on two giant monitors on either side of the ballroom. Filling the screen was daddy Danny Thomas, speaking from the grave about the thousands of sick children whose lives had been saved by St. Jude Children's Research Hospital, a *children's* charity that saved *children*. Children. Not grandpas. Children!

Above: President Ronald Reagan (on left) commending actor and philanthropist Danny Thomas, 1985. (Wikimedia Commons)

Had I been able to turn myself invisible like Mulligan's *Soap* character had done, surely this would have been the time!

When the video ended and the lights came back up, I could feel the cold stares coming at me from all directions. Even Suzanne was giving me the stink eye. What could I have possibly said at that point to save face? Oh, I don't know, maybe, "My grandfather was very childlike in his later years..." Or perhaps "My grandfather actually was a child ... when he first received treatment from St. Jude back in 1912."

Below: Author with Danny's actress daughter Marlo Thomas (a.k.a. *That Girl*), Los Angeles, CA, 2013.

And it's a damn good thing I didn't say that, because the lights no doubt would have dimmed again, with Danny's haunting face coming back on screen to remind everyone that his hospital first opened its doors in 1962 when the grandfather of William Keck would have been in his late 50s.

No, there was nothing more to say that could have saved us. We were exposed as the party crashers we were. There is, however, an amusing footnote. On the St. Jude webpage, it explains that St. Jude Thaddeus, for whom Danny named his charity, was known as "the patron saint of hopeless causes." And I like to think

157

that good-humored Danny, had he been alive and seated at the *Empty Nest* table, just might have chuckled—as he clocked me between the eyes with a dinner roll.

And as for the *Empty Nest* cast, I imagine they'd have cut me some slack for my dick move had they known their show's star had grabbed mine.

Lesson Learned: He who has no charity deserves no mercy. And he who grabs another's privates sacrifices his own right to privacy.

A WORD FROM MULLIGAN'S *SOAP* CO-STAR DIANA CANOVA

Source: Wikimedia Commons.

The Richard Mulligan I knew was a kind, complex and brilliant man. A natural who never ever stopped creating. He was also wicked funny. In the role of Burt Campbell on *Soap* he created a timeless character and I am so lucky that I was there to watch it happen.

When we weren't working, Richard was just a regular guy. He loved his wife. He was always warm and friendly. No actor ego. Just an all-around good person. So the incident that William speaks of when Rich "groped" him would be out of character for the man I knew.

I wasn't there, but I can't imagine that the guy I saw every day for four years, who had a sweet sensitive side, who could drink a little ... or a lot (I never saw him sloshed, but I was told he could put it away) would make a move like that unless it was in fun. A grab-ass moment, but certainly nothing sexual. Just a stupid, tough guy thing. All that said, these days that would be considered an assault, and if it made William at all uncomfortable, I bet Richard would apologize for doing it. I really bet he would.

PART III:
DANGEROUS DIVAS

DISCLAIMER: THE TERM "DIVA" (DĒ-Və), AS RELATED TO THE EXCEPTIONALLY TALENTED LADIES REFERENCED IN THIS SECTION, IS DEFINED BY THE MERRIAM-WEBSTER DICTIONARY AS "A GLAMOROUS AND SUCCESSFUL PERFORMER OR PERSONALITY." IN NO WAY DOES IT SUGGEST A REPUTATION THAT IS ANYTHING BUT 100% POSITIVE AND PROFESSIONAL.

Chapter 19
WANTED DEAD OR ALIVE

(BRITNEY SPEARS)

WHO: Britney Spears (b. December 2, 1981). Former Mouseketeer turned pop princess behind such hits as "Oops!... I Did It Again" and "Toxic." Winner of numerous awards, including a Grammy, an American Music Award and multiple Teen Choice, *Billboard* Music and MTV Video Music Awards.

WHAT: A high-speed pursuit of Brit and then-husband Kevin Federline on assignment for *USA Today*.

Britney Spears on stage during her 2009 Circus Tour. (Wikimedia Commons)

WHERE: L.A.'s 405 Freeway. Some rando gas station. K-Fed's ex's Orange County, CA, apartment complex.

Before I take you back to the crazy day I ended up in a high-speed chase with Britney Spears—the first of my "Dangerous Divas"—let me first share some recollections of my clashes and encounters with other legendary, larger-than-life ladies from the musical world.

Madonna: Back in 2001, the Material Girl and her new hubby, British film director Guy Ritchie, couldn't stop kissing at the Los Angeles premiere for his film, *Snatch*. Since Madonna seemed in a particularly cheeky mood as she came toward me on the red carpet, I asked her if she ever had to kiss someone to whom she was *not* attracted. But instead of answering with words, she puckered her lips, looked deeply into my eyes and came close as if she was about to … But before our lips touched, she turned on her heels in seeming disgust and walked away—before looking back over her shoulder and offering me a little wink to let me know it was all in good fun. A bitchy, ballsy, diva move that only made me love her even more!

Diana Ross: Outside Downtown L.A.'s Orpheum Theatre in 2004 covering the red carpet premiere for the action film, *Collateral*—which cast Tom Cruise as a villainous *gray-haired* assassin—I quizzed Diana Ross, then 60, about her own fabulous "do," in which not a single gray hair had ever been spotted. Interpreting my playfulness as impudence, Ross turned deathly serious, stared me down and said, "I dye it, okay? Are you happy?" (Not particularly.)

Whitney Houston: At a concert after-party in Las Vegas, I chatted up Whitney and then-husband Bobby Brown and asked Brown to share something people might find surprising about his diva wife. We all laughed as they opened up about her odd affinity for vacuuming their home at all hours of the night. Far less amusing now, considering tragic Whitney vacuumed herself to the grave … quite possibly with a vacuum bag bursting at the seams with crack cocaine.

Beyoncé: In the early 2000s, VH1 assembled a virtual petting zoo of divas for their annual "Divas" concerts, which aired live from Vegas' MGM Grand from 2002–2004. On the 2003 red carpet, I laughed with Beyoncé about over-the-top "rider" requests that some of her fellow divas (Mariah, Madonna, Janet) were rumored to have had written into their contracts. Private bathroom transformations was a recurring theme that kept coming up—from the installation of brand-new toilet seats to toilet paper in a very specific shade of pink. Yep, even divas take dumps—but they do so in style.

Celine Dion: At that same 2003 concert, dubbed "Divas Duets," I got scolded by the "My Heart Will Go On" chanteuse when I asked her what it was like being a diva. While Beyoncé, Mary J. Blige, Chaka Khan and all the other fabulous femmes performing that night told me they embraced being dubbed "divas," Celine—without a hint of humor—told me she most certainly was *not* one. "I don't even know what this term 'diva' means," she said, seemingly oblivious to the name of the concert at which she was about to perform.

162

Mariah Carey and Nicki Minaj: In 2013, it was double-diva trouble as both ladies served as judges on *American Idol*, reportedly clashing over everything from wardrobe selections to salaries. It was all anyone could ask about at a press panel comprised of Mariah, Nicki, fellow judges Randy Jackson and Keith Urban, host Ryan Seacrest and approximately 200 other journalists. I chose to liven things up by asking Mariah and Nicki to prove there was no awkwardness between them by each saying something nice about the other. After an explosion of laughter calmed, Nicki was the first to break the unbearable silence: "I say nice things about Mariah all the time … she's one of my favorite artists [who has] shaped a generation of singers. It's kind of crazy to be on a panel with her."

"That was obviously a very sweet thing to say," responded the chilly Christmas Queen, without giving her rival so much as a glance. "Nicki and I worked together very early on in her career … and I did feel that she was going to go very far, and still have that feeling. [I] am grateful for anything nice that she and anyone else have to say about me."

Offering up just that ounce of kindness had to be excruciating, particularly for Mimi, who a couple years later told an Australian radio interviewer that *Idol* had been "the worst experience of my life" and lamented having to "fake" nice things to say.

What Mariah, Nicki, Diana and Celine failed to realize, as Madonna, Beyoncé, Mary J. and Chaka had, is that the label "diva" is something to embrace. Being a diva comes with a priceless license permitting one to get away with devilish fun, often (but not always) at another's expense. And that's perfectly fine because it's what divas are born to do. What they're *expected* to do. Sure, the title does have several definitions. Diva can refer to a celebrated virtuoso female opera singer, such as renowned Greek soprano Maria Callas. And yes, it can also take on a negative connotation when applied to a woman (or gay man), often a celebrity, with a reputation for being extremely demanding, temperamental and hard to please. But for the sake of this "Dangerous Divas" section, let's play it safe and go with Merriam-Webster's purely complimentary definition, as referenced in my Part III disclaimer. Given that, it's my hope that Dame Joan Collins, Victoria Principal, Teri Hatcher and all the other fabulously talented "divas" mentioned herein, are flattered to be acknowledged as such. Perhaps they'll even enjoy a good laugh, as I did, revisiting our past encounters.

To kick off my salute to some of show business' all-time great divas, we begin with Britney Spears—a glamorous, wildly successful global superstar who, in recent years, has become less known for her musical talents and more for her personal struggles and increasingly out-there social media posts. (Be careful not to scratch that stripper pole with those kitchen knives, girlfriend!)

The 2021 documentary *Framing Britney Spears* and her own 2023 memoir, *The Woman in Me* (in which the troubled icon makes several references to being constantly hounded by the unrelenting paparazzi), provided a clearer understanding of the events that contributed to her tragic turn. Dating back to even before Brit put on her very first pair of *Mickey Mouse Club* ears at age 11, the pop princess-in-the-making was taken advantage of by the media, the paparazzi and even those who claimed they loved her. I should know. I was one of 'em.

It had not been 10 years since Princess Diana's tragic death as a result of a high-speed paparazzi chase, and George Clooney was leading the charge among the Hollywood community to halt "Open Season" on celebrities. Because the issue was such a hot topic at the time, in 2004 I got approval from my assignment editor at *USA Today* to spend a day with Mel Bouzad—one of L.A.'s most aggressive (and successful) paparazzi.

It was a fascinating glimpse into a viciously competitive world shrouded in secrecy. Bouzad had an inside network of fellow photogs, celebrity personal assistants and bodyguards on his payroll to help guide him to the most profitable photo ops. Understandably, not every shutterbug was anxious to let a reporter like me in on his tricks, since not all their tricks were exactly ethical, or even legal. But Bouzad was a showman who loved attention, so it didn't take much to convince him to let me and my own photographer Dan sit quietly in the backseat of his Mercedes SUV to observe where the day might take us.

Never in a million years could I have imagined just how wild this ride would get ... or who would end up as our prey of the day!

It started out quietly enough: a stakeout outside the Pro Gym in Brentwood waiting for *Underworld* actress Kate Beckinsale to emerge from a workout. When she did, Mel brazenly stepped out of his car, positioned himself in her path and easily snapped several sweaty pics. And that was that. Nice sighting of a usually glam celeb glistening in her workout clothes, but not quite enough to warrant an exposé in the Nation's Newspaper. The most interesting observation on this starry safari was that Bouzad paid zero attention to parking signs or traffic laws, explaining, "What's a $100 ticket when we can get a picture worth thousands?" Hard to argue with that!

While we waited for a fresh lead to come in, Bouzad entertained us with his celebrity war stories. He had some 200 celebrity addresses programmed into his GPS, 400 celebrity license plates in his database and had added 12,000 miles on his odometer in just the past four months. He also possessed an incredible knowledge of all the hottest celebs' daily routines. Among his random shares:

"Paltrow is renowned for wearing disguises and hiding in the trunks of cars."

"Flockhart will never go to the park (with her child) on a weekday."

"We all know Ashton's cheating." (Unconfirmed by this reporter!!)

"Aniston will only remain of interest for as long as she's married to Pitt." (Well, no one's correct 100% of the time.)

Just when it was beginning to look like my potential cover story might end up as nothing more than a caption to a sweaty Beckinsale snapshot, fortune intervened. Or perhaps it was *mis*fortune. Regardless, it sure was damn exciting! A call came in from one of Bouzad's secret sources, who somehow knew Britney Spears was about to accompany her then-husband, bad boy Kevin Federline, to Orange County. Their mission: to return his two-year-old daughter Kori to her mother, Federline's ex-girlfriend Shar Jackson. This was to be the women's first meeting, and—according to Bouzad—a photo of Spears captured with the *Moesha* actress ("a massive picture" is what he called it) would earn him a hefty payday.

(Wacky sidenote here. Only weeks before, I'd reported that Shar had made the painful decision to give up her li'l "Britney"—a precious lap dog that she'd named after Spears *before* the superstar up and ran off with her man! As Shar explained it to me, having the bitch in her home was just too painful a reminder.)

To make sure he got his photo, Bouzad had at least one of his photogs parked 24/7 outside Spears' hilltop Malibu home awaiting her departure. The waiting

165

seemed to go on forever until our stomachs all started growling. Bouzad begrudgingly drove us to Duke's, an oceanfront tavern just down the road. And sure enough, just as the waitress was bringing our meals to the table, a call came in at 1:15pm reporting some activity back at the Spears compound, indicating her departure was imminent.

"Brit's on the move!" announced Bouzad, grabbing his fries and dropping a wad of cash on the table before making a mad dash to his car. There'd be no waiting for anyone to catch up, he let it be known. And I had no doubt he'd be perfectly fine just abandoning us there in the parking lot if we didn't get our asses in gear. So, as much as I was dying to dig into my clam boat sandwich, I knew we had to rock and roll. Ah, the life of the paparazzi.

By the time we pulled out of Duke's, Bouzad had discarded his barely touched lunch and was on the phone trying to hire a helicopter. Yes, an actual HELICOPTER!!! It's like this guy was Bruce effin' Wayne!! Word came in that the Federlines were already on the Pacific Coast Highway headed south in her black Mercedes G500 SUV, with a trail of *seven* paparazzi in SUVs already in hot pursuit. This was not good news for Bouzad, because the more competition on Britney's tail, the less likely he'd be to get anything exclusive. But in Bouzad's mind, it was still worth the stakes of a high-speed chase. And oh how the speed climbed ... and climbed. By the time the caravan reached the 405 South, we were driving at speeds in excess of 90 mph, with all the reckless paps weaving in and out of lanes, crossing double yellow lines and illegally swerving into the carpool lane trying to dodge expendable "civilians." While I personally found it both thrilling and frightening, Britney appeared completely undaunted. Sitting calmly in the passenger seat with her bare feet propped up on the dash while slurping up her slushy, this was just another day at the office.

Then, as so often happened with Spears, nature called. Kevin suddenly pulled off the freeway and into the nearest gas station.

"Girl's got a weak bladder," explained Bouzad, who had sped straight through red lights to make sure he didn't lose sight of his prey.

While Britney hurried to retrieve the restroom key from a gas station attendant, we studied Federline in his wife beater, dangling a cigarette out his window and waiting for his lady to return. Bouzad made no attempt to hide his animosity.

"All Kevin wears are those wife beaters," he told us, annoyed with K-Fed for failing to diversify his wardrobe so that Bouzad's photos might command a higher price. "They're both trailer trash … and you can print that!"

There was no mistaking just how much Bouzad was getting off on this thrilling game of cat and mouse. At one point he radioed one of his boys and told him, "If we get this picture, I'll pay for the next lap dance."

I started to get the feeling that Mel was intentionally laying it on extra thick so I'd paint him in my article as a fearless rogue. Everyone seemed to be playing a role in this insane melodrama, including our leading lady, who appeared to be choreographing her every move so that her pursuers could get what they wanted. When she emerged from the bathroom to discover a little girl waiting outside with her autograph book in hand, everyone seemed in agreement this was an irresistible photo op that could benefit all.

But Bouzad was relentless. He wanted more, more, MORE!!

"The photo we want is Brit *with Shar*," Bouzad emphasized as the race to Jackson's gated community resumed. "If we get it, I'm going to ask for 50 grand." Dan and I shared a glance, silently communicating, "Dang, we in the wrong biz!"

When we finally made it to Jackson's home, Brit chose to remain in the car while Shar came out dressed in pink sweatpants to collect Kori. This complicated Bouzad's attempt for the two-shot he so desperately wanted. And he was about to learn that his day's work would not provide him the windfall he'd been anticipating. *Star* magazine, having just finalized the layout for their new issue, passed on the photos altogether. Bouzad shrugged, hoping *People* or *Us Weekly* might take the shots instead. No dice. (Sorry fellas, no lap dances tonight.)

In the end, a single shot of Brit's newly tattooed right hand would fetch a disappointing four grand. We can only guess the photo's added worth had her fingers been stained orange from Spears' favorite Nacho Cheese Doritos.

I, however, felt I'd hit the journalistic jackpot. It all made for such an exciting story that my *USA Today* editors deemed it worthy of placement on the purple *Life* section cover. On top of that, I'd be awarded a Hainer Award as the standout story of the whole issue—meaning I'd get a whopping 50-buck bonus added to my next paycheck. As if that weren't enough glory, I'd also be receiving another refrigerator magnet bearing the image of the award's namesake, Cathy Hainer, a much-beloved *USA Today* features reporter photographed with a scarf around her head in the weeks before she lost her valiant battle with breast cancer, just a few years before my hire.

Regretfully, not everyone shared my employer's enthusiasm for my day-in-the-life exposé on Ms. Spears. At the time, Miss Queen B had retained the services of the most aggressive and threatening publicist in New York: the dreaded Leslie Sloane (cue ominous *Phantom of the Opera* organ refrain). I'd already had a history with the family Sloane. Just a few years prior, when I was a reporter for the now defunct *Soap Opera Digest* (the only media outlet that would touch me after I'd quit the *Enquirer*), Leslie's sister, Stephanie Sloane, the mag's managing editor, had personally flown out from New York City to L.A. to surprise-fire me. As Stephanie explained it to me, my revelatory soap star profiles—a *Days of Our Lives* ingenue with a fondness for making home porn movies; an outspoken *Young and the Restless* actress with a disdain for environmental causes—had enraged too many executive producers and publicists, requiring frequent deliveries of apology muffin baskets.

(In hindsight, I'd most likely cooked my goose my very first week at *Digest* when the L.A. reporters all signed a congratulatory Hallmark greeting card for our NYC-based Editor-in-Chief, Lynn Leahey, who had announced she was expecting a baby. Instead of wisely keeping my message short and sweet as would behoove a new hire, I thought it would be oh so clever to mock an overused soap opera plot device. "Congratulations, Lynn," I scribbled on her card, followed by: "Hopefully you know who the father is." Safe to say my new boss didn't appreciate my inference that she was some ho.)

Besides Britney, Leslie's then-roster of celeb clients included Sarah Michelle Gellar, Shannen Doherty and another troublemaker whose off-screen antics I'd been routinely exposing: the infamous Lindsay Lohan. I was already on Leslie's radar as a nuisance she wanted to take down in flames, and now was the jaguar's time to pounce! And pounce she did!! HARD.

As I'd been told, Leslie assumed my article had been intentionally plotted from the get-go as a personal invasion of Britney's privacy under the fabricated "veil" of spending a random day with a member of the paparazzi. The fact that *USA Today*, a respected national newspaper, had climbed into bed with the enemy was a grievous sign in her eyes that journalism had sunk to a new low. And it was all the fault of this former tabloid scum ball.

I later came to learn what had really pissed off Brit-Brit and her team was one very specific observation in my story. From my vantage point in the backseat of Bouzad's car—just behind Kevin and Britney's speeding SUV—I could clearly see baby Kori's head bobbing up and down like a Bobblehead as the speeds increased. If this had been an actual rollercoaster ride at Disneyland, there's no way in hell little Kori would have passed the height requirement to ride. Although I'd been careful to point out that the tyke had been safely strapped into her car safety seat, my story had still handed Shar Jackson valuable ammunition. Because her relationship with Kevin and Britney was already highly antagonistic, she potentially could have used this info to prove that her daughter's life had been put in jeopardy. (She didn't, and Spears ended up filing for divorce two years later.)

As retaliation, Leslie crafted a truly scathing email labeling me as tabloid trash and sent it out wide, encouraging all her publicist friends to blacklist me. Fortunately, most of the recipients were already familiar with my reputation … and Leslie's. So, while it certainly presented me with some career hurdles for a while, it didn't take me down as Leslie had hoped. Ultimately, it only bolstered my confidence for future diva run-ins about to come my way.

Lesson Learned: When you allow yourself to get in a car with someone else behind the wheel, be prepared to go down some rocky roads you might not choose for yourself. And look both ways before crossing a diva ... or her publicist!

PRINCE AND THE PURPLE SUCKER

To be sure, men can be divas too. I've had my own fair share of diva moments, and I suppose it could even be considered "diva-ish" for me to have had the gall to approach one of the most private, media-shy personalities of all time in hopes of landing an impromptu exclusive.

It happened at the Beverly Hilton Hotel after the 2004 Golden Globe Awards when I was on assignment for *Entertainment Weekly*. For many years, the Globes party you really wanted to get into—before it reached capacity and the fire marshal barricaded the door—was the Warner Bros./InStyle party. I knew this particular year's party was going to be extra challenging to infiltrate because there was a rumor floating around that Prince might be performing. So, to make sure I got in, I hightailed it into the bash while servers were still setting up. And to my great shock, sitting all by himself against a wall and sucking away on a purple lollipop was Prince himself. No publicist. No security. No Apollonia.

Figuring it was worth a try, I casually sauntered over his way and introduced myself. Remaining seated and sucking away hard on his lolly, the only reaction I got from the "Artist" to my series of questions were coquettish glances that mildly acknowledged my presence.

Prince, circa 2008.
(MicahMedia at en.wikipedia)

"Not sure if you saw any of the ceremony, but could I ask what you enjoyed most...?" Crickets! "Were there any particular movies you were rooting for...?" Thud! "I'm assuming that's grape flavored...?" Silence!

He just kept batting his eyelashes and slurping on that purple sucker like Pamela Anderson working Tommy Lee's knob. As he was almost down to his candy's limp paper stick, I wished Prince good night and good luck on his performance. And while I can't be sure, it looked almost as though the corners of his mouth may have ever so slightly inched upwards. Now *that's* how a diva has fun with its prey!

Chapter 20
CHASING A LEGEND

(ELIZABETH TAYLOR)

WHO: Elizabeth Taylor (1932–2011). Violet-eyed screen legend known for her eight marriages, and, later in life, her AIDS activism, charity work and White Diamonds perfume commercials. Lead actress Oscar winner for her roles in *BUtterfield 8* (1960) and *Who's Afraid of Virginia Woolf?* (1966)

Elizabeth Taylor in one of her last films, the 2001 TV movie *These Old Broads*. (Columbia Tri-Star Television)

as well as the Motion Picture Academy's 1992 Jean Hersholt Humanitarian Award.

WHAT: Stakeout and high-speed chase outside her home, on assignment for the *National Enquirer*.

WHERE: Bel Air, CA.

Let's have a talk about legends, shall we? When I first arrived in Hollywood in 1990, it had been just eight months since the death of Lucille Ball—an indisputable legend who would have ranked high on my "Just Gotta Meet" list. Fortunately, several others on the Hollywood Legends Endangered Species list were waiting for me to pull a chair up to their tables at Spago and Le Dome. I did have the great fortune of getting to breathe the same air as many of them, including Gregory Peck, Jimmy Stewart, Sidney Poitier, Angela Lansbury and Sophia Loren. And I'm pleased to report that not a single one of them disappointed in the least.

Unlike Bacall, Hollywood legends Sophia Loren (above, in 2002) and Angela Lansbury (below, 2016) presented themselves to me as gracious and good-humored.

And then there was Lauren Bacall, a screen goddess with a strict opinion as to who among her peers was worthy of being called a legend, and who was not. Nicole Kidman, in her eyes, was most certainly *not*.

My interaction with Ms. Bacall took place at a November 2003 American Cinematheque gala honoring Kidman, where I was positioned on the red carpet next to my friend and colleague Monica Rizzo. Monica was covering the A-list arrivals for *People* magazine while I was on assignment for *USA Today*. At the time, Kidman was about to come out with two movies (*Dogville* and *Birth*) that paired her with Bacall, who turned up that night in support of both films.

Then 80, and every bit as venomous as she came off when she cameoed as herself in a 2006 episode of *The Sopranos*, Bacall for some reason seemed to take an instant dislike to Monica just as soon as my fellow red carpet soldier posed her introductory question: "What brought you out this evening?"

"What brought me *out*?" Bacall snapped back at her. "What do you *think* brought me out? They're honoring Nicole, in case you weren't aware."

Trying her best to recover from her public dressing down, Monica gently followed up with another softball question: "What makes Nicole a legend?"

And that's when Bacall really dug into her ... unnecessarily so.

"A *legend*?!!" Bacall practically screamed, turning heads from all within earshot—including the always lovely Geena Davis. "Nicole Kidman is *not* a legend. A fine actress, certainly. But a legend, maybe someday." And then Bacall turned to me and said, "Can you believe that? What a stupid question."

While Davis stepped in to offer Monica some much-needed TLC, it was my turn at bat with Bacall. And what I really wanted to ask her was, "And what makes you such a cunt?"

But of course, I didn't, and actually fared quite well with the wicked witch. To be fair, Bacall sorta had a point. Time reveals which stars become legends and which become nothing more than old actors who once starred in movies. (Pay attention all you superhero Chrises!)

Now Elizabeth Taylor, she was the real deal. In my eyes, the biggest of them all. And I attempted to chat her up on a few occasions. Once was in October 2000 at the Carousel of Hope Ball, a splashy, star-studded diabetes fundraiser held every other year at the Beverly Hilton Hotel. Though there was an unwritten rule not to disturb celebrities once they were seated at their tables, how could I resist an opportunity to get quotes for my *Entertainment Weekly* story? Not only from Liz, but from her "date": Prince of Pop Michael Jackson, who was not looking his best this particular evening. To be honest, both looked as though they'd been up all night playing with their Barbies and Kens, or whatever these two unlikely playmates did together in private. But suffice to say, all eyes in the ballroom were fixed on them.

I had just come from the silent-auction hall, where a collection of celebrity-painted plates were on display for bidding. MJ had painted one of a little boy (surprise, surprise!) that sold for a cool $4,500. So that seemed like an appropriate question to kick off what turned out to be my *second* shortest sit-down interview of all time. With him seated and me standing, this is how the conversation went:

"I saw your plate, Michael. It's very nice. What inspired you?"

"Children," he said in that eerie man-child whisper. "I have such a special place in my heart for children." (Not to mention *your bed*, I stopped myself from blurting out.)

I'm always surprised when I'm asked— even after all those damaging documentaries— if I think he really did all those terrible things. I haven't had so much as a shadow of a doubt since I'd first begun working leads from *Enquirer* sources who'd been employed at Jackson's Neverland Ranch. When you start hearing the same stories from different sources, such as Jackson allegedly installing floor sensors outside his bedroom that would activate warning lights whenever anyone approached, it's hard to brush them *all* away as rumors.

Jacko in 1997. (Georges Biard/Wikimedia Commons)

After Michael let me know he wanted to get back to his chicken fingers and tater tots (or whatever was on his plate), it was time for my #1 shortest interview of all time. With Dame Elizabeth.

Extremely medicated, poor disoriented Liz appeared completely mesmerized by the microcassette recorder I'd pulled out of my jacket pocket, so much so that Ms. Cleopatra took it in her hand, studying it like some unusual Egyptian artifact.

"What's *thiiiiss?*" she asked as if her own voice was being played back in slo-mo.

"It's my recorder I use to tape my interviews," I gently explained.

"Ohhhh," she said.

And that was my exclusive interview, before security politely yanked me away. Even if I'd had more time with Ms. Taylor, I'm afraid I wouldn't have been able to get much more outta the old girl, though it might have been fun to let her play with my car keys. Ah, Diazepam—gotta love it.

Five years earlier, the *Enquirer* assigned me to stake out her Bel Air compound. We'd received intel that Elizabeth would be driven that morning to a nearby hospital where this real-life Bionic Woman was to undergo another surgery on some body part. It might have been a shoulder; perhaps a hip. (When I recently reviewed my old reporter notebooks as part of my research for this book, they were filled with names of doctors and hospitals she frequented. Unfortunately, big shot celebrities like Liz never headed to downtown L.A.'s Keck Hospital of USC—named after my "fantasy" billionaire grampy, the late philanthropist William M. Keck—where I might have been able to use that convenient coincidence to my advantage.)

My job that Sunday morning was simple: Park my car outside 700 Nimes Road, wait until her car emerged from the gates and follow it to the hospital. I also jotted down the license plates of every car entering and exiting her estate, with the intention of running plate checks with the DMV (a right granted us media folk) to cultivate potential future Liz sources.

In just that one morning, 17 vehicles came and went: gardeners, flower deliveries and other service-oriented individuals who might likely be tempted to spill what they saw on the other side of the wall. I also distinctly remember hearing Elizabeth herself calling out for her beloved Maltese puppy: "Suggaaarr … mealtime. Come to mama, Sugar."

Since the *Enquirer* already had a source inside St. John's Hospital who would be providing a play-by-play of her surgical procedure, I'm not exactly sure why I was even needed. But it ended up being potentially cataclysmic for both Ms. Taylor and me. As soon as the gates to her estate opened and a car with tinted windows emerged, I turned on my engine and tried to follow from a safe distance. No easy task considering the multiple twisting roads in Bel Air that stem off in different directions as you make your way south to Sunset. Too much distance and you risk losing your prey.

So when they made a right turn, so did I. Followed by a left turn. And then another. When it became obvious I was following them, Ms. Taylor's driver sped up in an attempt to lose me. So, I did the same. The more they increased their speed, the harder my foot pressed down on my accelerator.

Though this was about a year before the high-speed paparazzi pursuit that ended Princess Diana's life, I was reminded of a tragic event earlier in Taylor's history that occurred not all that far from where we were now speeding. It was back in 1956 when Taylor's dear friend, movie idol Montgomery Clift, crashed his Chevrolet Bel Air sedan into a telephone pole after having too much to drink at Liz's then-residence on Beverly Estate Drive. Clift was lucky to have survived the violent wreck that forever robbed him of his gorgeous looks. As Elizabeth herself would later reveal, she single-handedly saved his life by rushing to the crash scene with Rock Hudson and sticking her fingers down his throat to extricate dislodged teeth that were blocking his airway. Though his face was rebuilt as best as surgeons of the time could, for the next decade Clift sunk into a bottomless pit of drugs and alcohol to escape his physical and mental anguish, right up until his death at the young age of 45.

Now here I was endangering the life of a treasured 60-something icon who was on her way to the hospital to undergo an operation! And this time I didn't have the excuse of being an "innocent" backseat passenger, as I was during the high-speed Britney Spears pursuit. No, this time I was behind the wheel. The choice was mine. So … I just stopped. Stopped and let them go. Who cares if I got in trouble for not tracking her like some wild animal? I damn sure wasn't up for extricating porcelain crowns from *her* airways.

While I was not always successful in making the morally responsible call, on that day I did. And had the relentless paparazzi pursuing Diana done the same, we'd still have the People's Princess with us today—likely hiding out with Harry and Meghan in Montecito and barbecuing with Oprah and Ellen.

Lesson Learned: A riff on an old proverb: *If you love an aging legend, set it free.* *If it comes back, it's yours and the world's to enjoy.* *If it doesn't, check Cedars-Sinai.*

Chapter 21
IN HER EYELINE

(JOAN COLLINS)

WHO: Dame Joan Collins (b. May 23, 1933). Winner and five-time Golden Globe nominee for her celebrated role as the villainous bitch Alexis Carrington Colby on the 1980s primetime soap *Dynasty*.

WHAT: On-the-record interviews for *Us Weekly* and *USA Today*. Celebrity cooking segment on *Home & Family*.

WHERE: Various Los Angeles locations for the filming of 1991's *Dynasty: The Reunion*. Filoli, the "Carrington" mansion estate in San Mateo County, CA, for the filming of the 2004 *Dynasty* reunion, *Catfights & Caviar. Home & Family* house, Universal City, CA.

Joan Collins, on the set of 1991's *Dynasty: The Reunion*. (Photo by author)

I'm routinely asked by dumbstruck younger gay guys why I waited until I was 30 to come out of the closet.

"Easy for you to say," I'll tell these lucky little bastards who, unlike me, grew up with *Glee, Will & Grace* and countless other positive representations of the LGBTQ community in TV shows, films and songs that empowered gay boys and girls to become their authentic "Born This Way" selves.

When I was coming of age in the 1980s, one of my only gay TV role models was the Steven Carrington character on the 1981–1989 ABC primetime soap opera *Dynasty*. But even Steven switched teams whenever Heather Locklear drove her Porsche into Denver to stir up trouble. Was Steven gay? Bi? Or just seriously confused? It sure as hell was confusing for the audience, particularly for closeted young gay boys trying to figure out if that's what being gay looked like.

Above: Author with reunited *Dynasty* stars (l–r) Pamela Bellwood, John James, Gordon Thomson, Pamela Sue Martin and Al Corley in 2015. Below: A dream come true! Getting a 2016 Krystle kiss from Linda Evans on the *Home & Family* set.

I can so clearly remember watching an episode of *Dynasty* with my mom, many years before she embraced the concept of unconditional love by becoming 100% accepting of my sexuality.

"Steven's such a handsome man," she sighed when the character (then played by Jack Coleman) came on screen. "What a waste …."

A waste: the implication being that the *Dynasty* character's life was of no value just because he was attracted to other men instead of women. "Yikes," little 15-year-old me told myself. "I'd better pray the gay away so *I'm* not a waste like Steven."

Now, all these years later, there is no one more supportive of my relationship with my partner than my mom. And my boyfriend and I have been having a total blast going back and re-watching all 220 *Dynasty* episodes from the beginning. As I write this chapter, Joan Collins' delicious Alexis Carrington Colby is plotting the marriage of her daughter Amanda to Prince Michael of Moldavia, while Blake Carrington has been making baby steps in accepting his son Steven's blossoming relationship with handsome Luke Fuller. I can now see Steven for who he is—an admirable son, father, business executive and romantic partner. Anything but a waste. (That the *Dynasty* writers elected to kill Luke off in Amanda's season-ending wedding massacre was the real waste.)

During my years producing *Home & Family*, one of my great joys was inviting the *Dynasty* stars to come on our show. I began with a splashy 2015 cast reunion of the actors who'd played the Carrington children—including original Steven actor Al Corley. Linda Evans, who was recovering from surgery, sent us a lovely letter to read on air and promised to come visit the show when she was back on her feet—a promise she kept.

With John Forsythe having passed in 2010, that left only Dame Joan—who'd declined to appear in my reunion—as my Holy Grail guest. But each time I extended an invitation via her longtime publicist Jeffrey Lane, he'd just keep putting me off. "Williammm, now's just not the right time," the sweet, diminutive, bald Brit would tell me time and again. "Let's just hold off a bit longer and then why don't we try to have Joan come on with Diahann?" Of course, I loved the idea of having Collins accompanied by her good friend (and another of Jeffrey's clients) Diahann Carroll—two *Dynasty* bitches for the price of one! But as the years passed, Joan's sister, romance novelist Jackie Collins, died in 2015, followed by Miss Carroll in 2019. I knew that any further postponing of Joan's visit was a luxury we could not afford. So I dialed Jeffrey one last time and told him point-blank, "I'm afraid if we wait much longer, I'll be producing Joan's In Memoriam tribute."

Within minutes, Jeffrey called back to let me know Joan would be delighted to join our hunky host, Cameron Mathison, in our kitchen set to prepare her famous Spaghetti Bolognese—a recipe she'd acquired from an old Italian woman while on location in Italy shooting the 1960 biblical romance *Esther & the King*.

While Joan couldn't have cared less when I shared with her that one of my very first jobs in Hollywood was working on her 1991 *Dynasty* reunion miniseries, I will give her this: She makes one helluva Bolognese.

Reconnecting with Collins over her Spaghetti Bolognese in 2020, on *Home & Family*.

Just two years after *Dynasty* had been cancelled, getting to work on that miniseries was a gift from the universe. I received the fancy-sounding title of "Assistant Production Coordinator" with a salary of $450 a week (a windfall at the time) and got to meet the entire cast of glamorous Carringtons and Colbys. Less glamorous was our dingy production office in a dilapidated 1960s San Fernando Valley office building adjacent to an overpass, crammed between a sketchy phone-sex operation and the Castle Park miniature-golf course, from which the occasional renegade golf ball would slam against one of our windows and scare us half to death.

I would come to learn that one of the reasons TV producer Aaron Spelling had been able to spend $45 million to build his swanky, 123-room, 56,500-square-foot Holmby Hills mega mansion, dubbed "The Manor" (which was back on the market in 2022 with a $165 million asking price), was that he shot many of his later shows in ridiculously cheap production facilities in the roughest parts of L.A. I remember the first time I dropped off a script at the *Beverly Hills, 90210* production office in dumpy Van Nuys and was shocked to discover the insanely expensive sports cars belonging to Jason Priestley, Luke Perry and Ian Ziering were parked in a scary alley behind a seedy adult bookstore. So, while Spelling's saintly daughter Tori was inside the *90210* studio filming her scenes as virginal Donna Martin, less than a block away guys were spanking their junk in adult video arcade booths.

One of my *Dynasty* duties was to field calls from those trying to reach our executive producer, Elaine Rich. It might be debonaire John Forsythe (who played patriarch Blake Carrington)—calling from his Santa Ynez ranch home needing assistance with his new fax machine—or Emma Samms (our Fallon Carrington) bemoaning having to go in for her mandated physical exam from the same "touchy feely" doctor who'd administered the cast's yearly check-ups during the series' original run. "He was ancient then," sighed Samms. "I can't believe he's even still alive."

And then there was a very memorable call I took from Aaron Spelling himself, phoning in response to a flyer that had been slipped inside his manor gates by our clueless location manager, desperate to secure an estate home to double for the interior Carrington mansion sets that had unfortunately all been destroyed after the series' cancellation.

"Hello, this is Aaron Spelling," said the unmistakable voice, as I pictured my kindly boss sitting back in his favorite burgundy leather chair, smoking his favorite pipe and swirling a cognac. "Apparently, you're interested in renting my house for our *Dynasty* miniseries."

I was at a complete loss.

"Oh, Mr. Spelling ... Sir," I fumbled, trying to find some composure. "You're not serious. You didn't receive one of those..."

"I sure did; right here in my hand," Mr. Spelling said, offering a laugh that instantly set me at ease. "While I do appreciate the offer, I hope you'll pass on to Elaine that I'm afraid my home's not available at this time."

While I'd always look forward to pleasant calls from Mr. Forsythe or Ms. Evans, both politely introducing themselves to me each time they phoned for Elaine, there was another individual who had a different approach.

"Is Elaine in?" the curt voice would ask, sounding more like a demand. Sometimes, if this woman was feeling extra warm and fuzzy, I'd get an "Elaine, *please*."

Even though I knew exactly whom this haughty British accent belonged to, I'd always respond with a cheery, oblivious "Who's calling, please?" which would reliably be followed by an annoyed, "*Humph*."

"It's JOAN," she'd practically scream in my ear.

The one and only time I ever dared follow that up with an inquisitive, "Um, *Joan...?*" the response I received was a very loud and dismissive, "COLLINS!!!"

"Oh, of course, Ms. Collins," I told her. "Let me put you right through."

Catching up with the Carringtons of *Dynasty* at the 2004 taping of *Dynasty Reunion: Catfights & Caviar*. From left: Gordon Thomson, Pamela Sue Martin, Linda Evans, Al Corley, John Forsythe (seated), Joan Collins, Catherine Oxenberg and me. (Courtesy CBS)

I can only imagine her immediately asking Elaine, "Who is that impertinent fool you have answering your phone? He should be fired at once!"

One day I offered to drive new script changes over to the location where Joan would be shooting her scenes. Upon my arrival to the soundstage where Alexis' posh condo had been reconstructed, I was warned to heed Collins' strict edict to avoid looking her directly in the eye while she was in the middle of shooting a scene. "Just stay out of her eyeline and you'll be fine," I was told.

But the thing is, when Joan Collins is anywhere even remotely within your field of vision, it's virtually impossible to look at anything else. Just try! So, before

I even realized, I was staring Medusa straight in her eyes—fortunate, I suppose, to not have been instantly turned to marble.

Like the most sensitive motion detector, Joan instantly busted me—stopping mid-scene and summoning over an assistant director. Within seconds, an announcement was made to the whole set over the PA system: "Please remember to keep out of Joan's eyeline while she is filming. Thank you."

Fifteen years later, I was reminded of Joan's stern rule on the set of the next *Dynasty* reunion special, *Catfights & Caviar*, when Collins herself announced to the entire crew, "There's a lot of movement. Even if it's someone putting their hand in their pocket, it distracts me."

But you see, that's also the thing about Joan. She's so damned sultry—even to gay dudes—that it's damn near impossible to not move some part of your body, involuntarily or otherwise.

While on set, Joan was never far from her longtime BFF/indentured servant Judy Bryer. This big-boned Collins lookalike—whose massive shoulder pads were, in actuality, her *real shoulders*—would have made an excellent stunt double for her mistress during those over-the-top Alexis/Krystle catfights. One afternoon outside Joan's trailer, Judy offered to have Joan personally autograph a glossy photo for me.

"Sure," I said, hoping there would be no witnesses to what would have been considered a professional no-no.

"Hold on; wait here," said Bryer, disappearing into Collins' trailer. Moments later, she emerged with a freshly signed glamour shot—personally autographed to yours truly!

"To William. Love, J Collins." Fabulous! Then, as I was watching the ink dry on my new treasure, an unmistakable voice shouted out, "Juddddyyyyy!!" We both turned to see Joan—walking out from set toward her trailer, which she had obviously *not* been in when the photo in my hand had been magically signed.

Totally busted, all Judy could do was smile sheepishly and hurry off to attend to her queen. (Read the sidebar for my second-best autograph story.)

Over the years, I would have the good fortune of landing future interviews with this diva of all divas. The next time was in 2001 when Collins was promoting the pretty dreadful TV movie *These Old Broads*. Collins was cast as a demanding actress alongside other larger-than-life Hollywood legends Elizabeth Taylor, Debbie Reynolds and Shirley MacLaine. Our entertaining chat—over the phone, which meant I didn't have to worry about looking her in the eye—revealed Collins' terrific sense of humor, along with a few sensitive subjects she clearly does not like to discuss. Ever.

I'd been forewarned about Joan's sensitivities—particularly when it came to the off-limits subject of plastic surgery—by the TV movie's screenwriter (and Debbie's daughter) Carrie Fisher. Spending a few hours with Carrie in her Coldwater Canyon home for a pair of interviews that appeared in the *Los Angeles Times* and *US Weekly* was surreal to say the least. How many hours, I thought, had I spent holding a 3¾-inch plastic version of this

The broads on plastic surgery

THREE'S COMPANY: Collins, Reynolds and MacLaine in Las Vegas, January 20

COLLINS: I haven't had any cosmetic procedures. You had better be careful. I have sued two English tabloids because they've said I had cosmetic procedures.

REYNOLDS: I had one face-lift. I don't know anyone who hasn't had their face done after 50 years old. If they say they haven't, they're just telling you a story.

MACLAINE: A face-lift a long time ago. But I wouldn't do it again, because it limits the parts you can play when they know how old you are. Did Joan admit to one?

woman (dressed in a tiny white Princess Leia Organa cape) while playing on the carpet with my *Star Wars* action figures and playsets? And now here I was about to be granted an in-person audience with the Princess herself! R2-D2, stand in line!

While offering me a tray of peanut-butter-flavored Rice Krispies Treats, Carrie, then 45, wasted no time lamenting to me that men were no longer interested in her sexually. When I told her, "I think you're still hot," she just shrugged.

"Sure," she said. "But you're gay."

Uh, not yet I wasn't! (At least not publicly.) As someone who'd discovered her second husband in bed with another man, this girl's gaydar was on fire. So when she caught me just staring back at her like a helpless gay deer caught in pink headlights, she nearly spit up her Diet Coke.

"Oh, come on," she said, having zero patience for a closet case who'd come to her home to ask personal questions about her own private life. So, after fessing up to having been far more into my Han Solo action figure than hers, we continued our talk.

When the discussion turned to Joan (whom I'd yet to interview), Carrie warned me I'd be in for a challenge. Having fielded several late-night calls asking for script changes the night before shoots, Carrie rolled her eyes and said, "It's like she's still on *Dynasty*."

The princess wasn't exaggerating. Out of all my *Old Broads* interviews— with Collins, Oscar nominee Reynolds and Oscar winner MacLaine (Elizabeth Taylor, also in the film, was too ill to participate)—only Collins had requested I submit my questions in advance. This is not a totally out-of-the-ordinary request. As recently as 2022, Jeff Bridges asked I do the same (of course, he was recovering from cancer *and* Covid at the time). But as a rule, it's something I always try to avoid simply because it ruins all spontaneity and pretty much guarantees flat, preconceived responses. But Collins was insistent, so I sent her my questions under the assumption it would help her prep for our scheduled phone interview. You can imagine my surprise when her publicist faxed me back short, written-out responses to each of my questions. I filed the fax away without giving it more than a glance, determined that our scheduled phone interview would be fun and off-the-cuff as I'd intended.

When Joan called at our appointed time, I thought it best to start by buttering her up, as I'd come to do so well. Since I'd been given an advance screener of *These Old Broads*, I was able to legitimately tell her, "I thought you stole the show."

"You did??!" she chirped, positively giddy. "Oh, how nice. I hope you're going to say that in your article...."

"Well, I can't offend the other ladies who did a fine job as well," I explained.

"*Yesssss*," she muttered, clearly displeased.

Then, when I tried posing my first question for the Q&A, she instantly cut me off. "I sent my answers off to the publicist, so I've done that."

"I'm sorry, Ms. Collins," I explained gently. "Your publicist was supposed to explain that your answers for this piece were meant to be ... *spontaneous*."

"Oh shit," she snapped back. "I spent a whole lot of time working on that."

"I'm so sorry."

"So, what's wrong with my answers?" she pouted, not getting the point. "I thought they were good."

"I'm sure they were just fine, but I actually never read your answers. I agreed to send over the questions to your publicist just to spark your thoughts. Not to be answered in advance of our talk today."

"Well," said Collins with a huff, "if what you're doing is a Q&A, I want to be quoted *exactly* and I want to be able to think about them. So, what you're going to do is write them all down again and send them to me. And then I'll have to do it all over again. Because a Q&A, from what I understand, is—because I've done them before—something you *write*. Not something you do off your head."

I took a deep breath and patiently explained that both Debbie and Shirley were going the spontaneous route in our scheduled phone interviews, which finally got her to concede defeat. But not before letting out a deep sigh and asking sadly, "None of the questions are going to be the same as the questions I was sent?"

"They're actually all the same, Joan."

"Then what's the problem?" she repeated, just not getting this.

"There really shouldn't be any problem," I said, fearing that Joan might hang up at any minute, thus leaving me no choice but to go with her crummy faxed answers. "I just want spontaneous conversational responses from you so the piece

186

flows more naturally. Again, I'm sorry. This was all supposed to be explained to you."

"Perhaps it was," she said, now softening a bit. "I didn't check my messages."

"Well, what do you say we try a few?"

"So, go...."

Phew. She was at last ready to play ball ... well, nearly. Collins asked if I wouldn't mind holding for a moment. When she returned, she informed me, "I'm just putting on my tape recorder."

"Okay, great," I said. "I have mine going as well," which all these many years later enabled me to transcribe our colorful conversation verbatim.

(NOTE: Should I ever be called before a judge, I've carefully catalogued all my interview recordings—much like Phyllis Diller's joke file. I remember all too well the media coverage of Joan's nasty 1987 divorce from ex-husband Peter Holm when she took the stand and masterfully eviscerated the poor fellow. He didn't stand a chance and neither would I.)

Now, here we were—facing off like two ghost-town outlaws—walking 20 paces and drawing our dueling tape recorders.

And, finally, our Q&A began:

KECK: "What does it mean to be an 'Old Broad?'"

COLLINS: "It means you get a wonderful role in a very funny film."

(*Ugh.* Super lame, I thought, suspecting she was repeating whatever answers she'd had faxed to me.)

KECK: "Okay ... are you an 'Old Broad?'"

COLLINS: "Well, the dictionary definition of a broad is a ... gosh, what was it ...? I wrote it down somewhere. You'll have to call me back on that one."

(It became apparent that Joan was, in fact, trying to remember her written responses which she just couldn't move past. Despite my best efforts, this was a seasoned actress skilled at line memorization. She simply wasn't going to be spontaneous. And with MacLaine scheduled to phone soon, I had no choice but to proceed.)

KECK: "What age would you go back to for one day, if you could?"

COLLINS: "Um ... 23, but knowing what I know today."

(Snooze. I knew the Joan Collins I'd seen give countless talk show interviews could do far better than this, so I tried helping her by throwing in some follow-up questions she hadn't seen coming. And that's when the fun started. As it turned out, there was no need for Joan to prep, as her wit was sharper than any drag queen who'd ever impersonated her.)

KECK: "Why 23?"

COLLINS: "You mean I have to give *reasons*?"

KECK: "Yes. This is the spontaneous part."

COLLINS: "Well, at 23 I was probably the most beautiful and sexiest of any time during my life."

Bingo! "You're pretty sexy and beautiful right now," I told her, feeling a need to jack off her ego just a bit. But it also happened to be true. Remaining as hot as ever into her nineties (judging from the bathing suit photos she posts on Instagram), this seemingly-immortal icon will no doubt give her embalmer a solid hard-on when the day comes. And her coquettish 23-year-old-like giggle told me my charms were doing the trick!

COLLINS: "Aren't you sweet."

KECK: "Okay Joan. We're doing great. Now, if you could meet any dead Hollywood legend, who would you choose and what would you ask them?"

COLLINS: "Marilyn Monroe. And I'd like to ask her, 'Who killed you, Marilyn?'"

She had me laughing out loud. I was in gay heaven.

KECK: "Do you own a tiara?"

COLLINS: "God no. I'll leave that to Elton John."

KECK: "What about a turban?"

COLLINS: "Oh yeah. I've got zillions."

KECK: "What about wigs?"

And this is where her guard started to come up. I was treading dangerously close to those two topics she despises more than any other: aging and plastic surgery.

COLLINS: "I have always worn wigs and hairpieces because who wants to spend two hours in hairdressing at 5:30 in the morning? Also, I have seen actresses on certain television shows who have lost half their hair after two seasons of back-combing, spraying and sitting under the dryer all day long."

(She was right. I thought of an old soap actress named Jeanne Cooper who I'd once seen without her wig on the set of *The Young and the Restless* looking very much like Dwayne "The Rock" Johnson.)

While Debbie Reynolds claimed to have 60 wigs, Collins estimated she had a mere 10, but I suspected there could be another zero added to that number. Joan may not have been fond of addressing her vanity, but her co-stars were more than game to spill all at her expense. MacLaine, for instance, called Collins "a makeup freak" who was constantly asking if she had lipstick on her teeth. MacLaine's sassy response: "Why don't you take 'em out and let the makeup man brush 'em off?" *Ha!*

No offense to Fisher's script, but *These Old Broads* would have been far more entertaining had it been presented as a behind-the-scenes reality show showcasing the actresses' actual dialogue. (One thing I love about MacLaine is that she'll openly ask what you think of her projects and you can be brutally honest. She could tell I thought *Broads* was a dud, just as we both would later trash the discombobulated mess her and Nicole Kidman's 2005 *Bewitched* movie had become following Will Ferrell's involvement.)

Because I knew it could be risky inquiring into which specific plastic surgery procedures each of the women had or had not undergone, I opted to ask each the same carefully worded stock question that would just simply *assume* they'd had work done: "What cosmetic procedure that you've undergone has made you feel more youthful?"

And my strategy worked ... at least on two out of the three of 'em.

Reynolds, refreshingly honest, told me about her facelift, and added, "I don't know anyone that hasn't had their face done after 50 years old. If they say they haven't, they're just telling you a story." MacLaine similarly copped to a facelift and asked me if Collins had admitted to having had one.

It probably comes as no great surprise that she did not. In fact, Collins stated emphatically, "I haven't had any cosmetic procedures. You had better be very careful about this, William, because I have sued two English tabloids because they have said I've had cosmetic procedures ... I am very litigious. If people print things about me that aren't true, I will sue them. So, I haven't had any cosmetic procedures."

She wasn't kidding. I would come to learn that Collins slaps suits about as often as her *Dynasty* character slapped poor Krystle. I knew I was dealing with a special-needs case and had to proceed with extreme caution for fear of being slapped myself.

But with all the plastic surgery jokes in Fisher's script, I couldn't just let the actress off that easily. Because she looked so amazing, I figured she at the very least must have undergone ... oh, like a chemical peel, right?

"Oh God, no!" she clarified. "I have far too delicate skin. I'm English, don't forget. I'm also extremely squeamish and loathe needles."

I'll tell you, MacLaine enjoyed a good laugh over the phone talking about Joan's answers. "If she hasn't had cosmetic surgery, she's the only one west of the Mississippi who hasn't," MacLaine cracked. "But I'll take her at her word. She lives in a bottle at UCLA Medical Center."

Fisher told me that Collins had gone so far as to object to *even her character* admitting she'd gone under the knife. Carrie recalled, "Joan came to me and said, 'There are far too many references to facelifts in the script. You must take them out because I haven't had any ... I know that everyone thinks that I have had all this liposuction, but I have not!!'"

I don't know why I thought I'd fare any better than Princess Leia had, but persist I did:

KECK: "What about some of the trendier rejuvenators? Like placenta or cow urine applied to the skin?"

COLLINS: *(robust guffaw)* "No! A seaweed wrap is the most unusual thing I tried, but I broke out in hives for a week. I don't want even someone's hands on my face."

(Meanwhile, I'd personally received a peel, microdermabrasion and Botox injections that week alone. After the ninth needle on my Botox punch card, I receive my 10th free!)

When Collins excused herself to prepare some instant coffee (and probably change tapes), I decided to give her a pass and move on. You see, this was an issue for Collins that was non-negotiable. Case in point: Just the previous year, the producers of *Will & Grace* had asked Collins to reprise her role as celebrated interior designer Helena Barnes, but she ended up backing out at the last minute, forcing the writers and casting directors to scramble to recast the character.

As Joan later explained to me of the mocking *Will & Grace* material she'd been given, "I got the script delivered at 9 o'clock the night before I was supposed to go in for a table read. And it was unacceptable, and I did not think funny. And totally not right for me. So as is an actor's right, I turned it down the next morning. I told my agent I wasn't going to do it."

Now, while *Will & Grace* certainly had its misfires, how bad could the script really have been? I mean, just a year later, Collins was vamping on the daytime soap opera *Guiding Light* as the third actress to play Alexandra Spaulding Von Halkein Thorpe. Was that honestly any better than a subpar episode of *Will & Grace*? But yes, it was most certainly her prerogative to decline.

Collins went on to tell me she was taking the *Globe* tabloid to court for printing an alternate version of the backstage *Will & Grace* drama, claiming, as Joan recounted to me, "... that I 'stormed off the set, screaming, turned on my designer heels ...' all the crap they like to pull out about me which isn't true. So, the *Globe* has just been slapped with a very large suit for professional damages. My professionalism is extremely important to me."

(For the record, your honor, I would like to state that I have never once observed any unprofessionalism on the part of Ms. Collins—a consummate pro if ever there was one! And considering I'm the one who got *my* way, with Joan submitting to *my* request to redo her entire interview, who was the real diva here?)

When Joan came back on the phone after a brief pause, we resumed our now-lively and breezy Q&A.

KECK: "If you could star in a project with one of today's hottest talents, whom would you choose?"

COLLINS: "Brad Pitt, by far, is the best looking. He's got great bones, hair and a terrific body. But this is absolutely ridiculous. You're asking me a stupid question."

I finally knew how Lauren Bacall must have made my friend Monica feel with her own "stupid" questions. But I wasn't going to let Dame Joan reduce me to tears, choosing instead to spontaneously turn the tables:

KECK: "What makes you cry, Joan?"

COLLINS: "Whenever I see pictures on television of children starving in Africa. I do a lot of charity work, but it's never mentioned. They'd much rather write about me storming off a set, which, at the moment, I'm suing a tabloid about." (Yes, you'd mentioned that.)

Suffice to say, Collins didn't disappoint in the slightest. But really, isn't this exactly the Joan Collins we want her to be? The world needs its Joan Collinses. Without them, we'd never appreciate our Linda Evanses.

Speaking of Evans, six years after *These Old Broads*, Collins reunited with her *Dynasty* rival in a touring stage production titled *Legends*, which opened in Los Angeles in January 2007. And you can bet I landed myself a ticket as well as a prime position on the red carpet to interview all the arriving stars. Though the play—with Evans and Collins exchanging barbs as two competitive, aging actresses (however did they come up with *that* casting?)—was almost universally panned by critics, the subpar material was tailor-made for these two dueling divas who did their very best with it. And I savored every second.

And the highlight of the evening by far was a truly disastrous wardrobe malfunction that befell poor Joan. The zipper on the back of her black dress slid down and got stuck, exposing the then 73-year-old's white bloomers to a theater packed with other '80s TV legends, including *Hart to Hart*'s Robert Wagner and Stefanie Powers, *Knots Landing*'s Michele Lee, *Falcon Crest*'s Lorenzo Lamas and her *Dynasty* children Gordon Thomson, Pamela Sue Martin and Al Corley.

I admit I really felt for poor Joan—already battling the flu that night—as she struggled to keep her dress up with one arm while delicately sidestepping her way across the stage so as to not reveal her tush to the now-howling crowd.

While I'd secretly hoped that Linda had sabotaged the gown—just as Alexis surely would have done to Krystle back in the day—Evans instead had made a valiant attempt to zip her co-star back up, telling me after the show, "I tried, but it just didn't want to stay."

Ultimately, Collins felt she had no choice but to break the fourth wall and acknowledge her "wardrobe malfunction," a term very much in vogue—it being just three years since Janet Jackson's renegade nipple had made its peekaboob debut during her 2004 Super Bowl halftime show.

What probably stung Joan the most was Linda's "nice ass" ad-lib, which earned Linda the biggest laugh of the evening. See Joan, that's what happens when you allow yourself to be a little spontaneous!!!

Lively — and revealing — 'Legends'

Broken zipper doesn't stop Joan Collins

By William Keck
USA TODAY

BEVERLY HILLS — Joan Collins showed off more than her talents at Tuesday night's opening performance of her traveling stage play, *Legends*, when the zipper on the back of her dress slid down, exposing the 73-year-old's lingerie-covered backside to a theater packed with '80s TV legends.

Among those who were treated to the moon: *Hart to Hart's* Robert Wagner and Stefanie Powers; *Knots Landing's* Michele Lee; *Falcon Crest's* Lorenzo Lamas; and *Dynasty's* Pamela Sue Martin, Al Corley, Gordon Thomson and Pamela Bellwood.

On stage, Collins' co-star and *Dynasty* rival, Linda Evans, 64, struggled in vain to zip Collins up. "I tried, but it just didn't want to stay," Evans sighed at the after-party.

So Collins momentarily broke the fourth wall, vocally acknowledging her "ward-

By John M. Heller, Getty Images

Wardrobe-ready — but with a catch: Joan Collins, right, wore Michael Kors, and Linda Evans wore Armani, on the red carpet before the premiere at the Wilshire Theatre.

robe malfunction" and inspiring Evans to ad-lib "nice (butt)." Collins, who also was battling the flu, spent the rest of the show delicately sidestepping her way across the stage, occasionally clasping her hands over her posterior.

ing antics of heroine Lucky Santangelo.

"How embarrassing," Joan said of the mishap. "But I had to make it fun, because if you're not having fun, neither is your audience."

Joan's husband, Percy Gibson, is a producer on the show, which casts Evans and Collins as aging actress rivals. After its two-week engagement in Los Angeles, the show will continue to Phoenix, Denver, Chicago and Boston before concluding in New Haven, Conn., on May 13.

It also was a night to remember those who could not attend. The most missed face was *Dynasty* patriarch John Forsythe, who had colon cancer surgery in September and was released from the hospital three weeks ago.

Forsythe's wife, Nicole, said her husband, who turns 89 Jan. 29, is cancer-free but is now fighting a leg hematoma. "He thinks he can get up and walk, because he's not getting any pain to his brain," Nicole said.

She planned to make the two-hour drive back to their Santa Ynez Valley ranch the same night so she would not worry her husband, who "saw me getting all dolled up."

"That poor thing; what a trouper," Powers said. "I once had a set fall down on me."

At the after-party, Collins shared a booth with sister Jackie, who just finished her latest racy novel, *Drop Dead Beautiful*, about the continu-

The dress debacle was of course the talk of the after-party (something I made sure of), with Stefanie Powers telling me, "That poor thing; whatta trouper!"

After being kept waiting for over an hour for an interview, I was finally escorted to a private booth in the back of the after-party where Collins was being comforted by her sister Jackie. Wisely, Joan opted to embrace the incident as one only could—with humor. "How embarrassing," she said. "But I had to make it fun, because if you're not having fun, neither is your audience." (Truth be told, we would have had fun either way.)

With the sub-header "Broken zipper doesn't stop Joan Collins," my article in *USA Today* declared, "Joan Collins showed off more than her talents at Tuesday night's opening."

193

I saw Collins on stage for the last time in a wildly entertaining one-woman show she was workshopping in Orange County, CA, in which she showed slides and clips from her many television and film appearances, embellished with juicy behind-the-scenes tales. My favorite: how she'd lost the big-screen role of Cleopatra to Elizabeth Taylor because Joan had declined to sleep with one of the film's producers. The obvious implication was that La Liz had done what Joan had refused. I let out my biggest chuckle that night when Joan went on to explain that her "dream of playing Cleopatra was ultimately fulfilled years later ... when I played the Queen of the Nile in a fabulous episode of *Fantasy Island*."

(Man, you just know Liz Taylor had to be kicking herself for not fucking Ricardo Montalban to land *that* plum role!)

After the slideshow, Collins kicked up the houselights and opened the room up to an informal audience Q&A, which surprised me. I mean, you'd assume she would have wanted to see our questions in advance, right? I, of course, was one of the first to raise my hand to ask, "Why didn't you mention anything about your role as the villainous Siren on *Batman*?"

Joan Collins as Cleopatra in "My Fair Pharaoh," a 1980 episode of *Fantasy Island*. (Columbia Pictures Television)

"Well," she hmphed. "Were I to go through every role I'd ever played, we'd be here all night, wouldn't we? Next question...."

After the show, I was escorted backstage where I reminded Joan that I'd covered her *Legends* premiere performance for *USA Today*. (I know. Bad idea. But I couldn't resist.)

Her eyes flared. "*You* were the one who wrote about my dress?" she admonished, before turning her back to me and signaling that my audience with the mummified Queen of the Nile had wrapped.

It was my Miranda Priestly "that's all" moment, and we should all be so fortunate at least once in our lives to be on the receiving end of such a delicious dressing-down.

I really do have to hand it to the unsinkable old broad, who outlived Debbie, Carrie, Liz, her younger sister Jackie and even a palm-full of the hunky *Dynasty* studs who'd filled Alexis' stable of lovers. She continued to work, stay relevant, throw shade and attract admiring stares … without having had so much as a hair plucked from her chinny chin chin.

Lesson Learned: Every so often, your idols turn out to be EXACTLY who you'd hoped they'd be. Thanks, Joan, for never failing to disappoint.

A WORD FROM JOAN'S *DYNASTY* CO-STAR GORDON THOMSON

Dynasty **stars Jack Coleman (left) and Gordon Thomson (right) with author, Los Angeles, 2002.**

I believe that all of us have at least two basic faces: one for showing ourselves to the world and the other for our private life. Joan is no exception. But in her case, her public identity is so inexorably connected to Alexis, that that is how she is almost always perceived. In fact I believe she often revels in it; the role made her the star she has always wanted to be, so why not?!

Privately, I cannot claim to be her close friend: Her family is, of course, her most loved connection. But I do claim to know what it is like to be a guest in her home. Joan is a sensationally good hostess: Nothing is missing to make you feel welcome in every way. And what makes the experience even rarer is that she makes it all appear utterly effortless.

I envy my friend and peer, Jack Coleman, who with his gorgeous wife, Beth, was invited to tea with Joan at her house in London. She could not have been warmer or more charming. (Which was no surprise at all.)

MY *SECOND*-BEST AUTOGRAPH STORY: RUSSELL JOHNSON

So, my *second*-best autograph story took place in 1995 when I spent a fun-filled afternoon interviewing actor Russell Johnson for the *National Enquirer.* Russell was famous for having played the Professor on *Gilligan's Island* (you know, the one who turned coconuts into transistor radios).

Russell Johnson's autograph "gift."

Russell had flown into L.A. from northern California to appear at a celebrity autograph show, where fans pay their favorite old-time stars for autographs and wax museum-like photo ops. Taking a break from the fans, Russell got up from his signing table to join me for a bite. Over lunch, we shared a very deep, intimate and emotional conversation about his love for his late son, David, a young gay man who had recently died of AIDS. After we dried our tears, I walked Russell back to his table and was incredibly touched when he asked if I'd like an autographed picture.

"Sure, Russell," I told my new pal. "That'd be awfully nice!"

With Russell Johnson, the Professor from *Gilligan's Island,* in 1995.

The Professor offered me a warm smile, pulled out a black Sharpie, signed the photo and, before I could even say "Thank you," handed me the 5-x-7 glossy and said, "That'll be 15 dollars."

Chapter 22
DANGEROUSLY OBSESSED

(VICTORIA PRINCIPAL)

WHO: Victoria Principal (b. January 3, 1950). A two-time Golden Globe nominee much beloved for playing Pamela Barnes Ewing on the CBS primetime soap *Dallas* from 1978–1987. Stepped back from acting to focus on her production company and Principal Secret skin care empire.

Principal as *Dallas'* Pam Ewing in the 1980s.
(CBS)

WHAT: Various on-the-record interviews for *USA Today*, which revealed my fanatical obsession with this intriguing star.

WHERE: Dr. Harry Glassman's plastic surgery office, Beverly Hills, CA. Southfork Ranch, Parker, TX. CUT restaurant, The Regent Beverly Wilshire Hotel, Beverly Hills, CA.

I once had an obsessive stalker who made my life hell. And the worst part was he lived in the condo right across the hall from mine, so there was really no escaping him. By that time in the early 2000s, I was out of the closet not only to Carrie Fisher, but also my family, friends and closest co-workers. But closer to home I chose to still keep things, as they say, "discreet" to maintain my privacy amongst my straight, mostly conservative neighbors. But those plans were thwarted while I was out of town on a two-week vacation when my stalker elected to mail out hundreds of letters to every neighbor in my condo complex, professing to be me. In the bizarre letter—headlined "I'M GAY, OK? (accompanied by name

197

and home address)—he (as me) announced (with italicized, bold and underlined accents to really get the point across) "There, it's done. ***I've come out.*** The truth sets one free. So, get over it!"

It went on to read, "Just think of me as 'Jack,' the character on *Will & Grace*, just as flamboyant, slightly bitter and, yes, babbling!" (He perhaps had a point on that last one.) "I'm usually lying at the pool in a baseball cap or watching my favorite soaps. Gay's don't bite! Otherwise, blah, blah, blah, I'm a freelance reporter divulging the latest juicy gossip about people in L.A."

This was followed by synopses of a selection of published articles I'd written that pertained in any way to gay stuff. (Stalker boy really spent some time on this.)

I only learned he'd gone to all this trouble when I checked my answering machine messages from the East Coast upon my return to the states from Egypt. "Hi William, this is Matt and Lois from the B building. We got your letter and just wanted to let you know we have a gay son, so we're completely fine with your lifestyle choice."

"Hello neighbor. My name is Don. I think it's just terrific that you're out and proud. We should grab a drink sometime."

I was beyond mortified. But it got even worse when I finally returned home to strange stares in the hallways and supportive letters in my mailbox. For example: this particularly odd one from Irena over in Building 250: "You came out. For myself, as a 66-year-old matronly woman, sexual preferences are of no consequence … Go for it!"

While I'm able to make light of it now, at the time the whole thing seriously freaked me out. I immediately filed a police report and sought a restraining order, which isn't easy to enforce when your stalker lives just ten feet across the hall! That gross invasion of privacy was the only time I ever came even close to experiencing how my unwelcome snooping into celebrities' private lives and exposing their secrets might have made them feel.

Karma, folks.

If I were ever to have pled guilty for having stalked someone, the object of my unhealthy obsession would have been eternally gorgeous *Dallas* actress Victoria Principal. While I enthusiastically followed the characters on all the primetime soaps, it was Principal's long-suffering Pamela Barnes Ewing who most captured my heart as she weathered one horrible crisis after another. Over the show's many seasons, Pam repeatedly lost Bobby Ewing (the great love of her life), attempted suicide, discovered a long-lost mother only to have her perish in a plane crash and received a shattering medical diagnosis: neurofibromatosis, an extremely rare tumor-forming genetic disposition (similar to the Elephant Man's condition) that prevented Pam from achieving her greatest dream: motherhood. As the seasons progressed, I kept hoping Pam would one day give Bobby an elephant baby they'd name Dumbo.

But then, on May 15, 1987, when I was a freshman in college, Pam learned from her OB/GYN that she in fact could carry a healthy baby to term. Oh, happy day! Driving back to the Southfork Ranch in her little red Mercedes, she dialed up Bobby to share the joyous news. But the momentary distraction of hanging up her car phone prevented Pam from seeing an oil tanker in her car's path. And

Fan obsession in the making: an enhanced photo I took of my childhood TV on May 17, 1985—the horrible night Bobby Ewing died (temporarily) in Pam's arms.

KABOOM!! An inferno lit up the screen the likes of which I'd only seen on the nightly news coverage of the Iran-Iraq War. I can't even begin to explain just how deeply that horrific TV moment forever scarred my psyche.

When I read in *USA Today* that Principal had quit *Dallas* and would not be returning to the show in the fall, I was beyond devastated. With apologies to beloved deceased members of my own family, the sudden impact of losing Pam was the one death from which I've never quite recovered.

Miraculously, poor charbroiled Pam survived her accident, only to be wrapped head to toe in bandages so viewers could no longer see her face. Having killed off the Bobby character two seasons prior, only to then have to reverse history by writing off an entire season as Pam's bad dream when actor Patrick Duffy

199

elected to return to the role, the writers wanted to keep Pam alive just in case Principal might one day similarly change her mind. After a few episodes appearing as a voiceless mummy, Pam just disappeared one day from the hospital. And Principal followed through on her vow to never again play Pam. Like Bobby, my heart too was broken. And I viewed this as a personal afront.

So when I moved to L.A. three years later, I was determined to track down Victoria and demand an explanation. And I was willing to go to any lengths necessary to get answers. For me, that would mean booking a consultation with her then-husband, renowned Beverly Hills cosmetic surgeon Dr. Harry Glassman.

I can so clearly remember entering Dr. Glassman's posh Beverly Hills office right off Wilshire Boulevard hoping I'd see some of my favorite done-over divas. Priscilla Presley, perhaps? Kim Novak, maybe? But absolutely *not* Joan Collins!!

When the receptionist called my name, I was ushered past Glassman's office to a consultation room. The door to his office had been left open just enough for me to catch a passing glimpse of Victoria's photo displayed in a sterling silver frame on his desk. Inching ever closer to my prey, I was determined to see this through.

I went ahead and scheduled a rhinoplasty with Dr. Glassman, and agreed to add on a little liposuction of my tummy fat. I remember the jovial doc cracking a joke about me having chowed down too much chili from Chasen's, the once-famous eatery to the stars that by that time had already closed its doors. (Time for some fresh material, Doc.)

But then—just days before I was to go under the knife— Glassman came *this close* to cancelling my surgery. When I filled out my initial paperwork, I very honestly listed the *National Enquirer* as my employer—a fact Glassman didn't discover for weeks. In his eyes, working as a *National Enquirer* reporter was akin to earning your living as a professional seal clubber. It probably would have looked better had I listed the Third Reich as my workplace. Over the years, the *Enquirer* had raked both him and Victoria over the coals on numerous occasions, and it was only natural for him to suspect that I could be setting him up for yet another damaging exposé.

I was summoned to Glassman's office, where he sat me down and asked point-blank, "Do you know what your paper has done to us?" As a longtime *Enquirer* subscriber, I had a pretty good idea, but I wisely stayed quiet and let him unload all his fury and disgust.

After I gave Glassman my God's-honest word that I was there just to have my nose shaved, and not to stick it in his private affairs, I was asked to sign an additional legal document before he agreed to put my surgery back on the books.

But now I was worried. Had I set myself up for this mad doctor to enact his revenge? Would I awaken from anesthesia with the word "SCUM" carved into my forehead? Or with my nose missing entirely, like Voldemort or Michael Jackson?

Then, on the night before my surgery—my head weary after a day of fasting—I was consumed by a more realistic fear. What if Dr. Glassman took advantage of my vulnerability under anesthesia to extract *Enquirer* secrets out of me? Or even worse, what if I started mumbling horribly inappropriate things about Victoria??! What if? What if?? *What if???*

Victoria Principal with plastic surgeon husband, Dr. Harry Glassman, at the 1987 Emmy Awards. (Alan Light/Wikimedia Commons)

Fortunately, all my fears turned out to be unfounded. Harry's a brilliant surgeon, and the procedure was a great success. I loved my new nose which later gave me the excuse I needed to approach Harry and Victoria at various charity functions. Our very first meeting was at a star-studded fundraiser for Hillary Clinton's run for the New York Senate. And Victoria could not have been kinder or more complimentary of her husband's work. But it would be several more years before I'd have my chance to get Victoria alone in a room to properly grill her. Appropriately, that grilling would take place at *Dallas'* Southfork Ranch, the site of so many contentious Ewing barbeques.

In 2004, it was announced that a *Dallas* reunion special would be shot on location at that iconic TV ranch in Parker, TX. Having wisely skipped a pair of seriously bad reunion movies, this would mark Principal's very first return to Southfork since she'd broken my heart by quitting the show. But she'd be returning not in character as Pam, but as herself to join the rest of the cast in looking back at the show's enduring legacy. Working then as a reporter for *USA Today*, I made sure I, too, would be at this once-in-a-lifetime shoot!

During breaks in shooting, I found familiar places at the ranch to interview each *Dallas* actor, who, after 13 seasons, felt like real family to me. I already mentioned back in my Larry Hagman chapter that this was the day when he recommended I get me some Texas "pussy." As sweet as that moment was, I have to say I got far more enjoyment out of my interviews with Hagman's co-stars—none of whom sent me out searching for poon.

Duffy took me for a stroll with his since-deceased wife, Carlyn, by the horse corrals. I accompanied Charlene Tilton (who had portrayed Pam's niece Lucy and was executive-producing this reunion special) to the old barn where her rebellious teenaged character had enjoyed consensual sex with ranch foreman Ray Krebbs before learning he was her biological uncle. *Ah, gotta love those Ewings!* Ken Kercheval, so endearing as Pam's "loser" brother Cliff Barnes, spoke with me by the Southfork pool where his character had discovered the floating corpse of J.R. Ewing shooter Kristin Shepard. I remember Kenny chain-smoking cigarettes throughout our interview despite having already lost one of his lungs to cancer and groaning to me, "I enjoy my smokes and I'm going to continue enjoying them until the day I die." (Which turned out to be April 21, 2019. R.I.P. Cliff.)

Miss Ellie's kitchen was the quiet place I selected to conduct my most important interview, and the primary reason I'd flown to Texas on *USA Today*'s dime. This was the big moment I'd been waiting for ever since 1987—when Victoria left me high and dry! So after a little friendly catch-up chit-chat around the kitchen table ("Harry sends his love …"), I cut right to the chase!!! "So, why'd you do it?" I asked her point-blank. "Why'd you leave the show and disappoint me and all your other fans?"

Catching up with the Ewings of *Dallas* at the 2004 taping of *Dallas Reunion: Return to Southfork*. From left: Patrick Duffy, my Victoria, Steve Kanaly, Charlene Tilton, Ken Kercheval (seated), Linda Gray, Larry Hagman and me. (Courtesy CBS)

Principal was caught completely off guard; and understandably so, as it had now been 17 years since she'd walked away from the role. Perhaps sensing that her husband's former patient was, in fact, a raving lunatic, Victoria (likely scanning the kitchen for the nearest exit) tried calmly explaining, "I needed to explore different things as a human being and as an actress." Among those different things were a string of starring roles in such Victoria Principal Productions as *River of Rage, Naked Lie* and … my personal favorite, *Don't Touch My Daughter*.

I was curious if she'd at least watched *J.R. Returns* and *War of the Ewings*, the two shitty *Dallas* reunion movies she'd wisely dodged. After a long pause followed by an extended, "Ummm...," Victoria admitted, "I saw a little bit ... and I didn't feel that they added to the memory of *Dallas* … When you see people 20, 30 years later, repeating the same sensual dynamics, there's something lost in the translation. Maybe Pam & Bobby and J.R. & Sue Ellen should be left in our collective memories the way they were. Because there comes a point where I don't see it as a reunion, I see it as potentially pathetic."

"Pathetic." Let's sit with that uncomfortable word for just a moment, shall we?

As much as I may not have wanted to ever hear the P word used to in any way describe a *Dallas* production, Principal had a point, didn't she? I mean, for every heartwarming *A Walton Thanksgiving Reunion* or *Return to Mayberry*, TV would deliver us such pitiful messes as *The Harlem Globetrotters on Gilligan's Island* or *The Bradys*—an undeniably PATHETIC attempt to turn the beloved half hour sitcom into a weekly, one-hour dramatic series that rendered Marcia an alcoholic and Bobby a paraplegic.

However, nostalgia junkie that I am, you know I tuned in to every damn one of those crapfests. Just as I most certainly would have done backflips all the way to Texas to see Victoria sign on for *DALLAS: A Southfork Wedding ... with The Oak Ridge Boys*.

So it was finally time for me to ask the million-dollar question: Would she ever consider reprising her role so that Bobby and Pam could at long last be reunited and live happily ever after? (With or without The Oak Ridge Boys.)

Without a moment's hesitation, Victoria told me flat out, "Pam's dead."

"But Pam's not really dead…" I insisted.

"No, Pam *is* really dead," she countered.

"But she ended up in the hospital ... wrapped in bandages," I reminded her.

"No, that was *their* idea," said Principal, refusing to even consider any alternative scenario. "Pam's DEAD. When I left, I asked that Pam truly die so the public would know that this was not a joke. That I was not going away and coming back in the future. That this was not a ploy for more money. I was leaving and that was the end of the storyline. And I told them I did not want some other actress coming in to play Pam. Pam belonged to *me*. Don't think they didn't try to find someone else to play Pam. They just couldn't. After nine years, it was very hard to introduce someone else. What happened the next season I had nothing to do with. It was totally out of my control. As far as I'm concerned, when Pam died in the car accident, Pam died."

I felt sweat building up on the back of my neck as if it were happening all over again. I was reliving Pam's death, practically feeling the heat from Pam's car explosion melting off my face right there in the Ewing kitchen where Miss Ellie had cooked up her buttery biscuits. Unlike author Stephen King's sweet, totally reasonable, sledgehammer-wielding mountain woman Annie Wilkes, who'd "convinced" selfish romance novelist Paul Sheldon to revive his killed-off *Misery* heroine, there would no changing Principal's mind. Ever. Since I wasn't about to kidnap Victoria and tie her to a bed, I had to accept her word as fact, and rethink my own "pathetic" perception of who I so desperately wanted Principal to be. She was not my beloved Pam. She was, in fact, a stranger who was being very kind to a reporter, who also happened to be her husband's former patient.

Two years later, after 21 years of marriage, Victoria filed for divorce from the doctor who'd given me my new nose. Around this time, her longtime publicist and friend, Alan Nierob (a true mensch who'd once trusted me to speak with his client Mel Gibson not long after the actor's embarrassing 2006 DUI arrest), called to tell me that Victoria was sending her regards and very much wanted to do another story with me for *USA Today* ("Cool!") … about the latest products in her skin care line ("Ugh!").

My editors weren't having it. "If she wants her products in *USA Today*, give her the number to our ad sales department," my editor Jacque told me. So, I politely declined.

When Alan came back to me, I explained there simply was no story … unless, of course, she'd be willing to open up about her divorce. I knew she'd never go for it, but, remarkably, Alan told me she would. "She won't go into great detail," he explained. "But she'll discuss it a little, sure."

Given that assurance, I went back to Jacque to pitch a post-divorce update that would also work in the skin care line by having newly single Principal select celebrities in their 30s, 40s, 50s and 60s who had the best skin. Jacque was aware of my Principal obsession and reluctantly gave the story a greenlight. But no more *Dallas*-related stories after this, she implored. This was it!

I allowed Victoria to choose a convenient meeting place. With her healthy skin regimen, I assumed we'd be lunching at the Vegan Cafe or The Good Earth. Instead, my carnivorous companion suggested CUT at the Regent Beverly Wilshire (the swanky hotel where they filmed *Pretty Woman*). At the time, CUT was THE place to be seen, as evidenced by Paris Hilton's parents, Kathy and Rick, lunching at a table just a few feet from ours.

Having spent the first half of our afternoon together discussing skin care and selecting our ageless Hollywood beauties, it was now time to get Victoria to talk about the divorce. As it so happened, my face was noticeably swollen from a recent chin procedure I'd undergone (*not* performed by Glassman). The results admittedly weren't looking great, and Victoria very compassionately advised I return for a consultation with her ex. "Despite whatever's happening personally between me and Harry, he really is a great doctor," she said. I thought that was extra classy.

I worked up the courage to ask if being married to a plastic surgeon had allowed her ... well, freebies. But she wasn't about to go there. "There are two areas that are off limits because they breach my personal privacy," she explained. "And that is plastic surgery and sex ... it's just none of your business." (Perhaps Victoria's truly priceless 1973 discussion about pubic hair with Johnny Carson on *The Tonight Show* had taught her something about discretion.)

With her ex now introduced into the conversation, I very softly said, "There's been a lot written about your divorce, Victoria. What do you want to say?"

Thud.

Principal stopped eating her steak salad and just about dropped her fork, shocked that I would go there. Clearly, she was not prepared for this invasive question.

"But Victoria," I tried to explain. "Alan told me you were open to discussing the divorce."

"Oh no; I'd never," she said. "Even if I wanted to, I couldn't. My lawyer wouldn't want me saying anything."

Aw, hell. I knew I'd be in hot water with Jacque, especially after submitting the pricey lunch bill. But eventually, Victoria did begin opening up on the record ever so slightly, admitting she was no longer speaking with her ex. "I spent almost 24 years in a relationship," she told me. "And now I'm learning to live my life about what *I* want instead of what *we* want. Some days it's incredibly exciting. And some days it's incredibly painful." (There was much more shared off-the-record, which I naturally will never reveal.)

While not spilling any headline-making Principal secrets as I'd hoped, I did feel I had barely enough to write up something. Jacque agreed and dubbed the article "evergreen," a newspaper term meaning it could be held to run anytime (or no time) to fill space on a slow news day.

And held it was. And held. And held. Every few weeks, Principal would have her beauty-line publicist, Briana, check in on the story's status, and each time I'd have to make up some excuse why it hadn't yet run. After a few of these calls, I was stunned when Briana phoned relaying a message from Principal herself: "She wants you to know you've lost her as a friend."

I felt awful for poor Briana being put in this awkward position. Still a true friend to this day, Briana has told me on several occasions how much anxiety that particular campaign caused her. I knew I had to find a way to get this story in the paper and be done with it once and for all. If not for me, then for Briana. So, here's what I came up with.

At the time, Victoria had shelled out a reported $200,000 to book one of the first seats on billionaire Richard Branson's Virgin Galactic SpaceShipTwo and was anticipating being shot into outer space in the summer of 2008. "I have a thing for speed," she told me. "Fast planes, fast cars...." So, I re-edited the story, making this spin its new focus, while still devoting a significant amount of space to hocking the skin care products. (Just try working revolutionary re-firming eye cream into a story about outer space. It ain't easy!)

In July 2021, SpaceShipTwo's maiden voyage finally launched without Principal, then in her 70s, among its passengers. She'd reportedly (and understandably) withdrawn from the program back in 2012 after several postponements. Alas, her only liftoff would be her Principal Secret make-up remover.

When my *USA Today* story was finally published, I received word from Briana that Victoria and I were friends again. And though I can't say whether or not Victoria would endorse this book, I will certainly and sincerely endorse her Principal Secret products, which I used for many years, enjoying great results. I've never been able to find a product to rival the line's discontinued pre-shave cream.

But alas, our renewed friendship was not to last long. Four years later, I was working as a Senior Editor and columnist for *TV Guide* and, not surprisingly, had taken a particular interest in TNT's *Dallas* reboot—which provided one last glimmer of hope for that Bobby/Pam reunion for which I'd so (pathetically) yearned.

Unfortunately, the reboot's producer, Cynthia Cidre, had other plans, and gave Bobby a brand-new wife fans had never met. Although Cidre told me she had no intentions of ever truly bringing Principal on to the show (and I won't reveal why so as not to taint *Dallas'* legacy), that didn't stop the producer from teasing fans with a mystery storyline that suggested Pam might very well turn up alive at Southfork.

Then, in my very own *TV Guide* "Keck's Exclusives" column, I quoted the show's Jesse Metcalfe as being "excited about the possibility of Victoria Principal coming back to the show" to play his mother. That quote—referencing *not* the Pam character, but her original portrayer by name—was quickly picked up by several other media outlets, and eventually reached Principal. With the actress feeling a need to immediately set the record straight, I received another call from Nierob on March 1, 2013. Per Principal's publicist, his client and I apparently were still friends, because Victoria had personally selected me to publish an exclusive statement she'd prepared, spelling out her feelings about a possible return to this new *Dallas*. Without revealing exactly what she wanted to say, Alan instructed me to write him an email asking for her comment on the matter.

Excited as I was to get an exclusive from Principal about Pam for my *TV Guide* column, I knew I had to be very careful how I handled this delicate situation. I was on very good terms with the show's producers and cast (including Duffy and Linda Gray) who had entrusted me with tons of *Dallas* secrets, so I thought it only fair that I alert Cidre to Victoria's intentions. The show was gearing up to finally reveal the secret of Pam's ultimate fate, which I knew the writers would want to protect, and having Victoria announce she was or wasn't returning would blow the whole story.

I shot an email off to Alan explaining that I'd reached out to the *Dallas* producers and would be in touch by day's end if I didn't get a response, which I didn't. I was just about to email Alan that I was ready to go with Victoria's statement when I discovered he'd just released my promised exclusive to one of my competitors. I was crushed.

Here's Principal's statement in its entirety:

Since the inception of Dallas, the creators and fans around the world have referred to Bobby and Pam as the 'Romeo & Juliet' of Dallas. I could not agree more. And since the original author of this scenario, William Shakespeare, felt compelled to make theirs a tragic love story of epic and unforgettable deathly loss, I think I shall respect that very successful example and leave the legacy of Bobby & Pam's tragic love story undisturbed and intact. When I filmed Pam's fatal car accident, for me that was the punctuation mark on my role as Pam. I cannot be held responsible for any choices made by producers once I left Dallas, but I do take responsibility for my decision, not to risk tarnishing Bobby & Pam's love story with a desperate reappearance. I made this decision a long time ago with a loving and respectful heart for Dallas, Bobby & Pam, and all the faithful fans.

When I phoned Alan to express my confusion and disappointment, he explained they had handed me a scoop on a silver platter, but I'd instead chosen to align myself with the producers.

And with that, the writers' plans to keep Pam's fate a mystery until the end of the season were instantly torpedoed, which certainly did not help the reboot's steady ratings decline. Cidre wasted no time pounding the final nail in the character's coffin by explaining Pam had undergone significant plastic surgery, developed pancreatic cancer (the very worst kind of cancer that you *really* don't want to get) and relocated to Abu Dhabi (a city in the middle of a dry, barren desert) for experimental treatments, only to die on the operating table. A particularly horrifying way to go. (Not unlike the extreme torture *Desperate Housewives* would employ to write out Nicollette Sheridan, as you'll read all about next.)

This entire ugly 26-year-long saga—from Pam's initial car crash, to my regrettable missteps with Victoria, to her character's horrific death—had left me devastated. It could not have gone worse, until I made it worse. Much, much worse. After more than a quarter decade holding on to the false hope of Pam and Bobby one day at long last getting their happily-ever-after (the fantasy of a grown child who could never reunite his own parents), the dream was now squashed, and I, in some small way, had been involved tangentially in the tragic denouement. I can't explain exactly why, but my brain went into an instant meltdown, with me taking all my anger and resentment out on the one person in all this whose character I once cherished more than any other in the history of television. More than even Lucy Ricardo. My Victoria. My Pam. And I was hardly alone in my adoration, evidenced by Victoria having graced the covers of 16 issues of *TV Guide*—behind only a very few other undisputed television icons including Johnny Carson, Bob Hope, Mary Tyler Moore, Michael Landon and record-holder Lucille Ball.

So, what did I do? I took to Facebook to voice my outrage, with a series of terribly unprofessional and unflattering public posts. I still cringe with embarrassment when I look back at them all these years later.

First, there was a photo I dug up of Pam's fiery car crash—my all-time worst *Dallas* memory ever, which I now coldly ID'd as my favorite. Ugh.

Then there was a close-up photo of Pam's post-crash mummified face, which I dubbed "Victoria Principal's best acting." *God, what was I thinking??!* It wasn't even her playing the character in that scene!! And it didn't end there.

I found a photo from one of *Dallas'* very first episodes that showed an unconscious Pam lying face-down on the hay-strewn floor of the Ewing barn after J.R. had caused her to fall from a ladder and miscarry Bobby's child. My psychopathic caption: "J.R. almost got her back in '78 at Southfork Ranch."

And for all my followers who were wondering if some lunatic had hacked my Facebook account (my friend David suspected I may have become a closeted cocaine addict), I made it crystal clear it was, in fact, me who had been authoring these demented posts. "What Victoria Principal did to me today (makes) Pam Ewing's fiery death … karmic justice!! Burn. Burn!!!!"

Clearly, I'd lost my fucking mind. Crazier than Kristin Shepard when she pumped J.R. full of lead. Nuttier than Clayton Farlow's sister, Jessica, when she kidnapped a bound-and-gagged Miss Ellie in the trunk of her car. Loonier than that jealous Katherine Wentworth when she shot Bobby Ewing in the head and then later plowed him down in cold blood. I only wished my psychotic Facebook postings could have been dreamt away as easily as Bobby's death had been. But there was no waking from this nightmare I'd caused.

As you'd might expect, it didn't take long for Principal's attorneys to contact my *TV Guide* editor in defense of their client who had, legitimately, been brazenly defamed. While the legal letter wasn't 100% accurate (it stated I'd "declined" Alan's exclusive statement), it was spot-on in comparing my actions to that of a "spurned lover" making "spurious and offensive" rants.

What can I say? I was heartbroken, and, as crestfallen lovers often do, I lashed out at the woman I loved most. *Sigh.*

Victoria, I'm speaking to you directly now. I'm deeply and sincerely sorry for my childish, bratty antics. Your elegant portrayal of the damaged but eternally hopeful Pamela Ewing touched me so deeply that, for some inexplicable reason, I just couldn't let you go. You were right. The *Dallas* producers did a disservice to your millions of fans by keeping the character alive off-screen and offering the forever-unfulfilled possibility of your return to Southfork. To Bobby. And to me. Just as I left the *Enquirer* behind to begin a new life for myself, so was it your right to move forward to accomplish all the amazing things you did after laying Pam down to rest.

Still, had you only embraced the Bobby/Pam reunion storyline scenario I'd pitched you during our talk in the Southfork kitchen: "Why not just make everyone happy by coming back as Pam for one damn movie with the explanation that your character's disfiguring third-degree facial burns had been miraculously healed by your Principal Secret rejuvenating face cream??!!" *Right??!* A total win-win! Alas, like Romeo and Juliet, that just wasn't meant to be. Fuck William Shakespeare!!

I'm just grateful I came to my senses before I did something really insane, as Joan Rivers did in 1986 when she gave out Victoria's unlisted home phone number live on air, prompting Victoria to receive a flurry of calls from crazies. Principal ended up hitting Rivers with a $3 million lawsuit. Though the terms of the settlement forbid the parties from revealing the undisclosed sum, when *TV Guide* asked her about the lawsuit's outcome in 1993, Victoria coyly invited her interviewer to "Come and see my Picasso." What a perfectly cheeky response!

One of the things I love most about Victoria is that, with her, you can always expect the unexpected. And after all I'd put her through, I never would have expected to receive a phone call from her in fall 2023 after I gave Nierob a heads-up about the publication of this book. For the better part of an hour, we discussed (off the record) all that had happened between us and celebrated the happiness we'd both found in our private lives today. What a healing gift that call was, and I will remain forever grateful to Victoria for having reached out.

As for the outcome of my own stalker ordeal, I ultimately felt I had no choice but to list my condo for sale before I came home to find my Lhasa Apso boiling in a pot on the stove. Sadly, it wasn't only my stalker's actions that left me feeling frustrated and powerless. The two police officers who'd come to my home to take down the report initially seemed to view the crime of mail fraud as a serious offense worthy of prosecution. But when one of the officers pointedly asked, "You're not gay, are you?" I was thrown.

"Not that it should make any difference, but yes I am," I told the cops. "But I don't discuss my private life with my neighbors, so I don't see how that's at all relevant."

I could see their demeanor instantly shift. As one of the cops casually closed his notepad and tucked it away in his pocket, he said, "Well if you're gay then it's not slander."

Any further attempt to explain that this psycho had still impersonated me and egregiously violated my privacy fell on deaf ears. They were done with a capital D (as in *Dallas*). And at that point I knew it was time to pack up all my feather boas, Judy Garland records, rainbow flags, glitter wands and—of course—my impressive collection of expertly, hand-carved African dildos, and relocate to what I hoped would be a more progressive community. For me, that ended up being a neighborhood right off Melrose Avenue adjacent to gay-friendly West Hollywood.

Ironically, it was right around this time that a *Melrose Place/Desperate Housewives* star would hold a mirror up to my face and force me to see an ugliness no plastic surgeon could change. Not even Harry Glassman. This time the change would have to come from within.

Lesson Learned: Don't waste your life living vicariously through the fabricated adventures and romances of TV characters. Turn off the damn TV and find the courage to carve out your own storylines. Take it from someone who did; it's worth the risk! After a few broken hearts, you may very well find your own Pam or Bobby Ewing amongst all those drunken Sue Ellens and cheatin' J.R.s.

Chapter 23
DESPERATE TIMES CALL FOR ...

(THE *DESPERATE HOUSEWIVES*)

Author on set with Longoria, Huffman and Cross during the 2012 taping of *Desperate Housewives'* series finale. Where was Teri Hatcher?

WHO: Marcia Cross, Teri Hatcher, Nicollette Sheridan and Eva Longoria, co-stars of ABC's 2004–2012 juggernaut, *Desperate Housewives.*

WHAT: On-the-record interviews for *USA Today* and *TV Guide.*

WHERE: Wisteria Lane/Colonial Street on the Universal Studios backlot, Universal City, CA. The private homes of the actresses, and series creator Marc Cherry, Los Angeles. The Polo Lounge at the Beverly Hills Hotel. The White House, Washington D.C.

During *Desperate Housewives'* delightfully entertaining eight-season run, my former neighbor, Eva Longoria—who lived just 10 houses up the road—made me huevos rancheros in her Hollywood Hills kitchen. Teri Hatcher served me sushi in her Studio City living room, and Marcia Cross baked me a basket of homemade muffins in her picture-perfect Santa Monica home that was worthy of its own spread in *House Beautiful* magazine … before making it crystal clear she wanted me out ASAP. And truth be told, were it not for Marcia calling me on my shit and opening my eyes to the reporter and man I was becoming, this chapter exposing my own missteps on the show's fictitious Wisteria Lane may instead have devolved into a juicy tell-all book exposing all the salacious, behind-the-scene secrets I learned as the reporter granted more access to the show than any other.

"Wisteria Lane" was actually Colonial Street—a sunny cul-de-sac on the Universal Studios backlot lined with facades of homes that over the years had been occupied by *The Munsters*, the Cleavers of *Leave It to Beaver* and now an entire community of often contentious, occasionally murderous neighbors. It was October 2004 and I was on assignment to write a cover story for *USA Today* about this new ABC drama series that right out of the gate had become a red-hot ratings phenomenon. On set, I was treated to a scripted screaming match between Hatcher's Susan and Longoria's Gabby. And then afterward, both women came up to assure me that the fireworks were strictly on-screen. Off-screen, they'd already become like sisters.

"We hate fighting with each other," said Longoria, who up until then had been known only for her short stint as loony stalker Isabella on *The Young and the Restless*. "After we finish, we're like, 'I don't want to yell at you. I'm so sorry. It's just awful.'"

Hatcher, meanwhile, seemed genuinely grateful that she'd been given a second shot at fame, having gone from Superman's main squeeze on *Lois & Clark* to hawking batteries as a spokesperson for Radio Shack. Upon completing her scene with Longoria, Hatcher confided, "When you feel like you've been kind of nowhere for four years, it makes you that much more appreciative."

I left the set feeling a similar sense of appreciation from Cross, who, having struggled to find work after her *Melrose Place* success, had gone back to get her master's degree and was about to abandon acting entirely for a career as a psychologist. Also basking in gratitude: Felicity Huffman, who'd previously received critical acclaim and a Golden Globe nomination for her role in the short-lived sitcom *Sports Night*, but knew this was the role that would finally make her a household name. Even Nicollette Sheridan seemed thankful for being back in the spotlight a decade after the cancellation of her previous primetime soap, *Knots Landing*.

THE NATION'S NEWSPAPER — 7? CENTS — NO. 1 IN THE USA

By Dan MacMedan, USA TODAY

Private lives of Wisteria Lane
Behind the scenes of "Desperate Housewives" ■ 1E

It was a very pleasant, drama-free visit that kicked off the first of many *Housewives* cover stories for *USA Today* and, later, *TV Guide*. The sub-header of that debut piece read, "Where there's a hit, there's a catfight—but only on screen."

Eight years later, when I was the sole journalist permitted on the closed set for the shooting of the show's final episode, Sheridan had been killed off and was suing the show for wrongful termination, while the tension amongst the remaining "family" had grown so toxic that Longoria, Cross and Huffman were no longer speaking with Hatcher. It had been that way for some time, ever since the discovery of a sweetheart deal Hatcher had secretly struck with the show's producers granting her Fridays off to spend quality time with her young daughter. But that was just one of many problems that had caused a divide so deep that the women couldn't even attempt to "fake it" when I came to observe the final scene the four would ever shoot together.

After eight long years of inflated egos, heightened sensitivities, that infamous *Vanity Fair* swimsuit cover debacle (where they'd all vied for the center spotlight) and some truly cringeworthy confrontations with yours truly, they all seemed exhausted and more than ready for the show to conclude. As was I. And here, Housewife by Housewife, I explain why.

When *Desperate Housewives* began, Marcia was the actress I was most looking forward to meeting, having been a huge fan of her psychotic *Melrose Place* character, Dr. Kimberly Shaw. When I made that first visit to the set, I told her I was throwing my annual Halloween party, and planned to dress up as a Jekyll & Hyde version of her—half Kimberly (with a grisly, exposed lobotomy scar) and the other half as her perfectly put-together *Housewives* homemaker, Bree Van de Kamp. Cross was so tickled that she asked for an invitation to attend with her girlfriends. She was of course invited, but never showed. And I probably should have done the same when she invited me into her own home in January 2008 for an intimate *USA Today* profile.

When I pulled up to her Santa Monica home, I was impressed by how inviting and understated it seemed. With no gates or guards, it very easily could have been one of the homes on Wisteria Lane. And she could not have made me feel more welcome. I was greeted by the sweet aroma of freshly baked muffins in her spotless kitchen. On the countertop was a crystal vase containing freshly cut red roses—a gift from her handsome husband, financial advisor Tom Mahoney. She was also whipping up cappuccinos and informed me that when her 10-month-old twins, Eden and Savannah, awoke from their naps, they'd be brought downstairs to make me feel even more welcomed. All that was missing were little animated bluebirds to wrap a scarf around my neck and whistle a Disney song in my ear.

The previous evening, I'd gone shopping for an adorable pair of velvet baby onesies for the twins—one purple, the other pink—hoping to make the best possible impression not only on my hostess, but also her publicist, Heidi Slan, a BWR Public Relations associate of Leslie Sloane (cue lightning bolt!)—my arch nemesis discussed back in my Britney Spears chapter. I knew Sloane had most likely warned Slan to beware of this former tabloid sleazeball, so now was my big chance to win back BWR's broken trust!

Had only fate not intervened.

Just minutes before reaching Cross' house, I received a text message from my then-boyfriend, who (by a freakish foreboding coincidence) shared the same name as Bree Van de Kamp's dead husband: Rex. "Have you seen this story about Marcia that just broke on Perez Hilton?" read the text, with a link to the tasteless gossip columnist's web page.

Oh crap! With a sense of dread, I pulled over to the side of the road and brought up the web page, which revealed newly resurfaced photos of a young Marcia caught outdoors entirely in the nude. Even though they were extremely tasteful—artistic even—they were clearly taken in private and never intended for public viewing.

Rex had presented me with a moral quandary: ignore or exploit to land a shady exclusive? Having a fairly good sense of my track record by now, you can probably guess which option I chose. But I did wrestle with the dilemma throughout the interview up until the very last minute. "God, this is going so well," I told myself. "Do I go there and risk ruining everything?"

With Marcia introducing me as promised to her precious twins—who made a rather grand debut in the arms of their two nannies—and the actress opening up freely about turning to costly in-vitro fertilization to help her become a mom at age 45, I fooled myself into thinking she might also be open to discussing those personal photographs taken so long ago.

I was dead wrong. A hint came when she mentioned how she'd recently dealt with pesky paparazzi at the neighborhood park she enjoyed visiting with the twins: "I tell them I will *kill* them." (Perhaps an intentional warning to mind my own manners.)

But my time had come to either shit or get off the pot. And I regrettably chose to take an epic crap right there on the polished, lemon-scented hardwood floors of Marcia's lovely living room.

I closed my notebook, folded my hands on my lap and said quietly, "There's just one last thing I need to bring up."

"And what's that?" Marcia asked, already on guard, with Heidi stepping in close like a protective lioness.

"The news story that broke this morning on Perez Hilton."

"What's Paris Hilton?" Cross asked.

"*Perez* Hilton," I corrected.

219

Cross was genuinely not familiar with the gossipmonger, which only made me further respect her. But it also made this already awkward moment even more drawn-out and excruciating.

"It's a celebrity gossip site," Heidi explained to her client.

"I never read any of that," Cross said. "In fact, I told Heidi I'd fire her if she ever brought any of that stuff to my attention."

I didn't doubt a word she was saying. And just as soon as I let Marcia know about the nude photos, she got up off the couch and returned to her kitchen, signaling that the interview was over. I apologized, trying to explain that my editor would be expecting me to ask.

"No, Will," Marcia corrected. "This was *your* decision. You made the choice."

And you know what? She was 100% right, and I felt about the size of one of her baby girls, who by now had been whisked upstairs and out of my sight. Making the most of her master's degree in Psychology, Marcia was able to see right through me. No editor had asked me to pose this question. It was residual tabloid brainwashing that pushed me to cross Cross by pushing her buttons just to seek a potential buzzworthy scoop.

"Are you planning on putting *that* in the story?" Marcia asked as I said my goodbyes.

"I haven't decided yet," I told her.

"Well, I'd be horrified if you did."

Ultimately, no mention was made of the photos, so I'd destroyed a perfectly lovely day for absolutely no reason. And I knew my twelfth-hour blunder was all she and Slan (not to mention Sloane) would take away from my visit.

I should have just left then and there with some remaining shred of dignity intact, but I ended up making things even worse. With Rex having texted me at the inopportune time he did, I'd been thrown off my game and left the twins' velvet onesies in my car. To Marcia and Heidi's great credit, they permitted me to go all the way back to my car and fetch the gifts, which Marcia agreed to open in front of the videographer I'd brought along to shoot an online video piece to accompany my article.

While Marcia displayed her typical elegance and class, gamely and generously offering up "coos" and expressions of gratitude while the camera rolled (and making me feel just slightly less parasitic), I could only imagine her tossing the onesies in the diaper bin the minute I was out the door. Which could not come soon enough. It was a horrible encounter, but also a "come to Jesus" moment that made me reassess the reporter I'd become and the man I wanted to be.

"No, Will. This was *your* decision," Marcia's words would continue resonating in my ear. "*You* made the choice."

Lesson Learned: Before you bring up something sensitive or potentially upsetting, question your true intentions and consider if the ends truly justify the means.

A WORD FROM MARCIA CROSS

Because Will is Will, and so much deeper than he gives himself credit for, he was open to hearing about my feelings concerning the question he asked at the end of our lovely time together, one for which he had felt terrible about asking ever since. To my embarrassment, I told him that I had absolutely no recollection of it! His lovely visit yes, the question, no.

I suspect I was beyond exhausted with my wonderfully full plate and didn't register it as anything truly hurtful. What I was disgusted and upset about was that someone had gone through my trash and found photos I must have accidentally thrown away. They were not "posed nudes," but rather me taking an outdoor shower the way one takes a shower, naked. I felt angry and violated and after paying $10k to supposedly make them "go away," I suddenly thought, *who cares?* I certainly don't. No one wants their privacy invaded, but with a little time and wisdom it truly didn't matter to me.

And now, at my age ... I should look them up as I would probably be thrilled with naked photos of my 25-year-old self!

Sadly, I have not spoken with Teri Hatcher (left, in 2012 on the *Desperate Housewives* set for her final shoot day) since that last interview with all the ladies up on Wisteria Lane for my *TV Guide* cover story. And that's a darn shame considering all the great fun Teri and I shared before things went south. Of them all, Teri was the one who felt closest to a friend.

Why, you may ask, was I even allowed on set to witness first-hand the obvious animosity between Hatcher and the other three? (Even ABC News' set visit had been pulled at the last minute!) I can only assume it was because everyone knew I'd been well aware for some time of just how badly things had deteriorated. And had kept my mouth shut.

But as *Housewives'* delicious plotlines taught us time and again, no secret lasts forever.

While Teri and I had indeed maintained an amicable relationship during the show's run, it had not been without the occasional hiccup. One of the show's senior producers, a woman with whom I remain friendly, called me up one day with a rumor relating to Teri having supposedly picked up the mysterious swine flu that was going around at the time. I wrote up a story for *TV Guide* magazine's website that was then picked up by PerezHilton.com. (Yes, *him* again.) But the sensationalized Perez version had been plussed with an unflattering photo of Teri sporting a crudely drawn pig snout in the middle of her face! I gasped when I saw the image because I knew this was not going to sit well with Teri, who, understandably, was incredibly protective of her public image and acted as her own publicist. With a little legal prodding from her attorney, we wasted no time taking down our story and the little Teri piggy went wee wee wee away. What was the motivation for that *Housewives* producer reporting this rumor to me in the first place? I can't be sure, but I have my suspicions it was to send a message.

Hatcher and I weathered a similar skirmish over what I felt to be a rather innocuous gossip item that ran as a sidebar to a lengthy *USA Today* cover story I wrote, timed to the publication of her amusing memoir, *Burnt Toast: And Other Philosophies of Life*. (If you'd like to know more about Teri, pick up a copy. It's a fun read!) But this time it wasn't Teri whom I pissed off, but her new "friend," Ryan Seacrest.

Teri had invited me to the modest Fryman Canyon home she and her daughter Emerson had lived in for many years. On my way to her front door, I passed her perpetually-under-construction swimming pool, and her groovy vintage VW van, from which she now broadcasts her delightful "Van Therapy" sessions on Instagram. (They're also worth checking out.)

When she opened the door, she was sporting an enormous gauze patch over her right eye, which (admittedly) I was excited to make part of my story. No, none of the other women had taken a swing at her. Rather, as she explained in her refreshingly humorous and reliably self-deprecating manner, the day before there had been an on-set accident involving a Christmas tree light exploding in her face and scratching her cornea.

After the requisite pirate joke, we settled into her cheery living room which had been decorated with throw pillows in the shapes of oversized candy bars. Over an impressive spread of sushi, Teri quickly cleared up a new rumor going around that she'd been dating her then-neighbor George Clooney. (She wasn't.) From there, we got to discussing the revelations in her book, of which there were many that helped explain how Teri Hatcher became Teri Hatcher. There was the childhood sexual abuse perpetrated by an uncle, a crime she believed later played a hand in the crumbling of her marriage to actor Jon Tenney of *The Closer*. Then there were her thick eyebrows, which promoted school bullies to call her "Hairy Teri." (As a former Mr. Unibrow, I could relate.)

Midway into my interview, I brought up Seacrest, with whom she had recently gone on a first date that also turned out to be their last. It was a total disaster that was mysteriously captured by the paparazzi. As Teri told me, "All I know is that I went to lunch and he kissed me, and there were pictures of it taken by *Us* magazine, and then he emailed me an hour after he dropped me off and said he didn't think he could see me anymore."

Believing the date had gone relatively well, Hatcher was totally blindsided. "I said, 'Wow, I thought we had a great time. I don't understand. Did I do something?' "

Seacrest's response was brief and to the point. "It just wasn't the right time for him and had nothing to do with me," Teri recalled him telling her before ending the call.

The obvious implication was that one (or perhaps both??) had tipped off the photogs in advance to capture a staged kiss for publicity purposes. But neither party would cop to it.

Seacrest later gave me his version, via a statement from his publicist: "We drove out of town to be away. She chose the restaurant. We were photographed. I assure you I did not know we were being photographed. However, it is not

Halloween in Wonderland **with Queen Teri and daughter Emerson.**

surprising ... Teri has her every move watched by photographers. That day had nothing to do with the evolution or lack of evolution of our relationship," adding that the actual reasons should "stay between us."

Hmmm ... *interesting*, right?

I gave them both a chance to tell their side of the story, and while Teri seemed to appreciate the opportunity, Seacrest did not. This would come to punish me a short time later. My producer friend Michael Levitt had hired me to write Seacrest's red carpet questions for E!'s Golden Globe Awards coverage,

224

but Michael told me Seacrest had asked him to *un*invite me following the Hatcher nonsense.

There was another Teri blip that took place at a Halloween charity fundraiser during the evening's auction. A one-of-a-kind Barbie had been created in Teri's likeness that she'd wanted to gift to Emerson, but the doll ultimately went to a higher bidder. In my cheeky *USA Today* coverage, I reported that Emerson had understandably burst into tears upon learning she wouldn't be getting the doll, having to settle for going home with the real, life-size one.

But that too we got through relatively smoothly.

Considering much of the female cast was no longer speaking with Hatcher by the final season, it's impressive that I lasted as long as I did. But I'd been very generous to Teri, not only giving her tons of mostly positive press, but also taking her on the adventure of a lifetime to our nation's capital.

For the second year in a row, I had been asked by *USA Today* to invite a big-time Hollywood celebrity to sit at our table at the annual White House Correspondents' Dinner. You'd think it would have been easy finding someone, considering the primo invite came with a pair of first-class airline tickets, hotel accommodations and, in all likelihood, a face-to-face meeting with the sitting president of the United States. But therein lay the problem. While President

Author meeting President George W. Bush at the 2006 White House Correspondents' Dinner.

George W. Bush is now regarded as a benevolent puppy dog in comparison to the orange menace who arrived a few years later, at the time he was not popular among the mostly liberal Hollywood community. I remember Eva Longoria telling me that she would have gladly accepted my invitation had there been a Democrat in the White House.

Since James Denton, the actor who played Hatcher's love interest, had been my guest to the previous year's dinner and

Posing with First Lady Laura Bush and *Desperate Housewives* actor James Denton.

had told Teri about his fabulous experience, she enthusiastically accepted my invitation without a moment's hesitation.

But there were a few logistical issues that arose before getting to D.C. As I mentioned, our initial invitation included *two* first class plane tickets for Teri and a guest, and Teri had chosen to invite her then-boyfriend, actor/director Stephen Kay. But then Teri asked if she could also bring Emerson. *Three* first class tickets. But then, of course, Emerson had to have a friend, so might it be possible for Stephen's daughter to come as well? Each time I had to go back to my increasingly annoyed editors to remind them that I'd managed to secure one of the hottest stars of the day and the investment would be well worth it. So, *four* first class tickets it was, with my sad, sorry ass seated wayyy back in coach to cut costs.

I had worked with *USA Today*'s White House liaison to arrange a guided tour inside the White House for Teri and her growing entourage, as well as for me and my parents. (Hey, if Ter could bring her family, then why shouldn't I do the same?) It took a lot of work and involved many clearances, but ultimately, I was very proud that I managed to pull it all off.

After we landed at Dulles International Airport, a limousine picked us all up. During the ride to our hotel, I noticed Teri quietly texting with a friend. That friend turned out to be our president's father—41st President George Herbert Walker Bush—who told Teri he was going to place a call to his sonny to arrange a VIP tour of the family's private, second-level living quarters, led by the President and First Lady Laura Bush themselves!

When Teri told me this, I admit the wind was taken out of my sails. My sad puppy-dog eyes must have communicated, "What about me and my parents?" because she told me she'd asked 41 if we could join the VIPs, but because I was a

member of the press it just wouldn't be possible. I would have to wait on the first floor while Teri, Emerson, Stephen and his daughter were escorted upstairs by the Secret Service.

So, while Teri and her gang were up with the Bushes being treated to a private piano recital from George W. (who Teri later told me was wearing Crocs), my parents and I enjoyed our own escapade. Being left alone in the foyer of the White House all by ourselves to explore the gallery of presidential portraits was without a doubt the most surreal experience of my life. (Even more surreal than that visit to a nudist colony with Tammy Faye Bakker.) To this day, my parents and I still have difficulty believing it all actually happened. But we have plenty of pictures with Abraham Lincoln and John F. Kennedy to prove it!

With my parents outside the **White House** (above), and my overjoyed **mom Nancy posing** with Teri inside (below).

Later that day, Teri and her group, along with my parents, went for lunch at a packed seafood restaurant. After waiting a near eternity for our food, our meals were finally brought out, only to be oddly abandoned on a tray to get cold. But instead of complaining, cheerleader Teri got right up out of her seat to play waitress. My parents and I were positively tickled.

227

Teri had also presented herself as a real trouper when, upon arriving to our Hilton after midnight with nary a single porter to be found, she commandeered a luggage cart and acted as our bell person—loading up all our suitcases and playfully wheeling the cart down a hall towards the elevators. "Remember what we talked about," she chirped to Emerson. "We're here to have an adventure."

The complete antithesis of a diva, right?

Yes, indeed; Teri and I enjoyed some truly wonderful memories leading up to our final encounter on that cursed Wisteria Lane during the shooting of the series finale. As I'd mentioned, midway through the show, Hatcher and the other women had a falling-out. Though I knew things were bad, even I was shocked when I saw what happened on set each time the director yelled "cut." Teri would physically walk away from the other three and keep busy on her cell phone without giving any of them so much as a glance. She only spoke with the others while in character as Susan. And I have to say all four should have been awarded special "Congeniality" Emmy Awards for how convincingly and quickly they snapped right back into their harmonious, neighborly alter egos.

Happier times: Moderating a 2009 PaleyFest *Desperate Housewives* panel with (from left): James Denton, Teri Hatcher, Doug Savant, me, executive producer Marc Cherry, Eva Longoria and Brenda Strong.

I couldn't help but be reminded of that very first set visit, when Longoria and Hatcher insisted that all the bickering was strictly for the cameras. Now, it was the complete opposite scenario. The on-set publicist told me we'd have to wait and see whether or not Hatcher would even speak with me.

After an hour or so, Teri took note of how much time I'd been spending chatting up Eva, Marcia and Flicka (Felicity's nickname). So finally, when the four of us took a photo together on Eva's character's front steps, Teri thoughtfully summoned me over to take a photo with her on her character Susan's lawn. She said I could even ask a few questions for my story. It was bizarre, and actually very, very sad to see all the love expressed between Susan, Gaby, Bree and Lynette not replicated in reality.

When my tell-*almost*-all series finale cover story came out in *TV Guide*, Teri sent me a scathing email saying she never should have trusted me, and that one day "you will look up at your reflection in your coffin and not like what you see." I shared this email with my ABC publicist friend who over the years had weathered so many *Desperate Housewives* storms and put out countless fires. Her hilarious response: "What kind of narcissist would have a mirror installed up inside their coffin?" (To be fair, if anyone would do something like that, it would probably be me!)

As one of Teri's magnanimous fellow Housewives recently told me, in hindsight, skirmishes that seemed so unforgivable at the time now no longer feel all that big a deal. And I'd imagine—seeing Teri over the past few years light up so many feel-good holiday movies—that same sentiment might ring true from her perspective as well. It certainly does from mine.

So what say you, Ter? Bygones…?

Lesson Learned: Never run into a dog (or cat) fight without expecting a nip or two in the butt.

Above: Interviewing **Nicollette** on the *Housewives* set. And below: **My 2009 *TV Guide*** cover story timed to the actress' exit.

By far the biggest real-life scandal that rocked *Housewives* during its tumultuous run was one to which I was given an exclusive advance peek: the nasty legal battle Nicollette Sheridan waged against ABC and the show's creator, Marc Cherry.

Prior to being cast as the other *Housewives'* trampy, man-hungry foil, Edie Britt, Sheridan had been popping up only in guest-starring roles in the ten years since she'd ended her run as young seductress Paige Matheson on the primetime soap *Knots Landing*.

Desperate Housewives had catapulted her to superstardom again, but five seasons in, after endless reported on-set headaches, Cherry decided to kill Nicollette off in a most dramatic fashion. And I'd been assigned by *TV Guide* to write the understandably resentful actress' one and only 2009 exit interview. So up I schlepped back to Wisteria Lane, but this time late at night in the rain (created by the show's special-effects wizards).

As Cherry's storyline was mapped out, tragic Edie had deteriorated significantly from the confident neighborhood hussy who'd once thought nothing of soaping up her car in super-short denims that left little to the imagination. In her final scenes, the despondent character had tried to hang herself, was nearly strangled by her psychotic husband and (for a scene I was to observe) had crashed her car into an electrical pole where she was to take her last breath.

When I was escorted to Sheridan, she had been positioned rather uncomfortably under a partially demolished car that was sparking and steaming. The actress' head was resting on the asphalt inches from a puddle, as a sudden surge of electricity was about to end the life of her once-vibrant vixen.

I recall squatting down to her with my tape recorder positioned in her face, and, understandably, Nic looked nothing short of miserable.

"How are you feeling?" I asked.

Her answer: "Cold and wet." She was clearly not having it. It was quite the scene, made even more macabre by the episode's director, Larry Shaw, vocally choreographing Edie's final moments for all to hear. But Shaw never referred to Edie. Rather, he said, "Nicollette dies ... she's dead ... dead ... dead ..."

Oh yeah, she dead!

"Someone really wanted her dead," Sheridan later told me, pointing her finger toward Cherry. "I think whoever Edie represented in Marc's life was somebody he didn't like. And he had a very difficult time distinguishing fact and fiction."

The groundwork was being laid for a bitter war of words between the two, both becoming increasingly bitchy towards the other.

But I do have to say, Nicollette was on to something. During her tragic time on Wisteria Lane, Cherry had:

• Burned her character's house to the ground.

• Rendered Edie swollen like a blimp after being severely stung by a swarm of bees.

• Run her over by a car steered by Hatcher's character, forcing Sheridan to shoot her scenes for several episodes while wearing a cumbersome cast.

And now, leading up to her excessively violent death scene, there were whispers of something very real having happened on-set between Cherry and Sheridan.

Since I had no knowledge of just how nasty Sheridan's ugly accusations would get, or that a lawsuit was in the planning stages, I couldn't understand why

I was having such difficulty getting the other Housewives to offer up kind memories of their soon-to-be ex-castmate for my "Farewell Nicollette" cover story. Eventually, all four did come through for me—each choosing her words carefully.

And I should offer a shout-out to the always-crafty Hatcher, the actress who'd remained the closest to Sheridan, for gifting her a colorful scrapbook illustrating their fun times together on and off set.

Because Sheridan was only able to give me a few moments to speak with her while shooting her death scene, ABC was to schedule a formal sit-down interview for the two of us. But Sheridan proved to be even more elusive than her co-stars, which left me sweating as my deadline neared. Even under the best of circumstances, naughty Nicollette was always one to keep me waiting.

One of those times was when the writers paired Edie with Longoria's character's husband Carlos (played by actor Ricardo Chavira). I was invited to set to shoot an exclusive behind-the-scenes video tour of all the beds where Edie and Carlos would be fuc…, *er*, making love. But I ended up being the one who got "made love to" the hardest!

I'd naturally been assured in advance that both Sheridan and Chavira were on board to lead the tour, but when I arrived, Chavira and I were kept waiting for a full hour while we watched Sheridan casually walking in and out of her trailer, just shootin' the shit on her cell phone, while offering us the occasional glance. Ultimately, when I was about to lose my cameraman, I had no choice but to have Chavira shoot the video solo. I was never given an explanation, much less an apology, for Sheridan's inconsiderate behavior.

But this time Nicollette was getting her very own *TV Guide* cover story—her last for *Desperate Housewives*. She had already spent a full day at a ritzy Beverly Hills estate that our magazine had rented to shoot her sexy cover image. (Those days are now long gone, with most celebrity magazines using handout art supplied by the studios.) All that was left was our sit-down interview, which after a few false starts, finally took place over lunch at the Beverly Hills Hotel's Polo Lounge.

And I have to say it was well worth the wait. Say what you will about Nicollette, that girl sure knows how to give an interview that packs a punch!

Though she wasn't quite ready to come completely clean with all her scathing accusations against Cherry—that he'd allegedly slapped her across the face while trying to demonstrate how a scene should be played (Cherry calls it a "gentle tap," which was corroborated in court by the testimonies of on-set witnesses)—she was certainly dropping enough clues. She told me she was hurt that she had never been added to the show's opening credits alongside the other four Housewives and felt Cherry rarely spoke of her in interviews. "When you have a jewel," Sheridan said of herself, "why not polish it and put it out there for all to see?"

Humble, Sheridan was not.

Prior to that Polo Lounge lunch, I'd already met with Cherry at his spectacular mansion where I'd attended several boys-only pool parties akin to those I imagine Rock Hudson having hosted back in his day. Over the years, Marc and I had become chums, and it should come as no surprise to *Housewives* fans that he's just as sharp, witty, fearless and unabashed as the characters he writes. But you don't want to get on Marc's bad side, as I'd come to learn first-hand.

By the start of *Housewives'* third season, our friendship was causing a real stink for ABC's head of publicity, who didn't appreciate Cherry sharing exclusive casting and storyline scoops with me for my column at the expense of competing journalists who began feeling shortchanged. So when I sensed Cherry was pulling back to appease his PR team, I turned to other well-placed show sources to deliver the goods I needed. Apparently my defiant digging rubbed Cherry the wrong way, as I would come to discover when I tuned into a new *Housewives* episode that introduced "Dr. Keck"—a respected member of the community who was exposed to be the neighborhood pedophile! (I think I would have preferred a good face slap!)

I would never cross Marc again.

Fortunately, it didn't take Marc long to bring me back into his circle of confidence. Regarding Sheridan's departure, he told me he'd been considering killing Edie off for the past two years as a message to Hatcher, Cross, Longoria and Huffman to back off on their increasing salary demands. He recalled telling his writers, "If we threaten one of the characters' lives, maybe they'll back off."

Sheridan was given a stay of execution, but only for so long. As the series was nearing its sixth season, the actress reportedly reached out to the other four to renegotiate their salaries in tandem, *a la* the *Friends* cast. So when ABC pressured Cherry to cut costs, it was obvious where he'd stick his knife. As Cherry reasoned, "Edie's already slept with most of the guys on the street and has caused about as many problems as she could." (He would very soon come to learn that Sheridan's troublemaking had barely begun, with her final playing card dragging him into a very ugly, years-long court battle.)

Besides saving him between $100–$200k per week, Sheridan's departure would spare him further clashes over what he told me were repeated storyline and line-delivery complaints. Sheridan admitted to me that she flatly refused Cherry's request to recreate her debut car wash scene wearing the same short shorts and tight t-shirt she'd worn four years earlier. Instead, she opted to go shopping for her own wardrobe—a huge Hollywood no-no, and a sign of great disrespect to the hard-working costume department. Her explanation was that the series had grown tired.

"Complacent," was the exact word she used. She wanted Edie to be given something fresh. Well, be careful what you wish for. Revenge is a dish best served fresh, cold and wet.

The day before the script revealing Edie's death was to be distributed to the cast, Sheridan was summoned to Cherry's office for a "story meeting." But right away, the actress said she "smelled a rat." She says Cherry seemed very uncomfortable and started speaking in circles before finally telling her, "I just wanted you to hear it here that Edie is going to get into a car crash. And she's going to die."

Cherry remembers he'd purposely left his office door ajar so that their interaction could be overheard by his assistant, Christine, who reported hearing Sheridan mutter "free at last" as she exited Cherry's office in a huff.

James Denton, who played Hatcher's husband Mike, and would be killed off himself in the show's final season, clued me in that "Marc told (the other housewives) ahead of time."

While Cherry had held nothing back in his reasoning for letting Sheridan go, he did pay her what he considered to be a "compliment," which I relayed to

Nicollette at our luncheon. I told her, "Marc said you performed the 'aging neighborhood tramp' better than anyone has ever done before."

Hearing this, Sheridan let out a sinister cackle. "That's so funny," she said. "Oh, he's such a *bitch*."

I realized my exit-interview article was transforming from a warm and fuzzy celebratory farewell tribute into a juicy, bitter exposé. And I give great credit to my editor, Debra Birnbaum, for allowing the article to run in its entirety, against ABC's wishes.

After our interview, Nicollette and I waited outside the front of the hotel for the valets to bring around our cars. With the tape recorder now off, Sheridan teased there was more to the story—something "explosive" that would soon be revealed. Perhaps to Larry King, she hinted. When I cautioned her that vocalizing any sour grapes could potentially hurt her chances of being hired in Hollywood, Sheridan told me, quite haughtily, "Sometimes you must follow your heart and do what must be done."

A few weeks later, Sheridan's attorney filed suit against both ABC and Cherry himself. The original case ended with a deadlocked jury and the judge calling a mistrial. There were various appeals and motions for retrials, and in 2017 a judge finally tossed out the suit. I was actually quite surprised that my name was never included on a witness list. Clearly, I would have had much to contribute.

When she guest-starred on *The Talk* in 2018 to promote her short-lived role as Alexis on the CW's *Dynasty* reboot, Sheridan laid it all out on the table: "I was a victim of assault and battery by my boss on the set, and I reported him and was retaliated against and fired off the show. All of which is illegal. There was nobody to stand up for me. I felt like I needed to stand up for myself."

In the ensuing years, the actress's acting roles have been few and far between, but in 2016 she appeared in the Hallmark Channel movie *All Yours* and was booked to promote the film on *Home & Family*—the show I was now working on as a producer. When Sheridan learned I'd been assigned to produce her segment, she demanded a replacement. To my knowledge, that is the only time a guest asked not to work with me.

Lesson Learned: Sometimes you actually can read a book (or a magazine) by its cover.

A WORD FROM *HOUSEWIVES* CREATOR MARC CHERRY

There was a time I loved showbiz gossip. The lives of glamorous celebrities fascinated me to no end. I reveled in the scandalous headlines of supermarket tabloids. And I believed every juicy tidbit the entertainment press served me. But then I created a hit show. That's when I learned it's all fun until someone gets hurt.

I met Will Keck at a party weeks after *Desperate Housewives* premiered. He was witty, engaging, sympathetic and more than willing to spill some of the tea he was in possession of. I'd never known a reporter before. I'd met plenty. But I wasn't friends with them. But Will was so damn charming, I decided to invite him to a few social gatherings.

Looking back, it was the oddest of friendships. I didn't realize that show runners of big hits NEVER hang out with the folks who write about them. It's a recipe for disaster. Some reporters get the details wrong. And some reporters lie. And some reporters wait for an idiot like me to say too much over shrimp cocktail. Yes, I ended up choking on some of the dirt Will spread. Because ... I sort of shoveled it for him. Ugh.

Now at this point I must say I never intentionally spilled the tea. But I did have conversations about my work, my frustrations, my bad days, like I would with any pal. As a result I sometimes dropped a few bread crumbs. And Will, being a good reporter, would start following those bread crumbs to where they led. And the publicity people at the studio and network would yell at me. And deservedly so.

It was at this time someone taught me the most valuable phrase in Showbiz Speak: "THIS IS OFF THE RECORD." The Writer's Guild needs to include that in its book of instruction to aspiring TV writers. It would have saved me a lot of anxiety over the years. And that one phrase is how I'm able to still hang out with Will. Because I know once I say it ... Will will take it seriously. And whatever comes out of my mouth remains private. Thank God.

So if you should ever meet Will Keck at a party, definitely introduce yourself. You'll have a good time and you'll learn some things. But don't start the conversation with "Hello." Start with "This is off the record." Trust me. It's safer.

EVA LONGORIA

I remember the first time I met Eva Longoria on the set of *Desperate Housewives.* She was the show's ingénue, so clearly destined to become the breakout star she is today. (Though who knew then that this stunner would come to add film director and social activist to her growing resume?) Instantly likeable, admirably ambitious and refreshingly candid, the actress, then 29, was newly divorced from *General Hospital* soap hunk Tyler Christopher (who sadly passed away on Halloween 2023 at age 50) and freely admitted to me that she hadn't been a good wife and was now faring better as the new girlfriend of NSYNC-er JC Chasez.

Flash forward to 2007. Now a household name with several product endorsement deals and a couple major motion pictures under her Gucci belt, this rising star had understandably become far more guarded—particularly when it came to providing me even the most minute morsel about her upcoming Parisian wedding to San Antonio Spurs star player Tony Parker. So, what did I do to get closer to the star? Well, in 2011 I sold my Melrose house and bought a 1920s Spanish three-bedroom in the Hollywood Hills—just ten houses down from where Eva lived! Yup, we were now neighbors.

I'd fallen in love with Eva's neighborhood (the 100-year-old Hollywood Dell, tucked away in a canyon beneath the Hollywood Reservoir) when she invited me into her colorful home to make me her famous huevos rancheros for a *USA Today* cover story I was writing about her.

Eva would often tell me how much she loved reading *USA Today*, and now—every morning when I'd walk my dogs past her home—I'd get a kick out of seeing my paper on her driveway. Before she left the neighborhood to start a family with her third husband, José Antonio Bastón (one of the most successful media titans in all of Latin America), I'd routinely hear the bark of her little dog or her unmistakable, hearty laugh echoing from across the canyon during one of her raucous celebrity game nights. It was times like these when I wondered if I wasn't a reporter constantly having to badger celebrities for scoop, might I, like Eva's good friend (and TV host) Mario Lopez, earned an invite to game night. Might we perhaps have had a chance to get to know each other as neighbors, like the ladies of Wisteria Lane? I will say I never took advantage of our close proximity. No late night garbage raids as I'd done to snoop for dirt on Kelsey Grammer. Our only semi-awkward exchange in the Dell was in early 2012 when Eva first discovered I'd moved into her hood.

"What are *you* doing here?!!" Eva yelled from her car when she saw me out on one of my doggie walks. When I pointed to my new home—with its bird's-eye view of hers—she surely must have thought I was a stalker.

I tried my very best to play it cool and bury my reporter instincts, but *Housewives'* top-secret final episodes were shooting at that time and I just couldn't resist trying to land an exclusive for my *Keck's Exclusives* gossip column in *TV Guide*. I'd just received a tip that one of the Househusbands was being killed off, and I was convinced it was going to be Eva's TV husband Carlos (played by actor Ricardo Chavira).

"Hey, by the way," I told Eva, just as she was about to take off down the road. "I heard about your husband ... so sorry."

Eva looked at me incredulously, and I immediately realized how what I'd just said could have been misinterpreted given that her marriage to Parker had ended following rumors of his infidelity. So much for making a good first impression as the new neighbor! I was mortified. I mean how incredibly tacky would that have been??!!

I wasted no time explaining that I was talking only about rumors I'd heard about the end of her on-screen *TV* marriage. "Ohhh…," Eva sighed. "I thought you were talking about Tony." Yep, I was right. *Oy!!!*

Eva cleared up that I had my info wrong. Her character, Gabrielle, wasn't the housewife who was about to be widowed, but she wouldn't reveal which of the others was. (Hatcher's Susan, interestingly enough, was the one whom Cherry chose to give a tragic ending.) "I'm not telling," Eva said as she offered me a coquettish wave, drove off and—I can only presume—speed-dialed her realtor to put her house on the market.

Lesson Learned: The expression "there goes the neighborhood" can just as easily be applied to you!

A WORD ABOUT FELICITY HUFFMAN

Of the four main *Desperate Housewives*, only Felicity Huffman—whom I found to be the most laid back of them all—never invited me to visit the home she shared with her actor husband William H. Macy. Instead, for her *USA Today* cover-story profile, we met at a gay Mexican restaurant in West Hollywood, along with two transgender actresses to promote what would become her Oscar-nominated role as a trans woman in the film *Transamerica*. Felicity was probably smart to keep her private world off-limits, and I guarantee that Marcia Cross (and perhaps the others) wished she'd done the same.

My very first interview with Flicka took place on the front porch of her character's Wisteria Lane home. I remember being surprised when she took time to ask about my own life, which I thought was very considerate. When I credited her for being a good mom to daughters Sophia, then 4, and Georgia, 2, she questioned the compliment, asking, "How do you know I am?" She went on to open up about the insecurities she was feeling having to be away from her daughters during their formative years.

The truly desperate lengths Felicity would be willing to go to for her girls became evident in 2019 when she would serve 11 days behind bars for her involvement in the college-admissions scandal. But I don't think about any of that. Flicka handled that unpleasant chapter with her usual honesty, dignity and class. What I *do* choose to focus on is the time I ran into Felicity a good while after *Housewives* had ended its run and invited her to appear as a guest on *Home & Family*. Not only did she come on the show for an on-camera interview, but she also agreed to cook her chewy pecan bars in an additional kitchen segment. She had such fun that she came back for a second visit with husband Bill in tow to prep a refreshing spring salad with poppyseed dressing.

All that yumminess—combined with Marcia's muffins, Eva's huevos rancheros, Teri's sushi and a healthy helping of crow along the way—amounted to one helluva buffet that gave me plenty of food for thought during my eight unforgettable years with the ladies. Gradually, this supposedly "reformed" *Enquirer* bad boy was becoming less desperate to prove his worthiness by poking into celebrities' private lives and more focused on finding a happy and healthy private life of his own.

Chapter 24
FLYING FUR

(ELLEN DEGENERES)

WHO: Ellen DeGeneres (b. January 26, 1958). Multiple Daytime Emmy-winning host of the 2003–2023 talk show, *The Ellen DeGeneres Show.* Winner of a Primetime Emmy Award for writing the 1997 coming-out episode of her 1994–1998 sitcom, *Ellen.*

WHAT: Event coverage for *USA Today.*

WHERE: The Shrine Auditorium, L.A.

When I began writing this book, the name "Ellen DeGeneres" was synonymous with "nice." That changed rather dramatically midway into the onset of our Great Covid Shit

Ellen DeGeneres, circa 2011.
(Glenn Francis/ Wikimedia Commons)

Show of 2020 when reports leaked of toxicity behind the scenes of her afternoon talk show. Suddenly, it seemed most everyone in Hollywood had their own Ellen story to tell. This is mine, which will probably leave you liking her more than you will me.

Before I share the stupid thing I did, let's go way back to when I was still "Billy," a little boy who idolized his Nana Ruth, my mom's mom, who pops up several times in these pages. Nana, who in my eyes could do no wrong, kept black poodles as pets. First there was Jockey, who got old and gray and died. And then came Romeo, a true lover who lived up to his name. Despite my severe pet allergy, I found it impossible to resist burying my face in the soft curls of his inviting fur.

But even more enticing: wrapping myself up inside Nana's big, fluffy, chocolate brown mink coat that had been a gift from her doting husband, Alfred.

Yep! Authentic skinned-from-the-still-warm-flesh fur!! Nothing but the very best. All the fancy ladies on TV wore them as status symbols. And it wasn't just the primetime soap divas. Sitcom characters like *Gilligan's Island*'s Lovey Howell, *The Jeffersons*' Weezy Jefferson, *The Facts of Life*'s Blair Warner, *Designing Women*'s Suzanne Sugarbaker, *WKRP*'s Jennifer

Family photo of my mom with Nana's poodle, Jockey.

Marlowe and *Green Acres*' Lisa Douglas (not to mention all the hookers who ever strutted into *Night Court*) proudly showed off this most prized gift that, as Lucy Ricardo tells Ethel Mertz, "every woman has always wanted from her husband." Back then, few (with the exception of *Friends*' Phoebe Buffay) gave even a passing thought about the torture inflicted upon the poor innocent woodland creatures whose lives were sacrificed in the name of luxury.

And even though I knew better, in a moment of weakness at a John Varvatos store on Melrose, I chose to purchase a tuxedo with a real fur collar when I found one in my size on the sale rack. Today, I fully understand that this was not only an unethical purchase, but perhaps even worse: a huge waste of money, as the tux looked completely ridiculous on me. As was typical, I just hadn't properly thought things out. And the first time I wore it, boy did I ever get a lecture!

It was backstage at the Shrine Auditorium for *The People's Choice Awards*, where I was on assignment for *USA Today*. As always, I was on the lookout for celebrities to interview, and across the room I spotted lesbian power couple Ellen DeGeneres and Portia de Rossi. It was January 2006, quite early into their relationship, and there was deep fascination with these two, so I couldn't let the opportunity go by without trying to land some quotes for the article I'd be writing.

I'd spoken with Portia many times during her years on *Ally McBeal* and *Arrested Development*, but this was my first-ever time meeting Ellen. Fortunately, when the *Enquirer* was trying to "out" Ellen back in the '90s, it was (not surprisingly) the female reporters who were sent out to the "girl bars" she was rumored to frequent. Shrewdly, the *Enquirer* never directly outed Ellen as gay. Rather, as was their style, they just printed a series of articles asking, "Why can't Ellen stay out of gay bars?"

I know—so ridiculous, right? Especially considering there were several closet cases right there on the *Enquirer* staff—my own self included!!

Portia de Rossi and Ellen at DeGeneres' 2012 Hollywood Walk of Fame star ceremony. (Angela George/Wikimedia Commons)

When I approached the ladies and introduced myself as a reporter for *USA Today*, both Ellen and Portia were very pleasant—a total reversal from the looks I used to get when I'd revealed my allegiance to the *Enquirer*. When I asked about the Christmas presents they'd recently exchanged, they gamely clued me in: a black Porsche for Ellen and a silver vintage Mercedes 280 SL for Portia. How charming.

It took me a moment before I realized Ellen was gently stroking my jacket's fur collar.

"This is lovely," she said. "It's not real fur, is it?"

Gulp!!

This was a moment when it would have behooved me to lie my ass off, but dumb naïve me decided to tell the truth.

"It is," I said, cringing sheepishly. "It was on sale at John Varvatos, and I just thought it was so beautiful."

Ellen instantly recoiled, pulling her hand back in horror as if I'd told her the fur had been harvested from a skinned Snuffleupagus. Portia also took a step back.

"Oh," said Ellen. "I liked you, but now I don't like you so much."

With the fur about to fly, I suddenly felt as though I might become the one skinned alive. I apologized and promised I would never make the mistake again.

"You don't have to apologize to me," Ellen said. "You need to apologize to the poor creature who gave up his life."

Ellen was right. I knew it, and there was nothing I could do but accept my punishment and try my best not to shrink away to nothing. I must have looked as though I were on the verge of tears, because, for whatever reason, Ellen took pity on me and said I could continue my interview.

Although that jacket still hangs somewhere deep within the recesses of a closet waiting to be buried in my backyard, I never wore it again. With just that one wearing, it turned out to be the most expensive "sale" item I'd ever purchased.

Regrettably, that wasn't my last time committing an ethically questionable fashion faux pas.

A short time later, I attended an industry function wearing black leather pants at a time when they were very much in fashion. I'd been sent here by the assigning editor of *Entertainment Weekly*, who phoned me midway through the event to ask if I might consider leaving early to cover another. No problem there; two events meant double the invoices!

The problem was that my leather pants ended up at a fundraiser for PETA (People for the Ethical Treatment of Animals)! Thank God Ellen and Portia weren't on the guest list; can you imagine?? But my primo spot on the red carpet did place me face-to-face with the militant organization's president, Ingrid Newkirk.

Hoping to avoid an embarrassing scolding, I tried my darndest to maintain eye contact with Ingrid by making odd, over-exaggerated facial expressions during our interview. Don't look down, Ingrid. Thatagirl. Stay with me now.

But I could see her curious eyes wandering south. And before she asked the question, I nipped it right in the bud. "Don't worry, Ingrid," I lied through my teeth with feigned confidence. "Pleather."

Lesson Learned: With the exception of David Hasselhoff, full body fur belongs only on the four-legged. And, yeah; I know I need to get rid of that fucking Varvatos tux. PETA recommends donating these items to the homeless. And in Ellen's name, I have.

Chapter 25
SCIENTOLOGY BLACKLIST

(KIRSTIE ALLEY)

Showtime press photo for *Fat Actress*, 2005.

WHO: Kirstie Alley (1951–2022). Winner of an Emmy and Golden Globe for playing bar owner Rebecca Howe on *Cheers* from 1987–1993. For three seasons, starred as the owner of a lingerie company in the sitcom *Veronica's Closet*. Films include *Look Who's Talking* and *Star Trek II: The Wrath of Khan*.

WHAT: Scientology-sabotaged on-the-record profile for *USA Today* to publicize her series *Fat Actress*.

WHERE: Cinerama Dome theater, Hollywood, CA. Sushi House restaurant, Hollywood, CA.

I love Scientologists. Truly, I do. I remember reading founder L. Ron Hubbard's Dianetics self-help book when I was a teenager and thinking, "Wow, this sounds awesome!! Sign me up!" And the members I've met over the years (both current, former, dead and jailed), including Tom Cruise, Katie Holmes, John Travolta, Kelly Preston and Priscilla Presley were all completely lovely human beings who treated me with kindness, respect and laser-sharp attention as if they were reading my mind.

But here's the one thing—you don't piss 'em off. You just don't, okay? We've all heard the scary stories, and thanks to brave escapee Leah Remini coming forward to blow the lid off so many "church" secrets, we have a somewhat clearer understanding of what goes on in the mysterious Castle Von Cruise.

To make it crystal clear, the Church of Scientology never did anything to me personally (so please, Church leaders, don't empty my bank account—there's nothing there anyway). And I've always heard IHOP has nothing on their pancake breakfasts.

However, for those needing a little background, Wikipedia (not I) identifies the Church as a business, religious movement or even (according to some disbelieving "suppressives") a cult that science-fiction author Hubbard founded back in the 1950s. Depending upon the source, global membership fluctuates anywhere between 40,000 to ten million (!!!). It has included amongst its disciples *Mad Men's* Elisabeth Moss, the late Lisa Marie Presley, Juliette Lewis (of *Natural Born Killers* and *Mixed Nuts*), Nancy Cartwright (the longtime voice of that rascal Bart Simpson) and cast members from *That '70s Show,* including convicted rapist Danny Masterson, now serving 30 years to life.

In 2005, I learned the Scientologists had reserved a special spot just for me on their list of suppressives, as a journalist not to be trusted. *Aw, shucks!* But it took me a little time to figure out exactly how that happened.

USA Today had assigned me to write a cover story on Kirstie Alley, the great comedic actress and fervent Scientologist whose death in December 2022 at age 71 came as a shock to us all. Besides her strong body of work on *Cheers* and *Veronica's Closet*, the Emmy and Golden Globe winner had gained infamy in an unforgettable 1991 Emmy acceptance speech. I was lucky enough to be seated in the Pasadena Civic Auditorium that evening to hear Kirstie thank then-husband Parker Stevenson as "the man who has given me the big one for the last eight years." (When I spoke with Parker in 2023 about that infamous zinger, he described it to me as "an appropriate summation of Kirstie's bawdiness and my discomfort with that." And on their limo ride home, he remembered telling her, "You don't have to mention me ever again in a speech." The couple ended up divorcing in 1997.)

More than a decade after that speech, I was super excited for my opportunity to sit down with Kirstie to discuss how she was embracing her curves as the star of the new Showtime mock reality series *Fat Actress.* But just before we finalized a meeting place, I received an upsetting call from her manager Jason Weinberg.

"Sorry, Will," he said. "The interview's not going to happen."

I was so confused. *"Why??!!!"* I asked.

I was told I'd done something involving Alley during my years writing for *Entertainment Weekly* that had alienated Scientology's Supreme Being, Xenu. There was just one problem with that: I'd never interviewed Kirstie Alley for *EW* or any other outlet. I'd never even met her. There had to have been a mistake. Somehow the Scientologists had confused me with some other William Keck.

Showtime publicity still for *Fat Actress,* **2005.**

But then a few days later it hit me. In fact, I *had* done something. But it was so miniscule that not even Weinberg remembered. Could *that* really have been the reason??

A few years earlier, I'd contributed a small gossip item to *EW* about all the *Cheers* actors who'd been guest-starring on the Kelsey Grammer spin-off series *Frasier.* Over *Frasier*'s 11 seasons, Ted Danson, Shelley Long, John Ratzenberger, George Wendt, Rhea Perlman and even Woody Harrelson had all popped up in episodes, leaving but one holdout who had yet to pay a visit to Seattle. And on an Emmy Awards red carpet, I asked Grammer (yes, getting in trouble with *him* again) why that was.

"Apparently, Kirstie will not do the show because I play a psychiatrist and psychiatry conflicts with her Scientology beliefs," I was told by Grammer, a reliably outspoken interviewee whose more recent public support for Donald Trump presented a real challenge to Paramount +'s protective PR team.

Grammer had handed me a juicy scoop which *EW* naturally wanted to run, but not before I reached out to Alley for independent confirmation and to offer her an opportunity to comment. And boy, did she ever! It had actually been Weinberg—the very same rep who was now telling me I couldn't speak with his client—who called me with Kirstie's exclusive quote. But before he'd email it to me, he prefaced that, per Kirstie, it could only run in *EW* if it was printed unedited. And *EW* had no problem doing so because it was hysterical! "The only way I'd ever do *Frasier*," Alley said, "is if I get to *do* Frasier."

It was a naughty little item that ran and was then quickly forgotten. Or so I'd thought. Apparently, that little blurb was viewed negatively by the Scientologists and landed me on their "do not speak with" list, which was now coming back to derail my *Fat Actress* profile.

I must give *USA Today* major kudos for refusing to reassign another reporter to the story. If Kirstie wouldn't speak with me, then the paper didn't want to speak with her about her new show! This is a crucially important journalistic policy that defends the journalist over the talent, aiding the paper in retaining a certain degree of power.

I would come to appreciate *USA Today*'s strict stance even more during my sometimes-challenging subsequent on-staff position as a senior editor and columnist for a magazine run by a smart, savvy editor … who kissed the ass of every star, publicist, producer and network executive in town to get them to come to her lavish company-paid parties. (If you think I've taken a lot of photos with celebrities, you should just see her massive collection.) If a certain publicist didn't want William Keck to interview a particular actor for her magazine, she had no problem assigning another writer without giving the switcheroo a second thought. The problem? This practice made the magazine a pawn of the various publicity departments and emasculated its own journalists, who felt unsupported and thus reticent to pose sensitive questions that the über-protective publicists might deem overly intrusive.

What was once a top-selling, well-respected and celebrated newsmaking periodical has now devolved into a paper-thin fanzine, which in part explains why this supermarket checkout line staple is now so increasingly difficult to find. Still, my six years working for this editor did provide me ample opportunities to engage many of the famous folk you're now reading about, such as … ah yes—Kirstie!

After Kirstie cancelled our interview, you can imagine my surprise when I received an invitation from Showtime to attend and cover their red carpet premiere screening of *Fat Actress* at Hollywood's historic Cinerama Dome. I called the network to make sure there was no mistake, and even confirmed with Weinberg that Kirstie wouldn't object to my attending.

"You can come," Weinberg told me. "But no guarantee Kirstie will stop for you. Let's see what happens."

What happened was this: Not only did Kirstie stop and speak with me on the carpet, but she invited me to join her at the Geisha House after-party for a longer conversation over sushi. (Clearly, she was regretting missing out on that cover story.)

I was genuinely appreciative of Kirstie's typical Scientologist warmth that evening, not to mention the mouth-watering spicy tuna rolls. So, I gave Kirstie and her new show a nice write-up in *USA Today*. One of my favorite quotes from the candid 54-year-old was that she was aspiring to become more promiscuous "because I have always aspired to promiscuity. But I've never been able to achieve it because I'm one of those people who can only sleep with people I love. How *boring*!"

To be sure, *gurl* never disappointed when it came to giving good quote!!

When my premiere coverage came out, I received yet another call from Weinberg, this time telling me that not only was Kirstie absolutely thrilled with my article, but I was the *USA Today* reporter she'd prefer to speak with going forward. *Uh-huh.* What a reversal! She'd even like to have me over to her home for that cover story I was going to write.

But as far as *USA Today* was concerned, that ship had passed. Reviews for *Fat Actress* had not been kind and, after just seven episodes, Showtime pulled the plug. Am I still persona non grata to the Church of Scientology? I have to assume not, as I was granted access to both Cruise and Travolta at subsequent Hollywood events. So perhaps I owe Alley for getting my name removed from her church's naughty list. If that's indeed so, I have dear Kirstie to thank for giving me "the big one" ... as in a second chance. Cheers, lady. You are missed.

Lesson Learned: The past (which, according to L. Ron Hubbard, began some 60 trillion years ago) inevitably comes back to haunt us.

Chapter 26
HORSE SPERM & SPOCK EARS

(WILLIAM SHATNER & LEONARD NIMOY)

WHO: William Shatner (b. March 22, 1931) and Leonard Nimoy (1931–2015). One-time best friends and co-stars of the 1966–1969 *Star Trek* TV series and its various big-screen spinoffs.

WHAT: On-the-record interviews for *Entertainment Weekly* and *USA Today*. Shatner's numerous visits to *Home & Family*.

WHERE: The Leonard Nimoy Event Horizon Theater at the Griffith Observatory, Los Feliz, CA. The *Home & Family* set and various other locations.

Shatner's Captain Kirk and Nimoy's Mr. Spock, circa 1967. (Wikimedia Commons)

All that Scientology talk in the previous Kirstie Alley chapter reminds me of a certain *other* long-running sci-fi franchise that's been compared to a religious cult with fanatical followers. But before revisiting a pair of enterprising interview questions that galactically perturbed *Star Trek* divas William Shatner and Leonard Nimoy, let me begin by confessing my very own *Trek*-related diva moment: one that taught me how *not* to get out of a parking ticket … at least not in Los Angeles.

On August 31, 2004, I was assigned by *USA Today* to cover the Hollywood Walk of Fame star induction ceremony for James Doohan, the actor eternally beloved for playing Scotty, chief engineer of *Star Trek's* U.S.S. Enterprise. Since I lived just a five-minute drive from where Scotty's star was to be installed on Hollywood Blvd., I waited until the last possible minute to get in my car and head out. Now, suddenly late to the show, I sped through the residential streets of Hollywood until I saw red lights in my rear-view mirror signaling me to pull over. *Aw, shit!*

When I lowered my window, I looked up at my own reflection in the stern LAPD officer's mirrored sunglasses and began my rather pathetic, privileged plea for leniency.

"I'm sorry, officer; you got me," I copped with an apologetic grin. "I'm actually a reporter for *USA Today* trying to get to Hollywood Blvd. to cover an important event that's just about to take place. Is there any way you'd consider letting me off with a warning so I won't miss it?"

Well, this take-no-crap cop lowered his shades and offered only a condescending snigger as he smugly began writing out my citation. "You actually expect me to give you a break after all the shit you journalists have put my department through?" he asked.

"Yeah, I get it," I shrugged. "But I'm just an *entertainment* reporter. I haven't done anything to you guys. I love the LAPD!"

Shockingly, my appeal fell on deaf ears.

By the time I made it to Hollywood Blvd. and found a parking spot, my next challenge was to navigate through an asteroid field of costumed Trekkies, many of whom—judging by their pungent humanoid smell that would make any authentic Vulcan wince—had been camped out overnight, and didn't appreciate being pushed out of the way by a pesky last-minute attendee.

Fortunately, I made it to my designated spot just in time to watch a smiling Doohan, then 84, tap on his wheelchair to the sounds of live bagpipers. A post-reception was held, oddly enough, in a replica of the *Cheers* bar erected in the long-since-shuttered Hollywood Entertainment Museum. As an invited guest, I was able to personally congratulate Doohan, who—now less than a year before his death—

had been severely weakened by diabetes and Alzheimer's disease and was unable to grant me an interview. But I got a sense of what the day meant to him by chatting up his fellow Enterprisers who'd turned up that day to honor their friend's legacy.

Nichelle Nichols (Uhura) shared with me that she'd taken Doohan's hand and whispered in his ear, "We made it, my darling. You're there for posterity." Hearing these words, Doohan sat up ever so slightly, smiled and whispered back, "Nichelle, it's the most wonderful day of my life."

"I don't want to sound maudlin," Walter Koenig (Chekov) came over to tell me. "But if you care about *Star Trek*, it's important to (appreciate) each moment you folks have left with us."

And indeed, we did, I reassured both Koenig and George Takei (Sulu) on behalf of all *Trek* fans.

Conspicuously absent that day were both Shatner and Nimoy, not to mention Kirstie the Scientologist, who would have fit in beautifully serving cocktails from behind that *Cheers* bar. As *Trek* fans are well aware, Alley had played the half-Vulcan/half-Romulan Lt. Saavik in 1982's *Star Trek II: The Wrath of Khan*, and—according to reports—had clashed with Shatner and Nimoy over such things as her inexperience as an actress, performance choices (as a stoic Vulcan, she dared shed tears at Spock's funeral!!!) and salary demands that lead to her role being recast for *Star Trek III: The Search for Spock*.

And, interestingly enough, Alley's not the only diva previously referenced in this section who'd crossed paths with Shatner. In the 1967 *Star Trek* episode "The City on the Edge of Forever," Dame Joan Collins shared a passionate kiss with Shatner's Captain Kirk. Despite both Shatner and Collins having singled out this episode as one of their favorites, Collins recalled in a 1994 interview with U.K. talk show host Clive James having observed Shatner in his makeup chair as a "rather short, very white-face man who is follically challenged." *Meow!!*

Then, after Shatner became the oldest human ever to travel to space when bazillionaire *Star Trek* fan Jeff Bezos comped the then-90-year-old's October 2021 flight on board his Blue Origin New Shepard spacecraft, Collins branded Shatner "a fool."

The 60-foot rocket's unmistakable similarity in appearance to a massive dick was no doubt a source of great amusement to those such as Takei who have considered Shatner himself to be one. I, however, am not of that opinion. I have gotten on just fine with Bill during our numerous interviews over the years. And he has always been refreshingly candid and generous with his answers to my personal questions.

The first time I ever remember poking into the star's private life was way back in 1997 when I visited the L.A. Pet Memorial Park in Calabasas, CA,

Beaming aboard the Enterprise with Shatner at a 2008 Long Beach *Star Trek* exhibit.

as part of a *National Enquirer* exposé on this historic cemetery where such legends as Charlie Chaplin, Humphrey Bogart, Steven Spielberg and Diana Ross have fossilized their fur babies. Under the guise of Tori Spelling's personal assistant looking to make burial arrangements for the *Beverly Hills, 90210* star's terminally ill Maltese, I was granted a private tour of the cemetery's hallowed grounds. Among the tour stops that stopped me in my tracks: the eerie showroom of miniature velvet-lined kitty and doggy caskets. A secret storage area where late *The Price Is Right* game-show host Bob Barker had reportedly kept his dead cats cryogenically frozen until the deaths of their four-legged siblings made it possible for the entire feline family to be cremated en masse and buried as one. And then— under the shade of a tree—was the grave marker of Shatner's late Doberman pincher, China, with the inscription "The Beauty Girl."

Jump to 2001, when I was invited by *Entertainment Weekly* to sit in with Bill when he recorded his commentary for the DVD release of *Incubus*, his bizzarro 1966 cult classic in which all dialogue was spoken in the artificially constructed late-1800s language Esperanto. In keeping with the kooky film's out-there plot (about a solider who falls in love with a sexy demon chick), cheeky Bill kept me guessing that whole afternoon if anything he was telling me for my interview was actually true. For instance, did you ever hear (as Shatner claimed) that *Star Trek* was also originally intended to be shot entirely in Esperanto? *Hmmm...???*

Our next meeting was in 2008 when I met Bill in Long Beach, CA, to promote the opening of the traveling exhibition, *Star Trek The Tour,* and our conversation was pretty much limited to how pissed he was that Nimoy—and not he—had been invited to reprise his *Star Trek* character in J.J. Abrams' 2009 feature-film reboot.

And then just a few months before his historic penis-rocket adventure, I produced Shatner's visit to Discovery Channel's *Josh Gates Tonight*, where he again was a total delight, regaling us with tales from his recent shark-diving encounters.

That all being said, I did have my own ever-so-brief skirmish with the man in 2017 when he came on *Home & Family* to promote his new book, *Spirit of the Horse: A Celebration in Fact and Fable*, which chronicles his lifelong love of horses.

The thing with Shatner is you've just got to know how to handle the guy. He'd be the first to admit he can be a bit standoffish with people. While he commands respect, he doesn't particularly appreciate being coddled. And if you dare present yourself as a fan, you'll be instantly relegated to the ranks of the crazed Trekkies who have simultaneously inflated his ego and haunted him for over a half century. It's a delicate dance I believe I've come to master. With his sense of humor remaining razor-sharp even into his nineties, I think Bill generally appreciates whenever I've busted his balls, just as he has mine. Take for instance the time I poked a little fun at that inflated ego by commissioning *H&F's* ingenious editor Michael Hinkley to create a portrait of bare-chested Bill during his studly *T.J. Hooker* era depicted as a mythical centaur posing in a grassy field (a nod to a pleasing dream Shatner once had). As Hinkley now recalls, his digital "painting"—a precursor to today's AI-generated art— was a creative composite that may also have included Hugh Jackman's chest, James Gandolfini's knuckles and Ellen Pompeo's front lawn. Presented to Bill as a surprise gift during his interview segment, his chuckle indicated he greatly appreciated the gesture. And some time later, Mr. Shatner told me the framed portrait was still prominently displayed in his home ... or more accurately, in his home's *garage*.

While that stunt went over better than I could have expected, I fared less well when I asked the Emmy winner what I thought was a rather innocuous question related to *Spirit of the Horse*. For many years, Mr. Shatner has kept horses as personal pets as well as breeding and racing them professionally. Several were referenced by name in his book. So, I thought it perfectly on-point to ask, "How many horses do you actually own, Mr. Shatner?"

Shatner as Centaur, a 2017 depiction presented to the actor on *Home & Family*.

Well, apparently asking rich people how many horses they have is a major faux pas, akin to asking Collins how many facelifts she's had (which is *none,* by the way.)

"William," he prefaced with a deathly serious tone. "Would you ever ask someone how much they make at their job?"

"No," I gulped.

"Well, asking someone how many horses they own is no different."

I certainly didn't see *that* coming and my mind instantly raced to several scenarios to explain his defensiveness. Either:

- William Shatner owned *hundreds* of horses and was breeding them illegally. Perhaps even selling their meat on the black market.

- He actually owned way *fewer* than what he wanted people to believe.

- It was authentically a rude question and I'd stepped in a steaming pile of metaphorical horseshit.

Fortunately, Bill and I were easily able to move past that awkward tête-à-tête and resume our friendly chit-chat. And all's been hunky dory ever since.

By the way, I would only learn the answer to that multiple-choice question in late 2019, when the actor filed documents to legally divorce his fourth wife, Elizabeth, after 18 years of marriage. In the terms of the divorce settlement, he was to be awarded all of their award-winning horses' semen and breeding equipment. (Shatner's very protective of who gets his seed, as well he should!) And to my great surprise, the court docs listed only four horses in his stable—of which he got to keep two: Renaissance Man's Medici and Powder River Shirley. A happy footnote: In 2023, it was reported that the exes had reconciled, keeping all that studly cum under one roof.

My beef with Spock was equally bizarre.

In 2007, when J.J. Abrams' *Star Trek* reboot was about to start rolling with *Heroes* actor Zachary Quinto having just won the coveted role of Mr. Spock, I thought it might be fun to try to have Quinto share some

Interviewing old and new Spocks, Leonard Nimoy and Zachary Quinto, at the Griffith Observatory, 2007. (Lost that lesbian haircut shortly after.)

quality time with his pointy-eared predecessor. I was certain Paramount Studios would squash my plan, but remarkably, within very little time, both parties agreed to meet for a story I'd write for *USA Today*. Mr. Nimoy chose the meeting spot: his Leonard Nimoy Event Horizon Theater at the Griffith Observatory. A perfect spot for the planets to align or, conversely, play host to a supernova of cataclysmic proportions!

Prior to our meeting, Mr. Nimoy asked if we might have a quick phone call. I think he really just wanted to hear my voice to make sure I wasn't some crazy *Star Trek* fan. *Ahem.*

Over the phone, Nimoy basically filled me in that he approved of Quinto's casting, couldn't spill any details about his own role in the film and was very much looking forward to getting to know his Vulcan successor. He also wanted to tell me a little about his theater, which he hoped (insisted) would be part of my story.

It was a very pleasant chat, up until the very end when the whole galaxy very nearly imploded.

I casually asked Mr. Nimoy, "Hey, do you still have the ears?"

"The *what?*" he asked, turning suddenly stern.

"A set of your old Spock ears. I thought it might be fun after you meet Zach to show him how to wear the ears."

Well ... almost like Dr. Jekyll and Mr. Hyde, Nimoy turned extremely dark. Frighteningly so. "Listen, *Keck*," he practically yelled into the phone, reminding me of when Milton Berle similarly admonished me as "William *PECK*." "You pull any of that ear shit and I'm OUT of this. That's *not* what this is about! Got it!!?"

I was terrified. But I for sure got the message. It was as if he'd invited me into his inner circle as a professional contemporary and then felt suddenly betrayed by my fanboy request. A little bit of an overreaction, wouldn't you say? I mean, it was just a set of prosthetic ears—not a prosthetic penis. But something about those ears obviously haunted this man.

Nimoy himself discussed his complex relationship with his iconic character and those defining ears, dating all the way back to 1964 when they were first presented to him on the set of *The Lucy Show* for a makeup screen test. (For those who may not know, my idol Lucille Ball was the one who first bought *Star Trek* creator Gene Roddenberry's "space Western" for her Desilu Productions.) Nimoy remembered Lucy's crew staring at him as if he were some kind of freak, and feared the ears would prevent him from ever being taken seriously as an actor. It certainly didn't help matters when the *Trek* writers added lines to the scripts referring to Spock as "a pointed-eared freak." Interviewers, like me, would routinely ask him to show up wearing the prosthetic auditory appendages. So with all that in mind, I gave old Leonard a pass and tried my best to backpedal to save both my interview and my ass.

"I apologize, Mr. Nimoy," I said sheepishly. "I thought it could be fun, but of course we don't have to do anything like that."

"I don't want any surprises," he said, still in attack mode. "I would not find that fun."

"Absolutely not, sir. No ears. No surprises."

"Good. I'll see you there." And with that, he hung up.

Honestly, I wasn't 100% confident he'd show, half-expecting a phone call from an irate publicist informing me that Mr. Nimoy had a scheduling conflict and would no longer be available.

On the day of the interview, I was on pins and needles not only hoping he'd arrive, but that he'd be pleasant. The Observatory had been closed to the public that day, so it was very, very dark and quiet inside. Spooky, actually. Zach arrived a few minutes early, so I took that time to interview him about *Heroes*, the NBC superhero show he was on at the time. We were met by a representative of the Observatory who asked if we'd like to be escorted into the theater where the interview would take place. I told Zachary to go on ahead while I waited for Mr. Nimoy to arrive.

It seemed like an eternity, but finally a door opened and the legendary actor, then age 76, walked from the darkness into the light. He appeared stern.

"You William Keck?" he asked.

"Yes, sir."

And you're not going to believe what Nimoy said next. Allowing his body to relax, he looked me straight in the eye and asked, "Did you bring the ears?" His kind, big toothy grin let me know he was sorry for the scolding, all was forgotten and he'd now come to play.

We shared a good laugh about the call and ended up having a thoroughly enjoyable afternoon.   Having had my experiences with Shatner and Nimoy—two extremely private, impassioned artists born just four days apart—I'd have to guess cosmic-sized egos may have contributed to the mysterious late-in-life demise of their decades-long friendship just a short time before Nimoy's 2015 passing.   It saddened me greatly when Bill told me he'd placed several calls to Leonard that were never returned, and that he was deeply stung when the Nimoy family opted not to invite him to the funeral.

I have to wonder if either of them had brought up the other's ears or sperm.

Lesson Learned: When someone you're speaking with turns suddenly volatile, don't automatically assume you've said something wrong.   If the reaction seems to defy logic, more often than not it has something to do with their own insecurities and nothing about you.

Chapter 27
NANNY, GET YOUR GUN

(KIM FIELDS & FRAN DRESCHER)

Sitcom stars Kim Fields, 2019 (left) and Fran Drescher, 2018 (right).
(Gage Skidmore/Wikimedia Commons)

WHO: Former child actress Kim Fields (b. May 12, 1969), who played Tootie Ramsey on the 1979–1988 NBC sitcom *The Facts of Life* before graduating to a successful, well-respected career as an NAACP Award-nominated actress, producer and director. And SAG-AFTRA President Fran Drescher (b. September 30, 1957), who played Fran Fine on the 1993–1999 sitcom *The Nanny*.

WHAT: Appearances on Hallmark Channel's *Home & Family*. Recruited by Fields to produce a never-made TV special honoring her life and career.

WHERE: *Home & Family* set, Universal City, CA. Field's L.A. apartment.

Long before I came to Hollywood, during my high school and college years, I worked a series of part-time jobs, as many of us do. I washed dishes at the family-run Villa Italia Ristorante in Slingerlands, NY, alongside the owner's ancient grandmother, Filomena, who'd routinely cut her hands on knives in the soapy dishwater and then hand me plates draped with soaked Band-Aids. (Not to worry; the long gone Villa Italia is now the Gold Coin Chinese restaurant.) I recklessly sliced cold cuts at a neighborhood delicatessen in Delmar, NY, fortunate to have never sliced off a finger. I worked for the Fuller Brush Company as a door-to-door salesman, cold knocking on neighbors' doors and hoping to WOW them with the jaw-dropping cleaning abilities of our revolutionary carpet sweepers. I worked as a customer-service agent at Crossgates Mall during the busy Christmas season, enthusiastically distributing gift certificates … without thinking to charge my customers' credit cards. (And was somehow *still* named Employee of the Month!) And in that same mall, I conducted market-research surveys, offering shoppers up to $20 apiece to follow me into a private room to answer a few questions or participate in taste tests.

One of my more aggressive female respondents ended up giving me my very first BJ after sharing her bread preferences. (Wonder Bread White, as I recall.) I remember her being less than thrilled when I then asked her to sign for the five bucks she'd earned for her time. To this day, I pray we weren't observed by anyone on the other side of the two-way mirror that was occasionally used by visiting clients.

That totally unexpected, teenage dream bonus was way more than I ever received from either Kim Fields or Fran Drescher, a pair of beloved sitcom vets who treated me as if I were their personal assistants.

Fields had already left a disappointing impression on me back in 2011 when I was working for *TV Guide* and invited her to join her castmates from the '80s sitcom *The Facts of Life* in posing for a recreation of their classic *TV Guide* cover shoot from 1982. But when we all gathered in New York City for the shoot, Fields curiously kept her easy-going co-stars waiting while she matter-of-factly "requested" she be gifted a framed portrait of the cast's original cover that I'd brought from my own personal collection as a point of reference for our photographer. (After some persuading, Kim did eventually agree to pose, and even joined the others in autographing my print.)

So I was already a bit on guard five years later when I asked the cast to reunite again in 2016 on *Home & Family* to honor Charlotte Rae, the bubbly actress universally adored for playing the show's affable housekeeper-turned-housemother Edna Garrett, after first introducing the character on *Diff'rent Strokes*. The tribute—celebrating Rae's 90th birthday and the release of her memoir, *The Facts of My Life*—was no easy task to pull off.

Top right: The original 1982 *TV Guide* photo, matted and autographed by cast (author's collection). Above: Recreating that photo in 2011 with *The Facts of Life* cast (from left: **Mindy Cohn, Nancy McKeon,** Charlotte Rae, **Kim Fields, Lisa Whelchel and yours truly**). (Courtesy Victoria Will)

I do have to say Fields was **particularly agreeable** each time I shifted the reunion's shoot date to accommodate the availability of Mindy Cohn (who'd played boarding school student Natalie), only to learn the actress never had any real intention of participating. As I was ultimately informed, Cohn was done making unpaid appearances to promote the *Facts* brand (as was certainly her right). And to the actress' credit, she did meet up with me at the eleventh hour to record a video for us to play for Charlotte claiming, "I so wish I could be with you all today." *Mm-hmm.*

When I broke the news to Charlotte (who'd pass away just two years later) that Mindy had declined our invitation, she was crushed. She told me Mindy had assured her she'd take part and now felt personally betrayed. Oh, well; what are you gonna do? As the catchy *Facts* theme song teaches us: "Ya take the good; ya take the bad." And there was plenty of good to be had, with participation from

Fields, Lisa Whelchel (Blair), Geri Jewell (Cousin Geri) and singer/soap star Gloria Loring (Robin Thicke's mama), joining us to sing the theme song she'd made famous!!

Above: My *Facts of Life* special reunited (from left) Fields, Todd Bridges, Whelchel and Rae, with a surprise greeting from George Clooney (with me below).

To fill the void, I secured additional video greetings from a pair of former cast members who had never before taken part in any *Facts* reunions: movie stars Molly Ringwald (who'd been let go after the first season) and George Clooney (who'd played handyman George for two of the latter

264

seasons). Ever the amiable rascal, George shared a naughty story about Charlotte and a banana that had to be the raciest thing to ever air on Hallmark.

And that wasn't all! I then lined up even more surprises for Charlotte. Nancy McKeon (who played tough girl Jo) Zoomed in from Texas, where she'd committed to attend her daughter's school play. And I secretly flew in Todd Bridges (Rae's only other surviving *Strokes* co-star) from Las Vegas.

All in all, it was a super fun show, with Fields gamely agreeing to take part in a DIY designer roller skates segment as a nod to her "Rollergirl" character Tootie. (Though she did make it crystal clear there was to be no actual on-camera skating.) As I watched all my wonderful surprises unfold perfectly, Fields seemed particularly shell-shocked by Clooney's appearance. As it turned out, she was so impressed that, after the reunion aired, she personally phoned to ask if I'd be at all interested in coming to work for her as a producer. The job offer was to help her develop a splashy, two-hour TV special celebrating ... KIM FIELDS! And naturally, she hoped another Clooney appearance might be part of the deal.

While I had serious doubts that *A Star-Studded Tribute to TV's Tootie* would ever get on the air, I took a couple days to consider Kim's kind invitation before telling her I was in. What did I have to lose? She was thrilled and invited me over to her L.A. apartment to begin hammering out the details.

When I arrived, my new boss was fresh out of the shower and answered the door with a towel wrapped around her head. My first assignment as her "producer" was to look after her adorable two-year-old son, Quincy, while Mommy continued getting ready. It'd just be a few minutes, she assured. Nearly a half hour later— after entertaining Quincy on the floor with toy dinosaurs and race cars—the doorbell rang. I wondered who it could possibly be. Perhaps Kim's date picking her up for dinner and a movie while I continued babysitting?

Kim finally emerged from her bathroom—now fully clothed—and opened her door to two close friends who I learned would *also* be producing her extravaganza. News to me!

Relieving me of my child care duties, Kim then asked if I wouldn't mind running across the street to pick up a couple gourmet pizzas she'd ordered for our production meeting. As I was schlepping the pizzas back to her apartment, it occurred to me that perhaps "producer" wasn't the most accurate description for the job I'd accepted.

Nothing much was accomplished at that meeting. Kim didn't particularly care for my pitch that we shop the show to BET, which had aired reruns of her sitcom, *Living Single*, or OWN, which featured Oprah Winfrey routinely catching up with former headline makers on the series *Where Are They Now?* Rather, Kim wanted her primetime special to air on NBC or Fox.

I left the meeting with zero talk of what she intended to pay me, if anything. Maybe it was a work-for-pizza deal. Anyway, she agreed with my suggestion that the first thing we needed to do was line up a video crew ASAP to get taped interviews from Rae and *Facts'* executive producer Norman Lear, who at the time was also in his nineties and lived to the ripe old age of 101. But before setting up these interviews, I tried my best to get Kim on the phone to discuss her budget for me and my crew. Though she left me a couple messages with her availability, our scheduled appointments conveniently slipped her mind.

Tootie was giving me the runaround as if she were *still* roller skating through the halls of Eastland Academy trying to escape Headmaster Bradley. Finally fed up, I channeled Rae's Mrs. Garrett and notified Kim that if we were to continue working together, we would have to respect each other's time and keep our appointments. I never heard back from her. Toot, toot, Tootie, goodbye!

While I was at least fed a few slices of pepperoni pizza from Fields in exchange for my nanny services, all I got was a verbal spanking from *The Nanny* star Fran Drescher, who also treated me more like her personal assistant than her producer. The controversial SAG-AFTRA president, whose nasally laugh still batters our brains decades after her '90s sitcom signed off, had been booked on *Home & Family* in 2018 to promote the children's animated film *Hotel Transylvania 3: Summer Vacation*. And I was assigned to produce her segment. For the third go-round, Drescher was voicing Eunice, the bouffant-haired Bride-of-Frankensteinish wife of Count Dracula. Since Fran, in each of her previous *H&F* appearances, had always insisted that talk of her Cancer Schmancer charity be worked into her interview segments, I came up with what I thought would be a clever tie-in. This *Transylvania* installment just happened to take place on a cruise ship, and as luck would have it, Fran's upcoming annual Cancer Schmancer Cabaret Cruise fundraiser would also be taking place out on the open waters in just a few months. We could have fun tying the two together! Or so I thought.

You can imagine my surprise during our phone pre-interview when Fran informed me that she had little interest in talking about *Hotel Transylvania*—as in none at all. "I haven't even seen the movie, and I honestly don't really even know what it's about," she said. "I have like three lines and you're only given the script pages that include your dialogue." *Sigh.*

When I received a follow-up call from the movie's publicist to find out how my chat with Fran had gone, I filled him in. The concerned rep then reported all I'd told him (about Fran's reluctance to discuss the film) to his boss, who then communicated this to her boss in New York, who communicated this to Fran's manager, who shared the info with Fran's personal assistant, who then of course spilled all to Fran. And that, friends, is how you piss off a celebrity!!

Word quickly reached me from the movie studio that I should brace myself for a stern talking-to when Fran arrived on set a couple days later to shoot her actual on-camera interview with our hosts. Prepped with this warning, I awaited the arrival of her black sedan with the most welcoming shit-eating grin I could muster.

When Fran stepped out of her car, she immediately addressed our transportation coordinator, Andrew. "Are you William Keck?" she asked. When Andrew told her he was not, she responded, "Okay, then I like you."

Aw, shit. At that point I probably should have just dropped my pants, bent over and took my nanny spanking like a man. Instead, Andrew pointed Fran to her trailer—and the real William Keck. Staring me down without a hint of amusement, Fran snapped, "You and I need to talk.

Fran Drescher giving another of her no-nonsense lectures in 2018. (Gage Skidmore/Wikimedia Commons)

Come with me!" With my head bowed to the pavement, I followed the actress into her trailer and let her rip me a new one.

"*Your* job is to make *me* look good," she scolded, as I suppressed my instincts to ask my new employer for a clear job description of my duties, and perhaps a raise. "Why would you tell the studio I'm working for that I don't want to support their project? I never said that."

Well, she kinda did. But I of course couldn't say that. So instead, I told Fran what she needed to hear: that I felt absolutely horrible, that I'd always been a huge fan and that I considered this whole matter a regrettable failure on my part as her producer.

And that pretty much did the trick. Fran immediately softened and opened her arms. "Okay, come here," she said, offering me a hug. Phew, I was off the hook!

In the spirit of paying it forward, I wrote her out a check for $100 to go toward someone's charity cruise ticket. While I could see she genuinely appreciated my gesture, she has yet to cash it.

By this time in my life and career, I was starting to notice the human beings behind the divas. Besides copping an unnecessary attitude, what was Fran's true crime here? As a grateful cancer survivor, she had pledged to raise as much awareness as possible for her charity to help spare others the pain and fear she'd endured. Slightly more important than promoting a kid's cartoon about monsters on a boat, wouldn't you say? Like her past *H&F* appearances, she got her life-saving message across with the same zeal she expressed in summer 2023 when, as SAG-AFTRA President, she led the charge in her acting community's strike against greedy Hollywood producers. Again, her mission was to improve the lives of others. So you go, Fran!

And as for Kim, was it really so bad getting to spend some playtime with Quincy? He was a sweet kid. And since I don't have any children of my own, it was an opportunity to be reminded of what life was like before Hollywood turned me into a jaded adult. Had my teenage self been told I'd one day get a chance to babysit Tootie's kid, I'd have been over the moon.

Kim and I are the same age, and like me, she'd reached a time in her life when she was looking back at all she'd accomplished and wanted to share her story. I can obviously relate. In my years-long process of writing this very book (about … WILLIAM KECK!), there were probably a few "volunteers" I should have properly compensated for their helpful notes and proofreading catches. A few slices of pizza at the very least!

Heading now into the book's final section, I'll be sharing stories of celebrities dealing with the personal highs (but mostly lows) of dating, marriage, divorce, childbirth, postpartum issues and parenting. All very real, human issues that it was time for me to recognize—and respect—if I truly wished to make a change.

Lesson Learned: If an offer seems too good to be true, it probably is. If they're not paying you, then they aren't your boss. And if they are paying you, is it enough for what's being asked of you? Know your worth, kids!

PART IV:
DOMESTIC DISTURBANCES

"THEY SAY MARRIAGES ARE MADE IN HEAVEN.
BUT SO ARE THUNDER AND LIGHTNING."
— CLINT EASTWOOD

Chapter 28
WEDDING CRASHER

(MEREDITH BAXTER)

Meredith Baxter at a 2014 Human Rights Campaign Gala. (Wikimedia Commons)

WHO: Meredith Baxter (b. June 21, 1947). Television actress best known for her roles on the '70s drama *Family* and for playing mom Elyse Keaton on the 1982–1989 NBC sitcom *Family Ties.*

WHAT: Crashing her wedding reception for the *National Enquirer.*

WHERE: The Hotel Bel-Air, L.A., CA.

At the very start of this book, I shared quite a bit about how my father's sudden passing when I was five led to an unhealthy obsession with death, which probably plays into why, over the years, my attendance at downer all-star funerals far outnumbered my presence at splashy celebrity weddings. Even so, I did still manage to infiltrate the "I dos" of several **boldfaced names** … to varying degrees of success.

There was 65-year-old **Clint Eastwood's** 1996 Las Vegas wedding to his 30-year-old bride (now ex-wife) Dina Ruiz, which turned into a wild-goose chase straight out of the movie *Bridesmaids* involving Dina's posse of 20 raucous gal pals, a suitcase loaded with booze, several belly dancers and a trio of male strippers. (Fortunately, none of the floozies ended up squatting in the middle of The Vegas Strip, Maya Rudolph style.)

ONLY IN THE ENQUIRER

INSIDE CLINT'S SECRET WEDDING

Intimate details of their wild weekend

NATIONAL

LARGEST CIRCULATION OF ANY PAPER IN AMERICA

ENQUIRER

$1.29/$1.59 CANADA   April 16, 1996

I'd brought along Stefanie, one of my very best friends, whose court reporter training made her a natural snoop. It was her enterprising idea to book a hair appointment in the Mirage hotel's salon at the very same time Clint's daughter, Alison, was to get her hair done. Stef's eavesdropping secured some key details, but, in the end, we lost track of Clint, Dina and all her hungover hussies when they loaded into a procession of stretch limos headed for the private gated home of Clint's best man, Sin City billionaire mogul Steve Wynn. Crestfallen after two days of non-stop sleuthing, all Stef and I could do was drive back to the hotel and bribe a maid to let us sniff around Dina's vacated room. But alas, no sign of a pregnancy test or prenup.

Child star Johnny Crawford with his *Rifleman* co-star Chuck Connors, circa 1960. (Wikimedia Commons)

Another time, I was invited to cover the wedding of **Johnny Crawford**, a former kid star from the 1958–1963 TV Western series *The Rifleman*. I'd been told the wedding was Great Gatsby-themed, so I persuaded my heavyset photographer Vincent (the very same put-upon Brit whom I'd asked to capture Lindsay Wagner at her father's funeral, Prince Frédéric von Anhalt's peekaboo Speedo, Phyllis Diller's elderly contest winner and the family of Larry Hagman's liver donor) to join me in wearing 1920s clothing I'd rented for us from a costume shop.

Vincent was less than thrilled with having to dress in costume, and even less so when we arrived at the Pacific Palisades wedding venue only to discover that Johnny and his bride, Charlotte, were the only two dressed in theme. Not even Crawford's best man, *Playboy* titan Hugh Hefner, came in Gatsby duds. Vincent threatened to never work with me again, and I could hardly blame him.

Author in '20s newsboy attire interviewing Crawford's best man, *Playboy* founder Hugh Hefner.

I had a secret source inside the wedding of **the Olsen twins'** father, David, to his former secretary, McKenzie, whom we so kindly dubbed the "blonde mistress." My story talked about how "inseparable" *Full House* twins Mary-Kate and Ashley, then 9, were "tragically ripped apart" like conjoined twins when Ashley opted to skip the church wedding to stay home and console their "shattered," "hysterically" sobbing mother, Jarnie.

Left as the sole maid of honor, "Mary-Kate looked so sad and lonely walking down the aisle all by herself," I quoted my source, who'd managed to snap a photo to illustrate just how heartbreaking this must have been for the guests to witness.

When my editor Jerry insisted I tell our readers what Ashley and her mother

'FULL HOUSE' TWINS TORN APART AS DAD MARRIES MISTRESS

Inseparable "Full House" twins Mary-Kate and Ashley Olsen were tragically ripped apart on the day their daddy married his blonde mistress.

The adorable 9½-year-olds were due to be maids of honor. But a few hours before the wedding their shattered mother Jarnie broke down and sobbed hysterically: "I'm going to be all alone!"

Alarmed Ashley stayed home to comfort her mom — while Mary-Kate went on to the March 10 nuptials between dad David, 43, and his former secretary McKenzie Taylor, 36.

"Mary-Kate looked so sad and lonely walking down the aisle all by herself," said an insider.

"She and Ashley had been practicing their march like little brides for months, and they'd been looking forward to it.

"Their father David was furious at his ex-wife for ruining his wedding. He told me: 'You have no idea how embarrassing it was explaining to all the guests that my little daughter had to stay home and babysit my ex-wife.'

"McKenzie also was angry. She told me: 'David and I spent $400 apiece for the twins' gowns — and now Ashley's will never even be seen!'"

David and McKenzie became romantically involved while she was working at his mortgage company. Jarnie, 41, has been heartbroken since he dumped her for his mistress in the summer of

SAD & LONELY Mary-Kate had to walk down the aisle without her sister Ashley when her dad married his mistress (above).

HAPPIER DAYS: Olsen twins with mom before devastating divorce.

1994, said the insider.

"Many days, Jarnie spends the whole day in bed.

"On the morning of the wedding, Ashley laid out her gown hoping she'd be able to go to the wedding.

"But Jarnie woke up crying that day. And when she poked her head into the girls' bedroom and saw their dresses laid out on the bed, she started sobbing uncontrollably.

"Jarnie cried: 'I'm going to be all alone!'

"So Ashley, who's very protective of her mom, stayed behind while Mary-Kate went off to the wedding at Los Angeles' Westwood Hills Christian Church.

"And while David and McKenzie were exchanging 'I do's' Ashley and Jarnie were in their pajamas watching a video of 'Cinderella' — which, ironically, is about a girl with a wicked stepmother."

— WILLIAM KECK

275

were doing while the wedding was taking place (something we couldn't possibly have known), I finally caved and conveniently quoted a secret "inside source" who told *Enquirer* readers that Ashley and her mom stayed home in pajamas watching a video of *Cinderella*—hissing at the film's wicked stepmother.

I personally attended (and photographed) the 1996 wedding of the Olsen twins' *Full House* co-star, **Candace Cameron**. But, as you can imagine, I never mentioned that to the Christmas Movie Queen when our paths crossed years later when we were both working for the Hallmark Channel. Before I was politely asked to leave Candace's reception, I made sure to group the bride with her *Full House* co-stars Dave Coulier, John Stamos, Lori Loughlin, Bob Saget, Jodie Sweetin, Scott Weinger and Andrea Barber for a reunion photo that ran in that week's *Enquirer*. (You know how much I wanted to jump into *that* shot!!)

Above: The author interrogating Candace Cameron's bridesmaids just before her 1996 wedding, which was covered in the *Enquirer* (below).

THE GANG'S ALL HERE: Candace Cameron and new hubby Valeri Bure celebrate their marriage with the "Full House" cast.

IT'S A FULL HOUSE AS TV CUTIE SAYS 'I DO'

By **WILLIAM KECK**

RADIANT Candace and Valeri are all smiles as they cut their wedding cake.

It was a "Full House" of stars when series cutie Candace Cameron tied the knot with her hockey player beau.

Candace's TV dad and Bob Saget headed the list of sitcom co-stars on hand as the 20-year-old beauty walked down the aisle on June 22 — her parents' 27th wedding anniversary.

"I feel so doubly blessed to have both my families — the Camerons and the 'Full House' gang — with me on my wedding day!" Candace beamed to The ENQUIRER.

And her new hubby, Russian-born Valeri Bure, 22, got the surprise of his life when his father flew in from Moscow unexpectedly just in time to join his mom, brother and grandmother for the big day.

Candace and Valeri met at a hockey rink two years ago and the Montreal Canadiens star proposed marriage last year on a street in Paris at midnight.

"I told him, 'Yes, Val — there's nothing thing old, new, borrowed and blue," her mom Barbara disclosed.

"What's old is her grandmother's Bible that every Cameron bride has carried at their weddings. Her pearl-embroidered wedding dress is new. Candace borrowed her aunt's pearl

But the most fun I ever had at a TV's star's wedding was in 1995 when *Family Ties* mom Meredith Baxter married *Turner & Hooch* and *Rent-a-Cop* screenwriter Michael Blodgett.

With the reunited cast of *Family Ties* at the 2011 TV Land Awards. (Courtesy Victoria Will) Clockwise from upper left: Justine Bateman, Meredith Baxter, Michael Gross, author, Tina Yothers and Michael J. Fox: a recreation of the cast's 1985 *TV Guide* cover portrait (author's collection, below).

I'd actually skipped Meredith and Michael's Westwood Presbyterian Church wedding, choosing instead to crash their elegant reception that was to be held at the Hotel Bel-Air, a posh slice of heaven known for its regal swans and lush, mysterious gardens. My date for this afternoon soirée was Kimberly Curry, a sassy Southern flight attendant I'd met while serving jury duty. (Incidentally, the case we were called to hear involved an armed robbery allegedly committed by an East L.A. gang member who went by the name "7-Up," perpetrated against his "Play Mama." The case proved very educational for both me and Kimberly, a righteous churchgoer and staunch feminist who would go on to pursue a career in law.)

Because of Kimberly's high moral compass, I opted not to tell her whose reception we were attending until we were pulling up to the valet. To say she was displeased would be an understatement.

"Hold on," said Kimberly, placing her palms on my car's dashboard. "Were you actually *invited* to this wedding?"

"Not exactly," I said.

"Well don't expect me to lie," she clarified in no uncertain terms. "You can say whatever you need to, but I'm not going to be part of this charade."

"Don't worry," I assured Kimberly. "I'll do all the talking. Just follow my lead."

To blend in with the roughly 100 other guests, I brought along a wedding gift—a $10 Target picture frame wrapped in fancy paper that cost more than the present inside. (Both items were written off on my weekly expense report.)

As we crossed over a bridge leading to a garden courtyard where guests were sampling fancy appetizers until the banquet doors were opened, I noticed a pair of security guards posted at the entrance. Not to worry, I told Kimberly, taking her hand and offering the guards a friendly smile and nod as we walked right past them.

The only issue we encountered was locating a table with two available seats, a problem we solved by just milling about sipping champagne by the check-in table until it became obvious that two place cards were likely going to be unclaimed. So just before the bride and groom made their grand entrance, we snatched up those place cards and took "our" seats.

"See," I told Kimberly. "Nothing to worry about."

Well, *nearly*. To Kimberly's horror, the plain-clothed gentleman seated to her immediate right introduced himself as the priest who'd just performed the ceremony. I mean what are the odds, right??!!

"How do you know Meredith and Michael?" asked the handsome padre. *Gulp!* Kimberly pivoted her head toward me, curious herself to hear the answer.

"We're guests of Michael through his teaching," I said, always trying to keep my fabrications short and sweet. Like any proper spy, I'd done some prep work and read somewhere that Michael taught writing classes when not selling scripts about crime-solving dogs. The priest bought my story, but Kimberly, I could tell, was reaching her limit.

It was super easy gathering details about the wedding ceremony we'd missed, simply by asking the reception guests, "So, what was your favorite part of the ceremony?"

"Oh," one would say, "it had to be when the boys walked their mother down the aisle."

When the question was turned on us, I'd just smile and say, "the vows." Again, short and sweet.

Fortunately, the salads arrived just in time to press pause on the chit-chat. I assured Kimberly we could leave just as soon as I snapped a photo of the cake cutting. Then, just as I was beginning to relax and enjoy my prime rib and scalloped potatoes, I received a sharp nudge in the side from Kimberly. Across the room, Meredith and Michael had put down their forks and were now making the rounds from table to table, warmly greeting each of their invited guests.

Zoinks!

With the newlyweds closing in, Kimberly and I excused ourselves for a trip to the restrooms, making sure not to return until Mer and Mike had moved on.

"Never again," Kimberly whispered sternly in my ear as we sat down to finish our dinners. "You lied ... to a priest."

"I'm sorry," I told Kimberly. "But you have to admit it's all kind of funny." (It would take another 10 years or so for her to fully appreciate the humor.)

Fortunately, Kimberly and the priest hit it off smashingly, talking about everything from theology to world travel, allowing me all the time I needed to secure myself a prime spot for the cutting of the cake and get my perfect shot!

My photograph of Meredith slicing through the frosting, flanked by her groom and two children, made it into the *Enquirer*, which no doubt left the bride scratching her head as to which of her guests (presumably Tina Yothers) had sold the shot for a fast buck.

In my magical unicorn mind, I imagined Meredith carefully cutting my article out of the *Enquirer* and displaying it proudly in the picture frame she'd received from a mystery guest who'd neglected to sign the card.

What I didn't know then was that Meredith and I had a little secret in common: We were both living lives in the closet. This was her *third* wedding to a man with a last name beginning with the letter B (first Bush, then Birney and Blodgett) before marrying wife Nancy Locke in 2013 at age 66. Yep, Bush is where the bride started, and where she'd end up finding lasting love.

ALL IN THE FAMILY: Meredith's daughter Mollie (blue dress) and son Peter were close by when the newlyweds cut their wedding cake.

The *National Enquirer* photo I snapped as a "guest" at Meredith Baxter's 1995 wedding.

I applaud Meredith for her brave later in life decision, remembering all too well the anxiety and exhaustion I experienced while living a life in the closet just to gain approval from others. Before I ended up mimicking my father's great charade by taking a bride of my own, I knew it would soon be time to come clean. Both to myself and to everyone in my life. But I also knew that if I wanted to find true happiness—and, ideally, authentic family ties of my own—some cleaning up had to be done in my professional life. No longer would I be able to make a living by telling lies and exposing the private struggles of celebrities.

Lesson Learned: It's way more fun crashing weddings than funerals, which is probably why there's never been a movie called The Funeral Crashers.

Chapter 29
PRAIRIE BRIDE

(MELISSA GILBERT)

WHO: Melissa Gilbert (b. May 8, 1964). Emmy and Golden Globe-nominated star of the 1974–1983 TV family drama *Little House on the Prairie* and *The Miracle Worker.* Recipient of a Hollywood Walk of Fame star. President of the Screen Actors Guild (2001–2005).

WHAT: Crashing Gilbert's wedding for the *National Enquirer* and harassing her at home. On-the-record sit-down profile interview for *Us Weekly.* Teaming up for a Hallmark Channel *Little House* reunion special.

WHERE: The private homes of **Melissa Gilbert** and her parents.

Another wedding. How we react to receiving invitations to our friends' and family members' nuptials depends entirely upon our relationships with the bride and groom; doesn't it? "Yay—isn't it just swell Todd and Lori are finally taking the plunge?" vs. "Crap—we have to buy another damn espresso maker."

One of the weddings I'll never forget attending was my college "girlfriend" Julie's nuptials to her now ex-husband Stuart. I was still bitter from Julie having dumped me at our Valentine's Day dance for her handsome karate instructor with a killer Cobra Kai body. (In hindsight, I can hardly blame Jules, as I never made even the slightest move on her ... for obvious reasons.) To drown my sorrows, I'd consumed so much vodka punch at that school dance, held in Julie's dormitory, that I vomited my guts out in the girls' showers. As I was told, the housekeeping staff was so disgusted by the mess I'd caused that they flatly refused to clean it up. For the remainder of the school year, the girls referred to throwing up as "kecking." Regrettably, one actual definition of my last name is "to retch or heave, as if about to vomit," though I far prefer its Germanic definition: "a brash, perky, cheekily self-confident young man." Regardless, before Julie and Stuart's wedding, we all placed bets in the synagogue parking lot as to how long the marriage would last, which wasn't long. But I'm happy to report Julie and I are still chums.

Truth be told, I never should have been at that wedding in the first place. But I was never one to allow the absence of an invitation deter my attendance.

By any chance have you ever seen the heart-wrenching final scene of the 1937 Barbara Stanwyck tearjerker *Stella Dallas* (remade as simply *Stella* in 1990 with Bette Midler)? The film concludes with poor working gal Stella gazing longingly through a window on a cold, rainy night as her estranged daughter marries a wealthy society man. Well, try picturing me as pathetic Stella when I celebrated New Year's Day 1995 by standing in the chilling cold spying through a window as beloved *Little House on the Prairie* star Melissa Gilbert became Mrs. Bruce (*Babylon 5*) Boxleitner.

But just a few months prior, it seemed as though I might actually score a legit invitation to the nuptials. The *Enquirer* had sent me to Gilbert's home to extend our congratulations on being newly engaged to Boxleitner, a handsome actor I first discovered on the lighthearted '80s spy series *Scarecrow and Mrs. King*.

"Doorstepping," as it's called in the tabloid world, is rarely pleasant. It was hard enough knocking on strangers' doors when I worked as a door-to-door carpet-sweeper salesman that one summer during college. But when you know the person on the other side of the door is a celebrity you're about to antagonize with some personally invasive question, you want to run the other way. Many of my fellow reporters adamantly refused to doorstep. "Just drive around for a while and say there was no one home," I remember Julia Coates, one of my senior colleagues, telling me. But I usually chose to just suck it up and knock, with dramatically differing results.

Whereas one celebrity might ... oh, I don't know, put me in a headlock and beat the crap out of me (more about that later!), at the other end of the spectrum was lovely *Home Improvement* TV mom Patricia Richardson. Taking a break from raking leaves on the front lawn of her Santa Monica home, Pat kindly offered me a glass of lemonade when I showed up out of the blue one summer day in 1995 to ask why she was divorcing her husband. How thoughtful of me, right? I ended up consoling Pat as she cried in front of me, expressing concern for her young children. Before I left, she even introduced me to her soon-to-be ex-husband Ray, who'd stopped by to visit the kids.

Little House on the Prairie's Melissa Gilbert. (NBC, circa 1975)

Now, with Melissa Gilbert, I figured it could go either way. I'd grown up adoring her as little Laura Ingalls (honestly, who hadn't?), but I'd also caught her on a 1992 episode of *The Tonight Show*, presenting herself as a mature, confident, sophisticated woman. Plugging her new sitcom, *Stand by Your Man* (pulled after just seven airings) Gilbert told Jay Leno it was airing on "Fox, Fox, Fox, Fox, Fox," which, as Leno noted, sounded more like "Fuck, Fuck, Fuck, Fuck, Fuck." Might I end up being the recipient of one of Gilbert's F-bombs? At least, I reassured myself, I had come doorstepping this time to discuss *happy* news.

To my delight, Melissa, like Pat, could not have been more welcoming. She invited me into her living room, showed off her gorgeous engagement ring and seemed tickled to spill all the personal details of Bruce's romantic proposal. She'd broken things off earlier that February, fearing he couldn't commit. But they'd quickly reconciled by Valentine's Day. To profess his love, he'd presented her with "Valentino," a pet cockatoo (not to be confused with the previously discussed cocka*tiel* belonging to Kelsey Grammer's former fiancée). And after a couple months, he proposed, telling her, "I can't live without you."

The wedding, Gilbert hinted coquettishly, would be "soon."

Well, when you tell your *Enquirer* editor that you received a warm reception from a certain celebrity, they figure it's perfectly acceptable to continue badgering that celebrity until he or she sends you either an engraved wedding invitation or a restraining order. I was asked to be persistent, so that's just what I did. Until, not surprisingly, Melissa grew increasingly annoyed and told me to stop calling. I don't blame her one bit. The very same thing happened with a couple of my exes. You just gotta know when to back the Fuck, Fuck, Fuck, Fuck, Fuck off, right?

Through the *Enquirer's* own means, we managed to find out where and when the wedding

Above: On the *Home & Family* set with Melissa Gilbert, 2015. Below: With Bruce Boxleitner at a Disney TRON event, 2022.

would be held: the evening of New Year's Day at the Encino home of Gilbert's mother, Barbara. That meant sayonara to my plans to accompany my friends on a long weekend holiday road trip. Instead, I'd be spending the first night of 1995 camped out on a long private driveway trying to identify arriving wedding guests. And that night, more than one tried handing me their car keys, understandably confusing me for a valet. (And don't think I didn't consider taking off in one of those swanky BMWs or Jags.)

Despite my hopes of seeing a covered wagon pull up transporting the entire surviving cast of *Little House on the Prairie*, Melissa had filled me in earlier that she and Bruce had jointly made the smart decision to not invite friends from any of their various shows, simply to avoid an 800-person guest list comprising the casts and crew of *Little House*, her new show *Sweet Justice* and his many series: *Babylon 5, How the West Was Won* and *Scarecrow and Mrs. King*. As Melissa explained to me, "It would have ended up being a media circus held on a Sony soundstage."

The highlight of my miserable evening had to be when Melissa's stepfather marched out to tell me and my photographer to stay off his well-manicured lawn or he'd call the police.

My hours of Stella Dallas window snooping yielded few specifics. Younger sister Sara Gilbert (of *Roseanne* and *The Talk*) had fulfilled her maid-of-honor duties beautifully, while violinists played songs from *West Side Story*. *"Tonight, tonight..."* The only other detail I managed to spot was a fleeting glimpse of what I thought was Melissa's white veil passing by the glow of candles. (Confession: I briefly contemplated taking a very *Enquirer* angle in my reporting by speculating that the haunting glow may, in fact, have been the ghost of Melissa's late *Prairie* Pa, Michael Landon, who had come to give away the bride. But remembering how my Mr. Brady ghost-story debacle had played out, I wisely reconsidered.)

As had happened so many times by now, the sweet, romantic story I turned in to my editors was rewritten by the dinosaurs in our Lantana, FL, bureau who took an unnecessarily sensationalized slant. "*Little House* Star Melissa Gilbert Weds After Warning: Marry Me or Else!" read the headline.

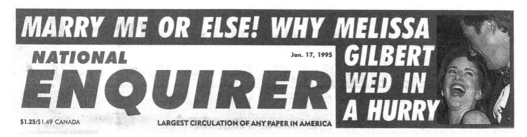

Remarkably, my relationship with Melissa improved over the following year. That is, until she named me in a lawsuit she filed against the *Enquirer* claiming I'd played a part in her nearly losing her newborn child. (Your Honor, I swear on my life I had absolutely nothing to do with these preposterous accusations. And really, I didn't!)

The horrible misunderstanding all started with me—the *Enquirer's* well-intentioned Pollyanna—writing an innocuous Mother's Day article praising Melissa, then pregnant with Bruce's son, as one of the "Best Moms" in all of Hollywood, inspired by the family values she'd learned from Landon during her *Little House* years. Not surprisingly, Melissa was 100% on board for the complimentary article, offering me details about how she made time in her busy career to put her six-year-old son Dakota first.

Well, apparently Dakota's then-out-of-work actor dad, Bo Brinkman—unhappy with his divorce settlement from Melissa—had read my Mother's Day piece and decided to come forward to another *Enquirer* reporter with his own version, painting his ex-wife as anything but Mom of the Year. Specifically, he called her a "Deadbeat Mom"!!

'Little House' star: I'm a better mom thanks to *Michael Landon*

"Little House on the Prairie" star Melissa Gilbert reveals that lessons she learned from her TV dad Michael Landon help her to be a better mom.

"Michael stood for positive family values," the 31-year-old actress told The ENQUIRER.

"I've tried to apply Michael's teachings in my own home.

"He loved children and it's no coincidence that his most remembered roles — as Little Joe on 'Bonanza'

and Charles Ingalls on 'Little House' — took place when folks relied on their families for survival as well as love."

Melissa played Landon's daughter Laura Ingalls on "Little House" and America watched her grow up on the hit series.

The actress, who stars in the series "Sweet Justice," is married to

actor Bruce Boxleitner and they are expecting their first child together. Melissa is also raising a son, Dakota, 6, from a previous marriage and is stepmom to Bruce's sons Sam, 14, and Lee, 9.

"The secret to being a successful mom is to shower your kids with unconditional love and support them in the paths they choose to follow," said the actress.

"The most important thing in my life is my family."

TV DAD Michael Landon was role model for Melissa Gilbert.

Melissa was naturally livid and somehow got into her head that I had concocted my Best Mom article solely to set her up as Brinkman's target. While that was complete bullshit, Melissa received major sympathy in the media when she claimed her ex's hatchet job had upset her so much that she'd gone into premature labor. Her baby boy, whom she'd named Michael after Landon, had been born with undeveloped lungs and was fighting for life in a hospital. Even though I wasn't to blame, I obviously felt awful about the whole situation and prayed for the infant's health. (To this day, I remain traumatized by the brutal *Little House* episodes that featured dead babies.)

I desperately wanted to get word to Melissa that she was totally wrong about my involvement, but the *Enquirer* lawyers forbade me from reaching out. I was never called to testify, and by the time the lawsuit settled, I had quit the tabloid to seek freelance writing assignments from more respectable entertainment publications ... including *Us Weekly*. And here's the kicker on that one: One of the first articles I was assigned by *Us* was a feature profile on ... you guessed it, Melissa Gilbert!

I mean you can't make this shit up, unless of course you're writing for the *Enquirer*.

I thought about turning down the assignment, but I was desperately trying to overcome my *Enquirer* past and really needed the cash. Well, you should have seen the look on Melissa's face when she saw me stand up to greet her at our agreed-upon meeting spot.

"You???" she said, aghast. "You've got to be kidding."

It says a lot about Half Pint (her *Little House* nickname) that she not only stuck around for the interview, but trusted me with very personal details about her past relationships with Rob Lowe, Dylan McDermott and Tom Cruise. (Damn, girl, look at you!!!) And she had me laughing when she referred to herself and Bruce as "two old, horrible Hollywood sluts" who had fun watching TV and exchanging stories of all the stars they'd slept with.

But Melissa also alluded to problems in her new marriage, primarily Boxleitner resisting her dream to adopt a baby daughter. Her quote: "There are times when I honestly want to say, 'OK, I'm done.' " She did admit she would be shattered if the marriage didn't work out, and the two managed to give it another 10 years before ultimately calling it quits. Not a bad run, I'd say. Particularly by Hollywood standards.

I risked torpedoing our friendly chat by daring to bring up that whole nasty "deadbeat mom" *Enquirer* saga, but once again Gilbert's marvelous sense of humor kept things light. With baby Michael having grown into a healthy boy, she was now able to poke fun at the *Enquirer*'s cruel label, joking that the tabloid no doubt would have had a field day had they witnessed her family's recent visit to her star on the Hollywood Walk of Fame. Melissa's mom had made her grandsons get down on their hands and knees with rags and a bottle of Windex, inspiring Melissa to dream up what would have been the perfect *Enquirer* headline: "Deadbeat Mom Forces Children to Clean Star."

Now that's what I call one helluva great sport! And my friendship with Melissa has remained intact, so much so that in 2015, Melissa called me up, agreeing to reunite with her *Little House* co-stars for a splashy reunion show I produced for Hallmark Channel. The two-hour special turned out to be great fun for everyone. I even got her to climb up into a covered wagon with her Ingalls family siblings—exactly as I'd imagined the cast arriving to Melissa's wedding so many years earlier!

Lesson Learned: It's never too late for old enemies to become new friends, particularly when both have a healthy sense of humor. Oh, and it's much, much safer crashing funerals, where you're treated to the same beautiful flowers, moving music and inspirational readings … but with a very slim chance of getting tossed out by the guest of honor!

Reuniting the *Little House* cast in 2015 for *Home & Family*. From left: Lindsay Greenbush, the late Hersha Parady, Melissa Gilbert, Dean Butler, Charlotte Stewart, me, Michael Landon Jr., Leslie Landon and Matthew Labyorteaux.

A WORD FROM MELISSA GILBERT

What can I say; there's just something about Will that makes one feel safe. Maybe it's his guileless sweetness … yes, I know … a guileless and sweet reporter for the *National Enquirer*—a piece of shit tabloid whom I sued for causing one of the most painful times in my life?!!!

Here's the thing; Will OWNS it. He owns it all! What's more, he is brave enough to apologize when an apology is warranted. I cannot fault any human who is willing to atone. In fact, I find it an incredibly courageous and inspiring thing to do.

Here's the other thing I just love about Will: He's a fan first and foremost. A fan of the highest order. As I read this book I could feel the true love he has for every show, every character, every actor or creative he has come in contact with. That love is palpable and overcomes any missteps or mistakes made in the process of expressing that love.

I also have to admit, as a fan of film and television myself, I found this book to be a big, juicy morsel. So read on my friends, and enjoy the rest of these stories from the great adventure that is the life of my friend Will Keck.

P.S. Will, I promise you'll get an invite to the next wedding … it'll be in my next lifetime, but I'll find you.

ANOTHER *LITTLE HOUSE* "BEST MOM" DEBACLE:
KAREN GRASSLE

Bizarrely enough, that ugly Melissa Gilbert misunderstanding was the *second* time one of my *Enquirer* "Best Mom" stories pissed off a *Little House* actress. Karen Grassle, who played Gilbert's Ma, Caroline Ingalls, agreed to come on the phone with me from her home in Louisville, KY, to take part in a two-page roundup spread I was writing timed to Mother's Day, offering updates on several beloved TV Moms that also included *The Jeffersons'* Isabel Sanford and *The Munsters'* Yvonne De Carlo. Our interview started off great, but quickly went south when I threw out what I thought was a softball question:

"What would you say you learned from Michael Landon about family values?"

"Family values?" Grassle repeated back to me. "What did *I* learn from Michael about *family values*?"

And with that, Grassle—clearly forgetting what outlet she was speaking with—launched into a bitter tirade about Landon, who had passed only a couple years prior, thus sealing his legacy as the most beloved TV dad of all time.

"You're asking me what *I* learned from a man who left his wife and kids for a much younger woman...," Grassle continued, throwing fuel on the fire. She went on to talk about how Landon was a hard drinker who allowed alcohol on the set and, as the show's executive producer, had fostered a "boy's club" mentality.

Uh oh. For all the cow pies on the prairie, I never could have seen this coming. It was as if Grassle had been holding in all this aggression and was finally being given an opportunity to let Landon have it. Then I asked, innocently again, if it had been disappointing for her to have to leave the series when Landon decided to relocate their characters, Charles and Caroline Ingalls, to another city.

KAREN GRASSLE

Karen Grassle ("Little House on the Prairie" 1974-1982) is a feminist who says of her TV husband (right), "There was no place for women on Michael Landon's Prairie." That's why she eventually quit. "I found it increasingly difficult to pour coffee for the men while they solved the town's problems. I felt like the highest-paid babysitter in the world." Karen went on to stage and movie roles including "Wyatt Earp" with Kevin Costner. A divorcee, she lives with her 11-year-old daughter Lily in Louisville, Ky. "I live just 10 minutes from the Actor's Theater of Louisville, where I'm offered challenging roles," Karen told The ENQUIRER. "And I've started dating!"

"*I'm* the one who made the decision to leave," the actress schooled me in no uncertain terms. "There was no place for women on Michael Landon's prairie. I found it increasingly difficult to pour coffee for the men while they solved the town's problems. I felt like the highest-paid babysitter in the world. A woman can only sit in a church pew cradling a baby in her arms and singing 'Bringing in the Sheaves' for so long."

So, after years of pouring coffee for husband Charles in their little house, fed-up Grassle had gone to Landon demanding her character get a job. And what job did Landon come up with for poor Ma? Pouring coffee in the town's restaurant!

So Grassle quit, and rather than kill off Ma, she told me Landon made the call to have both Ma and Pa move out of Walnut Grove (and off the show) together.

When I finally hung up the phone, I felt heartsick. My easy-breezy TV Moms round-up piece had just been soiled by a prairie woman scorned! Grassle had literally handed me the kind of story the *Enquirer* loves, and—blame me if you must—I chose to run with it.

But, as so often happens, Grassle's quotes came back to haunt her once she saw them in print. I still have the letter Karen sent to "thank" me for my article along with her promise that she'd never again repeat her mistake of trusting the *Enquirer*. I have to admit, that stung.

Flash forward to 2021 when Grassle released her own tell-all memoir, *Bright Lights, Prairie Dust,* in which she double downed on everything negative she'd told me about Landon, along with far more shocking on-set sexual harassment allegations. So, in hindsight, perhaps Ma was just pissed that I'd scooped her—25 years before she was ready to tell the very same stories in a book of her own.

Chapter 30
AN INCONVENIENT TRUTH

(DREW BARRYMORE)

WHO: Drew Barrymore (b. February 22, 1975). Golden Globe-winning actress and Emmy-nominated daytime talk show host.

WHAT: A bizarre movie date. Production assistant duties. On-the-record sit-down interview (along with Cameron Diaz and Lucy Liu) for *USA Today*.

WHERE: Various locations.

Back in 2006, I had a follow-up nose job to the one I'd had performed by Victoria Principal's plastic surgeon husband a few years prior.

Drew Barrymore circa 2007.
(David Shankbone/ Wikimedia Commons)

(And I promise, that's it! *No more.* I've promised my partner that I'm stopping before the man in the mirror looks like Michael Jackson!)

All these years later, I still cringe when I think back on that incredibly uncomfortable post-op procedure of having tampon-like cotton packing slowly extracted from my raw, stitched-up nostrils.

Hiding out at home in front of the TV with only my dog at my side, nothing in a million years could have persuaded me to break from my self-imposed exile as I waited for the massive swelling to go down. But then one day my phone rang. It was my friend John calling to see if I wanted to go the movies.

"Sorry," I told John. "I'm not ready to be seen in public."

"Oh c'mon, Will, you should come," he pressed. "It'll be good for you to get out."

"Thanks, but I'm not going anywhere for another week or so. Have fun, buddy."

"But I *need* you to go," he finally said, revealing an ulterior motive that was not uncommon for John.

"Oh yeah?" I asked. "Why's that?"

"It's sort of ... a double date."

"John!" I snapped. "You seriously think I'm going to go out on a *date* looking like this?!!"

"It'll be fun," he insisted. "It's my date Chris' roommate. You'll love her."

Her??? Had tampons also been shoved up my ears? John was as gay as I was, so I figured I must have heard him wrong.

"Just come," he said, clearly keeping some vital bit of intel from me. "You'll be happy you did."

"John, there's no way I'd set foot out of this house for the hottest guy on Earth, so you can just forget about me joining you on a double date with a *girl*!"

Then finally, he fessed up. "Okay, your date's Drew Barrymore."

"What time's the movie?" I asked.

Even a big, swollen schnoz couldn't keep me from a once-in-a-lifetime opportunity to go to the movies with Gertie from *E.T.*

So, off my swollen self went to join John, his new boyfriend Chris and Drew Barrymore to see the Al Gore documentary *An Inconvenient Truth*. When I arrived at the Arclight Cinemas in Hollywood, the trio were already in the courtyard waiting for me. Since I was extremely self-conscious about the nose thing, I decided to just acknowledge it right away.

While the boys said I looked just fine (LIES!!), Drew simply said, "Arnica."

"Huh?" I asked.

"Arnica. A homeopathic. Great for swelling after surgery," she said, giving me a wink to let me know she'd apparently been in a similar position herself.

"Ah..., okay. Thanks, Drew. I'll be sure to get some."

Once Vice President Gore's documentary about saving the planet began, John reached over to take Chris' hand. My date, however, had curled up into a ball and quickly fallen asleep. From my recollection, she must have been out for at least half the movie. But as soon as the credits started rolling and the theater lights came on, Drew opened her eyes like Snow White and told us how the film had completely transformed her view of the world. Starting first thing Monday morning there were going to be some serious changes at her Flower Films production office, starting with no more Styrofoam cups!

"We all have to do our part," she said, offering the same earnestness she's displayed as champion to numerous causes over the years.

With the bizarro movie date over, I was more than ready to grab some Arnica and a handful of E.T.'s Reese's Pieces and retreat back under the sheets with my dog. As for Chris, while his relationship with John soon fizzled, he and Drew remained friends for life, with Chris executive producing her popular afternoon talk show before moving on to helm Jimmy Fallon's *Tonight Show*.

That was actually not my first time meeting Ms. Barrymore, nor would it be the last. I made what I thought was the wise decision to not remind Drew of our earlier encounter back in the '90s when she was still a teenager emerging from a troubled childhood.

In 1992, I was working as a production assistant on a new Aaron Spelling primetime soap called *2000 Malibu Road*, a very expensive series about three women living together in a breathtaking beach house (that was primarily shot—like my *Dynasty* production office space—in yet another cheap-ass Spelling soundstage rental in Culver City).

Drew had been cast as one of the show's three stars (along with *Flashdance's* Jennifer Beals and Lisa Hartman of *Knots Landing*). One of my (near daily) tasks was to drive across town to the Beverly Center mall to fetch Drew her favorite pizza from California Pizza Kitchen. While Beals, Hartman and the rest of the cast and crew were just fine with whatever the caterer prepared each day, young Miss Barrymore—just 17 at the time—routinely craved CPK's BBQ Chicken pizza. (And if you've ever had one, you can probably sympathize with Drew's addiction.)

During the show's production, there was one very stressful weekend when I was trying to reach Drew, back in that prehistoric era without cell phones or the internet. Some last-minute script changes had come out for scenes shooting Monday, and my job was to deliver the revised salmon-colored script pages to her home. I then had to get confirmation from Drew herself that she'd received them.

Looking back, all I needed to do was leave one pleasant, concise message on her answering machine and I'd have done my job. But because I was anxious to get out of my apartment to join my friends for a day of rollercoastering at the Magic Mountain theme park, I left Drew at least three—each increasingly irritating than the one before.

Beeeep. "Hey Drew, it's Will Keck from *Malibu Road.* Hope you're having a great weekend. Just making sure you got those new pages. Call me back when you can. Bye."

Beeeep. "Hey Drew. Will again. You're probably out with your friends. Not sure if you got my earlier message about the salmon-colored script pages I left at your door. Can you please just let me know you got 'em? Thanks."

Beeeep. "Hi Drew. It's Will from the production office. The one who gets your pizzas every day. (Awkward giggle.) I hate to bother you again, but I have to make sure you got your new lines for Monday. I left them in a manila envelope on your front doorstep, if you could just confirm they were there. Thank you."

I can only imagine her playing back these messages, thinking I was a stalker like the deranged man who'd be arrested for harassing her in August 2023. How epically annoying, right?! And I don't blame her one bit for the passive-aggressive (but mostly aggressive) return message she finally did leave on my machine:

"Hey Will. It's Drew. I got your *50* fucking messages and I'm going to fucking kill you. (Little giggle.) Just kidding. I got the pages. See you Monday."

Fortunately, when we ran into each other back on set, the little *Firestarter* didn't use her pyrokinetic powers to turn me into charbroiled hamburger meat.

While *2000 Malibu Road* premiered as the most-watched show of the summer, the ratings then started eroding faster than a sandcastle at high tide. And after just six airings, Mr. Spelling pulled the plug. It would be eight years before Drew reentered my life, and Mr. Spelling was again involved, though tangentially.

Drew had secured the rights to produce and star in a big-screen remake of one of my favorite '70s TV shows, *Charlie's Angels,* which had been an Aaron Spelling Production. At the time, I was covering all the premiere red carpets for *Entertainment Weekly*—on the constant lookout for showbiz scoop. Because of my obsessive excitement over this top-

Interviewing a less-than-thrilled Lucy Liu.

secret project, I made sure I showed up at every Hollywood event where Drew was expected so I could be the first to report what she and her director pal McG had planned for her and Drew's fellow angels, Cameron Diaz and Lucy Liu.

Who'd be voicing Charlie...? Would any of the original angels turn up in cameos...? Many scoops were successfully broken by yours truly.

Then, three years later when the angelic trio reunited for its sequel, *Charlie's Angels: Full Throttle*, I was granted a sit-down interview with Barrymore, Diaz and Liu for a big *USA Today* cover story.

I still cringe when I recall how unnecessarily aggressive I was in that interview. The thing is, I was up for a staff position at *USA Today* to take over as their West Coast celebrity reporter—a primo gig that would allow me access to all of Hollywood's major events and celebs. And I wanted that job bad!! So, in an effort to wow the newspaper's editors, I pushed all politeness aside and dug extra hard to land provocative quotes for my article. While I ultimately did end up being offered the staff position, my *Full Throttle* feature very well could have cost me my angel wings.

Our interview took place in a Santa Monica oceanfront hotel suite with all three angels tightly squeezed together into one loveseat as if they were conjoined triplets gestating in a supermodel's womb. I sat across from them and asked about Barrymore's recent divorce from actor Tom Green, who'd appeared in the first film but was now absent. Liu protectively stepped in to deflect the question, allowing me to then ask what has to be the most intrusive—and if I'm going to be totally honest—downright RUDE question I've perhaps ever posed in a celebrity interview. It was a question about a subject matter most of us have been schooled by our parents to *never* ask anyone: salaries.

These days, talk of celebrity paydays (primarily as they relate to an unfair disparity between male and female actors) has become less shocking, but at the time it was a topic that was just not broached.

Barrymore, Diaz and Liu on a *Charlie's Angels: Full Throttle* promotional poster. (Columbia Pictures/Sony Pictures Releasing)

For taking part in the movie, it had been reported in the entertainment trade papers that Diaz was earning a whopping $20 million (plus profit sharing points), while Barrymore was collecting $14 mil (enhanced with profit sharing and a hefty producing fee), while Liu pocketed a comparatively low (but what now seems kinda generous) $4 million.

The way I posed the question was, "How do you, as friends, deal with the knowledge that you are paid such different salaries?"

What I got back were three blank stares, almost as if they were in a film scene that had come to an abrupt, inexplicable stop. Just as I was prepping for one, two or perhaps all three of them to ascend from their loveseat in slo-mo, taking the form of high-flying wire-fu angels with their pointed feet directed at my neck, Diaz finally broke the unbearable silence.

"We don't ... it's never ..." Diaz said, trying to form a sentence before Liu interjected, "I've actually never had money affect anything in my life."

"It just doesn't really have a place in our relationship," Diaz continued, having found her voice. "We never discuss it."

"It's weird," asserted Liu. "This is the first time ever, in the history of *Charlie's Angels 1* or *2*, that anyone's ever asked us this question."

Barrymore remained understandably silent.

That my interview with the Angels was able to continue from that point was a miracle. Had they stood up and left the room it most certainly would have cost me my dream job at *USA Today*. And for what? Out of all the interesting questions I could have asked, why did I feel it necessary to embarrass them so?

Years later, when I was working as a Hallmark Channel producer, I would come to understand the importance of keeping one's salary private. Our show's production manager, Susan, accidentally printed a highly confidential spreadsheet of our entire staff's salaries to a common printer shared by all the producers. That info was intercepted by one of my fellow female producers, also named Susan, who had been with the show longer than me but was earning considerably less than what I was being paid. This salary discrepancy scoop spread like wildfire amongst our entire producing staff, and there would be no putting the genie back in the bottle. For the duration of my time at the show, I strongly believe resentments stemming from that unfortunate error altered how I was perceived and treated by my co-workers, making me feel as though I constantly had to over justify my worth.

Karma perhaps? I'm sure the Charlie's Angels would tell you it was.

Oh, and to top off my messy *Full Throttle* interview with one additional poisoned cherry, for some dumb reason I felt it necessary to report in my article that Diaz had let out a deafening belch in the middle of answering one of my questions. Honestly, had I been in Diaz's position, I could very easily see myself having projectile vomited (again in slo-mo) directly toward my interviewer's face.

If any good at all came from this clusterfuck, perhaps I succeeded in tutoring future talk show host Drew how *not* to conduct an interview.

Lesson Learned: Taking Arnica after plastic surgery really does help reduce swelling resulting from severe body trauma. And I probably would have been wise to pop a precautionary dose before I sat down with Barrymore, Diaz and Liu.

Sorry Angels.

Chapter 31
SOAPED HARD

(BRUCE WILLIS)

WHO: Bruce Willis (b. March 19, 1955). Golden Globe and Emmy winner for the TV detective series *Moonlighting*. Star of such epic blockbusters as *Die Hard, Armageddon* and *The Sixth Sense*.

WHAT: Premiere after-party coverage for *USA Today*.

WHERE: The Hollywood-Highland complex, Hollywood, CA.

Bruce Willis, circa 2007.
(Wikimedia Commons)

Unlike Cybill Shepherd, Ben Affleck and Samuel L. Jackson, who have all had the privilege of sharing the screen with Bruce Willis in some of his most career-defining projects, I have no inside advantage to help me interpret the action star's often hard to read temperament. Was I truly bullied by the adored action star at one of his movie premieres, or was he merely engaging me in some good-natured sparring to test my mettle? I like to think the latter, because—at least in Hollywood—being branded a "bully" is right up there with racist, sexist, homophobic or Republican. (Though Bruce's Republican affiliation somehow never seemed to harm him in the slightest.)

Were you ever bullied? Not much fun, is it? I remember dreading school bus rides home from Bethlehem Central Middle School when jerky Joel Lieberman would corner me in the back seats to taunt me about being gay. "No, seriously; you like sucking d**k, don't you?" is how it might start.

299

But Joel wasn't the worst bully in middle school. Not by a long shot. BCMS's most feared tormentor was our macho, mustached gym teacher Jack Whipple. To give you some idea who this Whipple fella was, the personalized license plate on his flashy sports car read "THE WHIP." And damn if that douchebag didn't like to crack his—turning our sports field into his own personal plantation. Think *Glee's* Sue Sylvester, but without the compassion we'd occasionally see her display toward anyone with Down syndrome.

As an insecure kid who suffered from year-round allergies and asthma, I felt entirely at the mercy of this whip-wielding master.

I'll never forget a particularly high pollen count spring afternoon that had morphed my 14-year-old lungs into those of a hacking, 85-year-old habitual smoker with a five-pack-a-day habit. Ignoring my heavy wheezing and gasps for air, the Whip forced me to complete a mini-marathon around the running track long after the other boys had clocked their times. When I finally collapsed at the finish line, Whipple made sure to announce my humiliating finish time to all within earshot before recording it in his book. *Dick move*, Whipple.

Cut to just over a decade later when the Whip had been promoted to high school principal, and I was working for the *National Enquirer* out in L.A. According to a secret call-in source (that'd be my mom Nancy), Principal Whipple had apparently attended a banquet honoring the student president of his school's Students Against Drunk Driving chapter. Then on his drive home, Whipple ended up getting busted for a DWI and arrested by the Albany County Sheriff's Department. Thanks to yours truly (and of course my mom), what had been a smaller local news story—quickly forgotten—ended up being reported in the nation's #1-selling tabloid, thus reaching millions. Call it what you wish: irony, karma, sweet revenge; I sure as hell wasn't wheezing that day.

Last I heard, the Whip was living out his last days in a senior living facility. And I can only hope he's learned to treat his caregivers with more compassion than he offered some of his less athletically inclined students. And even more importantly, Jack Whipple, I hope you shaved off that ridiculous pornstache, you macho shithead!

But I will give Whipple this: He never threatened to burn down my house. And I can't say the same about action star Bruce Willis.

Yessiree. Makes all those other threats I'd received over the years—the "fuck you" from Lindsay Wagner, the "I'm going to fucking kill you" from Drew Barrymore and Kelsey Grammer's invitation for me to "fry in hell"—seem pretty tame in comparison, wouldn't you say?

What could possibly have provoked Bruce to say such a vicious thing to an "innocent" lad like me? Without his co-stars' insight, I can only imagine it relates to the enormous ego that comes with taking down terrorists, scaling skyscrapers, deactivating bombs, saving the world from asteroids and defeating a redneck gimp who'd bound and ball gagged you in his basement.

While none of those standout cinematic hurdles ever brought Bruce down, aphasia (the loss of one's ability to understand or express speech caused by brain damage) proved to be the ultimate insurmountable adversary that would put a cap on his blockbuster career. By the time the current and former Mrs. Willises—Emma Heming and Demi Moore—jointly revealed his heartbreaking diagnosis and retirement from acting in spring 2022, Bruce's ability to communicate had already been severely impaired.

It was a far cry from the fearless, outspoken man I'd encountered back in December 2004 when I covered the premiere of *Ocean's Twelve*, in which Willis cameoed as himself.

When Willis' limo pulled up outside the Grauman's Chinese Theatre, the actor stepped out onto the carpet with a freshly spray-tanned, 24-year-old buxom brunette dressed in red peekaboo lace and feathers. She turned out to be soap opera actress Nadia Bjorlin, who played *Days of Our Lives'* tragically

All in a lather

Head turners: Soap alums, a lady in red

By William Keck
USA TODAY

HOLLYWOOD — Like sands through the hourglass, so are the *Days of Our Lives*. And so was Wednesday night's star-studded black-tie premiere for *Ocean's Twelve*, a far-out heist caper (opening today, ★★★ review, 6E) with some soapy elements of its own.

Two *Ocean's* stars share surprising connections to the long-running NBC daytime soap opera. Cast member **Julia Roberts**, who skipped the premiere to stay home with her newborn twins, is a *Days of Our Lives* groupie. And **Bruce Willis**, 49, who pops up in the film as himself, brought *Days* actress **Nadia Bjorlin**, 24, as his date.

Bjorlin, who plays the soap's tragically disfigured soprano diva, Chloe Lane, rode to the premiere at Grauman's Chinese Theatre in a limousine with Willis' family.

Ocean's star **Matt Damon**, who is expected to shoot *The Bourne Ultimatum* in 2006, did a double take as Bjorlin strutted down the carpet in a shocking red lacy/feathered peekaboo gown designed by Mark Zunino for Nolan Miller. Without acknowledging a romance, Bjorlin, who had her hand on Willis' lap at the after-party, had this to say about her *Die Hard* hunk: "He's very sexy. Men who look like real men are sexy ... as are a lot of the men in this movie."

Bjorlin's *Days* co-star **Matt Cedeno** wasn't working this week and was surprised to learn of the Bjorlin/Willis pairing. "He's a very charismatic guy, and she's a little on the young side," he noted.

By Vince Bucci, Getty Images

There's that dress: Nadia Bjorlin arrives at the *Ocean's Twelve* premiere in a barely-there red gown.

disfigured nymphomaniac operatic soprano Chloe Lane on and off from 1999-2023.

"He's very sexy," Bjorlin cooed to me about Willis when she paused to offer me a few brief words. "Men who look like real men are sexy."

At the after-party following the screening, I noted Bjorlin and Willis getting cozy in a booth, with her hand resting on his lap. Then when I overheard he was getting up to take a leak, I approached him on the way to the men's room and introduced myself as William Keck, a reporter with *USA Today*.

While Willis was always a tough read, I still tried to get a sense of whether or not he recognized my name. Since the actor's split from Moore back in 2000, I'd devoted considerable ink in the nation's newspaper to both parties' post-divorce pursuits of younger paramours—including a rumor I'd shared a few months earlier that Willis, then 49, had become engaged to 26-year-old actress Brooke Burns while vacationing in Zimbabwe. I may also have had a bit too much fun in print commenting on the unusual relationship he'd fostered with Demi's then-boy toy Ashton Kutcher (fifteen years Demi's junior).

Or perhaps I'd ticked Bruce off by writing something seemingly innocuous about his suddenly-in-the-news daughters, Rumer, Tallulah Belle and Scout—such as his purchase of 12,000 boxes of Girl Scout cookies from Tallulah. I'd explained to my readers that all the cookies had been flown to our brave soldiers fighting in Afghanistan: an M16 assault rifle in one hand and a Thin Mint in the other! Kevin Pollak (of *The Marvelous Mrs. Maisel*) provided me a quote claiming that ever since he'd co-starred with Moore in *A Few Good Men*, he'd been forced to buy Do-si-dos from her daughters: "A very large man comes to the house and says, 'I'm here to collect for the Willis girls,' and you write a check instantly."

I found that amusing. But had Bruce? He probably didn't appreciate when I revealed that he'd brought along Tallulah, at age 11, to sit through the premiere screening of his R-rated *Sin City*—an excessively violent film featuring graphic depictions of torture, child molestation, prostitution, decapitations, castrations and cannibalism. Or that he'd squired Rumer, then 16, to the film's after-party, where porn king (and Tammy Faye Bakker BFF) Ron Jeremy was among the revelers.

All I know is that despite me delaying his trip to the boy's room, Willis did manage to form something akin to a grin after my initial introduction. But then after exchanging a few pleasantries about the film, his mood soured the second I asked, innocently enough, if he perchance was a fan of daytime soaps. No dummy, Bruce immediately picked up on the angle I'd planned to pursue and clearly wasn't having it.

"Well…, I'm just saying," I tried explaining coyly. "Demi was on *General Hospital*, and your lovely date tonight is on *Days of Our Lives* … so …"

Bruce stopped me dead in my tracks. "Don't go there," he interrupted. "Don't even go there."

But I couldn't stop myself. I was having too much fun.

"What??" I shrugged, feigning innocence. "Soaps are great. And the actresses are obviously beautiful. I just thought maybe that's how you …"

"Stop!" Bruce demanded, flashing that billion-dollar "I could snap your neck right now" smile that earned him bazillions. "What did you say your name was: *Keck*? I'll find out where you live, Keck, and I'll come burn your house down."

I laughed. He did not reciprocate.

"I'm not kidding," he repeated. "You write that in your article, and I'll burn it down and you'll have no place to live."

"Write *what??*" I wanted to ask. He hadn't provided me with any solid "thats" to write about. Did he mean to suggest that if I dared print that an alpha male the likes of Bruce Willis might secretly spend his afternoons enthralled in *The Bold & the Beautiful* or *Days of Our Lives*—on the lookout for his next movie-premiere dates—that I'd find my home in flames? Was *that* the "that" that got him all in a lather?

Whatever "that" was, it's fair to say he ever so slightly overreacted, wouldn't you agree? I mean, it would have been one thing if I'd followed him into the john and conducted my impromptu interrogation while we were hanging out over the urinals. But this was technically still a work function that I'd been invited by the film studio to cover to promote *Ocean's Twelve*'s upcoming release. And that's that!

The most likely explanation for his pyromaniacal pledge: the guy was just getting off by fucking with an intrusive reporter because that's what powerful Hollywood A-listers can do. And what bullies like Joel Lieberman and Jack Whipple do. Some of the more senior *National Enquirer* reporters would tell me how Frank Sinatra would routinely silence snoops back in his day with similar threats. Threats that on occasion became something more.

Who can explain the motivation of power-hungry bullies? In Bruce's case, it could possibly have been an early indicator of his frontotemporal dementia. There was no point in wasting time trying to analyze his actions. I had no choice but to let him get away with his threat and just hope I wouldn't wake up in the middle of the night to discover Bruce Willis on my front lawn wearing a black tank top, crouched at the knees and aiming a flame thrower at my Spanish two-bedroom—screaming at the top of his lungs, "Yippee-ki-yay, motherfucker!"

But I'm not one to be easily intimidated, and my premiere coverage did of course include my "playful" banter with Bruce about the soaps, albeit softened considerably by my *USA Today* editor. And to my relief, there was never a need to place a frantic midnight call to the fire department while running around hysterically in my pajamas. (I did, however, invest in an extra fire extinguisher … just in case!)

As I heard, Bjorlin was tickled by my reporting, which served as a memento of a brief fling that was, alas, not meant to last. (And in 2023, the actress chose to step away from Hollywood, more than a decade after it came out that she'd been targeted by sex trafficker Jeffrey Epstein when she was only 13.)

Looking back at my own dating history, I guess I can relate to Bruce. I'd prefer not to be asked by some punk on my way to pee if I'd picked up my date at a bar or by discovering him on *The Young and the Restless*. Like asking Shatner how many horses he owned, or quizzing Joan Collins on plastic-surgery preferences, this was a topic I'd know to skip the next time I crossed paths with Bruno. That is if I wished to avoid dying hard, soft or in some unfortunate condition in between.

Lesson Learned: Before you initiate a dance with the devil, check your insurance policy's fire coverage. Because you might very well get burned.

A WORD FROM WILLIS'S *MOONLIGHTING* CO-STAR CYBILL SHEPHERD

Do I think Bruce was serious when he threatened to burn down William Keck's house? I just can't see him doing something like that. I think he was just being funny. That's not to say he couldn't be naughty at times, which is one of the most charming things about the guy. Working alongside him on *Moonlighting*, it took everything I had to not constantly laugh out loud, because Bruce was just that funny.

And if I'm going to be perfectly honest, the very first time I ever met Bruce—when he walked into the room—my temperature went up ten degrees. I was very attracted to him. There was instant chemistry but we both knew we couldn't act on it. That's not to say we didn't have to work hard on that. We came so close. I remember one time we were in a La-Z-Boy chair that went so far back you're almost lying down. I think he was on top and we were feeling really turned on, and then all of a sudden he said, "You know somethin', I think maybe we shouldn't do this because we may be working together a long time." And Bruce was right. No regrets!

Although it's been years since we last spoke, and I of course know he's had his problems like we all do as we grow older, I think of Bruce all the time. In my dining room, I have a Zippo lighter that says "Bruce Willis Roast" with my name spelled correctly on it in a place of honor—right next to my Blue Moon Detective Agency business card that says "Madolyn Hayes."

Cybill Shepherd, circa 2007. (Wiki Commons/Petr Novak)

I guess what I'd like people to know about Bruce is that behind that tough guy exterior we saw in *Die Hard*, there is a serious side. A person of great depth who'll stand up for you when you need him. Over the course of filming 67 episodes, we went through everything together. There was one director who was having some issues with my performance, and it felt like everyone was watching me, waiting for me to do something wrong. And Bruce was there for me when I was feeling a tremendous amount of pressure. That's the kind of thing you never forget.

Chapter 32
SLUMMING ON SKID ROW

(ERIC DANE & REBECCA GAYHEART)

WHO: Eric Dane (b. November 9, 1972), hunky *Euphoria* actor best known for playing Dr. Mark "McSteamy" Sloan on *Grey's Anatomy*, and his then wife, actress and philanthropist Rebecca Gayheart (b. August 12, 1971), remembered for playing the late Luke Perry's love interest on *Beverly Hills, 90210*. That, and a tragic real-life 2001 vehicular manslaughter charge.

WHAT: On-the-record interview for *USA Today*.

WHERE: Chrysalis center, Skid Row, Downtown L.A.

Top: Eric Dane in 2017. (Gage Skidmore/Wikimedia Commons) Above: Rebecca Gayheart in 2019. (Glenn Francis/ Wikimedia Commons)

Over the past few years in Los Angeles and in other major American cites, homeless encampments have been popping up on streets the way Starbucks coffeehouses and CVS pharmacies once had. And in several instances, they have led to such franchises having to shutter for the safety of both their employees and patrons. A few summers back, I learned firsthand just how widespread this out-of-control problem was becoming when a mentally ill man set up camp in my backyard, where he would bring his daily intake of "found" treasures, including jewelry, knives and drug paraphernalia. That was fun.

But traditionally—dating way back to the 1930s—the majority of the city's tarped homeless encampments was restricted to Downtown L.A.'s Skid Row, home today to upwards of ten thousand individuals.

My first visit to Skid Row was back in 2007 when I was the third wheel on a romantic stroll through the rough area with a *Grey's Anatomy* star and his wife. Our "date" started off on the right foot, but ended horribly when I became privy to a devastating childhood secret that I have not written about until now.

My *USA Today* assignment began innocently enough (as so often they do) with a pitch from a publicist to spend a day with Rebecca Gayheart, the actress who had played Luke Perry's murdered bride Antonia on *Beverly Hills, 90210* and more recently appeared in Quentin Tarantino's *Once Upon a Time in ... Hollywood*. Besides her film credits, Gayheart's name unfortunately had also become linked to the tragic vehicular manslaughter death of a 9-year-old boy from Mexico whom she'd struck with her Jeep Grand Cherokee back in 2001. By the time of our interview, Gayheart was well on her way to completing her 750 hours of court-ordered community service and had become passionately involved with the organization Chrysalis, an incredible non-profit that helps homeless men and women get back on their feet. If you think there's nothing you can do to make a difference in your community, Rebecca would prove you wrong!

I thought it was a solid celebrity/human-interest story, but my editor saw the opportunity for a much bigger "get." Gayheart was newly married to actor Eric Dane who had shot to overnight superstardom on *Grey's Anatomy* (then TV's hottest show) when he emerged from a steamy shower clad only in a towel, instantly earning himself the nickname "McSteamy"—a play on co-star Patrick Dempsey's "McDreamy."

Suddenly, everyone wanted to know more about this sexy, sweaty, mysterious Greek god, and my editor mandated that we would only do the story on Rebecca's charity if she were accompanied by her husband. (See, it's not only the tabloids that exploit stars' personal lives to sell papers.) I thought Rebecca's reps would balk, but they agreed almost immediately.

So, the three of us met up at Chrysalis' Skid Row headquarters to begin our walk-and-talk interview in full view of men and women openly urinating, rummaging through garbage cans and shooting up heroin. Way worse than anything I saw during my *Enquirer* years.

Star couple give a hand on Skid Row

Photos by Dan MacMedan, USA TODAY

While Gayheart was very chatty and friendly with me throughout the day, Dane seemed withdrawn and distant. When I asked him back at the headquarters who had been his childhood role model, he simply walked away as if he'd not heard my question. It could have been interpreted as rude, but I sensed I'd touched a nerve.

"He never really had a role model," Rebecca explained to me, as Eric disappeared into a labyrinth of donated clothing. Though I elected not to probe any further, Rebecca nonchalantly offered up that Eric's father had committed suicide when Eric was just a 7-year-old boy. Wait, *what??!!* I was stunned! And I knew Eric would be livid with Rebecca for revealing such a whopper of a secret to a reporter they'd only met an hour earlier.

Now herein lies a dilemma reporters face whenever their interview subject tells you something during an interview—without prefacing the information with three essential words that make all the difference: "Off. The. Record." While many reporters would have swept this hugely personal reveal under the rug, I'd received my training as a reporter for the *National Enquirer*, meaning if they don't say "off

309

the record," it ain't. So, I discussed the matter with my *USA Today* editor who made the call that it was relevant information that I should include in my story. Would you agree with that decision? Today, I'm not so sure *I* would.

Further complicating matters for Dane was an out-of-the-blue call I received from his mother, Leah, asking me when Eric's story would be coming out in the newspaper. (I'd only ever experienced something like that once before after I'd written a mildly unflattering profile of actress Denise Richards and her mother phoned me to ask, "Why do you hate my daughter?") In that call with Eric's incredibly sweet mom, I mentioned to her the sensitive bit of news that Rebecca had let slip. While Leah was clearly startled that this private family secret had been revealed by her new daughter-in-law, she confirmed that yes, sadly, it was true. Within minutes, I received a frazzled call from Dane's publicist insisting that I had my information wrong.

This is what publicists are paid to when faced with potential scandals. Deny, deny, deny for as long as possible. But this time there was no backpedaling. There had been no misunderstanding. The truth had been stated very clearly by both Eric's wife and, now, mother, and no amount of publicist denials could take it back. As far as my editor was concerned, it was going into the story. Case closed. Still, I immediately felt regretful and sick to my stomach.

The genesis of this story was a pair of celebrities lending their names to a charitable cause, and I was turning it into something salacious. It was a test of my integrity and I'd failed. Badly. The publication of this scandal, I realized, could sully all I'd accomplished trying to put my tabloid ties in the past and achieve respect as a legitimate journalist. And not only that, I'd already earned myself a place on *Grey's Anatomy* creator Shonda Rhimes's shit list after I'd pissed her off royally with a profile I'd written on her new hire, fresh-faced ingénue Chyler Leigh, whom Rhimes had added to the cast as Lexie Grey, the half-sister of central character Meredith Grey (Ellen Pompeo). Neither Rhimes nor ABC appreciated the actress opening up to me on the record about a potentially fatal drug addiction she'd overcome—a dark past that contradicted the sweet innocence of her Lexie character. There was also my visit to the set of the *Grey's* spinoff series, *Private Practice*, that just happened to coincide with the cast's sexual-harassment training.

I couldn't help but overhear Kate Walsh, Tim Daly and most all the cast mocking their network-mandated seminars, with portions of their sexually charged quotes making it into my reporting. And then there was some crack I made about Patrick Dempsey's hair that didn't go over well.

So, I was already skating on Pompeo-thin ice over at Shondaland.

But then a little angel perched atop my shoulder had a thought. I wasn't working for the *Enquirer* anymore, was I? Maybe there was a way I could still make this right. I called my editor and asked how she'd feel about offering Dane a deal. If he'd come on the phone to share more details with me about his early years, we'd agree to bury the info about his dad's suicide. After some persuasion, both my editor and Eric's reps agreed.

While I'm sure he was doing so through clenched teeth, Eric was incredibly kind when he phoned for his "follow-up" interview. He even thanked me for negotiating the deal to protect his family's privacy. And though we'd never signed any official non-disclosure agreements, the story remained forever buried. The only reason I'm discussing it now is because Eric finally chose to open up about it himself in 2014.

I was floored that Rebecca opted not to rescind my invitation to her annual Chrysalis Butterfly Ball fundraising gala that was held just days later. Even so, she did avoid making eye contact with me throughout the uncomfortable evening. And I could hardly blame her. I shouldn't have been there.

Eric, on the other hand, was as warm to me that night as he continues to be every time our paths cross. And as the years went on, Rebecca warmed to me as well, even speaking with me on the record at her subsequent fund-raising balls.

Unfortunately, Eric and Rebecca wouldn't be able to bury an even bigger scandal that erupted two years later when an eXXXtra-McSteamy sex tape leaked showing the frisky couple cavorting naked in a bathtub with a former Miss Teen USA. In 2018, Rebecca filed for divorce citing the familiar "irreconcilable differences," but the divorce was never finalized. And in 2023, the two were photographed in Mexico holding hands—taking me back to the sweet day I saw them strolling down the streets of Skid Row, careful to avoid stepping in the frothing puddles of aromatic pee-pee.

Whether you're a strung-out junkie or a glammed-up movie star, our unpredictable paths can always end with a regrettable step into a big pile of Skid Row scat.

Lesson Learned: They say no good deed goes unpunished. Just make sure you're never the one punishing the good deed-doers.

Chapter 33
NO LOVE LOST

(THE CAST OF *LOST*)

Author (center) with *Lost* stars (clockwise l-r) Monaghan, Garcia, Andrews and de Ravin, shortly before it all imploded.

WHO: Dominic Monaghan, Jorge Garcia, Emilie de Ravin and Naveen Andrews, stars of the 2004–2010 ABC drama series *Lost*.

WHAT: On-the-record sit-down interview for *USA Today*.

WHERE: Langham Huntington Hotel in Pasadena, CA. Various locations in Oahu, HI.

During the early 2000s, when my career was in high gear as *USA Today's* West Coast Celebrity Reporter (so loved that title!), I had a few short-term relationships, but was mostly single. While it typically wasn't difficult finding "plus ones" to accompany me to movie premieres and award show after-parties, finding "the one" proved far more challenging. Like single celebrities, I too was having to ask myself if my dates were really interested in me, or just the perks that came with dating me. There was little doubt when it came to dating aspiring actors, the worst offender being a pretty Spaniard named Joseph who would slip away from me at parties to ingratiate himself to celebrities.

"Where did you disappear to?" I'd ask Joe, who would pull out his phone to show me all the selfies he'd taken with the stars. Behavior like this is just one of the many reasons they say "don't date actors."

That being said, my own behavior at celebrity functions could also have used some improvement. As the newspaper's *celebrity* reporter—unlike *USA Today's* more respected film, television and music journalists whose articles were more project-oriented than personal—part of my job was to report the kinds of gossipy stories one might read in *People*. Or the *Enquirer*. Yep, I was still digging for the

same scoop, only now I was collecting it in high-grade designer handbags instead of cheap plastic *Enquirer* poop bags.

Not long after I was hired by *USA Today*, ABC unveiled its truly epic 2004–2005 primetime TV schedule, which included the debuts of not only *Desperate Housewives* and *Grey's Anatomy* (whose stars you read about earlier), but a mysterious drama called *Lost* about the marooned survivors of an airplane crash. Because the show's diverse cast of overnight stars were sequestered in faraway Hawaii, I was routinely flown to Oahu to get to know many of them in their natural habitats. Memorable encounters included spontaneous skinny-dipping off a sandbar with Jorge Garcia (Hurley), a dolphin encounter with Maggie Grace (Shannon), whittling wood with Terry O'Quinn (Locke)

The author hiking with *Lost's* Josh Holloway (above). And (below) getting a "couples massage" with Yunjin Kim; on set in Oahu with Jorge Garcia and Michael Emerson.

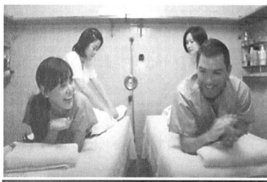

and picking up Josh Holloway (Sawyer) in my rental Jeep for an all-day island drive that found me buying Josh a pack of smokes because famous people rarely carry wallets. (I'll never forget when multi-millionaire singer Melissa Etheridge asked me to buy her popcorn at a movie screening because she'd assumed everything would be comped.)

But every so often, the Losties were sprung from their prison in paradise for quick visits to Los Angeles, allowing me to meet up with them for fun excursions on my own turf. These included a "couples" massage with Yunjin Kim (Sun) at a Korean Spa and touring the L.A. Zoo with Harold Perrineau (Michael) and Malcolm David Kelley (Walt) on an unfortunate afternoon when a monkey escaped from its cage, putting the entire facility on lockdown. And I can't leave out that time in San Diego when I had my ass playfully squeezed by that roguish Ian Somerhalder (Boone). Man, that sure left a lasting mark.

The only two lead actors I never profiled were Matthew Fox (Jack), whom I found to be consistently aloof, and Evangeline Lilly (Kate), who wanted nothing to do with me after I reported her "canoodling" with co-star Dominic Monaghan (Charlie) at the 2005 Golden Globe Awards. Even though both actors were single at the time and would continue on as a committed couple for the next three years, my scoop was picked up by all the major entertainment outlets, prompting Lilly to view my reveal as an unforgivable invasion of her privacy. From that point on, in her eyes, I was not to be trusted. Fortunately, Monaghan, a laid-back dude's dude, did not share his girlfriend's view and freely spoke with me on the record until his edgy rocker character was killed off in *Lost's* third-season finale.

Because the size of this ever-revolving cast was becoming so massive (for every fan favorite killed off, new island characters would magically appear in some underground hatch or newly revealed colony), it became impossible for me to give every actor his or her own individual *USA Today* profile. So, in January 2007, I invited a quartet of them to join me for what was intended to be a friendly roundtable discussion over Arnold Palmers at the ritzy Langham Huntington Hotel in Pasadena. I never could have imagined that this would end up going down as the most unpleasant sit-down interview of my entire career, with one of the four getting up in the middle of our chat and walking out—a regrettable moment that impacted how I would conduct interviews from that point on.

Joining me, Monaghan and Garcia was the heavenly Emilie de Ravin, who played the show's perpetually suffering Claire (and would go on to portray Belle on ABC's *Once Upon a Time*) and Naveen Andrews (Sayid), a no-nonsense Indian actor raised in London who treated me so poorly that afternoon that I hoped he'd be the next casualty of *Lost's* homicidal Smoke Monster.

Keenly aware that I'd be asking personal questions during our discussion, and knowing his girlfriend's protective nature of their relationship, Monaghan shrewdly requested to meet with me privately on the Langham patio before the others arrived. Among the more private topics we discussed was the bravery Lilly had shown following the total loss of her house to fire. (Had she pissed off Bruce Willis?)

When the other three joined us, talk quickly revealed just how frustrated they'd all become with the new cast additions cutting into their valuable screen time. By far the most outspoken of the group, Andrews wasted no time displaying his feathers by boasting, "Even though I like getting paid for doing nothing, it is nice occasionally to work." Specifically addressing his character's lack of storyline, the expletive-spewing actor griped, "What are we going to fucking say about it? Do we write the fucking thing? No!"

That promoted his protective publicist—who had been trying to listen in as unobtrusively as possible from behind a very large potted palm—to step in and remind his client to mind his language. I was half expecting the salty star to tell his rep to go screw himself. But as it turned out, he was saving that for me.

Sensing Andrews' sensitivity and short fuse, I elected to kiss his ass by offering what I thought was a compliment. His film career at that time was starting to heat up with roles in *Bride & Prejudice* and the Tarantino/Robert Rodriguez flick *Grindhouse*, so I asked if he might consider stepping away from *Lost* to focus full-time on film. Clearly displeased with my question, Andrews turned instantly confrontational, asking me, "How much do you make as a reporter for this paper?"

Gulp! I certainly hadn't seen *that* coming, as I was usually the one asking the *Charlie's Angels* that question. Monaghan and de Ravin remained quiet, lowering their heads and stirring their beverages, while Garcia gave me a supportive glance as if to say, "Good luck with that one, dude."

All I could think to whisper back was, "A lot less than you."

"Exactly!" Andrews shot back, adding that few individuals "make more than us ... I wouldn't have gotten nominated for awards *twice* (an Emmy and Golden Globe) if it hadn't been for this show."

Nor, I would write in my article, would the paparazzi have had any interest in capturing the actor "canoodling" with a mystery woman on an L.A. beach the previous summer while he was supposedly still in a committed relationship with *Beaches* beauty Barbara Hershey. I didn't dare bring that embarrassing scandal up in front of his castmates, as even I felt it would have been grossly inappropriate. But I did "go there" just enough about the current status of his relationship with Hershey for him to cut me off at the knees by muttering curtly that they were "fantastic and happy."

Ok, moving on then.

With the topic of their various romantic statuses having been introduced, Garcia was next to address the end of a year-long relationship with a live-in girlfriend. He took a very healthy, matter-of-fact approach, shrugging, "relationships end ... we talk very regularly." So now that left only Emilie, whom I'd profiled for *USA Today* the year prior just after her joyous engagement to a fella who, sadly, was now about to become her ex-husband. Talk about shitty timing. Just a week earlier, Emilie had announced her six-month marriage was coming to an end, and I'm sure was dreading being asked to comment about it: in a business setting. In front of close friends and colleagues. And seriously, who wouldn't feel exactly the same way?

So, in the softest, most compassionate voice possible, I gently asked, "Emilie, I'm sorry about your recent news. Is there anything you'd like to say?"

And just like that, Emilie—fighting back tears—announced, "I'm getting up to leave right now." And that's exactly what she did.

Ugh. I felt just sick. Just thinking about that moment *still* makes my stomach churn. Of course, there had always been the possibility in the back of my head of a peeved celebrity getting up and walking out of one of my interviews. Many of you may have seen clips on YouTube of Joan Rivers, Robert Downey Jr. and Robert Pattinson leaving their interviewers in the dust. But it had never happened to me, nor would it ever again, which I actually find quite remarkable given how often I poked the bear.

When Emilie ran off, a big part of me wanted to get up and follow her into the garden where she'd disappeared. The deafening silence at the table was first broken by Andrews who said he knew exactly what de Ravin was feeling and let me know how offensive he felt it was to expect them to discuss their private romantic statuses in a forum related to their work. And you know what? As tough as Naveen was on me that day, I have to give the guy major props for sticking up for his friend. He had a point—one that made me think long and hard about how I would conduct future group interviews. It's one thing to bring up personal matters in a more intimate 1:1 interview scenario. But it's quite another to do so in a group forum. I would not make that same mistake again.

Monaghan and Garcia did all they could to ease us back into civility so we could cordially wrap up the interview and continue with our days.

"We're all at a point in our lives where no one wants to talk about private issues," said Monaghan (without, of course, clueing in Garcia and Andrews that he'd already done just that before they arrived).

But the person who deserves the most praise here is Emilie, not only for bravely showing up to the interview in the first place when she easily could have canceled, but also for taking the totally unnecessary extra step of apologizing to me via her publicist, for "excusing herself abruptly from the table," as it was "a very sensitive and extremely emotional time." What an example of elegance and grace. If anyone owed anyone an apology, it was me to her.

Ever since that regrettable day—including during my multiple visits to the Vancouver set of her follow-up series, *Once Upon a Time,* and while joining me on Comic-Con panels I was asked to moderate—Emilie has shown me nothing but incredible kindness and respect. And I will always be enormously grateful to her for being among the first celebrities to partner with me on a virtual-classroom project I helped launch during the pandemic. She has become a friend with whom heart emojis are regularly exchanged, and I was tickled to have an opportunity to share this chapter with her in advance of publication. "So honest and open," is how she rather generously described what she'd read.

As for Mr. Andrews, I'll just say this. I have no problem being reprimanded when it's called for. Hell, in my *Desperate Housewives* chapter, I praised Marcia Cross for setting me straight with an appropriate wrist-slapping when I crossed the line in her home. But how Andrews treated me seemed … well, *different.* I personally felt as though he were deriving some perverse pleasure from publicly humiliating me, as I've only ever felt twice before during brief encounters with Uma Thurman and Jessica Lange. Had I similarly humiliated Emilie? It certainly hadn't been my intention. And nothing but instant anguish and regret came from it.

The last time I interviewed Naveen was by a lake in Vancouver, when he was fully costumed as the evil Disney villain Jafar for a guest-starring role on the short-lived ABC spin-off series *Once Upon a Time in Wonderland.* It was a pleasant exchange, as I felt we'd both been somewhat humbled. Sure, he was still pulling in a helluva lot more cash than I was, but at least I didn't have to carry around that silly serpent staff all day.

Lesson Learned: Any of us could be next in line to be killed off the island, so let's all play nice together in the sandbox.

A WORD FROM *LOST* SHOWRUNNER CARLTON CUSE

When I was making *Lost*, I crossed paths with Will Keck, who was covering our show for *USA Today* and *TV Guide*. Will was smart and worked hard to bring his publications interesting and fresh scoops. The experience of making a show like *Lost* that exploded into the zeitgeist was surreal, especially discovering the desire our audience had to know all our secrets. They wanted way more than just the episodes we were delivering up—they wanted inside information about the story we were telling and the actors who were telling it.

Enter Will, whose job it was to pry out those secrets. Now there were a couple of problems with that: We didn't want to reveal our secrets, and the cast wanted boundaries on their privacy. Most of our cast members were unknown to the public before the show aired. Suddenly, they became stars. And that was a seismic change. The one benefit they had was that they were living in Hawaii where we shot the show— far away from media centers, like Los Angeles. On the breezy island of Oahu, the residents were almost always respectful of their privacy. But enterprising journalists like Will got around this geographical barrier by flying to Hawaii and confronting the actors on their (new) home turf. They then had the difficult challenge of figuring out what was fair game for sharing with Will and what was not. Will was charming, but relentless in his pursuit of a good story. It was a tricky dance for them to navigate.

Ironically, I was so busy making the show that I knew almost nothing about what was going on in the private lives of our actors. My interactions with them were almost always about the work. So when I found myself reading Will's stories, I discovered he always knew way more about their private lives than I did. He also pressed me and my showrunning partner, Damon, for information. His questions went right to the heart of the story stuff we were trying to keep secret. It was always a challenge for us to protect ourselves from his snooping, but at the end of the day he respected the stuff that *really* needed to be kept secret, and we were grateful for all the coverage and attention Will gave our show.

Lost showrunners Damon Lindelof (left) and Carlton Cuse (costumed as Indiana Jones).

Chapter 34
HALLOWEEN HORROR

(PATRICIA ARQUETTE)

WHO: Patricia Arquette (b. April 8, 1968). Winner of the 2005 Primetime Emmy for Outstanding Lead Actress in a Drama Series for her role in the 2005–2011 supernatural series *Medium*. 2015's Best Supporting Actress Oscar winner for the film *Boyhood*.

WHAT: On-the-record interview for *USA Today*.

WHERE: Universal Studios Hollywood theme park, Universal City, CA.

Patricia Arquette, circa 2005.
(CBS/Paramount)

A few chapters back, I mentioned being bullied as a kid. What I failed to mention were the times *I* was the one doing the bullying, alongside my neighborhood's fellow freckle-faced juvenile delinquent Tommy Boyle. Our weaponry of choice in an ongoing turf war with the Freeman and Fink kids a few houses up from ours: water balloons. But not just any water balloons, mind you. Ours were … *augmented*.

Mark Freeman and his kid brother Kevin were good, kind-hearted, fair-haired mama's boys who only wanted to be our friends, as did their next-door neighbors, the lisping Billy Fink and his older adopted sister, Annie. As my mom explained it to me, Mr. and Mrs. Fink didn't think they could conceive biological children of their own, so they adopted Annie, only to discover a couple years later that Mrs. Fink was pregnant with Billy. Surprise!

Mark, Kevin, Annie and Billy became our rivals through no fault of their own. The only reason we singled them out was because they were easy, available targets, and everything on TV at the time—whether it be *Bonanza, The Bionic Woman* or *Batman*—showed us that every hero needed a nemesis to engage and conquer.

It was actually Kevin and Mark's fiery redneck father we despised. Whenever he'd catch us anywhere near his obsessively manicured lawn, Mr. Freeman would warn us he wasn't afraid to "kick a little ass." Granted, we weren't only retrieving renegade soccer balls that had accidentally landed on his property. Our intrusions were a little more creative than that. For instance, we were fond of hiding in a big bush on the Freemans' front yard and throwing rocks at passing cars. Another time, when the Freemans and Finks weren't home, we tossed all of the fireplace logs Mr. Fink had carefully stacked in preparation for winter over an adjoining fence into the Freemans' backyard. With each throw, we'd scream "Wooooooodchuck" and compete to see who could throw his log farthest. We'd also play "Robin Hood" by using my grandfather's old bow to randomly shoot arrows off into the neighborhood—never giving any consideration as to where (or through whose heart) they might land. Then there was the time Billy Fink snuck us into his parents' bedroom to show us his father's sex book and Trojan condoms, which we promptly ripped open and used to decorate a tree at the end of the Finks' driveway to welcome Billy's parents home from work.

What can I say? We were dumb kids with out-of-control testosterone. A much easier label to own up to than "bully."

But it was during the summer of '82 that our *Boyz in the Hood* war with the Freeman and Fink kids spiraled out of control. Having tired of our routine water-balloon attacks, we upped the stakes by assembling an arsenal of inflated balloons filled with ketchup, honey and maple syrup. The results were stupendous. A huge victory for the Keck and Boyle camp that left our opponents defeated in a web of sticky muck. But the victory celebration was cut short when a thoroughly livid Mrs. Freeman marched down the street with her traumatized sons' heavily syruped shorts, T-shirts, socks and underpants and handed them to my mother for me to wash. Although I didn't appreciate it at the time, that was a brilliant stroke of parenting on Mrs. Freeman's part: a protective mama bear sticking up for her sticky baby bears who were left with honey-drenched hair.

It should have ended there, but instead, Tommy and I instantly began plotting our ultimate revenge—a psychotic plot that very well could have sent us right to juvie.

Maple-syrup balloons were pretty ingenious, so where does one go from there? You go bigger. Much, much bigger, as in a 30-gallon Glad lawn bag. After we completely filled one of these with a garden hose, we carted the massive blob up toward the Freemans' house in the very same wheelbarrow we'd used to transport our stash of *Penthouse* magazines. When we arrived, we broke into the Freemans' home and carefully dragged that plastic bag all the way up the stairs and into Kevin and Mark's bedroom, positioning our Oppenheimer atomic aqua-bomb into an open window looking down onto the family's driveway. While I held onto the balloon, waiting for just the right time to drop the H_2O bomb over Upstate New York's Hiroshima, Tommy hurried back outside to find a kid (re: victim) to lure onto our bullseye below. Unfortunately for Annie Fink, she was at the wrong place at the wrong time. And fortunately for Tommy and me, our dropped incendiary device also ended up detonating at the wrong place, missing Annie's head by mere inches. While Tom and I were (of course) crushed that our mission failed, it no doubt prevented Annie from suffering a paralyzing spinal injury and sending us neighborhood bullies off to a detention camp where we'd no doubt have been brutally sodomized by bullies far bigger than we were.

Given all that, whatever childhood trauma Patricia Arquette and I may have inflicted upon two little girls should seem relatively minor in comparison, particularly considering it all had to do with an exciting, well-intended Halloween outing.

Halloween was always my favorite holiday, with my costume conceptualizing beginning weeks or even months before it was time to head out trick-or-treating. But my all-time best costume had to be one I wore to a college frat party—a daring choice that provoked a provocative response I hadn't seen coming. My mom was replacing one of our home's toilets, so I salvaged the crapper's seat and lift-up lid and decided to turn myself into a walking, talking commode. I created the candy corn-collecting toilet bowl from a papier-mâché-layered balloon, and an old *Star Wars* AT-AT Kenner toy box painted white became my tank. There was a hole cut in the top for my head, which would be adorned with a roll of toilet paper as my fascinator. I even had a little moveable flusher affixed to the side of the tank. What I hadn't properly considered was what could possibly happen at a booze-infused college party when a bunch of drunken frat boys with full bladders saw a dancing toilet headed their way. When more than one "whipped it out" from under their togas and tunics, I just narrowly avoided being used as a urinal.

It was a mess of a different sort I stirred up during Halloween 2006.

Each October, during my years as a *USA Today* reporter, the publicist for Universal Studios Hollywood theme park would reach out hoping I'd consider writing a story about their annual Halloween Horror Nights event. But because they were never able to attach a celebrity, I'd politely decline. But then one year something fun fell into place.

At the time, one of NBC's hottest shows was the spooky mystery series *Medium*, starring Patricia Arquette. Because Patricia's character Allison DuBois was a clairvoyant possessing supernatural psychic visions enabling her to assist with murder investigations, I'd been wanting to come up with a unique, perhaps slightly macabre, setting to interview the quirky actress. I'd previously invited Jennifer Love Hewitt (star of the similarly-themed *Ghost Whisperer* series) to the Hollywood Forever Cemetery as the backdrop for her eerie interview and photo shoot. So where to take Patricia? How about Horror Nights? Patricia loved the idea—but had one request. She was very close to the child actresses who played her character's three daughters and wanted to invite them and their moms along for our adventure.

So, on Halloween Eve, I met up with Patricia, 14-year-old Sofia Vassilieva (who played Allison's daughter Ariel) and 9-year-old Maria Lark (Bridgette) at the VIP entrance to the studio's spooky tram tour, which would take us to fun Halloween-themed attractions. There had been some discussion about extending our invite to Miranda and Madison Carabello, the 4-year-old twins who shared the role of youngest DuBois daughter Marie, but Patricia—who at the time was mom to her own 3-year-old daughter Harlow—worried that the chilly winter evening might prove too much for the toddlers. Good call there, as low temperatures would prove the very least of our concerns.

Me costumed as a demon with Patricia Arquette and her *Medium* daughters Sofia Vassilieva and Maria Lark at Universal Studios Halloween Horror Nights, 2006.

Everything started out perfectly fine, with Patricia costumed as a sailor, lovely Sofia arriving as a medieval fairy princess and quirky tomboy Maria taking on the part of a Roman gladiator pierced with bleeding flesh wounds.

What neither Patricia nor I had known was just how horrifically violent this attraction had become since its first family-friendly iteration way back in 1986. That year's inaugural event featured a spooky tram ride that was marred only by the accidental real-life death of a park employee who'd volunteered to perform as a character.

Our evening would take its own unanticipated ugly turn when it became starkly apparent that in place of the experiences we'd envisioned for little Sofia and Maria—bobbing for apples, jack o' lantern carving and perhaps a visit from Casper the Friendly Ghost—waiting for us instead were demented serial killers and grotesque, putrid-smelling zombies draped with decaying meat. Even Patricia and I found ourselves covering our eyes and noses.

Before I tell you what *really* happened that night, let me share with you how I seriously toned things down in my *USA Today* coverage of that unfortunate evening. While my story opened with a sensationalized kicker: "The girls who play Patricia Arquette's TV daughters on NBC's *Medium* shriek in terror and burst into tears," I opted to pacify the nervous theme-park publicists by glossing over the unpleasant particulars and give my readers the false impression that the girls went

325

on from there to partake in a healthy night of harmless merrymaking. *(Just like you and your entire family can enjoy on your next visit to Universal Studios Hollywood theme park!!)*

But that could not have been further from the truth. Things began going south from the moment we boarded the tram, when Patricia scared the shit out of her TV daughters by sharing a true story from her own past. "When I was 18, I kissed this really cute guy," her twisted bedtime story began. "But something about him gave me the creeps. He was the first guy I gave a fake number to. Years later, he killed a girl. So, you've got to trust your instincts."

Sofia and Maria, who'd arrived in an upbeat, playful mood, had been hanging onto their TV mom's every word, and the cautionary tale instantly rendered the impressionable young girls quiet and sullen. *"Might that cute guy I like in school also murder me???!"* they were perhaps asking themselves. While well intentioned, Patricia's age-*in*appropriate story was akin to reading children *Little Red Riding Hood*—only to reveal that the wolf sexually assaults the grandmother. Was this stunt really a good idea? I began to wonder. But the girls' mothers and the park publicist just shrugged it off, offering their well-liked, Emmy-winning meal ticket some obligatory "Oh, how awful" niceties.

When Patricia had first suggested bringing along the girls, she'd reassured me they were both thick-skinned, seasoned kid actors who'd grown up on a set that was routinely dressed with gory props and make-believe blood. On the *Medium* soundstages, guest actors walking around set in the form of corpses was as routine as Charo popping up with her maracas on an episode of *The Love Boat*. Yikes!! Oh, it's just *her* again.

Our reasoning: Whatever cheap props the Horror Nights team might have picked up at some rando Halloween store would be laughable in comparison to what the girls saw at work. Or so we thought. Those twisted Universal Studios special-effects wizards had gone overboard to ensure that even the most jaded teens would massively shit their pants.

As our private tram car set out toward a dilapidated recreation of the Bates Motel from Alfred Hitchcock's *Psycho*, a video montage up on our tram's TV monitor displayed chillingly realistic images of a serial killer slicing out a woman's eyeball. As the older of the two girls, Sofia tried her best to play it cool as if she were one of us fearless adults. When a drooling zombie rushed our tram car, Sofia flashed him the peace sign, screaming at the minimum-wage-earning actor to "Go get a facial!" And proving she was just as brave, our little gladiator Maria shouted out to the poor lanky kid portraying Norman Bates that he should expect a visit from *Extreme Makeover*. Okay, maybe these girls were mature enough to handle this after all.

But then ... *BZZZZZ!!!!*

On cue, an army of blood-thirsty, chainsaw-wielding zombies descended upon us from all directions, bringing our tram to a grinding halt. Sofia was first to crack, bursting into not whimpers, mind you, but loud, heaving sobs. Kudos to Patricia for springing into the role of protective mama bear—covering Maria's eyes and encouraging both girls to turn their heads from the onslaught of monsters who had come to eat our flesh.

"You're the gladiator," Patricia reminded Maria, trying to boost her scarred stamina. "You're supposed to protect us." But the deafening buzzing was now enhanced with the unbearable shrieks of torture victims. This sensory overload proved too much for even Maria, who had been reduced to a shrieking, inconsolable torture victim who wanted the fuck off that tram. Since this had been our idea, Patricia and I were her true tormentors, and it was now up to us to find a way to abort this ill-conceived mission STAT! And that's just what we did—piling off the tram and whisking the girls to a quiet, safe place.

A true Horror Night that well exceeded our naïve expectations. Had it been any of the ladies in my Dangerous Divas section instead of Patricia, the blame for this egregious lapse in judgment very easily could have been dumped all upon me. But that's not the way of the Arquette. When I looked over at Patricia to offer a heavy sigh expressing my incredulity over it all, she covered her mouth to conceal a devilish little giggle. She was finding this far more amusing than anyone else, myself included.

Patricia, like me, adored Halloween, and was taking delight in seeing the heavily commercialized holiday play out as she felt it had originally been intended. Not as a fashion show for girls to model precious, frilly Elsa and Anna princess gowns or for boys to suit up as their favorite Marvel superheroes, but rather a chilling evening meant to scare the bejesus out of us.

In the years that followed, Patricia would collect handfuls of awards—including 2015's Best Supporting Actress Oscar for her turn in *Boyhood*. Shot over a 12-year period, it prevented the actress (per the request of director Richard Linklater) from undergoing any plastic surgery. Walking the various award show red carpets, the paparazzi photos would occasionally (and unfairly) earn her the distinction "Worst Dressed." Fortunately, she never cared two shits what people thought of her natural aging and nontraditional fashion choices.

And how do I know this? That Halloween Eve after the dust settled, Patricia and I took a private moment to decompress. She recalled playing dress up as a child with her famous siblings, Rosanna, David and Alexis. They'd reach into their grandfather's old vaudeville leather trunks and pull out such items as scraggly beards made of actual human hair. She went on to share her fondness for DIYing what she called her "human baby teeth necklaces" made from the dislodged baby teeth of her then-teenaged son, Enzo. And she was very much looking forward to creating more of these unusual trinkets once baby Harlow's fangs fell out. Cute, though also the kind of thing you might hear from the written confession of a deranged mass murderer in a Discovery Channel true-crime docuseries.

Ever since, whenever I see Patricia out on the town, I always make sure to check that all her bling has been properly brushed and flossed.

And what, you may wonder, ever became of the two terrorized junior tram travelers? Clearly recovered from our zombie rampage, too-cool-for-school Sofia went on to star in such horror projects as *Stalker, Lucifer* and *Bad Stepmother,* while rambunctious Maria came out in 2021—right before *his* 24th birthday—as a transgender male named Feodor. Sounds like a good gladiator name to me!

Lesson Learned: When it comes to terrorizing tots—be it on Halloween or in the neighborhood—know when to pull back before well-intentioned playtime turns into ugly, brazen bullying.

Chapter 35
COX & FRIENDS

(COURTENEY COX)

Courteney Cox circa 2009.
(Felicia Sullivan/Wikimedia Commons)

WHO: Courteney Cox (b. June 15, 1964). Actress best known for playing Monica Geller on the classic 1994–2004 NBC sitcom *Friends*.

WHAT: On-the-record interview for *USA Today.*

WHERE: The Regent Beverly Wilshire Hotel, Beverly Hills, CA.

It's difficult to fathom as I write this that we're living in a world with six surviving Brady kids, but just five *Friends*.

Matthew Perry's death in October 2023 rocked us all and showed us that, yes, even Chandler, Ross, Joey, Phoebe, Rachel and Monica can suffer from what may at times seem like inescapable depression.

Back in the mid-2000s when I was writing for *USA Today*, postpartum depression was a hot topic. New mom Brooke Shields had come forward in 2003 with a shocking admission that the birth of her daughter Rowan had inspired suicidal thoughts. Oprah Winfrey devoted several of her shows to the widely misunderstood subject. And suddenly, admitting to depression—no matter the cause—was no longer taboo, as I would learn in a very personal interview I conducted with *Friends* star Courteney Cox.

If you're one of the few who has somehow managed to dodge depression, consider yourself extremely fortunate. Like a shadow monster, this albatross can creep up from behind and pull you down into a ditch so deep that at times you feel as though you may never be able to climb back out. My bout with severe, debilitating depression hit me hard at the start of my fifties when I was love bombed by a handsome, narcissistic Polish dude who was about ten years my junior. After meeting on New Year's Eve 2018 (Hallmark movie romantic, right?), his instantaneous, over-the-top adoration and constant gift-giving sent my endorphin levels soaring. He'd routinely take my hand and lead me up to the bedroom, fervently imploring me to take him. While I always try my best in bed to make sure both partners are getting their needs met, he insisted that all his pleasure came only from fulfilling me. When I'd refer to us having sex (or even the "F" word while in the throes of passion), he'd put his finger to my lips and correct me that what we were experiencing was "making love." It was beyond intense. I knew it was all much too much, much too soon, but the feelings he instilled in me were so intoxicating that I couldn't get enough of this guy and I found myself thinking about him morning, noon and night. I couldn't wait to get my next hit. Over dinner one night early into our relationship he told me he thought I might be "the one." For nearly six months I never felt more loved, desired and worshiped. Without realizing it, I'd become helplessly hooked on this drug I mistook for love.

Then, one night after eating hamburgers I'd cooked for us on the grill out on my deck, he announced we were done. He denied ever saying he thought I was "the one." He'd in fact never loved me at all and the sex apparently hadn't satisfied him for some time. (That last part really ticked me off, as I was always checking in to ask what I could do to please him.) I'd never been more blindsided in my entire life. Suddenly, he was out the door, taking with him all my warm, fuzzy endorphins (along with his French bulldog, Pyro, who pissed on my welcome mat on the way out). I felt empty. Gutted. I couldn't sleep and I completely lost my appetite. I dropped to a weight I hadn't been since my early teens and spent several months walking around like a zombie—just trying to get through each day. Hoping I'd wake up the next morning without this person occupying my every thought. How could this guy I'd only known for half a year have completely hijacked my brain? What had *I* done (or not done) to make his feelings change so dramatically? Was there anything I could do to get him back? Would I ever stop feeling this way?

Desperate, I signed up for exploitative online courses promising tricks for regaining lost loves. And I'd constantly be checking my phone for his texts that never came—discarding all others from true friends as unimportant. While I didn't go so far as to contemplate suicide, I felt completely trapped in my head and desperately wanted this pain to end. If I was going to continue feeling this way, what, I asked myself, was the point of living? It would be too unbearable. I invited God to take me if He saw fit to end the pain.

Instead, my friend John took me to Fantasy Island ... literally. On one of my darkest days, this former boyfriend, who knew me so well, gently took my hand and guided me through the Los Angeles County Arboretum and Botanic Gardens in Arcadia, CA, where sits the historic Queen Anne Cottage seen in the opening credits of Aaron Spelling's marvelous 1977–1984 *Love Boat* companion series, *Fantasy Island.* Marveling at the 1881 Victorian's bell tower, I could almost hear Tattoo (3'11" actor Hervé Villechaize) shouting out "da plane, da plane" as he

With my pal John at the *Fantasy Island* Queen Anne Cottage, 2019 (left). And (right) TV stars Ricardo Montalban and Hervé Villechaize at the same location in 1977. (ABC Television)

pointed up to the arriving seaplane that had brought so many lost souls like me to this mysterious locale.

Among those who sought out the mysterious Mr. Roarke (actor Ricardo Montalban) with hopes he might turn their lives around were many of the falling stars found within these very pages. Robert Reed, Florence Henderson, Maureen McCormick, Eve Plumb, Jayne Meadows, Andy Griffith, Max Baer Jr. and Adam West all had their greatest fantasies granted by Roarke. It was on this hallowed ground where Victoria Principal arrived the year before she landed *Dallas*. And where Joan Collins, at perhaps the lowest point in her career, came to fulfill her fantasy of playing Cleopatra—one year before her casting as *Dynasty's* Alexis. With a new lease on life, I vowed my story was not meant to end as Villechaize's had: with a self-inflicted bullet wound to the chest. No, that was not da plan, da plan.

Fortunately, with the aid of family (thank you, Mom and Jim), close friends who would take my endless calls at all hours (thank you Milena, Stefanie, Christine, Curtis, Randy, Rich and Eric), prescribed medication, tons of therapy and perhaps a little divine intervention from Mr. Roarke, the seemingly inescapable spell that had been cast upon me was at last broken. My appetite returned, I could sleep through the night without heavily sedating myself and I was able to find clarity in what had happened to me. My brain had been rewired and chemically altered, but not permanently.

All smiles with reunited *Mork & Mindy* co-stars Pam Dawber and Robin Williams, a few months before the comedian's tragic 2014 suicide. "Nanu, Nanu."

I emerged from that darkness with newfound empathy for those who do choose to end their lives, and thought of dear Robin Williams, whom I'd had the opportunity to meet on several occasions. The last time was just a few months before the universally-adored comedian hung himself with a belt strapped to his bedroom closet door in August 2014.

As you should well know by now, I'm an ardent fan of '70s and '80s classic TV, so when it came time for me to leave *TV Guide* magazine after a six-year run, it felt fitting that my final interview would be with Williams and his former *Mork & Mindy* co-star Pam Dawber, who had been cast as Robin's love interest on the third-to-last episode of his final television project, *The Crazy Ones*.

I was so excited to land this exclusive reunion interview that I went to a costume store the night before to buy a pair of the very same rainbow-striped suspenders that Robin's impish alien character Mork from Ork had worn throughout the sitcom's run. I hoped the two might get a kick out of my playful nod, and I was right. The problem was that I'd only been able to find those particular suspenders in a child's size, so as my interview with Robin and Pam progressed, I began feeling the straps pulling up on the crotch of my jeans and increasingly constricting my testicles, which have always been super sensitive even under the most ideal circumstances. Though I tried to continuously adjust my legs, the discomfort was becoming almost too unbearable to hide. So finally, when Pam made a casual reference to "balls," I admitted to them both that mine felt as though they were about to EXPLODE. When I explained why, they both laughed, with Robin deadpanning, "I will say your pants looked so tight I could practically tell what religion you are." Despite the delicate situation going on between my legs, this was music to my ears. Robin Williams had just recycled—on *me!*—one of his all-time most classic jokes about male ballet dancers' tights revealing whether or not they were circumcised.

But as much fun as the three of us were having that day on set, I couldn't help noticing a profound pensiveness in Williams I hadn't seen before. His energy level was extremely low and he seemed cloaked in a disabling darkness. That very same darkness that would try, unsuccessfully, to take me down five years later. I understood how Robin—who'd been diagnosed with debilitating Parkinson's disease—could have felt so trapped to the point of needing to escape. And for a comedian who was expected to always be "on," I can imagine it would have been even more difficult for him to expose the inner torment that was consuming him.

That's why I had nothing but tremendous respect for a world-famous celebrity like Courteney Cox, who seemingly had it all, to defy her Monica Geller persona by revealing that even she could experience suicidal fantasies at what should have been the happiest time of her life.

When I sat down with Courteney in the summer of 2004 in a cozy suite at the Regent Beverly Wilshire Hotel, it was not long after she and then-husband David Arquette (Patricia's brother) had welcomed their daughter Coco into their lives. I'd already had an opportunity to speak with Brooke Shields about her postpartum issues, so it seemed natural to ask Courteney if she could relate.

Like the Arquettes, Courteney has also struck me as someone who doesn't particularly give a crap what others think of her. While I'm sure she has her insecurities as we all do, she typically radiates a still confidence. Her answers to my interview questions were delivered with a refreshing honesty. But I admit I never expected for her to tell me—on-the-record with my tape recorder rolling—that not only had she experienced postpartum depression, but that she'd thought about driving her car right off the road to end it all!

"We all have this dark side of our personality when you're on Mulholland Drive and you're like, 'Well, I'm just going to drive over (the edge),' " she said matter-of-factly. *Wow!* While what she said was very relatable to me, I knew this was just the kind of sensational statement that would be picked up everywhere. And it was. *Access Hollywood* made it their lead story the night my article came out in *USA Today* (and then offered me a producer job which I turned down). Not everyone, however, was applauding my scoop. Cox's powerful publicist, the late, great Nanci Ryder of the public relations firm **BWR** (the "R" being for Ryder), was beyond livid.

Before the interview, Nanci had told me that her associate, Leslie Sloane— Britney Spears' publicist who had tried her best to take me down— had "warned me not to trust you, but I told her I always liked you and never had a problem with you." But now, having read my article that addressed her longtime client's suicidal thoughts, she was singing a far different tune. "Leslie told me not to trust you," she repeated, "and I *shouldn't* have. I made a mistake, but I won't again! I hope it was worth it, Will, because you'll never talk to my client again."

After initially trying to deny that Cox had ever said these things, Nanci backpedaled when I reminded her that the whole interview had been recorded on tape. Why publicists seem to forget this, I'll never know. Calming a bit, Nanci then took time to admit her primary gripe had not been that I'd printed Courteney's quotes, but that I hadn't given her a heads-up so that she could properly prepare for the resulting fallout. While that sounds understandable, that route always comes with the risk of torpedoing your exclusive. As was her job, Nanci would have done everything in her power to negotiate with *USA Today* to have those quotes killed. I'd seen it happen many times before.

As I viewed it, Courteney was a 40-year-old woman who'd given hundreds, if not thousands, of interviews over the years and was well aware she was sitting down with a reporter—not one of her *Friends*—for an on-the-record interview. It's not like I was a TMZ reporter waiting outside an airport terminal to ambush her with a question she hadn't seen coming. Just as Shields had so altruistically accomplished, she knew that what she was publicly revealing had the potential for good. To possibly help other new moms make sense of unanticipated, confusing feelings of hopelessness and anxiety that they were too ashamed to discuss with anyone. But most importantly, Cox's courageous confession would let these women know that these feelings were treatable. And temporary. She was offering hope. So why freak out, Nanci?

Fortunately, the vows routinely made in Hollywood to "never work with so-and-so again" typically have short shelf lives. Consequently, I was very pleased when Nanci cautiously invited me back into her circle of trust, allowing us to work together on other projects before she, sadly, (like Matt Perry) passed far too soon.

Lesson Learned: One of the most important lessons my Enquirer *bureau chief Jerry George taught me about relating to celebrities was to continually remind myself that "they're not your friends." While there are rare exceptions, the relationships between reporters and celebrities are rooted in a commercial exchange. I need them to give me something interesting to write about, while they need to bring awareness to their various projects, while hopefully being depicted by the journalist in a positive light.*

The celebrities themselves would be wise to also keep this in mind when sitting down with reporters who are not their friends. There's a mutual agenda that mustn't be forgotten so that there won't be any great surprises when quotes that are given in on-the-record interviews end up in print. Resulting freak-outs accomplish nothing. As I learned in the Landmark Forum personal development seminars, life is empty and meaningless. We are the ones who assign meaning to life events. Good/bad. Right/wrong. Positive/negative. And in the grand scheme of things, a TV actress opening her heart and sharing very human insecurities that others can relate to and perhaps find strength from is a brave and beautiful gift. The same as Perry would so courageously do before his death.

Chapter 36
FROM HERE TO MATERNITY

(SEAN PENN & ROBIN WRIGHT/
JOHN TESH & CONNIE SELLECCA)

WHO: Sean Penn (b. August 17, 1960) and ex-wife Robin Wright (b. April 8, 1966). He collected two Lead Actor Oscars for the films *Mystic River* (2003) and *Milk* (2008), while she is best known for the films *The Princess Bride* and *Forrest Gump* and won a 2013 Golden Globe for the TV drama *House of Cards*.

WHO: John Tesh (b. July 9, 1952) and Connie Sellecca (b. May 25, 1955). He's a Grammy-nominated pianist and former Emmy-winning host of *Entertainment Tonight*, while she is a TV actress best known for her roles on *The Greatest American Hero* (1981–1983) and *Hotel* (1983–1988).

WHAT: Crashing hospital emergency rooms and maternity wards on assignment for the *National Enquirer*.

WHERE (PENN/WRIGHT): Saint John's Hospital, Santa Monica, CA.

WHERE (TESH/SELLECCA): Cedars-Sinai Medical Center, L.A., CA.

While I do think everything worked out for the best in my life and I have little to regret (aside from most everything you've read in this book!), I hold some disappointment that I will never experience the joys that come with being a dad. (Of course, most all those idealistic lost moments I envision are primarily associated with Christmastime, Halloween or family outings to Disney World when parenting is relatively easy and fun.) Those "what could have been" fantasies will always be intertwined with thoughts of what my life might have looked like had my own dad not passed away when I was 5.

The July 16, 1966, wedding day of my parents, William Keck and Nancy Sporborg.

This may be the right place to share what little I know about my father, who by all accounts was a first-rate son, brother, friend and English professor, but a lousy husband. As my mom's shared with me on numerous occasions, she cried herself to sleep on her honeymoon night after my father informed her there'd be little sex in the marriage. It was a warning he apparently delivered on, much to the dismay of my mom, who seemingly had a libido on par with Florence Henderson and Phyllis Diller. I personally have no memories of William Aaron Keck to share; not even faint ones. And by the time my mom clued me in to the existence of film that had been shot of my dad teaching in his classroom, the reels had been long destroyed by the institution where they'd been stored. That discovery was devastating, as he'd never turned up in anyone's home movies to offer me a sense of who he was as a three-dimensional walking, talking human. What a rare, priceless gift those reels would have been.

When I ask my mom how she knew beyond a shadow of a doubt that her husband was gay, the evidence is circumstantial to say the least. Aside from his obsession with William Shakespeare, F. Scott Fitzgerald and everything Disney—she mentions his excessive drinking that would keep him out until all hours of the night, a handsome teacher from the art department with whom he seemed particularly smitten and solo day trips he'd take to New York City in search of rare books. While none of those things makes a man gay (except maybe the Disney thing), I ultimately have to trust the instincts of my mom—a very attractive woman who felt completely ignored in an unhealthy marriage that most certainly would have ended in divorce had William Aaron Keck lived.

Christmas 1970 with my father Bill.

But there was much more to the man than that. And from the many photos he took of me as a baby which he meticulously archived in albums, there's no denying how much he treasured being my dad. I only wish I'd had the chance to experience that love as a growing boy, adolescent and man. But I'm also old enough to know that growing up the child of an alcoholic would surely have presented its own challenges and heartaches.

Parenting in the 21st century, as I've come to learn from every single one of my traumatized friends who've so ~~foolishly~~ bravely taken on the role, ain't easy. That's why my partner and I are happy to be raising pets, who seem far less interested in online porn sites, vaping and vapid social media influencers. (Although I really have no idea what trouble our dogs and cat get into during the day, now do I?) But even Trick, Fallon and Valentino can be too much to handle at times. So to all you mommies and daddies out there raising your pandemic babies, I say best of luck.

Speaking of babies, it wasn't only the *Enquirer's* macabre "death watch" assignments that had me sneaking into hospitals with bouquets of flowers. Occasionally, I'd be dispatched on "baby watch" detail. And on rare occasions, those disparate missions sadly crossed. Here are two examples that demonstrate the incredible joy and devastating heartbreak that can accompany what should be the happiest of events: the arrival of new life.

Back on March 25, 1996—the day of the 68th annual Academy Awards—I spent the night with Best Actor nominee Sean Penn, but he never knew I was just feet away monitoring his every move. Penn was up for the first of his multiple

Lead Actor nominations, that particular year for *Dead Man Walking*—a title that aptly described how he appeared to me that night, pacing the floor of a waiting room at Saint John's Hospital in Santa Monica.

Robin Wright Penn and Sean Penn, circa 2006.
(Attit Patel/Wikimedia Commons)

Earlier that evening, as I was setting up for my annual Oscar viewing party, an *Enquirer* editor called with a tip he'd received from a hospital snitch that Penn's then-girlfriend (and future wife) Robin Wright was experiencing pregnancy complications and had been rushed by Sean and his actor brother Chris Penn to the ER.

After I made the disappointing—though by this time no longer surprising—calls to disinvite my party guests, I high-tailed it over to Saint John's and easily located Penn in a first-floor waiting room. With Chris at his side, Sean was sweating profusely, keeping vigil with his sweaty palms clasped in prayer. At this very time, Sean and Robin should have been holding hands in the Dorothy Chandler Pavilion, seated alongside fellow nominees Nicolas Cage, Anthony Hopkins and Richard Dreyfuss, waiting to hear which of their names would be called by presenter Jessica Lange. Instead, Penn was barely paying attention to the ceremony being telecast live up on a small monitor in a corner of the gloomy room. Despite Penn's volatile reputation—particularly as it relates to pesky reporters like me—this night he played only the role of caregiver, peeking through a small window leading to the surgical room where Wright was being operated on.

As a fly on the wall, I was among the first to learn—right along with Sean—that Robin was miscarrying what would have been their third child, after the arrivals of daughter Dylan in 1991 and son Hopper in 1993. The miscarriage was the result of an ectopic pregnancy (a life-threatening condition where the embryo develops inside a fallopian tube instead of the womb). While waiting for a nurse to escort him back to see his wife, Penn watched such stars as Kevin Spacey and Elisabeth

340

Shue rise from their seats as Cage joined Lange on stage to collect his Oscar for *Leaving Las Vegas*. Filled with overwhelming joy, Cage concluded his speech by thanking his "gorgeous" new bride of one year, Patricia Arquette, who was seated in the audience … not wearing any of her son Enzo's baby teeth (see Chapter 34).

Fortunately, Penn would receive four more Lead Actor nominations (winning twice), while Cage went on to receive four more wives (presumably losing tons of money in alimony payments).

To describe how I felt as "icky" would be a gross understatement, made all the worse when the article came out with cheesy, fabricated quotes chronicling what had transpired between Sean and Robin as they were getting ready to leave for the ceremony:

> The couple was giddy with anticipation when Robin suddenly slumped to the bedroom floor, gripped by excruciating stomach pains. "Oh Sean, something horrible is happening to me! Please don't let it be our baby," Robin cried out…. Sadly, the baby had been lost … but Sean's precious Robin was doing well. The much-relieved actor told a pal, "Nick Cage got the Oscar, but I get to take home my princess."

It's amazing to me that *Enquirer* readers actually bought this shit.

I should just count my blessings that Penn never discovered my identity, as I'm sure I would have required my own recovery room at Saint John's. While the couple ended up splitting in 2010, it was nice seeing photos emerge in 2023 of Sean and Robin reuniting for the first time in years for the sake of their now-grown kids, with Robin telling *E! News*, "We're always gonna be a family."

Two years before the Penns' hospital heartache, I was sent out on a more celebratory mission that once again found me arriving with a bouquet of flowers to my old stomping ground, Cedars-Sinai Medical Center. (I swear, I should have received that same robust greeting from the Cedars staff—*"WILLL!!!"*—that awaited beer-guzzling Norm Peterson each time he slumped into Cheers.)

Gorgeous brunette actress Connie Sellecca, who had starred on TV's *The Greatest American Hero* and Aaron Spelling's *Hotel,* had just given birth to the child of husband John Tesh, an *Entertainment Tonight* anchor and Grammy-nominated pianist whose heart is as big as his 6'6" frame. Because there had been complications with the baby's lungs during the breach birth, mother and baby were spending a few extra days at the hospital to gain their strength.

I managed to glide right past the nurses' station and enter Connie's room without attracting any eyeballs. There, I discovered Tesh cuddled in bed with his wife and their newborn preemie daughter, who had been delivered via cesarean section. While Connie's eyes remained fixed on her breastfeeding angel, John got one look at the floral arrangement I'd selected and beamed from ear to ear.

"Wowww. Who are these from?" John asked.

Without missing a beat, I answered, "Your friends at The Wave," referencing an L.A. radio station that regularly played his compositions. Yep, a shameless, bold-faced LIE that I suppose I'd been able to justify because I knew this was to be a feel-good story, as opposed to so many of those other monstrosities.

"Aw, isn't that nice," said John, with Connie offering a warm glance as her baby continued to suckle.

Having had ample time to plan exactly what I was going to say, everything, for once, went just as planned.

"Oh, your baby is so precious," I cooed. "A boy or a girl?"

"It's a girl," Sellecca whispered.

I inched just a bit closer to eyeball the babe, making sure she had all ten of her fingers and toes, and no extras. No horns or pig snout either. She was perfect, and my fabricated adoration instantly became genuine.

"Awww ... can I ask her name?"

"Prima," answered the proud mama.

At first, with my poor hearing (a result of chronic childhood ear trauma), I thought Connie had said "Preemie." But surely the Teshes would never have branded their child with a name reflecting her early arrival, three weeks before its due date. Just as no baby should be saddled with the name "Breech" or "Vaginal."

"How did you come up with that?" I prodded.

"My father was Primo Sellecchia, so we named her Prima after him," Connie explained.

Ahh, okay. *Prima*. Not Preemie. Much, much better! Like a prima ballerina. Lovely really, isn't it?

Having collected all the data I needed to fill in the blanks for my story, I hightailed it out of there before I was exposed. As a Sasquatchian 6'6", Teshy has a reputation for being an extremely benevolent Born-Again Bigfoot. But even so, I wouldn't have stood a chance had that protective Papa Bear turned on me.

The following year, as a nod to that rare, disaster-free hospital caper, I named my shiny new 1995 Toyota Celica convertible "Connie"—which I karmically crashed just months later.

Lesson Learned: Just leave dem babies alone.

A NOTE FROM JOHN TESH AND CONNIE SELLECCA

We don't really have to search our hearts for forgiveness as we have no memory of this violation of our privacy. We don't even know if it really happened! Jesus preached about repentance and changing our ways moving forward. Good on ya, William Keck. P.S. We did enjoy our phone conversation.

John Tesh, Prima Tesh and Connie Sellecca.
(Photo courtesy of the Tesh Family)

Chapter 37
HOLY HAWAIIAN BAT-PRISON!

(ADAM WEST)

Batman publicity photos of Adam West (above) and West with Burt Ward, circa 1966. (ABC/Wikimedia Commons)

WHO: Adam West (1928–2017). Famous for immortalizing the Caped Crusader in the campy 1966–1968 *Batman* TV series.

WHAT: *National Enquirer* investigation into West's daughter's imprisonment for attempted murder. Additional on-the-record interviews for *TV Guide* & an appearance on *Home & Family.*

WHERE: The Big Island of Hawaii. San Diego Convention Center, San Diego, CA. Various other locations.

At the risk of sounding as altruistic as Batman lecturing the good citizens of Gotham City, on those days when it seems we've lost all our heroes, it comforts me to think back on the late Adam West, a man whom I discovered to be as much a hero in real life as the Caped Crusader he played on TV.

There was no one quite like West. He was a larger-than-life personality, who—like William Shatner, Larry Hagman and Joan Collins—morphed over the

years into a living version of his most iconic television character. Having now lived in Los Angeles for more than three decades, I've witnessed the City of Angels struggle through one historic crisis after another. Police corruption and brutality. Violent rioting. Out-of-control homelessness. But on June 15, 2017, I could not have been more proud of my city when a ceremonial Bat-Signal was projected onto the side of downtown's City Hall in tribute to West, who'd passed away one week earlier. It took someone of his caliber, whose image had inspired and entertained so many, to wake my city up into doing something spectacular and out of the ordinary, budgetary concerns be damned.

I still have to smile when I think back on the last time I spent time with Adam … that horny little devil. It was November 2014 and he'd come on *Home & Family* to promote his camp classic's 50th anniversary. One story he shared left our hosts, Mark Steines and Cristina Ferrare, so shocked and speechless that it was deemed "un-Hallmarkable" and never made it to air. But no one was more shocked than me. As the producer of the segment, I'd conducted an extensive pre-interview with Adam over the phone so that I could properly prep Mark and Cristina on the questions he was expecting to answer. Adam and I had agreed he'd tell a sweet story in memory of his dear friend and *Batman* co-star, Frank Gorshin, the talented comic who rocked a bright green, skintight, question mark-dotted jumpsuit like no other as the maniacal Riddler.

"I was with Frank in the hospital on his deathbed," West had recalled to me in a teary, emotional voice. "Poor Frank was so weak and close to death, but I managed to get a smile out of my old pal by sticking one of his old headshots up on his heart monitor machine. It was like he was seeing himself on TV one last time. I'll never forget the smile on his face. Whatta guy."

By the end of the call, I was almost in tears myself and knew that would be a perfect story to share with our conservative Hallmark audience. But then I was thrown a real BatArang I never saw coming.

Riddler Frank Gorshin facing off against Adam West in a 1967 episode of *Batman*. **(20th Century Fox Television)**

When Steines prompted West to tell his Frank Gorshin story, as I watched on the studio floor from a few feet away, I could see West get a naughty gleam in his eye that worried me. "Are you sure we have time?" Adam asked.

"Oh, sure," Mark said, excited to hear West's sentimental deathbed memory.

But instead, this is the story West decided to share:

"I remember one night we got off work late and decided to head from the *Batman* set up to a party in the Hollywood Hills...."

Mark and Cristina flashed me a confused look—this was *not* the story any of us was expecting.

"Well…," West continued. "You can imagine our surprise when the door opened to the party and a wild orgy was in full swing. Everything you can imagine ... naked bodies twisted in all sorts of positions...."

Cristina covered her mouth, trying her best to hold back her laughs, while Mark let out a loud guffaw. Our entire crew was in stitches, as this kind of talk was never heard on our saccharine set. While West's orgy story would have been gold on any late-night talk show, I knew it would, alas, never air on Hallmark.

Now that I think about it, it's actually rather amusing just how many X-rated stories I've heard involving members of the Bat-family. When *Incredible Hulk* actor/bodybuilder Lou Ferrigno visited *Home & Family*, he shared with me (off camera) about his teenage crush on Yvonne Craig, the buxom actress who'd co-starred with West as Batgirl. Ferrigno clenched his hulkish hand into a rapidly-stroking masturbatory fist and told me in his nasally voice (a consequence of early childhood hearing loss), "I was so 'ot faw Yvonne, I use-a jack off tuh Baht-gawl."

Left: With Hulk actor Lou Ferrigno on the set of *Home & Family,* 2014—touching the fist that fantasized about Batgirl Yvonne Craig (right), circa 1968. (ABC/Wikimedia Commons)

And then there was actor Burt Ward, who'd portrayed West's sidekick, Robin the Boy Wonder. I first met Ward way back in 1995 when I took him to a screening of *Batman Forever* to get his exclusive first reaction to Chris O'Donnell's updated, edgier take on the Robin character. Ward and I so hit it off that he asked me to contribute a quote that would appear on the back cover of his naughty tell-all, *Boy Wonder: My Life in Tights*.

"Batman and Robin's onscreen adventures pale in comparison to what went on once the tights came off. You'll laugh louder than The Joker as Ward hurls one scathing BatArang after another," were the words I wrote to help sell Ward's memoir, which, among other sensationalized claims, revealed the great difficulty he'd experienced trying to stuff his "massive manhood" into his skintight costume.

While Ward divulged many titillating tales about his off-camera adventures with West, there are a couple amusing *mis*adventures he elected *not* to put in print, but have come up in our conversations over the years. Though Ward's stories may challenge West's gallant reputation, they're just too fun not to share!

Author with Boy Wonder Burt Ward (left) outside a 1995 screening *of Batman Forever*.

Take for instance the time Burt asked Adam to be best man at his 1990 wedding-at-sea to his now-wife Tracy. Adam accepted … but with a few very specific requests. You see, Adam was well aware that Tracy's daddy was a real-life Bruce Wayne billionaire who'd landed on the Forbes 400 list. As Burt told me, when he'd first informed his future father-in-law of his intentions to marry Tracy, the disapproving mogul offered Burt $10 million to *not* marry his daughter and put her on the first plane home. It was an offer Burt politely declined.

With Burt and Tracy's wedding moving forward despite the loud protests of her father, Adam informed the groom that he would require *eight* first class, round-trip plane tickets for him and his family to fly from their Idaho home to Los Angeles. (If you're counting, that's *double* the number of first class plane tickets Teri Hatcher requested of me!) While Burt begrudgingly agreed to those terms, he declined to contribute an additional $10k to rent a private Batcopter to whisk West north from the wedding yacht to a golf course where he was to receive a private lesson.

Then there was another time when West and Ward were appearing at an autograph show back east, when an enthused young fan approached West with a 1966 *Batman* movie poster he'd already had signed by Ward, Gorshin, Cesar Romero (The Joker), Burgess Meredith (The Penguin) and Lee Meriwether (Catwoman). The only outstanding signer was West, who of course knew that the addition of his name would make the poster extremely valuable. So in stepped Adam's longtime manager (and shrewd negotiator) Fred Westbrook, who—as Ward tells it—renegotiated Adam's signing fee from $100 to a whopping $600!!

The poor kid burst into tears while his mother became enraged, prompting the event organizer to put out the fire by offering to cover the $500 difference.

Left: Author with Julie Newmar (in Catwoman costume) at a 2001 Halloween event, and (right) with West, Newmar and Ward at San Diego Comic-Con 2014.

But despite Ward's stories, I only ever experienced Adam to be a man of honor. Our first encounter was in 1995 when the *Enquirer* flew me to Hawaii's Big Island to uncover the sordid details behind the actor's then-37-year-old daughter Jonelle's imprisonment for attempted murder—a story no one (especially a TV superhero) would ever want exposed.

I thought it best not to involve Adam in my investigation until the last possible minute, when we would need him to comment. Adam was living back in Idaho, but I worried he might use his influence to stop my sources on the island from speaking to me. I started my investigation by flying to Kailua-Kona to meet the story's original call-in source, the daughter's troubled Aussie photographer boyfriend, Paul, who was staying in a youth hostel called Patey's Place.

Paul had worked out a sweet deal for himself to stay at the hostel for free in exchange for painting psychedelic murals on its walls. And now Paul was wheeling and dealing with me! Besides revealing to me that Jonelle had attempted to murder both of her ex-husband's parents, Paul was in possession of private family photos he was looking to unload for a steep price. As part of the deal, he also wanted to be the photographer assigned to our story, meaning he'd be the one (if everything went according to plan) to photograph the elderly victims in their home, as well as Jonelle in her orange jumpsuit doing hard time in the county jail. But Paul proved to be unreliable and prone to angry outbursts, so as soon as I extracted enough details, I lost the guy. Public record court documents would be all I'd need to continue my investigation.

At that time, poor Jonelle was a beautiful but deeply troubled woman. Facing addiction issues, she'd accused her ex-husband Ron Rumley of molesting their two young sons and, for a while, was living in a tent on the beach. In the early afternoon of July 25, 1994, she became so enraged that she stormed into the swanky Kailua-Kona home of her wealthy ex in-laws, 68-year-old Margaret, and 81-year-old Preston Rumley, and demanded money for her kids.

I wasn't sure what to expect when I paid my own visit to the Rumleys, but both were happy to welcome me into their home and go on the record with their side of the story. According to Margaret, Jonelle was into witchcraft and devil worship. After a heated conflict ensued, Jonelle made "witch signs" with her hands and then hit Margaret over the head with a phone *(CLUNK!!!)* before trying to crush her skull with a flowerpot *(BAM!)*. Margaret further alleged that Jonelle kicked them both *(THWACK!!!)*, broke Margaret's wrist *(KAPOW!)* and repeatedly screamed, "I'm going to kill you!!" Per Margaret, a neighbor came to the couple's rescue just as Jonelle was about to do Margaret in with a garden hoe. Compared to The Joker's crimes on the *Batman* series (like, oh, attempting to turn Gotham City's water supply into strawberry gelatin, or feeding the dynamic duo to a giant clam), this was some serious shit!

When the Rumleys' son came to the home, he discovered both of his elderly parents in the fetal position and covered in blood. (I still have four notebooks filled with every unsavory detail of this tragic family nightmare.)

For her violent crimes, Jonelle was serving a year in the Hawaii Community Correction Center in Hilo—and, after much negotiating, I managed to score an in-prison interview. The night before I was to make the long drive to the other side of the island, the phone rang in my hotel room. Because I'd left my business card with all my contact info on the doorstep of Jonelle's mother and West's ex-wife, Ngatokoruaimatauaia Frisbie (which sounds like one of the wacky weapons in

Batman's arsenal), I assumed mama had to be the one calling. But instead, on the other end of the line was a silky smooth, deep, masculine voice that sounded … familiar.

"I'd like to speak to William Keck, please," said the caller.

"This is William," I answered.

"William, this is Bill Anderson."

(From having read court documents earlier that day, I knew Bill Anderson was Adam West's real name. Yup, I was on the Batphone with yet another of my childhood idols. *Holy time warp, Batman!!*)

"Apparently you are in Hawaii trying to speak with my family," he continued, surprisingly laying on the kindness and playing me like a fiddle.

"William," he said. "I want to thank you."

Say what??!!

"Thank me?" I asked, assuming I'd heard him wrong.

"Yes, thank you for taking the time to fly all the way out to Hawaii to get the facts right of this very sad story."

West was an absolutely brilliant negotiator, going so far as to offer to send me private family photos of him with Jonelle's young sons, whom he was now looking after until mommy got out of the slammer. (It had been Jonelle's wishes to get her boys off the island and away from their father and the Rumleys ASAP.) Though I didn't realize it at that very moment, Adam was writing his own tabloid story. (Let this serve as a lesson to any celebrity wishing to take control of a potentially scandalous exposé.)

The next day, Jonelle—dressed in an orange inmate jumpsuit—was brought to me from her cell in handcuffs. My heart immediately fell for this young woman who, because of drugs and mental challenges, had committed heinous acts that had separated her from her children. To add further salt to the wound, the day of our interview happened to be her son William's birthday, and all she'd been able to gift the boy was a handmade card scribbled with Crayolas. But I also remained ever cognizant of the frail, elderly Rumleys, who had nearly lost their lives. Unless you're The Penguin, you just can't go around hitting people over the head with flowerpots.

In our interview, Jonelle chose her words very carefully, almost as if she'd been coached what to say by her famous father. She expressed her great gratitude for West, whom she credited with teaching her prayer and meditation to get her through the remaining months of her sentence. Six months sober and exploring her creative side via poetry and art, Jonelle had also enrolled in a computer class and anger management courses, which she hoped might teach her how to fight calmly with words instead of lethal household objects.

GRANDPA BATMAN TO THE RESCUE!

FLASHBACK: Adam West in the role he made famous. Now he's taken on another challenge in real life.

TV's "Batman" Adam West has rescued his grandchildren from a horrifying family nightmare! Their father was forced to battle child abuse accusations. Their mother — West's 37-year-old daughter Jonelle — is in prison for beating and threatening to kill her in-laws.

TV's Adam West saves grandsons after their mom is jailed for brutal attack on her in-laws

So a heartbroken West has given a home to the ex-couple's two boys William, 8, and Preston, 6, and is raising them as his own.

"I'm no hero — I'm just a man who loves his grandchildren and wants to bring some joy to their sorrowful lives," West, 67, sadly told The ENQUIRER in an exclusive interview.

"My daughter Jonelle is an alcoholic who needs help. My former son-in-law Ron Rumley was accused of child molestation. And his mother is trying to destroy Jonelle's life.

"The least I could do was **" I just want to bring some joy to the boys' sorrowful lives?**

look after Jonelle's sons while she serves her sentence. So my wife Marcelle and I are providing William and Preston with a proper home environment for the first time in their young lives."

The family troubles first exploded into scandal two months after Jonelle's May 1994 divorce, according to Ron, 41, who lives with his parents in Hawaii.

"Jonelle was abusing drugs and alcohol, and jumping from one man to another — and she falsely accused me of molesting our sons during my visitations with them," Ron told The ENQUIRER.

He took a lie detector test and psychological exams that resulted in the charges against him being dis-

CARING Adam West is now raising grandsons Preston (left) and William as his own.

KIDS' DAD Ron Rumley

MARGARET RUMLEY

PRESTON RUMLEY

TROUBLED daughter Jonelle says West is "even more heroic than Batman."

911, but Jonelle ripped the phone out of the wall and hit me over the head with it. I fell to the ground. Then she threw my husband to the ground. She tried to crush my head with a

Correctional Center in Hilo.

But West — who's raising his grandchildren at his Idaho ranch — says that Margaret is the real villain. "She may look like a harmless grandmother,

But Jonelle couldn't hold back when it came to sharing disturbing accusations about her children's father and grandparents, claiming, "My husband (Ron) wanted to partake in sexual acts that I was not interested in that were against my religion." Questioning her sentencing, she asked, "Why am I here instead of my husband and his parents?" She called her former mother-in-law "a witch" who kept pornography in their home. She also claimed that, in 1981, two police officers in Utah had cuffed her and initiated sex, prompting a visit from West to defend his daughter and get the perpetrators kicked off the force. Way to go, Batman!

After a childhood spent in Malibu followed by 15 years of island life, Jonelle, upon her release, planned to move to her father's home in Idaho.

When I returned to my hotel room with all the information I needed (and then some!), I celebrated by buying a ticket to my first luau.

Then, one week later, the Adam West story hit stands, the headline reading "Grandpa Batman to the Rescue!" It was filled with exclusive quotes from West, demonstrating to *Enquirer* readers what a real-life hero he was. (Not to mention shrewd as a serpent.)

"I just want to bring some joy to the boys' sorrowful lives," is how he was quoted. And one of the last lines in the article is a quote I got from Jonelle about her famous dad being "even more heroic than Batman."

In a truly tragic twist of fate, Burt Ward has had to silently endure his own family heartache. Since 2018, Ward's daughter, Lisa, has remained motionless in a coma. As Ward's wife, Tracy, shared in an emotional Facebook post, Lisa's heart stopped after experiencing the onset of an asthma attack. To give you an idea of the close father/daughter bond Burt and Lisa had once shared, I quote this sweet sentiment Lisa expressed in a 2014 interview with Bat-fan Dan Greenfield: "My dad would have already been a superhero in my eyes even if he didn't play one on TV, as probably most little girls love their daddies; but to actually know he was one made me very proud and I felt very protected." Burt, our prayers are with you, Lisa and your family.

There is at least one happy footnote to Jonelle's sad saga. Shortly before his death, Adam filled me in that his daughter had served her time, gotten her life together and found work in the film industry. And I gotta say, for stepping in to raise his grandkids *and* turning a potential tabloid hatchet job into a glorified puff piece, that gracious grampy deserves an orgy in heaven with Egghead, King Tut, Lola Lasagne and the whole damn *Batman* cast!!!

WHACK! BOFF!! SPLATT!!!

Lesson Learned: Even seemingly-impervious superheroes like the Dynamic Duo have major bat-guano to clean up back at the Batcave. Keeping that in mind may just help the rest of us mild-mattered citizens from climbing the walls.

Chapter 38
ASSAULTED!

(?)

WHO: Prohibited from revealing the identity of the sitcom star who physically assaulted me.

WHAT: Confrontation stemming from a *National Enquirer* tip regarding possible infidelity.

WHERE: Outside the celebrity's Studio City, CA, home.

Who was my mystery celebrity assailant? For legal reasons I can't say. Instead, let's imagine me tussling in this chapter with Bogie, a 650-pound North American brown bear.

Speaking of **WHACK! BOFF!! SPLATT!!!**, I guess I had it coming to me sooner or later, didn't I? But considering all the many celebrities I antagonized during my *Enquirer* years, it's actually remarkable that only twice did my confrontations turn physical. Unfortunately, per the terms of a legally binding contract, I can only reveal the identity of one of my two attackers—a 650-pound North American brown bear named Bogie.

For a truly bizarre pictorial assignment dreamed up by one of the editors in Lantana, FL, I was asked to meet up with an exotic animal stunt coordinator, former Ringling Bros. and Barnum & Bailey circus lion tamer Brian McMillan, at his Hollywood Animals sanctuary in Santa Clarita, CA, to wrestle a bear. Billed as a "celebrity animal performer," Bogie's biggest credit at the time was the 1994 TV movie, *The Gambler V: Playing for Keeps*, starring Kenny Rogers, Dixie Carter,

Loni Anderson and a 30-year-old Mariska Hargitay, just five years before she'd begin her quarter-century-plus run on *Law & Order: Special Victims Unit.*

Author facing off with the real Bogie in 1994.

"Unlike bears that wrestle people at fairs and carnivals," I wrote in my super cheesy first-person survival narrative, "this bear hadn't been declawed and wasn't wearing a muzzle—so he was a formidable opponent. When the beast laid eyes on me, he started drooling. I could almost hear him thinking: 'Yum—150 pounds of fresh meat!' "

My charming *Enquirer* editors rewrote my copy to describe me as both a "flimsy card table with a Toyota on top" and a "helpless mouse caught under a fur-covered grand piano." (Gee, thanks.) And for some inexplicable reason, I'd also felt it would be fun to reveal to *Enquirer* readers an embarrassing memory from my high school gym years: that I'd set a new Bethlehem Central wrestling record for getting pinned in just 4.7 seconds. In my defense, I'd been paired with a hunky jock and my only concern was trying to get through the match without sporting a noticeable bulge in my singlet.

Apparently, such concerns are not uncommon, based upon an amusing discussion thread I discovered on Quora titled, "Is it common to get aroused when you are wrestling? How can you prevent this? Does it mean I'm gay?" A supposed erection expert named Nicholas Christo chimed in with some helpful advice to relieve students of their anxiety: "If it happens to you, ignore it or make a joke of it. Once, I heard a wrestler apologize by saying that he left the coat hanger inside his singlet. The boner will go away if you ignore it."

My favorite response to Christo had to be from Mark G, who answered, "Yes, a lot of wrestlers while on the mat get erections. It doesn't mean you are gay. It's what you do with it that says it all. If you try to kiss your opponent and stick your dick in his ass while on the mat you are probably gay." Truer words have never been spoken, Mark.

Anyway, I assure you I did *not* get aroused in my *Enquirer* scuffles with either that heavily salivating brown bear or a mystery human celebrity who, one year later, left me bloodied and bruised on the street outside his Studio City home. Because of a signed confidentiality agreement barring me from revealing the identity of this barbaric multiple-Emmy winner (not to mention how much more fun it is having an image in your mind of the celebrity at the center of my various skirmishes), let's just go ahead and refer to this unnamed sitcom star as … Bogie the bear.

The comparison's not all that far off. Similar to the bear (who towered nearly seven feet on his hind legs), my wild-haired *human* attacker was also quite tall, intimidating and suffered from questionable hygiene and foul breath. So from here on out, my unnamed "he" will be referenced as either "Bogie" or "the bear."

It was the day before Valentine's Day 1995 at the height of Bogie's popularity when I received (yet another) tip from my bureau chief Jerry—this one alleging that the bear was keeping company with one of the many former wives of movie actor Dennis Hopper.

I had absolutely no idea whether or not any of this was true, so I started my investigation by contacting my secret source on the bear's TV sitcom. This young woman had recently leaked me details about a top-secret storyline (a cosmic reveal about Bogie's character) that turned out to be 100% accurate, so I asked if she could also provide his home address in Studio City. My assignment was to confront the bear directly about these reports and ascertain his reaction. So over Coldwater Canyon I drove to his cul-de-sac to knock on his door.

What I had absolutely no way of knowing was that, earlier that very same day, a reporter from a competing tabloid had been caught peeping in one of Bogie's windows, thus frightening either his elderly mother or girlfriend (two different versions of the story were offered). A confrontation of some kind apparently ensued between this unidentified reporter and a home-security patrol officer that had royally pissed off the bear and prepared him for battle.

As luck would have it (and by luck I mean terrible, *terrible* misfortune), Bogie was pulling out of his driveway in his white Lexus just as I arrived. And sitting there in the passenger seat was his girlfriend. As I'd later learn, they were on their way to a yoga class. When I hurried over to the car, the bear lowered his driver-side window. I informed him that I was a reporter and that I needed to ask him about something of a confidential nature out of his passenger's earshot. But Bogie told me anything I had to say could be said in front of her. I tried stressing that it would *really* be much better if we could speak privately, but he was growing increasingly aggressive and demanded to know what I'd come to say.

"Spit it out!" Bogie growled.

So, I told him. And well, let's just say he was one unhappy bear.

Bogie got out of his Lexus, grabbed me by my shirt and pushed me down onto the street. He then challenged me to fight him, but I didn't dare engage the beast. Instead, I tried apologizing and talking him down. But there was no placating this bear. He got me in a stranglehold and dragged me across the pavement. I screamed for help so loud that a couple of his neighbors came out onto their doorsteps to watch the drama unfold. To *watch,*

The bear getting me from behind.

mind you. Not intervene, despite my anguished pleas for help.

"Call the police!" I screamed. "He's going to kill me!!" But the neighbors just stood there staring as if this was a pay-per-view wrestling match.

"Sure, go ahead, call the police!!" Bogie shouted out to his neighbors as he tried dragging me toward his front door. "I'll have you arrested for trespassing!"

In the scuffle, the bear's dirty, untrimmed fingernails cut my nose and the thumb of my left hand. As I tried desperately to break free of his stronghold, I told him I was sensing an asthma attack coming on and begged him to please let me at least fish my inhaler out of my back pocket. But still he refused to release his grip.

Finally, as other curious neighbors congregated on their front lawns, Bogie heeded his girlfriend's advice to let me go. Returning to his car, he noticed what I assume was *my* blood on his hand and shouted, "Look what you made me do!" There was also blood on my notebook, which he grabbed from my hand to read. When I informed him that he was stealing my property, that really set the bear off. He chased after me, screaming that I was a "scumbag piece of shit!!"

Bogie making me his Lauren Bacall bitch.

Bogie then got ahold of my shirt collar and dragged me toward his front gate, telling me he was taking me into his house—the last place I wanted to end up! I knew if this grisly bear succeeded in getting me in his cave, he could legally claim I was an intruder who'd broken in and I'd be toast. With my gasps for air growing increasingly noticeable, Bogie finally released his hold so I could take a couple puffs of my inhaler. That brief pause provided the moment I knew I needed for him to come out of his psychotic spell.

Finally, he got back in the car and drove off, leaving me alone to shout out to the neighbors, "Did you see that? He attacked me! I'm bleeding!! Did anyone call the police? Are they coming?!!!"

But not a single one of them could be bothered to come to my aid. With the show over, they all went back into their homes. In this era before cell phones were commonplace, I had no choice but to wait it out to see if the police might come, which, of course, they did not.

When I finally made contact with Jerry, I was encouraged to go to the hospital to make sure I was okay and have photos taken of my bruises and the bleeding cuts on my hand and nose. At the Daniel Freeman Marina Hospital, I received an exam, a tetanus shot and a Vicodin prescription for my pain. I also filled out an official police report with the LAPD. The *Enquirer* supported me fully in setting me up with one of their top attorneys to go after Bogie for reparations. I wasn't looking for a huge payout, mind you, just something to compensate me for the (legitimate) pain and suffering I'd endured from this brutal attack that stemmed from an animalistic, Hulk-like rage the likes of which I'd only ever experienced one other time: on the University of Southern California campus.

That was a whole other nightmare. A few years earlier, I'd been enrolled in USC Film School's Filmic Writing Program when a fellow film student whom I considered to be a close friend turned on me in the most brutal and unexpected manner. The two of us had just returned to Los Angeles from a fun, drama-free road trip to San Francisco when my friend—a strapping former boxer from Mexico City—pulled into a corner gas station on Franklin Ave. in Hollywood to fill the tank of his sports car. The last few miles had been strained as I struggled to comprehend his explanation of a custom called "la mojadera" (generally practiced in Panamanian carnival celebrations), whereby revelers are hosed down until they are soaked. I'd never heard of anything remotely like this and wasn't entirely sure he wasn't making the whole story up just to mess with me. So, I laughed it off. Now, looking back, he must have taken my response as an insensitive cultural affront.

Before I knew it, he hurled off and sucker-punched me hard in the head … neglecting to put on his boxing gloves. When I came to, I was dumbstruck. *Had that actually just happened??!!* He ended up driving off and leaving me at the gas station to be tended to by total strangers. Over the next couple of weeks, there were back-and-forth threats of retaliation before he tracked me down in a campus classroom during a guest lecture from the screenwriter of Disney's *The Rescuers Down Under*. After getting me in a chokehold, the guy dragged me out into a hallway where he pummeled my head until it was swollen. It took a couple of professors to pull the guy off me. For a variety of reasons—not the least of which were concerning stories he'd told me about his wealthy and influential family's "dealings" in Mexico—I elected not to press charges.

I ultimately made the same decision with Bogie after his powerful lawyers informed mine that their remorseless client was determined to take full advantage of his substantial financial resources and hold out until he could present *his* version of the events to a judge. He knew full well that a jury, in all likelihood, would side with a beloved TV star who made them laugh every week over a tabloid scumball who got just what he deserved. And my own attorneys ultimately agreed. So, on what was my 27th birthday, after Bogie rejected several attempted out-of-court settlements, I opted not to pursue a lawsuit and settled for a paltry sum to cover my medical costs—a good percentage of which was paid to my lawyers. The little he shelled out was probably what he earned in his first ten minutes on set.

Though nothing could make up for what he'd put me through, I'll admit there was some small sense of karmic satisfaction many years later when all the world discovered this man's true nature with the very public reveal of a deeply disturbing scandal that ended his career.

As for me, well, my pre-Valentine's Day massacre was an epic wake-up call. I'd originally joined the *Enquirer* to meet my favorite stars, *not* get pummeled by them. A change had to come. And it would. I was about to proclaim to my bureau chief, *"I'm out of here, Jerry!"*

Lesson Learned: Before making any major decisions that could impact your future, be sure to ponder what's really in your best interest. Sure, my family got a kick out of seeing photos of their "Billy" wrestling a bear in the National Enquirer. *And even though I was fortunate enough to not have my face ripped off, I ended up at the office of a high-priced Beverly Hills chiropractor with a bill that was immediately rejected by Blue Cross after the insurance company learned my injuries were the result of voluntary animal wrestling (a cruel practice I'd now never engage in).*

And was a $3,641.87 payout really worth sacrificing my right to call out my attacker by name in a book I'd one day write? If I had to do it all over again, I'd flatly refuse to sign the confidentiality agreement, give Bogie the finger and tell him, "Here's looking at you, kid!"

Chapter 39
BEING RAQUEL

Raquel Welch circa 2010.
(Justin Hoch/Wikimedia Commons)

The years of trauma and guilt that resulted from "attending" weddings and funerals to which I hadn't been invited, spying on dying legends in their homes and hospital beds, digging through garbage, engaging in dangerous high-speed chases and fielding threats from angry publicists had left me emotionally and physically drained. I was more than ready to tell Tony Soprano I wanted out of the tabloid family. For good.

During my tenure with the *Enquirer*, I'd seen so much: from the exploitation of the O.J. Simpson case to the tragedy of Christopher Reeve's paralyzing equestrian jump. But for me, the final hurdle that broke the Kryptonian's back wasn't anything particularly "chapter worthy," on par with getting beaten up by one star and fondled by another. What ultimately opened my eyes and forced me to permanently separate from the tabloid world and the business of exposing and exploiting celebrity dirt was a totally unexpected "ah-ha" moment—that wonderful term Oprah popularized to describe something that suddenly inspired her to look at life from a different perspective. My "ah-ha" was a quiet realization I experienced on a warm summer day 2,500 miles removed from the Hollywood bubble.

I'd taken a week off from celebrity hunting to attend my college roommate Mike's wedding on Staten Island—an over-the-top Italian extravaganza worthy of a Corleone with a buffet that took me a full week to digest. My date for the event was my *Enquirer* colleague Suzanne, who'd been at my side when we crashed that

St. Jude gala and, earlier, stalked Lana Turner at one of the screen goddess' final public appearances. And oh man, was *that* an unforgettable evening, the highlight being when Turner's protective daughter Cheryl Crane— the very one who'd fatally stabbed her mother's abusive lover Johnny Stompanato way back in 1958—tried to shield frail Lana from the vicious

A 1994 photo I snapped of Golden Age movie star Lana Turner as her daughter tried to shield her from the aggressive paparazzi.

paparazzi, who in turn retaliated by screaming at Cheryl and calling her a "MURDERER!!!"

Way to hold a grudge, eh?

My fellow reporter Suzanne in Times Square during her bout with "cancer."

I'd chosen to take Suzanne not only because she's a guaranteed good time, but also because she was a pretty girl with long blonde hair who'd serve me well as a "beard" to help me play it straight at Mike's Catholic wedding. It would be an understatement to say I was less than thrilled when—just days before we were to leave for the wedding— Suzanne elected to shave her head bald to mimic the sexy "butch" look Demi Moore had just revealed for her upcoming role as *G.I. Jane*. Oh, swell. Now everyone would assume gay Will had brought some militant lesbian as his date.

With Suzanne's plane ticket already purchased and Kimberly (my date to Meredith Baxter's wedding) still holding a grudge, my only choice was to shrug it off and whisper to everyone at the wedding reception that Suzanne had cancer. (Though no one asked, it obviously would have been hair cancer.) Suzanne began suspecting something was up when one Italian woman after another (including a nun) came up to take her hand in theirs and tell her how brave and beautiful she was and that God was watching over her. When I finally fessed up, G.I. Suzanne was so pissed that I thought she might grab the nearest shrimp fork and stab me in the eye.

After the reception, Suze and I took a long, uncomfortable ferry ride back to Manhattan. As we deboarded on to the Whitehall Ferry Terminal, we were excited to see that a newsstand had put out the new edition of the *Enquirer*. Since we'd been away from the office when that week's issue had been put to bed, we were both curious to see which of the stories the newsroom had been working on had made it onto the cover. If one of our stories was selected that meant there'd be a nice bonus in our next paycheck. Well, none of our stories were on the cover. Instead, the main image was an exploitative headline claiming that *Good Morning America* host Joan Lunden was an "emotional wreck" because her "gay pal" died in the recent TWA Flight 800 plane crash that killed all 230 people on board. *Jesus.* It wasn't bad enough that they were taking advantage of Lunden's heartache over losing a close friend, but I knew the inclusion of the word "gay" in the headline was deliberately included to stir speculation that this could have been the straight morning host's secret lesbian lover. At that time, the tabloid was weirdly obsessed with stirring speculation over stars' sexuality. On that same cover they'd included a sensationalized tease about one of their favorite suspected lesbian targets, Rosie O'Donnell, promising to reveal "The *Real* Reason She Hates Her Dad."

But it wasn't the unnecessarily heartless Lunden story nor the nasty Rosie exposé that struck me hardest. Sadly, these were typical tabloid fare. Rather, it was a large paparazzi photo they'd purchased of sultry cinema star Raquel Welch, caught with her head tilted downward and eyes closed on what appeared to be a bridge, but could also have been the rooftop edge of the Empire State Building. Though the star of *One Hundred Million Years, B.C.* had perhaps been meditating,

365

praying or going over her grocery list, the set-up also could have been interpreted as the final photo of a suicidal woman before she leapt into the sea or onto the pavement of 34th Street to end it all. As someone who has battled depression throughout life (as discussed a few chapters back), I found the image extremely relatable.

I was embarrassed and repulsed that this private human moment had been deemed appropriate to publicly display on newsstands with the extremely distasteful headline "Raquel's Bizarre Lonely Life: Sex Goddess Hasn't Had a Man for Years." And to really stick it to her, they included a smaller inset photo of "glam Raquel" as she was expected to present herself each time she left her home. *Ick!* It made me ill to just look at that *Enquirer* cover, much less be associated with it in any way. I could easily see my face in place of Raquel's with the headline: "Will's Bizarre Lonely Life: Sex God (we'll keep that part) Hasn't Had a Woman for Years."

When I got back to Los Angeles, I began to make it clear to Jerry and the other editors that I had no interest in continuing to exploit stars' sorrows. Ever since joining the *Enquirer,* I'd made it my mission to routinely pitch *People* magazine-type positive stories, such as catching up with our most treasured TV Moms and Dads, or "at home" pieces with our favorite celebs sharing yummy recipes. Not surprisingly, my campaign for "puff pieces," as the editors called them, was not well received. I was no longer their dependable monkey who'd been trained to infiltrate dangerous arenas and perform fun circus tricks like fooling doctors into telling me the *real* reason their patients had died. But I was still receiving the same circus-monkey salary I'd negotiated for myself when I'd carried out all those nefarious missions documented earlier. We all knew this couldn't go on, so in 1997 I flew to the *Enquirer's* home offices in Lantana, FL, to meet with editor-in-chief Steve Coz and his #2, David Perel, to discuss if I had a future with the tabloid. I honestly wasn't sure myself.

"Will, we value you here as a reporter," Coz told me. "But the kinds of stories you're now wanting to do just aren't the ones that sell papers." Sadly, he was right. Depression, death and divorce were what made the *Enquirer* America's top-selling source of celebrity news for so many years. Not backyard gardening with Doris

Roberts and her cute little gray bunny rabbit. Their offer to me, I have to say, was generous given my strict parameters. They'd invited me to remain on staff, but at half my salary. I was given a day to think it over before making my decision. While I already knew what it would be, the choice was made crystal clear when I laid back in my bed at the Hawaiian—a dilapidated, 1960s-era, bed bug-ridden Palm Beach motel where the *Enquirer* put up reporters and guests who they *weren't* trying to impress. I knew exactly how I'd be valued and treated by the editors and other reporters if I'd accepted their offer, and that wasn't for me. By that point, no amount of money would have made me happy. I was ready to find a new home where my skills and work ethic would be appreciated. So, the next morning, with one signature, I forever relinquished my position as a tabloid reporter.

And it really was time. Most all the old stars I'd come west to meet were now either dead, posing with me in photographs, or both. My initial treasure-hunting mission as tabloid reporter had been achieved, and now it was time for new adventures.

One of the more fabulous opportunities that came my way, as I've mentioned several times, was my seven-year run working as a talent producer on Hallmark Channel's *Home & Family*. Being the antithesis of the *Enquirer*, this much-beloved (and sorely missed) show's sugary-sweet segments tackled such sensitive topics as cherished Christmas memories, cupcake recipes and "fur baby" adoptions.

Long gone were my days of probing stars for invasive details about their private lives. My job now was to make our guests feel as secure and comfortable as possible. And one of those guests, on January 27, 2016, turned out to be none other than … Raquel Welch.

While everyone was excited to welcome this legend to our home set, Raquel was in no way a typical *Home & Family* celebrity visitor. Our guests were expected to be out of their hair and makeup trailer and camera-ready by 1pm sharp to shoot our show "live to tape," meaning—although it was recorded to air the following day—we always started right on time and taped straight through for two hours with no breaks or edits. But not this day. We'd been given a heads-up by Raquel's rep that she would require "a little extra time" to check her lighting and camera angles before shooting her segment. That "little extra time" stretched into nearly an hour—the equivalent of a band's sound check—with Raquel repeatedly darting back and forth between the guest sofa where she'd be seated and the various cameras to carefully inspect and adjust her angles and lighting. Once satisfied, she then turned her attention to the artwork on the wall behind her, which she preferred be removed.

As this continued, producers would take occasional breaks from their desks to check in on the whackadoo "Raquel Show." It was nothing short of ... *fabulous*. But for me, it took on extra significance. I realized that if Raquel—who'd obviously had a significant amount of facial work done—was this protective of her on-camera image, which would be protected and enhanced with our show's very best hair, makeup, wardrobe, lighting and camera angles, I could only imagine the deep humiliation and devastation she must have felt to have appeared on that *Enquirer* cover back in 1996. Dressed in sneakers with disheveled hair and not a hint of makeup, Raquel had been caught by a photographer who'd profited by sharing that image with roughly 2.5 million *Enquirer* readers. Blood money. A sick business catering to diseased appetites. I thought back to the insensitive crack I'd made about *Brady Bunch* kid Susan Olsen's appearance, and thanked God that I'd gotten out of the bullying biz before it was too late to change course.

Having by then undergone several cosmetic procedures to combat ageism and my own insecurities, I had a clearer understanding of what it meant to be a Raquel trying to remain relevant in a no-win world that attacked the once young and beautiful for transforming themselves into plastic "freaks," or—perhaps even worse—carelessly letting themselves go.

Despite their great fortune and privilege in life, celebrities are people too. And Celebrity Lives Matter.

Lesson Learned: Know when to get out ... and then get the hell out without looking back.

EPILOGUE

In 2023, your humble author got his chance to live life as a "Dangerous Diva" when *General Hospital* executive producer Frank Valentini cast me as a villain on the long-running ABC daytime drama. My role was Russell, the conniving

My May 2023 guest appearance on ABC's *General Hospital* opposite the divalicious Morgan Fairchild.

minion of veteran soap actress Morgan Fairchild's Haven de Havilland, the host of *Home & Heart*—a fictional TV show with a title curiously close to *Home & Family*, wouldn't you agree?

That bizarre experience with Ms. Fairchild—from catching a glimpse of the 73-year-old step out of her car in the studio parking lot with her hair done up in curlers to getting all dolled up to be *my* scene partner—naturally brought back a flood of memories of the many other legendary divas whose air I got to breathe during my years with *H&F* before the show's abrupt Covid-related cancellation. Among them, Joan Collins, Linda Evans, Donna Mills, Joan Van Ark, Michele Lee,

Dancing with a carousel of divas on *Home & Family*. From left: the late Suzanne Somers, Priscilla Presley and music legend Dionne Warwick.

369

Jaclyn Smith, Linda Gray, Patti LuPone, Susan Lucci, Suzanne Somers, Priscilla Presley and Dionne Warwick, to name but a few.

Though none of these ladies succeeded in altering the space-time continuum as Raquel Welch had so masterfully achieved on our set, some were more sensitive and particular than others when it came to their on-camera appearances. But rather than stepping on these stars and exploiting their very human insecurities as I'd once been called to do as a tabloid flunky, my job now was to do all I could to help mask their cracks and make them feel as beautiful and confident as possible. (Something I've naturally found far easier to do as I've matured right along with them—wrinkles, gray hair and all.)

My 10-year-old self all "Dolly-ed"up for the 5th-grade Halloween parade (above) and (below) with the real Dolly in 2016. Dolly's priceless autograph reads: "To Will, Dolly II. Love, Dolly Parton, Dolly 1."

My most special *H&F* guest of all-time had to have been larger-than-life country music icon Dolly Parton, whom I brought on the show back in 2016 to cook her fried green tomatoes and craft a DIY coat of many colors. Before the show, I had a chance to sit with Dolly privately in her trailer. We chatted about several personal topics, including her kinship with her many gay fans and how ridiculously long it took

for me to come out to my mom. When I showed Dolly an old snapshot of my 10-year-old self, costumed as *her* for Halloween in a big blonde wig and a tight turtleneck bursting with boobs, she took one look and deadpanned rather incredulously, "… and honey, your mama didn't know you was gay??!!"

Yep. I'd sure come a long way from being that scared, insecure kid in Carrie Fisher's home when she called me out for trying to pass myself off as straight. But in between the extremes of Carrie and Dolly, there was another standout actress who played a significant role in my self-discovery and acceptance: Judith Light—the Emmy-nominated TV actress best remembered for her maternal roles on the polar opposite "sitcoms" *Who's the Boss* and *Transparent.*

In the period between my discovery of that unflattering paparazzi photo of Raquel Welch on the cover of the *National Enquirer* and quitting the tabloid world, I found it increasingly unbearable to justify some of the more intrusive assignments I was still being given. With this stress gnawing at my self-esteem, I enrolled in the Landmark Forum, an intensive, soul-bearing, personal-development seminar designed to help people become their authentic selves and achieve both their personal and professional potentials. (I know, *gag*, but it actually works!!) Coincidentally, one of the other participants in my seminar was Judith, who understandably expressed legitimate concerns about exposing her innermost fears, insecurities and desires with a tabloid reporter in the same room.

The fact that Judith chose not only to remain in the course, but also trust that I would not betray her confidence was a major turning point for me. Having alienated so many friends during my years with the *Enquirer*, I'd yearned to be trusted and desperately wanted to be taken at my word. As the three-day seminar progressed, I became so comfortable with Judith—a staunch, lifelong human rights advocate—that I did something I hadn't expected to do. I came out. First to Judith, then to the whole room of participants. No longer doomed to live in the darkness of duplicity as my father and Mr. Brady had, I was free at last. And it felt great!

But I soon gave Judith another reason to be fearful when I announced my desire to invite my *Enquirer* mentor Jerry and a couple of other tabloid colleagues to our "graduation night" in hopes that they too might consider signing up for the transformative seminar. Judith ultimately gave me her blessing to extend the invitations, and although he ended up not enrolling, Jerry did show up to support me that night, just as he did a short time later when I finally handed him my letter of resignation.

Jerry. You've read his name many times in this book, starting with this book's dedication. In that tribute, I credited the man as my mentor for teaching me essential "Lessons Learned"—including my concluding chapter's takeaway: Know when to get out. And now I'll bring things to a close with his most valuable lesson of all, one connected to so many of the others found herein: Always be true to yourself. Once you've mastered that, all of life's other lessons tend to take hold organically.

Jerry and his wife Michelle had two biological sons of their own, but that never stopped him from assuming a protective, fatherly role toward me from the minute I joined his staff. I remember one time in particular being called into Jerry's office for a serious heart-to-heart in which he admonished me not to "make the same mistakes in life I did." Since Jerry, like me, had aspired to be a screenwriter, I assumed he was advising me to not abandon my writing dreams. I would only learn the true meaning behind Jerry's warning a few years later when I was still in the closet and covertly slipped into a Venice, CA, gay bar called Roosterfish, only to discover Jerry sitting at the bar nursing a beer.

"Looking for directions, Kecky?" he quipped.

I was stunned. Not only had my secret been blown, but what the hell was Jerry doing in a *gay bar* just a few miles from the Santa Monica Catholic church he attended each Sunday with Michelle and the kids? (The very same church, by the way, attended by Kelsey Grammer and his former fiancée Tammi!) Jerry explained he and Michelle were separating, having only recently made her aware of his late-in-life epiphany.

"So, this is what you were trying to communicate to me that day in your office?" I asked.

Jerry nodded, patted the stool next to his and ordered me a Heineken. We spent the next several hours talking about being true to oneself, something I knew I would have never truly been able to do while continuing to violate the privacy of others. Within a very short time of coming out to Judith and Jerry, I did the same with my friends (who all already knew) and then my mom during a miserably long and weepy day at Disneyland. Despite what you may have heard about Mickey's theme park, it's not *always* the happiest place on Earth.

With alimony to pay his ex-wife, as well as those two sons (one with special needs) to support, Jerry understandably elected to remain in the tabloid world until they washed their hands of him in 2013 after 28 years of loyal servitude. But Jerry had also managed to discover a new life for himself, ultimately finding a soulmate in doting husband John.

Several years would go by without seeing Jerry. But then a marvelous, miraculous twist of fate reconnected me to my fairy godfather—with a gay bar curiously once again serving as our magical portal.

One Sunday night, I'd decided to make a quick clothing donation at a drop-off center in West Hollywood located next to the since-shuttered Gold Coast bar. As I was navigating my Jeep through a tight squeeze, I accidentally knocked a side-view mirror off a car parked on the side of the road. *Aw shit!* "No good deed …," I thought, damning the universe. At least it was a crappy car, I shrugged.

I placed the car's dislodged mirror—along with a note of apology I scribbled on the back of a Bed, Bath & Beyond 20% Off coupon—on the car's windshield and braced myself for an angry call. Instead, two days later I was stunned to receive a call from Jerry telling me, "I got your 20% Off coupon, Kecky."

Wait, *whaaatt*??? No freaking way!!!

Yup, it was Jerry's car I'd hit while he was throwing back some afternoon beers at the Gold Coast. I mean, what are the odds? I'll tell you what they are: impossible, unless God or some other higher power was intervening to bring us together.

Never had I been so grateful for being involved in a car accident. Not only did I of course offer to reimburse Jerry for the damages, but I insisted on taking him out for dinner. Over cocktails, Jerry shared how the previous few years had been rough. To make ends meet, he was washing dishes and driving Uber. But that didn't matter. He was living an authentic life and earning an honest living. All that mattered to Jerry was that his sons Zack and Patrick were doing well and he and John were still in love and going strong.

Not long after that, in August 2019, I received a call from John informing me that my fatherly mentor had dropped dead of a heart attack while walking home in the early morning hours from a gay bar in Palm Springs. *Yep, another damn gay bar!!* I was devastated. Jerry was only 63. I was well into writing this book and was so looking forward to handing him a signed copy.

(Top) With my late *Enquirer* mentor Jerry George, circa 1996. (Below) Reuniting with my fellow *Enquirer* vets at Jerry's 2019 memorial. From left: me, Mike Glynn (who'd brought me into the tabloid), Marc Cetner (my co-conspirator on many Kelsey Grammer stories), Darryl Wrobel (our assistant turned ace journalist) and Suzanne Ely, with her lovely locks grown back out.

I shared the remarkable story of our serendipitous sideswipe to many of our former *Enquirer* colleagues when we reunited in Playa del Rey at the Knights of Columbus Hall to honor our dear friend. I concluded my little speech by speaking directly to my mentor:

"Sure, Jerry. I'll try my best to be true to myself and not make the same mistakes you did. But I'll try even harder to continue being the honorable man you always succeeded in being—even in a backwards tabloid world that reserved its deepest praise for undertaking the most dishonorable of acts."

In the interviews I conduct today—celebrity or otherwise—I still employ my same old tabloid-learned tricks of the trade to get inside my subjects' heads with the goal of extracting fascinating, never-before-revealed stories. But I now do so with the added responsibility of protecting them from themselves. Making sure their own words won't come back to bite them in the keister.

Why do I do this? Because, somewhere along the way, that insecure, shit-stirring tabloid bad boy grew up—finally finding the happiness, self-acceptance and peace that had long eluded him. And essential to maintaining that equilibrium is helping instill those qualities in the people I'm fortunate enough to interview.

It's been a great privilege getting to speak with so many legendary entertainers who left their mark on the world in one or another; many of them— from the Bradys to the Bionic Woman and Batman—cherished idols who'd made my childhood a little less lonely and a whole lot more fun. Remembering all the joy they've given to me and so many of you, I'm careful to honor the legacies of those we still have left. My 11-year-old self would have it no other way!

Just the other day I was interviewing a veteran actor who most assuredly would have come off as bitter and unlikable had I not taken the extra time he needed to help him focus—not on his life's many disappointments, but on gratitude for all the remarkable and wonderful things he'd experienced. Before long he was laughing and sharing relatable, life-affirming stories that I knew would endear him to the public. Had he been speaking to *Enquirer*-era William Keck, this naïve man would surely have dug his own grave.

My intentions were much the same when writing this book. Not to dredge up the past and recycle old celebrity scandals, but to pay homage to the many fabulous Hollywood stars who'd enthralled me on screen before our paths crossed—for better or worse—in person as adults in the real world. In some instances, this book has already helped heal old wounds.

Like trying to guess when Dean Martin might die, we can never be sure when our own Brave Last Days will arrive. For all we know, they may already be upon us. Whenever our time comes—despite the meaningless opinions and critiques of the gossipy Enquiring Minds constantly buzzing around us—it's important that we're happy and at peace with who we are, with whom we share our lives and how we choose to spend our days and treat those around us.

And that, folks, is ON the record.

MY OTHER TV FAMILIES
(ADDENDUM TO THE MANY REUNITED CLASSIC TV CAST PORTRAITS FEATURED IN THE PREVIOUS CHAPTERS)

LEAVE IT TO BEAVER (1957–1963)

Author (in cap) with *Leave it to Beaver* **stars (from left) Jerry Mathers and the late Tony Dow.** **Santa Monica, 2007, honoring the sitcom's landmark 50th anniversary.**

GILLIGAN'S ISLAND (1964–1967)

Author (center) with *Gilligan's Island* **stars (from left) Bob Denver, Dawn Wells, Tina Louise and Russell Johnson.** *TV Land Awards*, **2004.**

THE PARTRIDGE FAMILY (1970–1974)

Author (far right) with *Partridge Family* stars (from left) Danny Bonaduce, Shirley Jones and the late David Cassidy—reuniting to judge VH-1's *In Search of the Partridge Family,* 2004.   Their big discovery: future Oscar winner Emma Stone, who was cast as the new Laurie Partridge.

THE WALTONS (1972–1981)

Author (in overalls) with (from left) *The Waltons* stars Judy Norton, Kami Cotler, Richard Thomas, Michael Learned and Mary McDonough. Series creator Earl Hamner provided the voiceover for this 2015 *Home & Family* reunion, just one year before he passed.

THE BOB NEWHART SHOW (1972–1978)

Author (center) with the sitcom's Bob Newhart and Suzanne Pleshette at The Paley Center in Beverly Hills, 2007. Just four days after her release from the hospital for cancer treatment, a weakened Pleshette arrived in a wheelchair and would pass just four months later.
(Courtesy of The Paley Center for Media.)

M*A*S*H (1972–1983)

Author (up front) with *M*A*S*H* stars (from left) William Christopher, Kellye Nakahara, Alan Alda, Mike Farrell, Loretta Swit and Wayne Rogers. *TV Land Awards*, 2009.

HAPPY DAYS (1974–1984)

Author (center) with *Happy Days* stars (from left) Don Most, Ron Howard, Henry Winkler, Marion Ross and Anson Williams at a 2019 fundraiser for The Garry Marshall Theatre. The only other surviving co-star, Scott Baio, was not invited.

LAVERNE & SHIRLEY (1976–1983)

Author (far left) with *Laverne & Shirley* stars (clockwise from bottom left) Michael McKean, sweet as pie Cindy Williams, sour as vinegar Penny Marshall and David Lander. *TV Land Awards*, 2012. (Courtesy of Adam Olszewski.)

ONE DAY AT A TIME (1975–1984)

Author (top left) with *One Day at a Time* stars (from left) Bonnie Franklin, Mackenzie Phillips, Pat Harrington Jr. and Valerie Bertinelli. *TV Land Awards*, 2012. Co-star Glenn Scarpelli was also in attendance and delivered a highly emotional coming-out speech on stage that was cut from the broadcast for time. (Courtesy of Adam Olszewski.)

SOAP (1977–1981) & BENSON (1979–1986)

A final gathering of the stars of *Soap* and its spin-off *Benson* (seated from left), including honoree Robert Guillaume (died 2017), Katherine Helmond (d. 2019) and Robert Mandan (d. 2018). Standing (from left): René Auberjonois (d. 2019) and the sole survivors: Keck and ventriloquist Jay Johnson (holding dummy Bob). *Home & Family* reunion, 2015.

WKRP IN CINCINNATI (1978–1982)

Author (center) with *WKRP in Cincinnati* stars (from left) **Tim Reid, Jan Smithers, Loni Anderson** and the late **Howard Hesseman** at **The Paley Center for Media, 2014.**

DIFF'RENT STROKES (1978–1986)

Author (center) with *Diff'rent Strokes* stars **Todd Bridges and Dana Plato**, a couple of years before her death in 1999. Their TV sibling **Gary Coleman** declined to join us for this *Enquirer* reunion photo, and then organized his own (more lucrative) reunion shoot with our *Globe* competitor.

THE LOVE BOAT (1977–1986)

From left: Author with *Love Boat* stars Gavin MacLeod, Jill Whelan, Cynthia Lauren Tewes, Bernie Kopell, Fred Grandy, Charo and Ted Lange. A *Home & Family* Christmas reunion, 2015.

HART TO HART (1979–1984)

Author (right), moderator of a tribute to *Hart to Hart* with stars Robert Wagner and Stefanie Powers at The Paley Center for Media, Beverly Hills, 2010. Wagner surprised me by freely discussing his deceased wife Natalie Wood.

THE THORN BIRDS (1983 Miniseries)

Author (right) with reunited *The Thorn Birds* lovers Richard Chamberlain and Rachel Ward at the 2012 Television Critics Association press tour. (Courtesy of Don Flood.)

DESIGNING WOMEN (1986–1993)

Author with *Designing Women* stars (from left) Annie Potts, Jean Smart, the late Dixie Carter and Delta Burke at the Museum of Television & Radio, Beverly Hills, 2006, shortly after I orchestrated Dixie's and Delta's reconciliation after years of estrangement. (Courtesy of The Paley Center for Media/photographer Kevin Parry.)

FULL HOUSE (1987–1995)

Author (far left) with (from left) *Full House* co-stars Dave Coulier (holding Mr. Woodchuck), Jodie Sweetin, Andrea Barber and former Hallmark Channel darling Candace Cameron Bure, who helped me pull together this *Home & Family* reunion. Our executive producer, Woody Fraser, forbade me from inviting the late Bob Saget due to a past conflict between the men.

LIFE GOES ON (1989–1993)

Reuniting the cast of *Life Goes On* with the show's (from left) Chris Burke, Kellie Martin and Patti LuPone, who insisted her TV husband Bill Smitrovich *not* be invited to this 2015 *Home & Family* reunion.

ALL MY CHILDREN (1970–2011)

My *All My Children* cast reunion featured from left: *Home & Family* host Mark Steines, Eva LaRue, *H&F's* Debbie Matenopoulos, Peter Bergman, Taylor Miller, me, Susan Lucci, Eden Riegel, Kathleen Noone, Laurence Lau, Kim Delaney, Michael E. Knight and Jill Larson.

GENERAL HOSPITAL (1963–)

Author (center) moderating *General Hospital's* 50th-anniversary panel at The Paley Center for Media in Beverly Hills with stars (top row) Jacklyn Zeman, Finola Hughes, Kimberly McCullough, Jason Thompson and John J. York. Bottom row: Maurice Benard, Genie Francis, Tony Geary and Jane Elliot. (Courtesy of The Paley Center for Media.)

KNOTS LANDING (1979–1993)

Author (far left) with *Happy Days'* Henry Winkler, producer of 2005's *Knots Landing Reunion: Together Again* with the show's cast (top row from left) Kevin Dobson, William Devane and Ted Shackelford. Bottom row from left: Michelle Phillips, Joan Van Ark, Julie Harris, Michele Lee, Donna Mills and Lisa Hartman. Photo taken at the actual "Seaview Circle" cul-de-sac in Granada Hills, CA. Nicollette Sheridan participated via a pre-taped interview. (Courtesy CBS.)

FALCON CREST (1981–1990)

A 2010 30th-anniversary cast reunion organized by the author at The Paley Center for Media in Beverly Hills with (top row from left) David Selby, series creator Earl Hamner, me, Lorenzo Lamas & Robert Foxworth. Second row: Jamie Rose & Ana Alicia. Bottom row: Abby Dalton, Susan Sullivan & Margaret Ladd. A letter was read from Chao-Li Chi, who died four days later. (Courtesy of The Paley Center for Media.)

LOST IN SPACE (1965–1968)

Author (front left, with friend Curtis Wayne Brown, front right) moderating a 50th-anniversary *Lost in Space* panel in 2015 with cast members (back row from left) Mark Goddard, **Marta Kristen**, June Lockhart, Angela Cartwright, Billy Mumy and the Robot.

STAR TREK: THE NEXT GENERATION (1987–94)

A 2016 *Star Trek: The Next Generation* gathering on *Home & Family* marking the 30th anniversary with (from left) LeVar Burton, Michael Dorn, Denise Crosby, me, **Marina Sirtis and** Jonathan Frakes. (Brent Spiner and Gates McFadden sent video greetings.)

INDEX

(Alphabetically by First Name)

M

N

O

P

COMMENTARIES & SIDEBARS

ACKNOWLEDGMENTS

I've met and interviewed countless authors over the years, and not one of them ever told me what a monumental and exhausting undertaking it is to actually write … and finish (!!!) a book. Had I known, well … I probably would have done it anyway. But no way in hell could I have accomplished this without a support team dating wayyyy back to 1990 when I first arrived in Los Angeles.

So first and foremost, I must express enormous gratitude to every employer in Hollywood who took a chance on me with the words "You're hired," granting me access to all the celebrities you've just read about in these pages. They include:

Staff Pro, the company that hired me as a security guard and sent me to the Emmy Awards where I got groped by Richard Mulligan. (Today, I could easily sue you, Staff Pro.) The CBS and NBC Page programs, with a special shout-out to my peacock supervisor, Ronilyn Reilly. Aaron Spelling Productions' Gail Patterson and the late Doris Braden. The *National Enquirer*'s Steve Coz. *Soap Opera Digest*'s Alan Carter, the only sucker in town who'd hire me after I quit the *Enquirer*. *Entertainment Weekly*'s Cable Neuhaus, the late Carole Willcocks and Thom Geier. *Us Weekly*'s Todd Gold. The *Los Angeles Times*' Betsy Sharkey. *USA Today*'s Susan Weiss, Jacque Janssen and Dennis Moore. *TV Guide Magazine*'s Debra Birnbaum. *Closer*'s Carol Dittbrenner. Hallmark Channel. *Home & Family*'s Woody Fraser, Stacey Patterson and Tracy Verna. Discovery Channel's Mark Keizer, Aaron Schoonhoven and Josh Gates.

And then (after a fierce bidding war between all the top New York publishing houses … *ahem*), Jacobs Brown for seeing the potential in this book and not being afraid to go for it. Thanks most especially to: Steven Kates and Marc Cushman for wining and dining me at that Denny's off the 405 where the deal went down; Mark Alfred—what a wit you are, sir; and lastly, *I Dream of Jeannie* fan Rebecca Varga.

My good friend and backup proofreader Jack Bowers, who never misses a single spelling mistake. You really are the absolute brest!! (Note: Jack previously proofread countless screenplays of mine that are—incredibly—STILL AVAILABLE for optioning!! Among them: *Revenge of the Hollywood Mummies*,

The Minimals, *The Vagenie* and *Disco Hospital*. Interested parties please contact my agent, Brad Rosenfeld.)

Damonza, the company that designed this book's fun cover art.

All my reader pals who so charitably suffered through far shittier earlier versions of this manuscript, which at various times were titled *My TV Family Album, Cringeworthy, Horribly Wrong, Catching Falling Stars* and (very briefly considered during a dog walk) *Bad Will Hunting*. Thanks, guys and gal: Dan Abraham, Mark Mottern, Jim Colucci, Michael Schneider, David Sperber, Suzanne Ely, Alan Carter, Eric Wilkerson and Marc Cetner.

My hardworking publicist Harlan Boll, who, in all likelihood, is the reason you all became aware of this book. Also, my other publicist chums Jeffrey Lane, Heidi Schaeffer, Joe Trainor and Sheri Goldberg for your special celebrity favors.

And I must thank every celebrity and producer whose generous endorsements made this book something extra special—beginning with Linda Gray and Marcia Cross, the first to say "yes" and thus paving the way for Henry Winkler, Christopher Knight, Rich Little, Sheree J. Wilson, Tammi Baliszewski, Diana Canova, Gordon Thomson, Marc Cherry, Carlton Cuse, Melissa Gilbert, Cybill Shepherd, John Tesh, Connie Sellecca, Julie Newmar, Lindsay Wagner, Michael Learned, Dee Wallace, Mark Steines, Cynthia Lauren Tewes, Catherine Bach, Barbara Eden, Morgan Fairchild, Joan Van Ark, Donna Mills and Linda Evans. Wow.

My best friend and life partner, Emil, for encouraging me to finally complete this book, and reminding me that there was tremendous value in that accomplishment alone.

And last, but most certainly not least, my parents, Nancy and James Green, for their limitless support and generosity. I am so fortunate to have had you by my side throughout the years. I told you that letting me stay up late on school nights to watch *Hart to Hart, Dynasty* and *Knots Landing* wouldn't rot my brain … much.

ABOUT THE AUTHOR

William Keck began his career working for TV titan Aaron Spelling and as an NBC and CBS studio page before turning his focus to journalism and television production. He has worked as a staff reporter for the *National Enquirer* and *USA Today*, a senior editor and columnist for *TV Guide*, a regular contributor to *People, Us Weekly, Closer Weekly, Entertainment Weekly, Disney twenty-three* and the *Los Angeles Times*, and as a senior talent producer for NBC, Discovery Channel and Hallmark Channel's *Home & Family*. He lives in Los Angeles with his Austrian partner, two naughty dogs and a pussy cat who knows all their secrets.

Thinking about writing your own memoir? Find more information at WhenYouStepUponAStar.com.

f When You Step Upon A Star

X @StepUponAStar

@WhenYouStepUponAStar

You may also enjoy these books from Jacobs/Brown Press:

Beaming Up and Getting Off: Life Before and Beyond Star Trek
by Walter Koenig

Previously on X-Men: The Making of an Animated Series
by Eric Lewald

Mary: The Mary Tyler Moore Story
by Herbie J Pilato

The Show Runner: An Insider's Guide to Successful TV Production
by Cy Chermak

Swords, Starships and Superheroes: From Star Trek to Xena to Hercules
by Paul Robert Coyle

These Are the Voyages – Star Trek: The Original Series
in three volumes, by Marc Cushman with Susan Osborn

These Are the Voyages – Star Trek: The Original Series, Season One
(Audio Book) by Marc Cushman and Vic Mignogna

Irwin Allen's Voyage to the Bottom of the Sea: The Authorized Biography of a
Classic Sci-Fi Series
in two volumes, by Marc Cushman and Mark Alfred

Irwin Allen's Lost in Space: The Authorized Biography of a Classic Sci-Fi Series
in three volumes, by Marc Cushman

Long Distance Voyagers: The Story of the Moody Blues
in two volumes, by Marc Cushman

Jacobs/Brown Media Group, LLC
Jacobs/Brown Press

"Where truth is better than fiction."
www.jacobsbrownmediagroup.com